Advance Praise for *The Way I Rememb*…

"*The Way I Remember* is inarguably the most important book yet to be published for the preservation of the Cree language and an understanding of the importance of the oral tradition to Cree culture and education. Through his personal stories, poems, lessons, and retellings of sacred stories, Solomon bears living witness to the extermination of Indigenous cultures, but also to how they survive, not just in memory but through the practice of remembering. With remarkable honesty and creativity, Solomon's enduring and endearing positivity shines through as a testament that the restoration of Indigenous languages and stories is foundational to surviving and transcending the traumatic legacies of cultural genocide. This is a memoir that goes beyond the individual self, as it provides a framework for continuing Cree oral traditions based in the most contemporary educational technologies and transformations of cultural practices, breaking open the colonial barriers to learning the language and stories to a universal community and a new generation of Cree language students. You honour us all. *kinanâskomitinân.*
—JESSE ARCHIBALD-BARBER, editor of *kisiskâciwan: Indigenous Voices from Where the River Flows Swiftly*

"As he looks back over his life journey reclaiming, breathing new and old life back into our beautiful language, Solomon credits the late Reverend Edward Ahenakew for helping him 'put the pieces together.' *kîsta mîna*, dear Solomon, *êkosi ê-tôtamawiyâhk*. This is an important book because you have also put pieces together for us so that we can have a good journey. *kinanâskomitin*." —MARIA CAMPBELL, author of *Halfbreed*

"Sol is an international treasure the whole world should enjoy."
—BUFFY SAINTE-MARIE

"As a mother-tongue speaker of Cree, equally fluent in English, Solomon Ratt has unflaggingly shared his knowledge with countless language learners over the years. Using Syllabics, SRO, and English translations, he roots his written texts in traditional oral storytelling practices, providing masterful examples of formal and informal Cree. This book is a gift to future generations—half memoir, half sacred stories—a collection representing a cultural and linguistic wealth that is impossible to measure. Full of humour and resilience in equal measure, these Cree/English bilingual stories offer us a glimpse into a world as it was, and a future that could be."
—CHELSEA VOWEL, author of *Indigenous Writes*

OUR OWN WORDS 2

kâ-pî-isi-kiskisiyân

ᑳ ᐲ ᐃᓯ ᑭᐢᑭᓯᔮᐣ

The Way I Remember

Solomon Ratt

Edited with an Introduction by Arden Ogg

Cree Literacy Network

FIRST NATIONS UNIVERSITY OF CANADA

Printed and bound in Canada at Imprimerie Gauvin. The text of this book is printed on 100% post-consumer recycled paper with earth-friendly vegetable-based inks.

COVER AND TEXT DESIGN: Duncan Noel Campbell
COPY EDITOR: Arden Ogg
PROOFREADER: Kathryn Nogue
COVER PHOTO: Trevor Hopkin, University of Regina Photographic Services
SYLLABIC FONT: BJCree UNI by Bill Jancewicz

Library and Archives Canada Cataloguing in Publication

TITLE: kâ-pî-isi-kiskisiyân = The way I remember / Solomon Ratt ; edited with an introduction by Arden Ogg.

OTHER TITLES: Way I remember

NAMES: Ratt, Solomon, author. | Ogg, Arden C. (Arden Catherine), 1960- editor, writer of introduction. | Container of (work): Ratt, Solomon. kâ-pî-isi-kiskisiyân. | Container of (expression): Ratt, Solomon. kâ-pî-isi-kiskisiyân. English.

SERIES: Our own words ; 2.

DESCRIPTION: Series statement: Our own words ; 2 | Syllabics in title unable to be transcribed. | Text in Cree Syllabics and romanized Cree (th-dialect), and in English translation.

IDENTIFIERS: Canadiana (print) 20220449260 | Canadiana (ebook) 20220449821 | ISBN 9780889779150 (hardcover) | ISBN 9780889779143 (softcover) | ISBN 9780889779174 (PDF) | ISBN 9780889779167 (EPUB)

SUBJECTS: LCSH: Ratt, Solomon. | LCSH: Ratt, Solomon—Childhood and youth. | LCSH: Cree language— Dialects—Texts. | CSH: First Nations—Saskatchewan—Biography. | CSH: First Nations—Saskatchewan—Residential schools. | CSH: First Nations—Education—Saskatchewan. | CSH: First Nations— Saskatchewan—Social life and customs. | LCGFT: Autobiographies.

CLASSIFICATION: LCC E99.C88 R3813 2023 | DDC 971.24004/973230092—dc23

10 9 8 7 6 5 4 3 2 1

University of Regina Press

University of Regina, Regina, Saskatchewan, Canada, S4S 0A2
TEL: (306) 585-4758 FAX: (306) 585-4699
WEB: www.uofrpress.ca

We acknowledge the support of the Canada Council for the Arts for our publishing program. We acknowledge the financial support of the Government of Canada. / Nous reconnaissons l'appui financier du gouvernement du Canada. This publication was made possible with support from Creative Saskatchewan's Book Publishing Production Grant Program.

Canada Council for the Arts Conseil des arts du Canada
Canada
creative SASKATCHEWAN

nikiskisitotawâwak kahkithaw awâsisak
êkâ kâ-kî-ohci-kîwîcik ikwa mîna aniki kâ-kî-paspîcik.

ᓂᑭᐢᑭᓯᑐᑕᐚᐘᐠ ᑲᐦᑭᖬᐤ ᐊᐚᓯᓴᐠ ᐁᑳ ᑳ ᑮ ᐅᐦᒋ ᑮᐑᒋᐠ
ᐃᑿ ᒦᓇ ᐊᓂᑭ ᑳ ᑮ ᐸᐢᐲᒋᐠ᙮

Remembering all those children
who did not come home and those who survived.

Contents

ᐋᒐᖫᐦᑮᐏᓇ

kâ-pî-isi-kiskisiyân / The Way I Remember

kiskisiwina / Memories

âcathôhkîwina / Sacred Stories

Introduction

Reflecting on forces that have shaped his life, Solomon Ratt often claims that his education was interrupted by his schooling. Torn away from family life on a trapline near Stanley Mission, Saskatchewan (*âmaciwîspimowinihk*), he was deposited as a child of six into Canada's residential school system, a harsh, new institutional world, operated in a language he could not yet understand, far from the love and comfort of home and family. Memories of these realities and life-long challenges they provoked are reflected in the stories gathered here.

Solomon's *âcimisowina* "personal, autobiographical stories" form the core of Part 1 of this volume. Written over a period of ten years or more, these pieces of varying length and style are gathered thematically to build a memoir of Solomon's life: before, during, and after residential school. In many ways, these stories reflect the experience of thousands of other Indigenous children across Canada, collected between 2007 and 2015 in hearings of the

National Truth and Reconciliation Commission.[1] But Solomon's stories also stand apart in significant ways.

As a Native speaker of Woods Cree or *nîhithowîwin*, Solomon is one of those rare residential school students blessed with full retention of his mother language. Solomon was not punished for speaking his own language at school, unlike generations of students before him. Sadly, many of his classmates had already lost their traditional languages thanks to harsh punishment endured by parents and grandparents during their own schooldays. Solomon, on the other hand, returned each summer to parents who spoke nothing but Cree. This interaction with mature speakers supported his continued linguistic development and taught him to express himself well in Cree.

At the Saskatchewan Indian Federated College (affiliated with the University of Regina, now First Nations University), Solomon's studies with Dr. Jean Okimāsis gave him a command of reading and writing in Cree in contemporary standard spelling (SRO). Through Dr. Ahab Spence, he learned the Cree Syllabics system and rekindled his interest in traditional stories. Where Cree-speaking members of prior generations could only share their stories orally, narrating or recording them for others to transcribe and translate, Solomon acquired the ability to write for himself.

Solomon's reminiscences of residential school escapades almost always end with a close call and a smile. Solomon acknowledges the luck that helped him stay ahead of bullies and disciplinarian principals or priests, but he also remembers with gratitude the friends who shielded him from sharing the consequences, even when they were caught in the very same pranks. Even when the memories are dark, Solomon's particularly Cree sense of humour shines.

1 "Truth and Reconciliation Commission." Government of Canada website, last modified June 11, 2021. https://www.rcaanc-cirnac.gc.ca/eng/1450124405592/1529106060525.

Reading and Writing in Cree

To this day, many residential school survivors feel shame at their language loss and their inability to read and write in their ancestral languages. In no way is this shame deserved. In any language, reading and writing are skills that must be taught. With the residential school system promoting linguistic and cultural genocide, and children held captive within that system, there was literally no opportunity whatever for children to acquire reading and writing skills in Cree—or any other Indigenous language—even if they maintained the language orally.

It is really only since about 1970, when the "Red Paper" laid the groundwork for Indian Control of Indian Education, that a concerted effort was launched to teach standard spelling for Cree. Pioneers like the late Ida McLeod trained Dr. Freda Ahenakew in Saskatoon; Dr. Jean Okimāsis in Regina received her earliest training from Anna Crowe. Until the twenty-first century, universities were virtually the only places where Cree speakers could find instruction in standard spelling for reading and writing Cree.

In Solomon's writing, we see a significant generational leap, as he composes his own stories (and poems, teaching materials, and even social commentary) without intervention. All are written first in his own fully fluent Cree, for which he then prepares his own translations in equally fluent English. This writing process charts a path for others to follow. It embodies and enacts each of the language- and culture-related Calls to Action of the Truth and Reconciliation Commission report.[2]

2 National Centre for Truth and Reconciliation. *Honouring the Truth, Reconciling for the Future: Summary of the Final Report of the Truth and Reconciliation Commission of Canada,* Calls to Action 13 to 17. https://ehprnh2mwo3.exactdn.com/wp-content/uploads/2021/01/Executive_Summary_English_Web.pdf

Cree Literary Tradition

At the same time as Solomon's writing advances language revitalization, his autobiographical impulse is a clear example of long-standing Cree cultural and intellectual tradition. In her 2022 book, *Autobiography as Indigenous Intellectual Tradition*, Deanna Reder demonstrates how that tradition has been maintained, even when the language has not. Reder draws parallels between stories collected in Cree (for example, by Wolfart and Ahenakew), and English language writings of Edward Ahenakew and others (published and unpublished). All reflect *nêhiyawi-itâpisiniwin* "Cree worldview or way of seeing" and *nêhiyawi-mâmitonêyihcikan* "Cree consciousness or thinking." Whether in Cree or in English, these *âcimowinisa* are valuable examples of Indigenous literature.

In Part 2, the stories shift from the *âcimisowina* "personal, autobiographical stories" to *âcathôhkîwina* "sacred stories," the more formal and commonly recognized style of traditional Cree literature. Solomon explains in the *kiskinwahamâkîwina* or "lessons" that open Chapter 9: in a world uninterrupted by colonialism and its agenda of genocide, these traditional stories would have formed the winter curriculum of a Cree child's education.

Solomon's traditional education continued during summers at home, as we see in Part 1. But when he was taken away to residential school, the remainder of his traditional education was suspended and replaced with Anglican church-based, Western-style "schooling." Solomon had only his preschool years in which to listen and learn from his mother's annual tellings of the *âcathôhkîwina*. Absence from the family over the winter kept him from hearing the annual retellings that were essential in the oral tradition for securing the stories within listeners' memories. Many of his peers had no such opportunities at all.

In live storytelling sessions, Solomon has spoken about how his memory of those winter nights was reawakened. As an adult, he found a 1929 article from the *Journal of American Folklore,* titled

"Cree Trickster Tales." In that article, the Reverend Edward Ahenakew presents, in English only, the same *âcathôhkîwina* Solomon had heard from his mother as a young child. (As an aside, we might also note that Edward Ahenakew, who passed away in 1961, may have been the only other fluent reader and writer of Cree to use those skills for prolific creative expression until Solomon began to do so.)

Solomon describes the process of using the written records to supplement his personal memories: "In the process of reclaiming the traditional stories from the English back to Cree, I've appropriated some passages directly. I am grateful to Edward Ahenakew for writing the stories, as they helped to put the pieces together in my jigsaw-puzzle memory."

The *âcathôhkîwina* that form Part 2 call upon all of Solomon's skills as a speaker, a writer, a storyteller, and a writer of Cree. To honour their oral spirit, he first creates audio or video recordings of his storytelling performances before an in-person or online audience, alternating in his performance between Cree and English to accommodate listeners of different levels. The recordings are then transcribed word by word for online or print presentation.

Considering this book as a whole, what it represents of Solomon's life, and his passion for reclaiming and restoring the Cree language, it's not difficult to see Solomon as an *owawiyasihiwîw ayamihâw-kiskinwahamâtowikamikohk ohci*, a "residential school trickster." In spite of the system's blatant intent to kill the Indian in the child, in spite of its effort to silence traditional languages and erase traditional cultures, Solomon Ratt evaded all those plans. He has worked persistently ever since to recover all that was taken. He calls on others to join him on the Trickster's metaphorical raft, to reclaim and share, and to breathe life back into Cree language and culture.

Editorial Notes

Additional Cree Genres

Besides the *âcimisowina* "personal, autobiographical stories" of Part 1, and the *âcathôhkîwina* "sacred stories" of Part 2, this volume also includes *nikamowini-pîkiskwîwin* "poetry," *kiskinwahamâkîwina* "lessons," and *sîhkimâwasowina* "counselling speeches" or "encouragement." Some smaller pieces are designated *kiskisiwinisa* "little memories," or *mâmitonîthihcikana* "thoughts." A genre is suggested for each individual piece in "Notes to the Texts" at the end of this book, though some pieces, with their layers of teachings and memory, might deserve several.

Dialect

All of the stories in this book are presented in the language of Solomon's childhood: *nîhithowîwin*, the th-dialect, also known as Woods or Woodlands Cree. Woods Cree is spoken across northern Saskatchewan, and extends into northern Manitoba.

In Solomon's book, *nîhithaw âcimowina / Woods Cree Stories* (2014, xiv–xvi), editor Arok Wolvengrey details dialect features that differ between Solomon's th-dialect and other western dialects. His summary chart is reproduced here:

	th ~ y ~ n	î / ê	VhC
Dialect	"I; me"	"go home"	"I hear it"
Woods	nî**th**a	kîwî	nipi**h**tîn
northern Plains	ni**y**a	kîwî	nip**î**htîn
southern Plains	ni**y**a	kîw**ê**	nip**ê**htên
Swampy	nî**n**a	kîw**ê**	nip**ê**htên

Through many years of teaching, Solomon has learned to switch fluidly between his own th-dialect and the y-dialect (*nêhiyawêwin*, or Plains Cree) that has been more common in the classroom. His day-to-day writing may be in either. Some stories, previously published in y-dialect, have been converted to the th-dialect for the purposes of this book (and are identified in "Notes to the Texts").

All of the writing gathered here is presented both in Standard Roman Orthography (or SRO), and in Syllabics, with English translation. Most of the individual pieces have appeared on the Cree Literacy Network (creeliteracy.org) at some point over the last ten years. There, they are accompanied by Solomon's own audio recordings. These audio-assisted readings allow students to advance more quickly by working simultaneously on linguistic and reading fluency. Specific URLS and additional publication details can also be found in "Notes to the Texts" at the end of this book.

Syllabic Writing Style

nîhithaw âcimowina / Woods Cree Stories (2014, xvi–xx) also provides an outline of Woods Cree Syllabics. This book differs somewhat from that model. In this book, as in Solomon's classes at First Nations University, the characters ᐃ and ᐄ are used to distinguish the short vowel [i], and its long counterpart [î]. Although the th-dialect lacks the [ê] vowel sound, some northern communities prefer to use the symbol ᐁ [ê] in place of ᐄ [î]. We depart from this northern convention in this book: consistent use of the characters ᐃ [i] and ᐄ [î] has been found to reduce confusion for students reading multiple dialects. Our Syllabic chart looks like this:

	i	î	o	ô	a	â	[finals]
[vowels]	ᐃ	ᐄ	ᐅ	ᐆ	ᐊ	ᐋ	
w	ᐏ	ᐑ	ᐓ	ᐕ	ᐘ	ᐚ	ᐤ
p	ᐱ	ᐲ	ᐳ	ᐴ	ᐸ	ᐹ	ᑊ
t	ᑎ	ᑏ	ᑐ	ᑑ	ᑕ	ᑖ	ᐟ
k	ᑭ	ᑮ	ᑯ	ᑰ	ᑲ	ᑳ	ᐠ
c	ᒋ	ᒌ	ᒍ	ᒎ	ᒐ	ᒑ	ᐨ
m	ᒥ	ᒦ	ᒧ	ᒨ	ᒪ	ᒫ	ᒼ
n	ᓂ	ᓃ	ᓄ	ᓅ	ᓇ	ᓈ	ᐣ
s	ᓯ	ᓰ	ᓱ	ᓲ	ᓴ	ᓵ	ᐢ
y	ᔨ	ᔩ	ᔪ	ᔫ	ᔭ	ᔮ	ᐩ
th	ᖨ	ᖩ	ᖪ	ᖫ	ᖬ	ᖭ	ᙾ
	l: ᓬ	r: ᕒ	h: ᐦ	hk: ᕽ	[period]: ᙮		

A small sample of a letter to Solomon from his mother, Alice, illustrates the same omission of character ∇ (ê) and corresponding consonant-plus-∇ Syllabic characters:

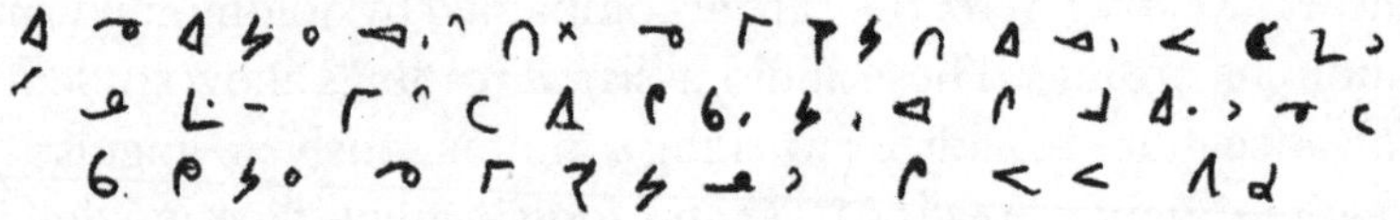

ᐄ ᓃᐦᐃᖬᐊᐧᐢᑏᐠ ᓂᒥᖩᐧᖩᐦᑏᐣ ᐄ ᐋᐧᐸᐦᑕᒫᐣ
ᓇᒫᐧᐨ ᒥᐢᑕᐦᐃ ᑮᑲᐧᖬ ᐋᒋᒧᐃᐧᐣ ᓂᑕᖭᐣ
ᑲᐦᑭᖬᐤ ᓂᒥᖭᐧᖭᓈᐣ ᑭᐹᐹ ᐱᑯ

î-nîhithawastîk nimithwîthihtîn î-wâpahtamân
namwâc mistahi kîkwaya âcimowin nitayân
kahkithaw nimithwâyânân kipâpâ piko

I am happy to see that.
I don't have much news to tell.
We are all well (except) your father only

Another interesting detail of the letter is the use of Syllabics for names. This was common practice for people with Syllabics as their only writing system.

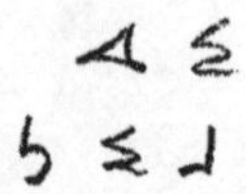

ᐊᖨᐢ (written as "alis") for "Alice."
ᓴᖨᒧ (written as "sal[o]mo") for "Solomon."

Many, many conventions followed in this volume reflect the practices for Cree-bilingual books established by Freda Ahenakew and H.C. Wolfart through the 1980s and 1990s, and replicated more recently in volumes edited by Arok Wolvengrey in the First

Nations Language Readers series from the University of Regina Press. Having assisted with that earlier work myself, it is an honour to contribute to this volume, a significant demonstration of what fully fluent Cree literacy in the twenty-first century can mean.

Arden Ogg, Director, Cree Literacy Network

References

Print

Bear, Glecia, et al. 1998. *kôhkominawak otâcimowiniwâwa / Our Grandmothers' Lives as Told in Their Own Words.* Edited by Freda Ahenakew and H.C. Wolfart. Regina: Canadian Plains Research Center.

Ratt, Solomon. 2014. *nîhithaw âcimowina / Woods Cree Stories*. Regina: University of Regina Press.

Reder, Deanna, 2022. *Autobiography as Indigenous Intellectual Tradition: Cree and Métis âcimisowina.* Waterloo: Wilfrid Laurier University Press.

Wolvengrey, Arok, ed. 2007. *wawiyatâcimowinisa / Funny Little Stories*. Regina: University of Regina Press.

Online

Cree Literacy Network: https://creeliteracy.org

Ahenakew, Edward. 1929. "Cree Trickster Tales." *The Journal of American Folklore*, 42(166). https://www.jstor.org/stable/i223502

Indian Chiefs of Alberta. 2011. " Citizens Plus" [The Red Paper]. *Aboriginal Policy Studies*, 1(2). doi:10.5663/aps.v1i2.11690

National Centre for Truth and Reconciliation. *Honouring the Truth, Reconciling for the Future: Summary of the Final Report of the Truth and Reconciliation Commission of Canada.* https://ehprnh2mw03.exactdn.com/wp-content/uploads/2021/01/Executive_Summary_English_Web.pdf

Santos, Eddie. Syllabics App. https://syllabics.app

The *itwêwina* Online Dictionary: https://itwewina.altlab.app

ᑳ ᐲ ᐃᓯ ᑭᐢᑭᓯᔮᐣ

ᑖᐱᑲ ᐋᒐᖫᐦᑮᐏᓇ
ᑕ ᑮ ᐲ ᑮᐑᒪᑲᐦᑭ

ᑳᐏ ᒥᐦᑐᑎᕽ ᐲᑐᐦᑏ ᐑᓴᐦᑮᒑᕽ,
ᐑᓴᐦᑮᒑᕽ ᑳᐏ ᒥᐦᑐᑎᕽ ᐲᑐᐦᑏ᙮
ᓂᑕᔭᒥᐦᒋᑮᐏᐣ ᑲᑮᐱᐢᑲᑦ
ᓂᑭᐢᑭᓇᐧᐦᐊᒫᑯᓯᐏᐣ;
ᓂᐲᑭᐢᑮᐧᐏᐣ, ᓂᓃᐦᐃᖬᐚᑎᓯᐏᐣ,
ᓇᔩᐦᑖᐏᐦᐃᑯᐤ ᐋᑲᖭᓰᒧᐏᐣ᙮
ᑳᐏ ᒥᐦᑐᑎᕽ ᐲᑐᐦᑏ ᐑᓴᐦᑮᒑᕽ,
ᐑᓴᐦᑮᒑᕽ ᑳᐏ ᒥᐦᑐᑎᕽ ᐲᑐᐦᑏ
ᑳ ᒪᑏᐧ ᒐᒍᐦᑲᐦᐊᕽ ᓂᐱᐩ ᐊᒥᐢᐠ ᐅᓱᐩ ᐅᐦᒋ᙮

ᑭᐢᑭᓯᐃᐧᓇ

1
ᐄ ᐋᐸᓵᐸᐦᑕᒫᐣ

1. ᐄ ᐊᑎ ᐳᐋᐧᑕᒫᐣ

ᓂᑮ ᑭᑕᐦᐊᒫᑲᐧᐠ ᐄᑳ ᑕ ᐲᑭᐢᑮᐧᔮᐣ ᓃᐦᐃᖬᐄᐧᐃᐧᐣ
ᓂᐲᑭᐢᑮᐧᐃᐧᐣ ᐃᑕ
ᑳ ᑭᐢᑮᖨᐦᑕᒫᐣ ᐃᑲᐧ ᑳ ᐃᐧᐦᑕᒫᐣ ᓂᑕᐢᑭᐩ᙮
ᓂᓇᐦᐊᐢᑖᓱᐃᐧᐣ,
ᓂᑎᖨᓃᓯᐃᐧᐣ,
ᑳ ᐃᓯ ᓃᐦᐃᖪᐋᐧᑎᓯᔮᐣ
ᑮ ᓂᑐᓇᒪᐧᐠ – ᒫᑲ ᑮ ᐹᐧᐦᐱᓃᐊᐧᐠ –
ᑕ ᒦᐢᑯᑕᐢᑖᒥᐠ ᓂᑎᑏᖨᒥᓱᐃᐧᐣ
ᑳ ᐃᓯ ᓃᐦᐃᖪᐋᐧᑎᓯᔮᐣ
ᒪᓯᓇᐦᐃᑲᓈᐱᐢᐠ ᑕ ᐱᓯᑲᐧᐢᑏᐠ
ᐃᑕ ᑕ ᐅᐦᐱᑭᐦᑖᓄᐃᐧᐠ ᐅᐢᑭᔮᑎᓯᐃᐧᐣ
ᐃᑲᐧ ᐅᐢᑭ ᐃᑕᑭᓱᐃᐧᐣ
ᐃᑕ ᓂᓃᐦᐃᖪᐋᐧᑎᓯᐃᐧᐣ
ᐄ ᒦᐢᑕᐦᐃᑳᑏᐠ ᐃᑲᐧ ᐄ ᑳᓲᐦᐃᑳᑏᐠ

ᐃᑲ· ᐊᓂᐦᐃ ᐃᑏᔨᒥᓱᐃ·ᓇ,
“ᐅᑮᐢᑮ·ᐲᐢᐠ,” “ᐅᑭᐦᑎᒥᐤ,” “ᒪᒑᔨᓯᐃ·ᐣ,” ᐃᑲ· ᑲᐦᑭᔭᐤ ᑮᑲ·+
ᑳ ᐃᓯ ᒪᒋ ᐃᑏᔨᐦᒋᑳᓱᐟ “ᐃᔨᓂᐤ”
ᐊᓇ ᐅᑭᒫᐃ·ᐃ·ᐣ ᑳ ᐅᔭᐢᑖᐟ
ᐃᑯᑕ ᐱᓯᑲ·ᐢᑏ ᒪᓯᓇᐦᐃᑲᓈᐱᐢᑯᕽ ᑕ ᐅᔭᐢᑖᓂᐃ·ᐠ᙮
ᑮ ᐹ·ᐦᐱᓃᐊ·ᐠ!

2. ᐄ ᒪᐢᑲᒥᐦᐟ ᐅᒐᐋ·ᓯᓰᐃ·ᐃ·ᐣ

ᒋᑰᒋ:
ᐄ ᐊᐋ·ᓯᓰᐃ·ᔭᐣ, ᐄ ᐸᐹᒥ ᒦᑕᐄ·ᔭᐣ,
ᐄ ᐸᐹᒥ ᑳ·ᐢᑯᐦᑎᔭᐣ, ᐄ ᐃᐢᑳ·ᐦᑕᐃ·ᔭᐣ ᒥᐢᑎᑲ·ᐠ,
ᐳᑯ ᑮᑲ·+ ᐄ ᒫᒪᐢᑳᑕᒪᐣ,
ᐄ ᑭᐦᒋᓈᐦᐅᔭᐣ ᐄ ᓵᑭᐦᐃᑲᐃ·ᔭᐣ
… ᑮᑕᐦᑕᐄ· ᐊᔭᒥᐦᐃᑭᒫᐊ·ᐠ ᑳ ᐱ ᑳ·ᓯᐦᐃᐢᑳ·ᐤ᙮

3. ᑳᑭᑮ ᓂᑲ ᑭᐢᑭᓯᐣ

ᑳᑭᑮ ᓂᑲ ᑭᐢᑭᓯᐣ
ᑳ ᑮ ᐊᐋ·ᓯᓰᐃ·ᔮᐣ
ᐃᐢᐲ ᑳ ᑮ ᑳ·ᓯᐦᐃᑲᐃ·ᔮᐣ ᓃᑭᕽ ᐅᐦᒋ
ᑕ ᓂᑕᐃ· ᐊᔭᒥᐦᒋᑮᔮᐣ ᐅᐦᐱᒦ, ᐋ·ᐦᔭᐤ ᓃᑭᕽ ᐅᐦᒋ᙮
ᑮᐢᐱᐣ ᐊ·ᓂᑭᐢᑭᓯᔮᓂ
ᓂᑲ ᒦᑕᐋ·ᑳᑖᐊ·ᐠ
ᑲᐦᑭᔭᐤ ᐊᐋ·ᓯᓴᐠ ᑳ ᑮ ᐊ·ᓂᐦᐃᐦᒋᐠ,
ᑲᐦᑭᔭᐤ ᐊᐋ·ᓯᓴᐠ ᑳ ᑮ ᓂᐸᐦᐃᐦᒋᐠ,
ᓇᒫ·ᐨ ᓂᑲ ᑭᐢᑏᔨᒥᐦᐋᐊ·ᐠ
ᑮᐢᐱᐣ ᐊ·ᓂᑭᐢᑭᓯᑐᑕᐊ·ᑳ·ᐃ·᙮
ᑮᐢᐱᐣ ᐊ·ᓂᑭᐢᑭᓯᔮᓂ ᓂᑲ ᐊ·ᓂᐦᐅᐣ᙮
ᑮᐢᐱᐣ ᐊ·ᓂᑭᐢᑭᓯᔮᓂ ᓂᑲ ᐊ·ᓂᐦᐋ·ᐤ ᓂᑕᐦᒐᕽ᙮

4. ᐋᑑᐢᐲᐃᐧᓈᑲᐧᐣ ᐸᐸᑭᐋᐧᔮᓂ ᑮᓯᑳᐤ

ᐊᓄᐦᐨ ᐆᒪ ᐋᑑᐢᐲᐃᐧᓈᑲᐧᐣ ᐸᐸᑭᐋᐧᔮᓂ ᑮᓯᑳᐤ ᐃᑕ ᑳ ᑭᐢᑭᓯᔭᕽ ᐊᐋᐧᓯᓴᐠ ᑳ ᑮ ᑳᐧᓯᐦᐃᐦᒋᐠ ᐄᐧᑭᐋᐧᕽ ᐅᐦᒋ ᐅᐦᐱᒦ ᑕ ᓂᑕᐃᐧ ᐊᔭᒥᐦᒋᑮᒋᐠ, ᐊᔭᒥᐦᐋᐧᐃᐧ ᑭᐢᑭᓈᐧᐦᐊᒫᑐᐃᐧᑲᒥᑯᕽ ᐄ ᐃᓯ ᑳᐧᓯᐦᐃᐦᒋᐠ ᒥᑐᓂ ᐋᐧᐦᖬᐤ ᐄᐧᑭᐋᐧᕽ ᐅᐦᒋ᙮ ᒥᐢᑕᐦᐃ ᒫᓇ ᑮ ᑳᐦ ᑭᑎᒪᐦᐋᐧᐊᐧᐠ ᐃᑯᑕ ᐊᐋᐧᓯᓴᐠ, ᐊᐦᐴ ᒦᓇ ᐋᑎᐦᐟ ᐃᑯᑕ ᑮ ᓂᐸᐦᐋᐧᐊᐧᐠ᙮

ᓃᐢᑕ ᓂᑮ ᑳᐧᓯᐦᐃᑲᐃᐧᐣ᙮ ᐃᐢᐲ ᓂᑯᑖᐧᓯᐠ ᐄ ᐃᑕᐦᑐᐱᐳᓃᔮᐣ ᓂᑮ ᑳᐧᓯᐦᐃᑲᐃᐧᐣ ᑭᐢᑕᐱᓈᓂᕽ ᐃᓯ᙮ ᑖᐦᑐ ᐊᐢᑭᐩ, ᐃᑯᑕ ᓂᑮ ᓂᑕᐃᐧ ᐊᔭᒥᐦᒋᑳᐣ᙮ ᒥᑖᑕᐦᐟ ᐲᓯᑦ ᐃᑯᑕ ᓂᑮ ᑭᑎᓂᑲᐃᐧᐣ᙮ ᑳ ᓃᐱᕽ ᒫᓇ ᐳᑯ ᑳ ᑮ ᑮᐋᐧᔮᐣ᙮ ᓇᒫᐧᐨ ᓃᖬ ᓂᑮ ᐅᐦᒋ ᑭᑎᒪᐦᐃᑲᐃᐧᐣ, ᓇᒫᐧᐨ ᒦᓇ ᓂᑮ ᐅᐦᒋ ᐊᐧᓂᐦᑖᐣ ᓂᐲᑭᐢᑮᐧᐃᐧᐣ᙮ ᑭᔮᐱᐨ ᓂᓃᐦᐃᖬᐋᐧᐣ ᐄᐧᖬ ᑲᐲ ᒫᓇ ᐄ ᑮ ᓃᐦᐃᖬᐄᐧᒋᐠ ᓂᓃᑭᐦᐃᑲᐧᐠ ᐃᐢᐲ ᑳ ᑮᐄᐧᔮᐣ ᑳ ᓃᐱᕽ᙮

ᒫᑲ ᐆᒪ ᑳ ᒫᒥᑐᓃᖮᐦᑕᒫᐣ; ᓂᑭᑖᐸᐦᐆᑎᐣ ᓂᐱᒫᑎᓯᐃᐧᐣ᙮ ᒥᐢᑕᐦᐃ ᑮᑲᐧᐩ ᓂᐲ ᐋᐧᐸᐦᐆᑎᐣ ᑳ ᑮ ᐃᓯ ᐊᐧᓈᐦᐃᑯᖬᐣ ᓂᑭᐢᑭᓈᐧᐦᐊᒫᑲᐃᐧᐣ ᐃᑯᑕ ᐅᐦᐱᒦ ᐊᔭᒥᐦᐋᐧᐃᐧ ᑭᐢᑭᓈᐧᐦᐊᒫᑐᐃᐧᑲᒥᑯᕽ᙮

ᓇᒫᐧᐨ ᐊᐋᐧᓯᒦ ᐃᑯᑕ ᓂᑮ ᐅᐦᒋ ᐲᐦᐅᑎᐣ ᐋᒐᖮᐦᑮᐃᐧᓇ᙮ ᐃᔭᑯᓂ ᐊᓂᐦᐃ ᐋᒐᖮᐦᑮᐃᐧᓇ ᑳ ᑮ ᑭᐢᑭᓇᐧᐦᐊᒪᐋᐧᒋᐠ ᐅᓃᑭᐦᐃᑲᐧᐠ ᐅᒐᐋᐧᓯᒥᓯᐋᐧᐊᐧ ᑖᓂᓯ ᑕ ᐃᓯ ᐅᐦᐱᑭᐦᐋᐧᐊᐧᓱᒋᐠ, ᒦᓇ ᑖᓂᓯ ᑕ ᐃᓯ ᐱᒫᑎᓯᐠ ᐆᑕ ᐊᐢᑮᕽ᙮ ᑲᐦᑭᖬᐤ ᑮᑲᐧᐩ ᐃᑯᑕ ᐋᒐᖮᐦᑮᐃᐧᓂᕽ ᑮ ᑭᐢᑭᓇᐧᐦᐊᒫᑮᐊᐧᐠ ᐅᓃᑭᐦᐃᑯᒫᐊᐧᐠ᙮ ᓇᒎᖬ ᑮ ᐃᐢᐸᖮᐣ ᐃᔭᑯᓂ ᑭᐢᑭᓇᐧᐦᐊᒫᑮᐃᐧᓇ ᑕ ᑭᐢᑭᓇᐧᐦᐊᒫᑲᐃᐧᔮᐣ ᐄᐧᖬ ᑳ ᐱᐳᕽ ᒫᓇ ᑳ ᑮ ᐋᒐᖮᐦᑳᓂᐃᐧᐠ, ᐃᐢᐲ ᐅᐦᐱᒦ ᑳ ᑮ ᐊᔮᔮᐣ᙮

ᓇᒎᖬ ᒫᒪᐢᑳᐨ ᑳ ᐲ ᑭᑎᒫᑭᓯᔮᐣ ᓂᐱᒫᑎᓯᐃᐧᓂᕽ: ᓂᑮ ᑭᑎᒪᐦᐃᑯᐣ ᒥᓂᐦᑮᐧᐃᐧᐣ ᒦᓇ ᒪᒋ ᒪᐢᑭᐦᑭᔭ; ᓂᑮ ᐄᐧᐱᓈᐊᐧᐠ ᓂᐋᐧᐦᑰᒫᑲᐣ ᐃᑲᐧ ᒦᓇ ᓂᑕᐋᐧᓯᒥᓴᐠ; ᓇᒎᖬ ᓂᑮ ᐅᐦᒋ ᒥᒋᒥᓃᐣ ᐊᑐᐢᑮᐃᐧᐣ᙮ ᐲᖮᐢᐠ

ᓇᒨᔭ ᐊᐦᐴ ᓈᓂᑕᐤ ᐃᑕ ᓂᑮ ᐅᐦᒋ ᐑᑭᐣ᙮ ᐆᑏᓈᕽ ᒦᐢᑲᓈᕽ ᐲᔨᐢᐠ ᓂᑮ ᐑᑭᐣ᙮ ᐹᑎᒫ ᑳ ᓇᑲᑕᒫᐣ ᒥᓂᐦᑹᐏᐣ ᐃᑿ ᒪᒋ ᒪᐢᑭᐦᑭᔭ ᑳ ᐊᑎ ᑲᐢᑭᐦᑖᔮᐣ ᐊᑐᐢᑮᐏᐣ ᑕᒥᒋᒥᓇᒫᐣ; ᐹᑎᒫ ᑳ ᓇᑲᑕᒫᐣ ᒥᓂᐦᑹᐏᐣ ᐃᑿ ᒪᒋ ᒪᐢᑭᐦᑭᔭ ᑳ ᑮ ᑲᐢᑭᐦᑖᔮᐣ ᑕ ᒥᔨ ᐱᒫᑎᓯᔮᐣ; ᐹᑎᒫ ᑳ ᓇᑲᑕᒫᐣ ᒥᓂᐦᑹᐏᐣ ᐃᑿ ᒪᒋ ᒪᐢᑭᐦᑭᔭ ᑳ ᑮ ᑲᐢᑭᐦᑖᔮᐣ ᑕ ᒥᔨ ᐸᒥᐦᐊᒁᐤ ᓂᒐᐚᓯᒥᓴᐠ ᐃᑿ ᓅᓯᓯᒪᐠ᙮ ᑲᔮᐢ, ᒥᑐᓂ ᑮᑲᐨ ᓂᐢᑐᒥᑕᓇᐤ ᐊᐢᑮᐏᐣ, ᑳ ᑮ ᓇᑲᑕᒫᐣ ᐃᔭᑯ ᓂᐱᒫᑎᓯᐏᐣ᙮

ᓂᓇᓈᐢᑯᒧᐣ ᐊᓄᐦᐨ ᑳ ᐃᓯ ᐱᒫᑎᓯᔮᐣ: ᓇᒲᐨ ᐊᐘᓯᒦ ᓂᒥᓂᐦᒁᐣ ᒦᓇ ᓇᒲᐨ ᓂᑖᐸᒋᐦᑖᐣ ᒪᒋ ᒪᐢᑭᐦᑭᔭ, ᐃᑿ ᒦᓇ ᓂᐢᑐᒥᑕᓇᐤ ᐊᐢᑮᐏᐣ ᓂᐲ ᐊᑐᐢᑳᑏᐣ ᐆᒪ ᓂᑕᑐᐢᑮᐏᐣ᙮ ᓇᒪ ᐑᐦᑳᐨ ᓂᑲ ᐘᓂᑭᐢᑭᓯᐣ ᐃᑕ ᑳ ᐲ ᐅᐦᒋ ᐸᓯᑯᔮᐣ, ᐃᑕ ᑳ ᐲ ᐃᓯ ᑭᑎᒫᑭᓯᔮᐣ᙮ ᑕᐦᑐ ᑮᓯᑳᐤ ᓂᑲᑹ ᒥᔨ ᐱᒫᑎᓯᐣ᙮

5. ᑮᐢᐱᐣ ᐄᑳ ᐄ ᑮ ᐅᒐᐚᓯᒥᓯᔮᐣ

ᐅᑖᑯᓰᕽ ᓂᑮ ᓂᑕᐏ ᐚᒋᒧᐢᑕᐚᐘᐠ ᐅᑭᐢᑭᓇᐧᐦᐊᒫᑲᓂᓯᓴᐠ ᑖᓂᓯ ᑳ ᑮ ᐃᐢᐸᔨᐦᐃᑯᔮᐣ ᐃᐢᐲ ᑳ ᑮ ᓯᐲᐧᐦᑕᐦᐃᑲᐏᔮᐣ ᑕ ᓂᑕᐏ ᐊᔭᒥᐦᒋᑮᔮᐣ ᐊᔭᒥᐦᐚᐏ ᑭᐢᑭᓇᐧᐦᐊᒫᑐᐏᑲᒥᑯᕽ᙮ ᐃᐢᐲ ᑳ ᐳᓂ ᐋᒋᒧᔮᐣ ᓂᑮ ᑳᐦ ᑲᑹᒋᒥᑿᐠ ᐊᐚᓯᓴᐠ ᓇᓈᑐᕽ ᑲᑹᒋᐦᑮᒧᐏᓇ᙮

ᐱᔭᐠ ᐊᐚᓯᐢ ᓂᑮ ᑲᑹᒋᒥᐠ: “ᒧᓲᒼ, ᑭᑮ ᒥᔩᐧᔨᐦᑏᐣ ᒌ ᑳ ᑮ ᑮᓯ ᐊᔭᒥᐦᒋᑮᔮᐣ?”

“ᐄᐦᐄ,” ᓂᑮ ᐃᑖᐤ, “ᓂᐢᑕᒼ ᐅᑎ᙮ ᒫᑲ ᓂᑮ ᒥᐢᑳᓱᐣ ᐄᑳ ᓈᓂᑕᐤ ᐃᑕ ᐄ ᑮ ᐅᐦᒋ ᑏᐱᐢᑲᒫᐣ, ᐄᑳ ᓈᓂᑕᐤ ᐃᑕ ᐄ ᑮ ᑎᐲᔨᐦᑖᑯᓯᔮᐣ᙮ ᓇᒨᔭ ᐊᐚᓯᒦ ᓂᑮ ᑎᐲᔨᐦᑖᑯᓯᐣ ᓂᑎᐢᑯᓂᑲᓂᕽ, ᓇᒨᔭ ᒦᓇ ᓂᑮ ᑎᐲᔨᐦᑖᑯᓯᐣ ᐅᑏᓈᕽ, ᐋᔩᑕᐚᔨᕽ ᐃᑯᑕ ᓂᑮ ᒥᐢᑳᓱᐣ, ᐄ ᑮ ᐘᓂᐦᐅᔮᐣ ᐋᔩᑕᐚᔨᕽ ᐊᐢᑭᔭ᙮”

ᑯᑕᐠ ᐊᐚᓯᐢ ᑳ ᑲᑮᐧᒋᒥᐟ: “ᒧᓲᒼ, ᑖᓂᓯ ᒫᑲ ᑳ ᑮ ᐃᓯ ᐸᐢᐲᔭᐣ?”

“ᑭᐣᐑᐢᐠ ᓂᑮ ᐚᐦ ᐘᓄᐦᑖᐣ,” ᓂᑮ ᐃᑖᐤ, “ᒫᑲ ᐲᖬᐢᐠ ᓂᑮ ᒥᐢᑮᐣ ᓂᑕᑐᐢᑮᐏᐣ, ᐆᒪ ᐊᑐᐢᑮᐏᐣ ᐄ ᒥᖭᐧᖬᐦᑕᒫᐣ᙮ ᐆᒪ ᑳ ᐲ ᑭᐢᑭᓇᐧᐦᐊᒫᑭᔮᐣ ᒦᓇ ᑳ ᓈᐦ ᓃᐦᐃᖬᐘᓯᓇᐦᐃᑮᔮᐣ᙮ ᐃᔭᑯᓂ ᐆᐦᐅ ᑳ ᑮ ᐸᐢᐲᐦᐃᑯᔮᐣ᙮ ᓂᓇᓈᐢᑯᒧᐣ ᐑᖬ ᐊᖬᐢᐠ ᒥᐦᑮᐟ ᓂᐑᒋ ᑭᐢᑭᓇᐧᐦᐊᒫᑲᓇᐠ ᐃᑯᑏ ᐅᐦᒋ ᐊᔭᒥᐦᐋᐏ ᑭᐢᑭᓇᐧᐦᐊᒫᑐᐏᑲᒥᑯᕽ ᑮ ᐅᓵᒥ ᐘᓂᐦᐅᐘᐠ, ᐋᖭᑕᐚᖬᕽ ᓃᓯ ᐊᐢᑭᔭ ᐑᖬᐚᐤ ᐄ ᑮ ᒥᒋᒫᐧᒌᒋᐠ᙮”

ᑮᐢᐱᐣ ᐁᑳ ᐅᐦᒋ ᓂᑕᐚᓯᒥᓴᐠ ᓂᑲ ᑮ ᒥᒋᒧᓯᓂᐦᑕᕀ ᐋᖭᑕᐚᖬᕽ ᐊᐢᑭᔭ᙮ ᓂᓇᓈᐢᑯᒧᐣ: *I am grateful.*

6. ᑲᑮᐹᑎᓴᐠ

ᑮ ᑲᑮᐧ ᓂᐸᐦᑖᐘᐠ ᓂᐲᑭᐢᑮᐧᐏᐣ
ᐃᐢᐲ ᑳ ᑮ ᑭᐢᑭᓇᐧᐦᐊᒪᐏᒋᐠ:
ᑲᑮᐹᑎᓴᐠ!
ᓂᑮ ᑭᐢᑭᓇᐧᐦᐊᒪᐏᑲᐧᐠ
ᑖᓂᓯ ᑭᑕ ᐃᓯ ᐸᓯᑰᐦᑖᔮᐣ
ᐊᓂᒪ ᑳ ᑮ ᓈᐢᐱᑎᐦᑳᐧᒥᐢᑲᐦᑳᐧᐤ᙮

2
ᐄ ᒪᐧᔩ ᓂᑕᐃᐧ ᐊᓴᒥᐦᒋᑮᓵᐤ

1. ᓂᒑᐦᑯᓲᐃᐧᑲᒥᑯᐣ

ᐃᐢᑮᐧᔫᓂᕽ ᑳ ᑮ ᑭᔭᑲᐊᐧᐤ ᓂᑳᐄᐧᐸᐤ ᓂᑮ ᐋᒋᒧᐢᑖᐤ ᐃᐢᐲ ᑳ ᑮ ᓂᐦᑖᐄᐧᑭᐊᐧᐤ:

ᐃᑯᐢᐲ ᐄᓴ ᐄ ᑮ ᒥᑭᐢᑳᐤ, ᑲᐢᑲᑎᓄᐃᐧᐲᓯᐟ ᐄ ᑮ ᐊᑭᒥᐦᐟ, ᑳ ᑮ ᐸᒨᐦᑏᐦᐅᒋᐤ ᓂᓈᑭᐦᐃᑲᐧᐤ ᐃᑳᐧ ᐅᓅᑏᒥᐋᐧᐊᐧ, ᐊᐧᓂᐦᐃᑮᐢᑲᓈᕽ ᐄ ᑮ ᐃᑐᐦᑏᐦᐅᒋᐤᐤ᙮ ᑖᐃᐧᐨ ᐆᒪ ᐄᓴ ᐄ ᑮ ᐅᑖᐸᐦᐊᐢᑎᒦᐧᒋᐤ ᐃᐢᐲ ᑳ ᑮ ᐊᑎ ᐋᐦᑯᓯᐟ ᓂᑳᐄᐧᐸᐤ, ᐊᔦᐢᐤ ᐄᓴ ᐃᑯᐢᐲ ᐄ ᑮ ᑭᑭᐢᑲᐋᐧᐊᐧᓯᐟ; ᓃᔭ ᐆᒪ ᐄᓴ ᐃᑯᑕ ᐄ ᑮ ᑭᑭᐢᑲᐃᐧᐟ᙮ ᐃᐧᐦᑕᒪᐄᐧᐤ ᓄᐦᑖᐄᐧᐸᓇ ᐄ ᐄᐧ ᐋᐧᐦᑯᓯᐟ, ᐅᒑᐸᓈᐢᑯᓯᕽ ᐄᓴ ᐄ ᑮ ᐹᓯᐟ ᐄᐢᑳᐧ ᓄᐦᑖᐄᐧᐸᐤ ᐄ ᐱᒥᑎᓴᐦᐊᐢᑎᒦᐧᐟ᙮

ᓰᒫᐤ ᑏᐹᐧᑏᐤ ᐅᐄᐧᒌᐋᐧᑲᓇ ᓄᐦᑖᐄᐧᐸᐤ, ᐄ ᐃᐧᐦᑕᒪᐋᐧᐟ ᐄ ᐄᐧ ᐋᐧᐦᑯᓯᔦᐟ ᓂᑳᐄᐧᐸᓇ᙮ ᑖᐲᐧ ᐹᑳᓂ ᓈᑕᑳᐨ

ᐃᓯ ᐅᑖᐸᐦᐊᐢᑎᒦᐘᐤ᙮ ᐃᑯᑏ ᓀᑏ ᑮᐚᑎᓄᕽ, ᓰᐸᓇᑭᒥᐘᓄᕽ ᑳ ᑮ ᐊᑎ ᑭᐱᐦᒌᒋᐤ᙮ ᐚᓵᑲᐣ ᐃᑯᑕ ᐄ ᑮ ᐊᑎ ᒫᓄᑮᒋᐤ᙮

ᐘᐦᐘ+, ᑲᐧᔭᐢᐤ ᐄᓴ ᑮ ᓲᐦᑭ ᐊᑐᐢᑮᐘᐤ ᐊᓂᑭ ᓈᐲᐘᐤ, ᐄ ᑮᐢᑲᑕᐦᐃᐦᑕᑹᒋᐤ, ᐄ ᐐ ᐚᐢᑲᐦᐃᑲᓃᐢᑕᒪᐚᒋᐤ ᓂᑳᐐᐸᓇ ᐃᑕ ᑭᑕ ᓂᐦᑖᐏᑭᐘᐤ᙮ ᒥᐢᒋᑯᓴ ᐄ ᑮ ᐊᐸᐦᑫᐧᒋᐤ ᑭᓯᐤ ᒦᓇ ᒪᐢᑮᑲᐧ ᐄ ᑕᐦᑯᐦᑕᐢᑖᒋᐤ ᐊᐸᐦᑳᐧᓂᕽ᙮ ᓇᒨᔥ ᑭᐣᐐᐢᐤ ᐃᐢᐲ ᑳ ᑮᓯ ᐚᐢᑲᐦᐃᑲᓂᐦᑮᒋᐤ ᐃᐢᐲ ᑳ ᐱ ᓂᐦᑖᐏᑮᔮᐣ᙮

ᓂᑳᐐᐸᐣ ᓂᑮ ᐃᑎᐤ: “ᐄ ᑮ ᐋᐦᑯᓰᐏᑲᒥᑯᐦᑳᑲᐏᔮᐣ ᐃᑯᐢᐲ᙮”

2. ᓴᕒᐊᒨ ᐃᑳᐧᓂ ᐸᑯ ᐊᕒᐋᐧᐟ

ᓇᒨᔥ ᑮᑲᐧ+ ᑯᑕᐤ ᓂᐐᐦᔦᐏᐣ ᐊᔦᐢᐤ ᐃᐢᐲ ᑳ ᑮ ᓂᐦᑖᐏᑮᔮᐣ ᐱᔭᐤ ᐊᐘ ᐊᔭᒥᐦᐃᑮᒫᓯᐢ (ᐅᓈᐲᒪ ᐊᓇ ᐃᐢᑮᐤ ᑳ ᑮ ᐸᒥᐦᐃᐐᐏᐟ “*Solomon*” ᑮ ᐃᓯᔦᐦᑳᓱᔦᐘ, ᐃᔭᑯ ᐄ ᑮ ᐅᑹᒦᓯᔮᐣ) ᓂᑮ ᑭᐢᑭᓇᐚᒋᐦᐃᐤ, ᑖᐱᐢᑰ- ᐄ ᑮ ᓰᑲᐦᐊᐦᑕᐏᐟ ᓀᑏ ᐘᓂᐦᐃᑮᐢᑲᓈᕽ ᐄ ᑮ ᐃᑏᐧᐟ “ᓴᕒᐊᒨ ᐃᑳᐧᓂ ᐸᑯ ᐊᕒᐋᐧᐟ.”

ᐃᐢᐲ ᑖᐲᐧ ᑕᑮ ᓰᑲᐦᐊᐦᑖᑲᐏᔮᐣ, ᓀᑏ ᐊᔭᒥᐦᐃᑲᒥᑯᕽ ᐋᒪᒋᐐᐢᐱᒧᐏᓂᕽ, ᐊᔭᒥᐦᐃᑮᒫᐤ ᓇᒫᐧ- ᑮ ᐅᐦᒋ ᐸᑭᑎᓇᐨ ᑯᑕᐤ ᐐᐦᔦᐏᐣ ᑭᑕ ᒦᔦᑲᐏᐘᐤ ᐊᔦᐢᐤ ᓵᓴ+ ᐄ ᑮ ᑭᐢᑭᓇᐚᒋᐦᐃᑲᐏᔮᐣ “*Solomon.*” “ᐃᑳᐧᓂ ᐸᑯ” ᑳ ᐋᑲᔮᓰᒧᓈᓇᐏᐤ “*that is all.*” ᓀᔮ ᐆᒪ ᓴᕒᐅᒨ ᐃᑳᐧᓂ ᐸᑯ ᐊᕒᐋᐧᐟ.

3. ᐊᒍᐢᑮᐏᓂᓴ

ᑳ ᑮ ᐊᐋᐧᓯᓰᐏᔮᐣ ᒥᐢᑕᐦᐃ ᒫᓇ ᓂᑮ ᐊᑐᐢᑮᐦᐃᑲᐏᐣ᙮ ᐆᐦᐅ ᐊᒍᐢᑮᐏᓂᓴ ᓂᑮ ᐃᑑᑏᐣ: ᓂᑮ ᓈᒥᓂᐦᑖᐣ, ᓂᑮ ᓂᑯᐦᑖᐣ, ᓂᑮ ᑖᐸᑳᐧᐣ᙮ ᓂᑮ ᐐᒋᐦᐋᐤ ᓅᐦᑖᐐᐸᐣ ᑕ ᐸᑭᑕᐦᐋᐧᐟ ᐃᑲᐧ ᑕ ᓈᑕᔭᐲᐟ᙮ ᓂᑮ ᐲᑲᐧᑕᐦᐆᐹᐣ ᑕ ᑳᐧᐱᑮᔮᐣ᙮ ᓂᑮ ᓇᑲᐧᑎᓱᐣ᙮

ᑲᐦᑭᖬᐤ ᐆᐦᐅ ᐊᒍᐢᑮᐃᐧᓂᓴ ᓂᑮ ᐄᐧᒋᐦᐃᑯᐣ᙮ ᐃᑯᓯ ᐆᒪ ᑳ ᑮ ᐋᐧᐸᐦᑕᒫᐣ ᐃᑯᑕ ᐄ ᑎᐲᖬᐦᑖᑯᓯᔮᐣ, ᐄ ᐄᐧᒋᐦᐅᐄᐧᔮᐣ᙮

4. ᐄᐧᒋᓵᓂ ᑲᐦᑮᐧᖨᐦᑐᐃᐧᐣ

ᐃᐢᐲ ᑳ ᑮ ᐊᐋᐧᓯᓰᐃᐧᔮᐣ ᒥᐦᒌᑖᐧᐤ ᒫᓇ ᓂᑮ ᑭᑎᒪᐦᐃᑲᐧᐠ ᓃᑎᓵᓇᐠ᙮ ᓇᒨᖬ ᒫᓇ ᓂᑮ ᐸᑭᑎᓂᑲᐧᐠ ᑕ ᐄᐧᒋ ᒦᑕᐄᐧᒪᑳᐧᐤ᙮

ᐱᔭᑳᐧᐤ ᐆᒪ ᐄ ᐱᐳᕽ ᐄ ᑮ ᓵᐦᓲᐢᑲᐧᒋᐄᐧᒋᐠ, ᒫᑲ ᓇᒨᖬ ᓂᑮ ᐸᑭᑎᓂᑲᐧᐠ ᑕ ᐄᐧᒋᒦᑕᐄᐧᒪᑳᐧᐤ᙮ ᓂᑮ ᑮᐄᐧᑎᓴᐦᐃᑲᐧᐠ᙮ ᓂᑮ ᐊᑎ ᑮᐄᐧ ᒫᑐᐣ ᐃᑯᑕ ᐅᐦᒋ᙮ ᓂᑮ ᑭᑎᒫᑭᓇᐃᐧᐠ ᓅᐦᑖᐄᐧᐸᐣ᙮ ᐃᑯᑕ ᓰᒫᐠ ᑮ ᐊᑎ ᐅᖬᑕᐦᐊᐨ ᒥᐢᑎᐠ, ᓇᐸᑭᑖᐸᓈᐢᑲᐧ ᐄ ᐄᐧ ᐅᖬᑕᐦᐄᐢᑕᒪᐃᐧᐟ᙮ ᓇᒨᖬ ᑭᐣᐄᐧᐢᐠ ᓵᓴᐩ ᑳ ᑮᓯ ᐅᖬᑕᐦᐋᐧᐟ ᓂᓇᐸᑭᒑᐸᓈᐢᑯᓴ᙮ ᑲᐧᔭᐢᐠ ᓂᑮ ᒌᐦᑮᖨᐦᑏᐣ ᐃᐢᐲ ᑳᐃᐧ ᑳ ᓂᑕᐃᐧ ᓲᐢᑲᐧᒋᐄᐧᔮᐣ ᐃᑕ ᑳ ᓲᐢᑲᐧᒋᐄᐧᒋᐠ ᓃᑎᓵᓇᐠ᙮

ᓂᑮ ᓇᓅᖬᒋᒫᐊᐧᐠ ᐊᖨᐢᐠ ᓃᖬ ᐳᑯ ᐄ ᐊᔮᐊᐧᐠ ᓇᐸᑭᒑᐸᓈᐢᑯᐢ᙮ ᐃᑳᐧᓂ ᓂᑕᑎ ᓲᐢᑲᐧᒋᐋᐧᐣ᙮ ᐊᐧᐦᐋᐧ ᓂᐱᐢᑕᐦᐋᐧᐤ ᒥᐢᑎᐠ! ᒥᑐᓂ ᐄ ᓈᐦᑖᐧᓯᒪᐠ ᓂᓇᐸᑭᒑᐸᓈᐢᑯᐢ᙮ ᑲᐧᔭᐢᐠ ᑮ ᒪᑏᐧ ᐸᐦᐱᐊᐧᐠ ᓃᑎᓵᓇᐠ᙮

5. ᐄᐧᓴᐦᑮᒑᕽ ᑏᐧᐦᐅᐤ ᐊᐧᓂᐦᐃᑮᐢᑲᓈᕽ

"ᐋᐤ, ᐄᐧᓴᐦᑮᒑᕽ:

ᐊᐱᓰᐢ ᑲ ᒪᓯᓇᐦᐊᒫᑎᐣ᙮

ᓂᑭᐢᑭᓯᐣ ᓂᔮᓇᐣ ᐄ ᑮ ᐃᑕᐦᑐᐱᐳᓃᔮᐣ ᐊᐧᓂᐦᐃᑮᐢᑲᓈᕽ ᐄ ᒦᑕᐄᐧᔮᐣ ᒥᐢᑲᐧᒦᕽ, ᐄ ᒪᑯᓰᑮᓯᑳᐠ ᐃᐢᐲ ᑳ ᑏᐧᐦᐅᔭᐣ ᐱᒥᖭᑲᓂᐢ ᐄ ᐋᐸᒥᐦᑖᔭᐣ᙮ ᑭᐊᐧᖬᐄᐧᔮᐦᑕᐋᐧᐣ ᒥᓯᐄᐧ ᐄ ᒦᐢᑯᓯᐦᐅᔭᐣ ᒥᓯ ᒪᐢᑭᒧᐟ ᐄ ᓇᔭᐦᑖᔭᐣ᙮ ᐃᑯᑕ ᓂᓃᐸᐃᐧᓈᐣ, ᐄ ᒫᒪᐢᑳᑕᒫᕽ᙮ ᐃᑲᐧ ᑳ ᐅᑎᓇᒪᐣ ᑮᑲᐧᔭ ᑭᒪᐢᑭᒧᑎᕽ ᐅᐦᒋ, ᑭᒫᐦ ᒦᖬᓈᐣ ᑳ ᐃᑕᐦᑕᐧᓯᔮᕽ ᓃᖬᓈᐣ

ᐊᐚᓯᓴᐠ, ᓲᐃᐧᕇᓴᐠ ᐃᑿ ᒦᑕᐚᑲᓇ᙮ ᐃᑿ ᑳ ᐅᐦᐸᐦᐅᔭᐤ, ᑮᐚᑎᓅᕽ ᐃᓯ᙮ ᑭᑮ ᐃᑏᔨᒥᑎᐤ ᐄ ᑮᐚᑯᒥᓂᔭᐤ, ᒫᑲ ᐄᑐᑮ ᑯᑕᑭᕽ ᐊᐧᓂᐦᐃᑮᐢᑳᓈᕽ ᐄ ᐃᑕᑯᒥᓂᔭᐤ ᑕ ᐸᐦᐱᐦᑮᐧᐦᐊᕆᐠ ᑯᑕᑲᐠ ᐊᐚᓯᓴᐠ᙮

ᓂᔦ ᑭᔫᑏᐟ,

ᓴᕓᐊᔫ

6. ᑖᐳᑮᔨᐦᑕᒧᐃᐧᐤ

ᑲᔮᐢ ᑳ ᑮ ᐊᐚᓯᓲᐃᐧᔮᐤ ᓂᑮ ᐹᐦ ᐱᒧᐦᑏᐦᐅᓈᐤ ᒫᓇ ᒥᓯᐚ ᐃᑏ ᒫᐦᑖᐃᐧᓲᐲᕽ᙮ ᐱᔭᑳᐧᐤ ᐄ ᓲᑳᐧᕽ ᓂᑮ ᐚᐸᒫᓈᐤ ᒨᓴᐧ ᐄ ᐋᓱᐊᐧᐦᐊᕽ ᓵᑲᐦᐃᑲᐤ᙮ ᑮᓯᐢᑲᐤ ᑮ ᐅᑎᐦᑎᓇᐨ ᐲᒥᓈᐦᑳᐧᐤ ᓅᐦᑯᒥᐢ ᐃᑲᐧ ᑮ ᐊᑎ ᑖᐸᑮᐧᐄᐧᐱᓃᐤ ᐃᔭᑯᓂ ᒨᓴᐧ᙮ ᒫᑲ ᐊᓇ ᒨᓴᐧ ᑲᐧᔭᐢᐠ ᓂᑮ ᓲᑭᐦᐃᐠ ᐊᔨᐢᐠ ᒥᑐᓂ ᑭᐦᒋᐋᐧᐠ ᑮᒫᓂᕽ ᐃᑕ ᑳ ᐊᐱᐊᐧᐠ ᐄ ᐲ ᐃᓯᒋᒦᐟ᙮ ᐲᔨᐢᐠ ᐋᑕᐄᐧᔦ ᑮ ᓂᐸᐦᐄᐤ ᐃᔭᑯᓂ ᒨᓴᐧ ᓅᐦᑯᒥᐢ ᐄ ᒪᐧᐲ ᑲᐧᑕᐱᐢᑲᒪᐧᐠ ᑮᒫᓂᐢ ᐃᐢᐲ ᑳ ᑮ ᑲᑮᐧ ᑕᐸᓲᐦᐊᐠ ᐊᓇ ᒨᓴᐧ᙮ ᐊᐄᐧᓇ ᐄᑐᑮ ᓇᐊᐧ ᑮ ᓲᑭᓯᐤ, ᓀᔦ ᐊᐃᐧᑳᑮ ᑮ ᐊᓇ ᒨᓴᐧ? ᒪᑖᐤ ᑮ ᐄ ᑮ ᓂᑕᐃᐧ ᐚᐸᒫᐟ ᓅᓲ ᒨᓴᐧ ᒥᓂᐢᑎᑯᕽ ᐃᑕ ᑳ ᑮ ᓂᐦᑖᐃᐧᑭᔨᐟ ᐅᐢᑳᔨᓯᓴ?

7. ᐅᐦᐸᐦᐅᐃᐧᐲᓯᐢ

ᑕᐦᑐ ᐊᐢᑭᐩ, ᐊᓄᐦᐨ ᑳ ᐃᐢᐸᔨᐠ, ᓂᑮ ᐲ ᓈᑕᐦᐅᑲᐃᐧᓈᐤ ᒫᓇ ᑕ ᓂᑕᐃᐧ ᐊᔭᒥᐦᒋᑮᔮᕽ ᐚᐦᔫᐤ ᓃᑭᓈᕽ ᐅᐦᒋ᙮ ᐃᑯᐢᐲ ᓇᒫᐧᐨ ᑮ ᐅᐦᒋ ᑕᑲᐧᒧᐤ ᒦᐢᑲᓈᐤ ᐋᒪᒋᐚᐢᐱᒧᐃᐧᓂᕽ᙮ ᐅᐦᒋᑕᐤ ᐳᑯ ᒫᓇ ᑕ ᐲ ᓈᑕᐦᐅᑯᔮᕽ ᐱᒦᔭᑲᓇ, ᑭᑕ ᐅᐦᐸᐦᐅᔮᕽ᙮ ᐱᔭᑳᐧᐤ ᓂᑮ ᑲᑮᐧᒋᒫᐤ ᓂᑳᐚᐸᐤ ᑮᐢᐱᐤ ᐃᔭᑯᐦᒋ "ᐅᐦᐸᐦᐅᐃᐧᐲᓯᐢ" ᑮ ᐃᒋᑳᓲᐟ ᐊᐊᐧ ᐲᓯᐢ᙮ ᑮ ᒥᔦ ᐸᐦᐱᐤ ᒫᑲ ᓂᑮ ᐄᐧᐦᑕᒫᐠ "ᐅᐦᐸᐦᐅᐃᐧᐲᓯᐢ" ᐊᐊᐧ ᐲᓯᐢ ᐃᑖᐤ ᐊᔨᐢᐠ ᐃᑯᐢᐲ ᒫᓇ ᓲᓲᐱᓯᓴᐠ ᐃᑲᐧ ᓂᐢᑭᓯᓴᐠ ᐄ ᐊᑎ ᓂᐦᑖ ᐅᐦᐸᐦᐅᕆᐠ᙮

3
ᓂᐢᑕᑦ ᐄᐧᓴᑮᔨᐦᑕᒧᐃᐧᐣ

1. **ᒫᒥᑐᓃᔨᐦᑕ ᐆᒪ!**

ᒌᐢᐟ!

ᒫᒥᑐᓃᔨᑕ ᐆᒪ:

ᐄ ᐊᐋᐧᓯᓰᐃᐧᔭᐣ᙮ ᑮᐄᐧᑎᓄᕽ ᐱᑲᐧᑕᐢᑮᕽ ᐄ ᐄᐧᒑᔮᒪᒋᐠ ᑭᓃᑭᐦᐃᑲᐧᐠ, ᑮᑎᓵᓇᐠ, ᒦᓇ ᑭᐋᐧᐦᑰᒫᑲᓇᐠ, ᑲᓈᑕᐢᑮᕽ ᐄ ᐱᒫᒋᐦᐅᔩᐠ᙮ ᒫᐦᑖᐃᐧᓰᐲᕽ ᐄ ᐸᐹᒧᐦᑏᐦᐅᔩᐠ, ᒫᒥᕽ ᐃᓯ ᐃᑲᐧ ᑳᐃᐧ ᓇᑕᒥᕽ, ᐋᐢᑲᐤ ᒫᓇ ᐄ ᓂᑕᐃᐧ ᑭᔫᑏᔩᐠ ᒥᐢᑕᐦᐃ ᓵᑲᐦᐃᑲᓂᕽ᙮ ᑭᑮ ᒥᔪ ᐱᒫᑎᓯᓈᐋᐧᐤ᙮ ᑭᑮ ᒌᐦᑮᔨᐦᑏᐣ ᐄ ᐄᐧᒋᐦᐅᐄᐧᔭᐣ ᐃᑕ ᑳ ᐱᒪᐦᑲᒥᑭᓯᒋᐠ ᑭᓃᑭᐦᐃᑲᐧᐠ ᒦᓇ ᑭᐋᐧᐦᑰᒫᑲᓇᐠ᙮ ᑭᑮ ᒌᐦᑮᔨᐦᑏᐣ ᐄ ᒦᑕᐄᐧᔭᐣ ᐱᑲᐧᑕᐢᑮᕽ, ᑲᓈᑕᐢᑮᕽ᙮

ᓇᒨᔭ ᑭᑮ ᐅᐦᒋ ᐋᐧᑲᔮᓰᒧᐣ, ᑭᑮ ᓃᐦᐃᔪᐋᐧᐣ ᐳᑯ᙮ ᑭᑮ ᒫᐦ ᒥᔪᐦᑏᐣ ᐋᐧᒐᔫᐦᑮᐃᐧᓇ ᐃᐢᐲ ᑳ ᐱᐳᕽ᙮

ᑮᑕᐦᑕᐑ ᑳ ᐲ ᓈᑎᑲᐏᔮᐣ, ᐄ ᓯᐲᐧᐦᑕᐦᐃᑲᐏᔭᐣ ᑕ ᓂᑕᐏ ᐊᔭᒥᐦᒋᑮᔮᐣ ᐊᔭᒥᐦᐋᐏ ᑭᐢᑭᓇᐧᐦᐊᒫᑐᐏᑲᒥᑯᕽ᙮

ᐲᑐᐢ ᐊᐢᑮᕽ ᑭᑮ ᐃᑐᐦᑕᐦᐃᑲᐏᐣ᙮

2. **ᑭᐢᑭᓇᐧᐦᐊᒫᑐᐏᑖᐸᓈᐢᐠ**

ᑮ ᒥᔭ ᑮᑭᓰᐹᔮᐤ ᐃᐢᐲ ᓂᐢᑕᒼ ᑳ ᑮ ᓯᐲᐧᐦᑕᐦᐃᑲᐏᔮᐣ ᓃᑭᕽ ᐅᐦᒋ, ᐅᐦᐱᒦ ᑭᑕ ᓂᑕᐏ ᐊᔭᒥᐦᒋᑮᔮᐣ᙮ ᓂᑯᑖᐧᓯᐠ ᐃᑯᐢᐲ ᓂᑮ ᐃᑕᐦᑐᐱᐳᓈᐣ᙮ ᓇᒨᔭ ᓂᑮ ᐱ ᐑᒌᐏᑯᓈᓇᐠ ᓂᓃᑭᐦᐃᑯᓈᓇᐠ ᒥᓯ ᑖᐸᓈᐢᑯᕽ ᐃᓯ ᐑᔭ ᓂᑳᐑᐸᐣ ᐋᐦᑯᓰᐏᑲᒥᑯᕽ ᐄ ᑮ ᐊᔮᐟ, ᐄ ᑮ ᑲᑑᐦᐱᓃᐟ ᐃᑿ ᓄᐦᑖᐑᐸᐣ ᐄ ᑮ ᐴᓯᐟ ᐄᑳ ᐄ ᑮ ᓄᐦᑏ ᐚᐸᒥᑯᔮᕽ ᑕ ᓯᐲᐧᐦᑏᔮᕽ᙮

ᐃᒁᓂ ᓂᑑᓯᓯᓈᓇᐠ ᒥᓯ ᑖᐸᓈᐢᑯᕽ ᓂᑮ ᐃᓯ ᐑᒌᐏᑯᓈᓇᐠ᙮ ᓃᔭ ᐃᑿ ᓂᐢᑏᐢ ᐃᒁᓂ ᓂᐢᑕᒼ ᐄ ᑮ ᓯᐲᐧᐦᑏᔮᕽ, ᐄ ᐊᑎ ᐑᒌᐚᔮᐦᒁᐤ ᓂᒥᓯᓈᓇᐠ, ᓵᓴᐩ ᐑᔭᐚᐤ ᑮ ᓵᐦ ᓯᐲᐧᐦᑏᐘᐠ, ᑭᐢᑕᐱᓈᓂᕽ ᓵᓴᐩ ᐄ ᑮ ᓂᑕᐏ ᐊᔭᒥᐦᒋᑮᒋᐠ᙮

ᐃᒁᓂ ᓂᑮ ᐴᓯᓈᐣ ᒥᓯ ᑖᐸᓈᐢᑯᕽ᙮ ᒥᐢᑕᐦᐃ ᓵᑲᐦᐃᑲᓂᕽ ᐅᐦᒋ ᐃᐢᑯ ᑭᐢᑕᐱᓈᓂᕽ᙮ *All Saints Indian Student Residential School* ᑮ ᐃᒋᑳᑏᐤ ᐃᑯᑕ ᑭᐢᑕᐱᓈᓂᕽ ᐊᓂᒪ *residential school* ᑳ ᑮ ᐃᑐᐦᑕᐦᐃᑲᐏᔮᐣ᙮ ᑭᐣᐑᐢᐠ ᐃᑯᐢᐲ ᓂᑮ ᐱᒥᑖᐸᓲᓈᐣ, ᓇᒨᔭ ᑮ ᐅᐦᒋ ᒥᔭᐧᓯᐣ ᒦᐢᑲᓇᐤ ᑖᐱᐢᑰᐨ ᐊᓄᐦᐨ᙮

ᐃᐢᐲ ᑳ ᑮ ᐊᑎ ᓯᐲᐧᑖᐸᓲᔮᕽ ᐴᓲᑖᐸᓈᐢᑯᕽ ᓂᑮ ᐊᑎ ᒫᒧᓯᐣ, ᐄ ᒪᐏᐦᒁᑕᒁᐤ ᓂᐚᐦᑰᒫᑲᓇᐠ᙮ ᐱᔭᐠ ᐊᐘ ᐅᐢᑭᓃᑮᐢ ᓂᑮ ᑭᑎᒫᑭᓇᐏᐠ; ᑲᐲ ᓂᑮ ᐊᑎ ᐅᑕᒥᐦᐃᐠ ᐃᑯᐢᐲ, ᐄ ᐋᐦᐊᒋᒧᐢᑕᐏᐟ ᐳᑯ ᑮᑿᐩ᙮ ᐲᔭᐢᐠ ᓂᑮ ᑕᑯᑖᐸᓲᓈᐣ ᑭᐢᑕᐱᓈᓂᕽ᙮

ᐲᔭᐢᐠ ᓂᑕᑯᑖᐸᓲᓈᐣ ᑭᐢᑕᐱᓈᓂᕽ᙮ ᐚᐦᐚ! ᓂᑮ ᒫᒪᐢᑳᑏᐣ ᐃᔭᑯᕽ ᐄ ᑮ ᒫ ᐦᒥᓵᑭ ᐚᐢᑲᐦᐃᑲᓇ᙮

ᑮᑕᐦᑕᐑ ᓂᑕᑯᑖᐹᓯᓈᐣ ᓂᑭᐢᑭᓌᐦᐊᒫᑐᐏᑲᒥᑯᓈᕽ᙮ ᓂᑮ ᑲᐹᓈᐣ ᒥᓯ ᑖᐹᓈᐢᑯᕽ ᐅᐦᒋ ᐃᑿ ᓂᑮ ᓃᐸᐏᐦᐃᑲᐏᓈᐣ ᐄ ᐲᐦᐅᔮᕽ ᑭᑕ ᓂᑐᒥᑲᐏᔮᕽ ᐃᑕ ᐆᒪ ᑳ ᐑ ᑭᑏᐥᒥᑲᐏᔮᕽ᙮ ᓂᑮ ᐲᐦᑏᐣ ᓂᒥᓴᐠ ᐄ ᒪᑜ ᑏᑈᑎᐦᒋᐠ ᐃᑿ ᐃᑯᑏ ᓃᐢᑕ ᓂᑮ ᑲᑹ ᐃᑐᐦᑖᐣ ᒫᑲ ᓂᑮ ᑭᐱᐦᑎᓂᑿᐠ ᓃᒋ ᓈᐲᓯᓴᐠ᙮

ᐃᑯᑕ *residential school* ᓂᑮ ᐋᔮᐣ ᒥᑖᑕᐦᐟ ᐲᓯᑦ ᑕᐦᑐ ᐊᐢᑭᐩ, ᓇᒪ ᐑᐦᑳᐨ ᓂᑮ ᐅᐦᒋ ᑮᐚᐣ ᑳ ᒪᑯᓰᑮᓯᑳᐠ ᐹᑎᒫ ᓂᑯᑤᓯᑯᓵᑊ ᑳ ᑮ ᐃᑕᐦᑐᐱᐳᓃᔮᐣ᙮

ᐋᑕᐑᕦ ᑕᐦᑐ ᓃᐱᐣ ᒫᓇ ᑳᐏ ᓂᑮ ᑮᐚᐣ᙮

3. **ᓂᑮ ᑖᑐᐱᑎᑲᐏᐣ**

ᑭᑳᐑᓇᐤ ᐊᐢᑮᕽ ᐅᐦᒋ:
ᑲᓈᑕᐢᑮᕽ ᐄ ᑮ ᐑᑭᔮᐣ᙮
ᓂᑮ ᑖᑐᐱᑎᑲᐏᐣ ᐃᑯᑕ ᐅᐦᒋ
ᑕ ᓂᑕᐏ ᐊᔭᒥᐦᒋᑮᔮᐣ
ᐊᔭᒥᐦᐋᐏ ᑭᐢᑭᓌᐦᐊᒫᑐᐏᓂᕽ᙮

4. **ᓂᒪᓯᓇᐦᐊᒪᐚᐤ ᓂᑳᐏᐩ**

ᓂᑭᐢᑭᓯᐣ ᐃᐢᐲ ᐅᐦᐱᒦ ᓃᑭᓈᕽ ᐅᐦᒋ ᑳ ᑮ ᓂᑕᐏ ᐊᔭᒥᐦᒋᑮᔮᕽ:

“ᑖᓂᓯ ᒫᒫ,

ᑖᓂᓯ ᐃᑿ? ᓃᕦ ᐑᕦ ᓂᒥᕧᐧᔮᐣ᙮ ᒨᒋᑲᐣ ᓂᑕᔭᒥᐦᒋᑮᐏᐣ ᒫᑲ ᒥᐢᑕᐦᐃ ᓂᑳᐦ ᑲᐢᑮᐥᐦᑏᐣ᙮ ᒪᐦᑎ ᐲ ᐃᑎᓴᐦᐊᒪᐏᐣ ᐸᐦᑹᓯᑲᐣ᙮”

ᓂᐢᑕᑦ ᐃᑯᓯ ᓂᑮ ᐃᓯ ᑮᐑ ᒪᓯᓇᐦᐃᑳᐣ ᒪᔭᐤ ᐄ ᑲᐢᑭᐦᑖᔮᐣ ᑕ ᒪᓯᓇᐦᐊᒫᐣ ᐋᑲᕧᓰᒧᐏᐣ᙮ ᑕᐦᑤᐤ ᑳ ᑮᐑ ᒪᓯᓇᐦᐃᑮᔮᐣ ᑖᐱᑕᐤ ᒫᓇ ᓂᑮ ᒪᓯᓇᐦᐄᐣ “ᐲ ᐃᑎᓴᐦᐊᒪᐏᐣ ᐸᐦᑹᓯᑲᐣ᙮”

5. ᒨᓂᔮᐤ ᐲᓯᒧᔮᐱᔭ

ᓂᑯᑖᐧᓯᐠ ᐳᑯ ᓂᑮ ᐃᑕᐦᑐᐱᐳᓈᐣ ᓂᐢᑕᑦ ᑳ ᐚᐸᐦᑕᒫᐣ ᐆᑏᓇᐤ᙮ ᒥᐢᑕᐦᐃ ᑮᑲᐧᐩ ᓂᑮ ᒫᒪᐢᑳᑖᐸᐦᑏᐣ᙮

“ᑖᐲᐧ ᒨᓂᔮᐘᐠ!” ᓂᑮ ᐃᑏᔨᐦᑏᐣ ᐃᐢᐲ ᐄ ᑮ ᐊᑎ ᐱᒥᑖᐹᓲᔮᕽ ᑭᐢᑭᓌᐦᐊᒫᑐᐏᑖᐹᓈᐢᑯᕽ ᑭᐢᑭᓌᐦᐊᒫᑐᐏᑲᒥᑯᕽ ᐃᓯ᙮ ᐄ ᑮ ᑲᓇᐚᐸᐦᑕᒫᐣ ᐚᐢᑲᐦᐃᑲᓇ ᐃᑲᐧ ᐄ ᑮ ᑯᐢᑳᐧᐱᓯᓂᔮᐣ ᐲᓯᒧᔮᐱᐩ ᒧᐦᒋᕽ ᐄ ᐅᐦᒋᐸᔨᐠ ᐅᐘᔨᐑᑎᒥᐢᑳᐧᑏᒥᕽ ᐱᔭᐠ ᒨᓂᔮᐤ᙮

“ᒫᒪᐢᑳᐨ ᐆᑯ! ᐄ ᑲᐢᑭᐦᑖᒋᐠ ᑕ ᐅᓰᐦᑕᒫᓱᒋᐠ ᐲᓯᒧᔮᐱᐩ!”

ᒥᑐᓂ ᒦᐧᐢᑕᐢ ᑳ ᑮ ᐊᑎ ᑭᐢᑮᔨᐦᑕᒫᐣ ᐆᒪ ᓂᐱᐩ ᓯᓯᐑᐑᐱᓂᐦᑳᐣ ᐄᓴ ᐄ ᑮ ᐋᐸᒋᐦᑖᒋᐠ᙮

6. ᐄ ᑮᐑᐦᑕᐦᐃᑲᐏᔮᐣ

ᑭᑲ ᐋᒋᒧᐢᑖᑎᓈᐚᐤ:

ᐃᐢᐲ ᑳ ᑮ ᐊᐚᓯᓰᐏᔮᕽ ᐅᐦᐱᒦ ᓂᑮ ᑳᐧᓯᐦᐃᑲᐏᓈᐣ ᑭᑕ ᓂᑕᐏ ᐊᔮᒥᐦᒋᑮᔮᕽ ᓃᑏ ᑭᐢᑕᐱᓈᓂᕽ᙮ ᒥᑖᑕᐦᐟ ᐲᓯᒪᐧᐠ ᐃᑯᑏ ᓂᑮ ᐊᔮᓈᐣ ᐃᑲᐧ ᐃᐢᐲ ᐄ ᐊᑎ ᐶᓂ ᐊᑭᒥᐦᐟ ᐅᐱᓂᔮᐏᐲᓯᑦ ᓂᑮ ᑮᐑ ᑖᐹᑎᑲᐏᓈᐣ ᒥᐢᑕᐦᐃ ᓵᑲᐦᐃᑲᓂᕽ ᐃᓯ, ᒥᓯᑖᐹᓈᐢᑯᕽ ᐄ ᐶᓯᔮᕽ᙮

ᐃᑳᐧᓂ ᓂᒥᓴᐠ ᓂᑮ ᐃᑐᐦᑕᐦᐃᑯᓈᐣ ᓂᒧᒌᒥᐸᐣ ᐑᑭᕽ, ᐃᑲᐧ ᑮ ᒫᒋ ᓂᑐᓇᐑᐘᐠ ᓂᓃᑭᐦᐃᑯᓈᓇ᙮ ᒥᑐᓂ ᓃᓯ ᑎᐱᐢᑳᐤ ᓂᑐᓇᐑᐘᐠ, ᐲᔨᐢᐠ ᐋᑕᐑᔭ ᑮ ᒥᐢᑲᐑᐘᐠ, ᐋᑳᒥᕽ ᐄᓴ ᐄ ᑮ ᐑ ᓃᐱᓂᓯᔨᐟ, ᓃᑎ ᑲᔮᓯ ᐚᐢᑲᐦᐃᑲᓂᕽ ᑳ ᐃᒥᑳᑎᐠ᙮

ᐃᑳᐧᓂ ᑳ ᐲ ᐋᐧᐸᕽ ᓂᓯᓯᐸᐣ ᓂᑮ ᐃᑖᐦᐅᔥᑯᓈᐣ ᐅᑑᑎᕽ, ᒫᑲ ᓂᑮ ᐊᑎ ᑭᑎᐢᑎᓈᐦᐅᑯᓈᐣ ᐋᓰᐊᐧᐦᐅᓈᓂᕽ ᓰᐢᑳᐧᐨ ᐃᑯᑕ ᓂᑮ ᑲᐲᓯᓈᐣ ᐱᔭᐠ ᑎᐱᐢᑳᐤ᙮ ᐃᑯᑕ ᓂᑲᐲᓰᐃᐧᓂᓈᕽ ᓂᑮ ᓭᓭᑭᑎᓯᓂᐣ ᑳ ᑎᐱᐢᑳᐠ, ᐄ ᑲᓇᐋᐧᐸᒪᑳᐧᐤ ᐊᑌᐦᑯᓭᐠ ᐃᑲᐧ ᑎᐱᐢᑲᐃᐧ ᐲᓯᑦ᙮

ᑳ ᐲ ᐋᐧᐸᕽ ᓂᑮ ᒥᓭᑳᓈᐣ ᑲᔮᓯ ᐋᐧᐢᑲᐦᐃᑲᓂᕽ᙮ ᐃᑯᑕ ᓈᑕᑳᑦ ᑳ ᐋᐧᐸᒪᐠ ᓂᑳᐄᐧᐸᐣ ᐄ ᓃᐸᐃᐧᐟ, ᑲᐧᔭᐢᐠ ᓂᑮ ᒋᐦᑮᔥᐦᑏᐣ ᐃᐢᐲ ᑳ ᐋᐧᐸᒪᐠ᙮

7. ᐃᐢᑳᐧᔮᐨ ᑎᐱᐢᑳᐤ ᐄ ᒪᐧᔥ ᐅᐦᐸᐦᐅᔮᕽ

ᐃᑯᐢᐲ ᐆᒪ ᒫᓇ ᑳ ᑮ ᐃᐦᑭᕽ ᑳ ᑮ ᐱ ᓈᑎᑲᐃᐧᔮᕽ ᑳᐃᐧ ᑭᑕ ᓂᑕᐃᐧ ᐊᔭᒥᐦᒋᑮᔮᕽ ᑭᐢᑕᐱᓈᓂᕽ, ᐊᔭᒥᐦᐋᐃᐧ ᑭᐢᑭᓇᐧᐦᐊᒫᑐᐃᐧᑲᒥᑯᕽ᙮

ᑮ ᒫᐦ ᒥᓭᑳᐊᐧᐠ ᒫᓇ ᐃᔥᓂᐊᐧᐠ ᐅᐦᐱᒦ ᐅᐦᒋ ᐃᑏ ᑳ ᑮ ᓃᐱᓂᓯᒋᐠ᙮ ᓂᑑᑏᒥᓈᓇᐠ ᒫᓇ ᓂᑮ ᐲ ᓈᑎᑯᓈᓇᐠ ᑕᐄᐧᒋ ᒦᑕᐄᐧᒫᔫᐦᑳᐧᐤ, ᐊᐢᐱᐣ ᑳ ᑮ ᐱ ᑮᐄᐧᔫᕽ ᑳ ᑮ ᐊᑏ ᓃᐱᕽ ᐃᐢᑳᐧᔮᐨ ᑳ ᑮ ᐋᐧᐸᒫᔫᐦᑳᐧᐤ᙮ ᑲᐲ ᓃᐱᐣ ᒫᓇ ᓃᔥᓈᐣ ᐋᒪᒥᐄᐧᐢᐱᒧᐃᐧᓂᕽ ᓂᑮ ᓃᐱᓂᓯᓈᐣ, ᓃᔥᓈᐣ ᓃᒋᓵᓇᐠ ᐃᑲᐧ ᓂᓃᑭᐦᐃᑯᓈᓇᐠ᙮ ᑲᐲ ᐄ ᐅᑖᑯᓯᐠ᙮

ᓂᑮ ᒫᐦ ᒦᑕᐋᐧᓈᐣ᙮ ᓂᑮ ᒨᒋᑭᐦᑖᑯᓯᓈᐣ ᐄᑐᑮ᙮ ᑳ ᐲ ᑮᑭᓰᐸᔮᐠ ᓂᑲ ᐅᐦᐸᐦᐅᓈᐣ ᐃᑯᑕ ᐅᐦᒋ᙮

ᑲᔮᐢ ᑳ ᐊᐋᐧᓯᓰᐃᐧᔮᐣ, ᓇᒫᐧᐨ ᓄᐦᒋ ᒫᒥᑐᓃᔥᒫᐊᐧᐠ ᐊᓂᑭ ᓂᐋᐧᐦᑰᒫᑲᓂᓈᓇᐠ ᑳ ᑮ ᓇᑲᑖᔫᐦᑳᐧᐤ᙮

ᒫᑲ ᐊᓄᐦᐨ ᐆᒪ ᓂᒫᒥᑐᓃᔥᐦᑏᐣ:

ᐱᔭᐠ ᐄ ᐅᑖᑯᓯᐠ ᑮ ᒨᒋᑭᐦᑖᑯᓯᐊᐧᐠ ᐊᐋᐧᓯᓴᐠ ᐄ ᒦᑕᐄᐧᒋᐠ;

ᑯᑕᐠ ᐄ ᐅᑖᑯᓯᐠ ᑮ ᑭᐱᐦᑐᐄᐧᐤ; ᑭᐱᐦᑐᐄᐧᐃᐧᐣ ᐳᑯ ᐊᐢᑏᐤ᙮

8. ᑭᒍᐦᒋᑲᓂᐢ

ᐱᔭᑿᐤ ᓂᑮ ᑭᒧᑎᐣ ᑭᑐᐦᒋᑲᐣ ᐋᒪᒋᐚᐢᐱᒧᐏᐣ *Co-op*ᐃᕽ ᐅᐦᒋ᙮ ᓂᑮ ᐃᑖᐤ ᓂᐢᑏᐢ ᑕ ᐊᓴᐚᐸᒫᐟ ᐅᑭᒫᐘ ᐃᑿ ᓃᔭ ᓂᑮ ᓲᑯᐚᐱᓃᐣ ᑭᑐᐦᒋᑲᐣ ᓂᐸᐸᑭᐘᔫᓂᕽ ᐃᑿ ᓂᑮ ᐘᔭᐚᐣ ᐊᑖᐏᑲᒥᑯᕽ ᐅᐦᒋ᙮

ᒥᑐᓂ ᐄ ᑮ ᓇᓇᒥᐸᔨᑭ ᓂᐢᑳᑕ ᐃᐢᐲ ᑳ ᓈᓯᐲᔮᐣ ᑕ ᐲᐦᐅᔮᐣ ᑕ ᐅᐦᐸᐦᐅᔮᐣ ᒥᐢᑕᐦᐃ ᓵᑲᐦᐃᑲᓂᕽ ᐃᓯ ᐃᑕ ᑕ ᐆᓯᔮᐣ ᐋᐘᑕᐚᓯᓷᑲᐣ ᐊᔭᒥᐦᐋᐏ ᑭᐢᑭᓈᐦᐊᒫᑐᐏᑲᒥᑯᕽ ᑕ ᐃᑐᐦᑕᐦᐃᑯᔮᕽ᙮ ᓂᐢᑳᑕ ᑮ ᓇᓇᒥᐸᔨᓈ ᐃᐢᐲ ᑳ ᑲᐹᔮᐣ ᐱᒥᔫᑲᓂᕽ ᐅᐦᒋ ᐃᑿ ᑳ ᐆᓯᔮᐣ ᐋᐘᑕᐚᓯᓷᑲᐣ᙮

ᐄ ᑮ ᐃᑏᔨᐦᑖᒫᐣ ᑕ ᑲᐦᒋᑎᓂᑲᐑᔮᐣ ᓂᑭᒧᑎᐏᐣ ᑭᑐᐦᒋᑲᐣ ᐅᐦᒋ, ᒫᑲ ᓇᒷᐨ ᓂᑮ ᐅᐦᒋ ᑲᐦᒋᑎᓂᑲᐏᐣ ᐃᑯᐢᐲ ᓂᑮ ᑮᒨᒋ ᓂᑐᐦᑏᐣ ᑭᑐᐦᒋᑲᐣ ᐃᐢᐲ ᑳ ᑎᐱᐢᑳᐠ ᒥᐦᑕᐘᑲᐩ ᓂᑐᐦᒌᑲᑲᓂᓴ ᐄ ᐋᐸᒋᐦᑖᔮᐣ᙮ *Beatles, Cream, Hendrix* ᓂᑮ ᒥᔦᐦᑕᐚᐘᐠ ᐃᑯᑕ ᓂᑭᒧᑎ ᑭᑐᐦᒋᑲᓂᕽ ᐅᐦᒋ᙮

4
ᑳ ᐊᑎ ᐅᐢᑭᓃᑮᓯᔮᐣ

1. **ᐄ ᒪᐢᑲᒥᑲᐏᔮᐣ ᓂᐹᐦᑮᑭᓇᐢᑭᓯᓇ**

ᐅᐦᐸᐦᐅᐏᐲᓯᐟ:

ᓂᑳᐑᐸᐣ ᒦᑭᓯᐦᑳᒋᑮᐤ; ᐄ ᑲᐢᑭᒀᑕᒫᑯᔮᕽ ᐅᐢᑭ ᐹᐦᑮᑭᓇᐢᑭᓯᓇ ᑭᑕ ᑭᑭᐢᑲᒫᕽ ᑳᐏ ᐃᑐᐦᑏᔮᐦᑭ *residential school* ᑭᐢᑕᐱᓈᓂᕽ᙮

ᓅᒋᐦᐃᑐᐏᐲᓯᐟ:

ᓂᑭᑭᐢᑮᐣ ᓂᑐᐢᑭ ᐹᐦᑮᑭᓇᐢᑭᓯᓇ ᑭᐢᑕᐱᓈᓂᕽ ᐃᓯ᙮ ᐃᑯᑕ ᑳ ᑕᑯᓯᓂᔮᕽ ᓂᒦᐢᑯᑕᔭᐏᓂᓵᓈᐣ᙮ ᓂᒪᐢᑲᒥᑲᐏᐣ ᓂᑐᐢᑭ ᐹᐦᑮᑭᓇᐢᑭᓯᓇ᙮

2. "*Dog Biscuits*"

ᐃᐢᐲ ᑳ ᑮ ᐊᐋᐧᓯᓰᐃᐧᔮᐣ ᓂᑮ ᓂᑕᐃᐧ ᐊᔭᒥᐦᒋᑳᐣ ᐅᐦᐱᒦ ᓂᑎᐢᑯᓂᑲᓂᕽ ᐅᐦᒋ᙮ ᑭᐢᑕᐱᓈᓂᕽ ᒫᓇ ᑳ ᑮ ᓂᑕᐃᐧ ᐊᔭᒥᐦᒋᑮᔮᐣ, ᐃᑯᑕ *residential school* ᐄ ᑮ ᐃᑐᐦᑕᐦᐃᑲᐃᐧᔮᐣ᙮ ᒥᐢᑕᐦᐃ ᒫᓇ ᓂᑮ ᑭᑎᒪᐦᐃᑲᐃᐧᓈᐣ, ᒫᑲ ᓇᒎᔭ ᐃᔭᑯ ᓂᐄᐧ ᐋᑐᑏᐣ, ᓂᐄᐧ ᐋᒋᒫᐊᐧᐠ ᓃᒋ ᑭᑎᒫᑭᓴᐠ, ᓃᒋ ᑭᐢᑭᓈᐧᐦᐊᒫᑲᓇᐠ᙮

ᐹᐦ ᐱᐢᑫᐦᐨ ᒫᓇ ᓂᑮ ᑭᑏᔨᒥᑲᐃᐧᓈᐣ; ᐱᔭᑲᐧᐣ ᑲ ᐃᑕᐦᑐᐱᐳᓃᔮᕽ ᐄ ᐃᓯ ᑭᑏᔨᒥᑲᐃᐧᔭᕽ᙮ ᐃᑲᐧ ᒫᓇ ᐋᑎᐦᐟ ᑳ ᒥᓯᑭᑎᒋᐠ ᓈᐲᓯᓴᐠ ᑮ ᑳᐦ ᑭᑎᒪᐦᐄᐊᐧᐠ ᐊᓂᐦᐃ ᓈᐲᓴᐠ ᓇᐊᐧᐨ ᑳ ᐊᐱᓰᓯᓯᔨᐟ᙮ ᐃᑲᐧ ᒦᓇ ᑮ ᓈᐦ ᓅᑎᓂᑐᐊᐧᐠ ᓈᐲᓯᓴᐠ ᒪᐦᑎ ᐊᐄᐧᓇ ᓇᐊᐧᐨ ᑳ ᒪᐢᑲᐃᐧᓰᐟ᙮

ᐃᑯᓯ ᐆᒪ ᑳ ᑮ ᐊᑎ ᐃᐦᑭᕽ᙮ ᐊᓇ ᓇᐊᐧᐨ ᑳ ᒪᐢᑲᐃᐧᓰᐟ "*First Boss,*" ᑮ ᐃᑖᐤ ᐃᑲᐧ ᒦᓇ ᑯᑕᐠ "*Second Boss,*" ᐃᑲᐧ ᒦᓇ ᑯᑕᐠ "*Third Boss.*" ᓃᔭ ᐄᐧᔭ "*Last Boss,*" ᐊᔨᐢᐠ ᐄ ᑮ ᐊᐱᓰᓯᓯᔮᐣ ᐃᑲᐧ ᒦᓇ ᐄ ᑮ ᐹᐊᐧᓃᓯᔮᐣ ᐃᑯᐢᐲ ᒦᓇ᙮ ᓇᒪ ᓈᓂᑖᐤ, ᑭᔮᑦ, ᓂᑮ ᐃᑏᔨᐦᑏᐣ ᒫᓇ ᐄᐧᔭ ᒫᓇ ᓂᐢᑏᐢ ᐄ ᑮ ᓈᐦ ᓈᑕᒪᐃᐧᐟ᙮

ᐱᔭᐠ ᐊᐊᐧ ᓈᐲᓯᐢ ᓂᑮ ᐸᑳᐧᑎᐠ; ᑲᐲ ᒫᓇ ᐄ ᑮ ᑲᑮᐧ ᓅᑎᓂᐟ᙮ ᒫᑲ ᑮ ᑯᐢᑏᐤ ᓂᐢᑏᓴ᙮ ᓂᑮ ᐸᐢᐹᐣ᙮ ᐱᔭᐠ ᐊᐢᑫᐩ ᒫᑲ ᓂᐢᑏᐢ ᓇᒫᐧᐨ ᑮ ᐲ ᓂᑕᐃᐧ ᐊᔭᒥᐦᒋᑮᐤ, ᐊᔭᔮ, ᓂᑮ ᑯᐢᑖᒋᐣ, ᓂᑮ ᑯᐢᑖᐤ ᐊᐊᐧ ᓈᐲᓯᐢ ᑳ ᑮ ᑲᑮᐧ ᓅᑎᓂᐟ᙮ ᐅᐦᒋᑕᐤ ᐳᑯ ᑕ ᑲᑮᐧ ᑲᐢᑭᒪᐠ ᐊᓇ *First Boss* ᑕ ᓈᑕᒪᐃᐧᐟ᙮

"*Frank* ᒥᐢᑎ ᓯᑳᐠ" ᓂᑲ ᐃᓯᔨᐦᑳᑖᐤ ᐊᓇ ᓈᐲᓯᐢ ᑲᐲ ᑳ ᑲᑮᐧ ᓅᑎᓂᐟ, ᐃᑲᐧ "*Joseph* ᒥᐢᑎ ᑭᔮᐢᐠ" ᓂᑲ ᐃᑖᐤ ᐊᓇ *First Boss.*

ᓂᑮ ᐋᐦᐊᐃᐧᐦᐋᐤ ᒫᓇ ᐊᓇ *First Boss* ᓂ*comic book*ᐃᒪ, ᐃᑲᐧ ᒦᓇ ᓂᑮ ᑲᑮᐧ ᐊᓯᑕᒪᐋᐧᐤ ᑕ ᐊᑐᐢᑳᑕᒍᐊᐧᐠ ᐅᑕᑐᐢᑮᐃᐧᐣ᙮ ᐱᐦᑕᐤ ᒫᑲ ᑮ ᐋᑕᐄᐧᔨᐦᑕᑦ ᑲᐦᑭᔮᐤ ᑮᑲᐧᐩ, ᐊᐦᐴ ᒦᓇ ᐊᓂᐦᐃ ᓂᓰᐃᐧ ᒦᒋᐃᐧᓇ

ᑳ ᑮ ᐃᑎᓴᐦᐊᒪᐊᐧᐠ ᑕᐦᑖᐧᐤ ᑳ ᑮ ᒦᒋᓱᔮ᙮ ᐦᐊᐩ, ᓂᑮ ᐊᑎ ᐊᐧᐋᐧᓃᔫᐦᑏᐣ ᐊᔫᐢᐠ ᑮᑕᐦᑕᐄᐧ ᓂᑲ ᑲᐦᒋᑎᓂᐠ ᐊᓇ *Frank* ᒥᐢᑎ ᓯᑳᐠ᙮ ᑖᓂᓯ ᒫᑲ ᐆᒪ ᑕᑮ ᐃᑑᑕᒫᐣ?

ᑕᐦᑐ ᑎᐱᐢᑳᐤ ᒫᓇ, ᐄ ᒪᐧᔫ ᑲᐃᐧᓯᒍᔮ᙮ ᓂᑮ ᐊᓴᒥᑲᐃᐧᓈᐣ ᒫᓇ ᐱᔭᐠ ᐄ ᒥᓯᑭᑎᐟ ᐱᐢᑭᐟ᙮ ᑲᐧᔭᐢᐠ ᒫᓇ ᓂᑮ ᐄᐧᐦᑭᐹᐧᐤ ᐃᔭᑯ᙮ “*Dog biscuits*” ᒫᓇ ᓂᑮ ᐃᓯᔫᐦᑳᑖᓈᓇᐠ ᐃᔭᑯᓂᐠ ᐱᐢᑭᑎᓴᐠ᙮

ᐦᐋᐧᐤ, ᐱᔭᑳᐧᐤ ᓂᑮ ᐃᑎᓴᐦᐊᒪᐋᐧᐤ *Joseph* ᒥᐢᑎ ᑭᔮᐢᐠ ᐃᔭᑯᓂ, ᑮ ᒥᔫᐧᔫᐦᑕᑦ! ᓂᑮ ᐊᑎ ᓂᐹᐣ ᐃᑯᐢᐲ ᐄ ᔓᐦᑏᐦᑲᑏᔮᐣ ᒫᑲ ᓂᑮ ᒋᐦᑮᔫᐦᑏᐣ ᐊᔫᐢᐠ ᐃᑳᐧᓂ ᐄ ᑲᐢᑭᒪᐠ *Joseph* ᒥᐢᑎ ᑭᔮᐢᐠ ᑕ ᓈᐦ ᓈᑕᒪᐃᐧᐟ ᐃᐢᐲ ᐊᓇ *Frank* ᒥᐢᑎ ᓯᑳᐠ ᑲᑮᐧ ᔔᑎᓂᒋ᙮ ᐃᑳᐧᓂ, ᐃᑯᐢᐲ ᐅᐦᒋ ᑕᐦᑐ ᑎᐱᐢᑳᐤ ᓂᑎᓴᐦᐊᒪᐋᐧᐤ *Joseph* ᒥᐢᑎ ᑭᔮᐢᐠ ᓂ*dog biscuit*ᐃᒪ᙮ ᓇᒨᔭ ᐊᐊᐧᓯᒦ ᓂᑮ ᑯᐢᑖᐤ *Frank* ᒥᐢᑎ ᓯᑳᐠ᙮

ᑭᐣᐄᐧᓲᐢ ᐃᑯᓯ ᓂᑮ ᐃᑑᑏᐣ᙮

ᑕᐦᑐ ᒫᑎᓈᐃᐧᑮᓯᑳᐤ ᒫᓇ ᓂᑮ ᑲᓇᐋᐧᐸᐦᑏᓈᐣ ᒋᑳᐢᑏᐸᔫᐦᒋᑲᓇ᙮ ᐃᑲᐧ ᒫᓇ ᑳ ᑮᓯ ᑲᓇᐋᐧᐸᐦᑕᒪ᙮ ᐃᔭᑯ ᓂᑮ ᒦᑕᐋᐧᓈᐣ ᐃᔭᑯᓂ ᒋᑳᐢᑏᐸᔫᐦᒋᑲᓇ ᐄ ᓇᓈᐢᐸᑖᑕᒫ᙮ ᐃᑯᓯ ᒫᓇ, *Pirates, Cowboys and Indians*: ᑲᐦᑭᔭᐤ ᑮᑲᐧᐩ᙮ ᓂᑮ ᓇᓈᐢᐸᑖᑏᓈᐣ᙮ ᐱᔭᑳᐧᐤ ᓂᑮ ᑲᓇᐋᐧᐸᐦᑏᓈᐣ *The Great Escape*.

ᐊᔮᔫᐦᑭᐣᐄᐧ! ᐃᑯᐢᐲ ᑳ ᑎᐱᐢᑳᐠ, ᑭᐣᐄᐧᓲᐢ ᐊᐢᐱᐣ ᐅᐦᒋ ᑳ ᑮ ᐊᑎ ᑲᐃᐧᓯᒍᔮ᙮ ᓂᐲᐦᑕᐋᐧᐊᐧᐠ ᓈᐲᓯᓴᐠ ᐄ ᐋᐧᐦ ᐊᐧᔭᐃᐧᐦᑕᐄᐧᒋᐠ ᐋᐧᓲᓇᒫᓂ᙮ ᐅᐦᒋ᙮ ᑮᑕᐦᑕᐄᐧ *Joseph* ᒥᐢᑎ ᑭᔮᐢᐠ ᑳ ᐲ ᓈᓯᐟ᙮

“ᐦᐋᐧᐤ, ᐋᐢᑕᑦ! ᐄᐧᒌᐃᐧᓈᐣ!” ᓂᑎᑎᐠ᙮

“ᓇᒨᔭ ᑲᑖᐨ, ᐅᔮᑦ ᔓᐦᑖᐃᐧᐩ ᑳᐃᐧ ᓂᑲ ᐲ ᐃᑎᓴᐦᐅᐠ” ᓂᑎᑖᐤ᙮ ᓂᐋᐧᐸᐦᑏᐣ ᑮᑲᐧᐩ ᐄ ᒥᒋᒥᓇ᙮, ᒪᐢᑭᒍᒋᐢ ᐄᓴ᙮

“ᑮᑳᐧᐩ ᐊᓂᒪ?” ᓂᑎᑖᐤ, ᐄ ᐃᑕᐧᐦᐊᒪᐧᐠ ᐅᒪᐢᑭᒍᒋᐢ᙮

“ᓂᓃᒫᐃᐧᐤ ᐆᒪ,” ᐃᑏᐧᐤ, “*Dog biscuits!*” ᐃᑳᐧᓂ, ᐊᐢᐱᐤ ᑳ ᐊᐧᔭᐄᐧᔮᐦᑕᐄᐧᐟ ᐋᐧᓯᓇᒫᓂᕽ᙮

ᐃᑳᐧᓂ ᐃᐢᑳᐧᔮᐨ ᐄ ᑮ ᐋᐧᐸᒪᐠ᙮ ᑲᐦᑭᔭᐤ ᐊᓂᑭ ᓈᐲᓯᓴᐠ ᑳ ᑮ ᑕᐸᓲᒋᐠ ᑳᐃᐧ ᑮ ᐲ ᐃᑐᐦᑕᐦᐋᐊᐧᐠ, ᒫᑲ ᓇᒫᐧᐨ *Joseph* ᒥᐢᑎ ᑭᔮᐢᐠ᙮

ᐃᑯᐢᐲ ᑳ ᑎᐸᐢᑳᐠ ᓇᒫᐧᐨ ᓂᑮ ᐅᐦᒋ ᓂᐹᐧᐤ᙮ ᓂᑮ ᑯᐢᑖᐤ *Frank* ᒥᐢᑎ ᓯᑳᐠ᙮

3. ᐄ ᑮᒎᒋ ᐊᔭᒥᐦᒋᑮᔮᐤ

ᓇᒎᔮ ᓂᑮ ᓂᓯᑐᐦᑏᐤ ᐋᑲᔮᓰᒧᐃᐧᐤ ᐃᐢᐲ ᐅᐦᐱᒦ ᑳ ᑮ ᓂᑕᐃᐧ ᐊᔭᒥᐦᒋᑮᔮᐤ᙮ ᒫᑲ ᓇᒎᔮ ᑭᐤᐄᐧᐢᐠ ᓂᑮ ᐊᑎ ᓂᓯᑐᐦᑏᐤ ᐄᐧᔭ ᑕᐦᑐ ᑮᓯᑳᐤ ᐄ ᑮ ᐱᐦᑖᒪᐤ, ᐃᑲᐧ ᒦᓇ ᑕᐦᑖᐧᐤ ᑳ ᒫᑎᓈᐃᐧ ᑮᓯᑳᐠ ᐄ ᑮ ᑲᓇᐋᐧᐸᐦᑖᒫᕽ ᒋᑳᐢᑏᐸᔦᐦᒋᑲᓇ᙮ ᓂᑮ ᒦᔦᐧᔦᐦᑏᐤ ᒦᓇ ᑭᑕ ᐊᔭᒥᐦᒋᑮᔮᐤ᙮ ᑕᐦᑐ ᑎᐸᐢᑳᐤ ᓂᑮ ᐊᔭᒥᐦᑖᐤ ᐋᒋᒍᐃᐧᓂ ᒪᓯᓇᐦᐃᑲᓂᓴ ᐃᑲᐧ ᒦᓇ ᑭᐦᒋ ᒪᓯᓇᐦᐃᑲᐤ, ᔩᐹ ᓂᑕᑯᐦᐱᒥᕽ ᒫᓇ ᐄ ᐋᐸᒋᐦᑖᔮᐤ ᐋᐧᓴᐢᑯᒦᐱᒋᑲᓂᐢ ᑕ ᑮᒎᒋ ᐊᔭᒥᐦᒋᑮᔮᐤ᙮

ᐱᔭᑳᐧᐤ ᐄ ᑎᐸᐢᑳᐠ ᓂᑮ ᐊᔭᒥᐦᑖᐤ *comic book*ᐊ ᔩᐹ ᓂᑕᑯᐦᐱᒥᕽ᙮

ᑮᑕᐦᑕᐄᐧ ᑳ ᐲᐦᑕᐊᐧᐠ ᐊᓇ ᑳ ᑲᓇᐄᐧᔦᒥᑯᔮᕽ ᓈᐲᐤ ᐄ ᐲ ᐃᑑᐦᑏᐟ ᓂᓂᐲᐃᐧᓂᕽ ᐃᓯ᙮ ᑮᓯᐢᑲᐤ ᐊᓂᒪ *comic book* ᑳ ᑮ ᐊᔭᒥᐦᑖᔮᐤ ᐃᑲᐧ ᓂᑐᑎᐦᑎᓃᐤ ᑭᐦᒋ ᒪᓯᓇᐦᐃᑲᐤ᙮ ᐃᐢᐲ ᑳ ᐄᑲᑏᐱᑕᕽ ᓂᑕᑯᐦᐱᒡ, ᐊᓇ ᓈᐲᐤ ᓂᒥᐢᑳᐠ ᐄ ᐊᔭᒥᐦᑖᐊᐧᐠ ᑭᐦᒋ ᒪᓯᓇᐦᐃᑲᐤ᙮

“ᐦᐋᐤ, ᐦᐋᐤ ᒫᑲ, ᑖᐲᐧ ᑭᐦᒋ, ᑭᔮᒡ ᐊᔭᒥᐦᒋᑭᔭᓂ᙮”

ᐊᑎ ᓯᐲᐧᐦᑏᐤ ᐃᑲᐧ ᑳᐃᐧ ᓂᑐᑎᓃᐣ ᓂ*comic book*ᐃᑦ᙮ ᐃᑯᐢᐲ ᑳ ᐊᐢᑮᐃᐧᐠ ᒥᐦᒌᐟ ᑳᐧᒥᐠ ᐸᑲ ᓂᑮ ᐊᔭᒥᐦᑖᐣ, ᓇᒪ ᐄᐧᐦᑳᐨ ᓂᑮ ᐱᓯᐢᑮᖨᒥᐠ ᐊᓇ ᓈᐲᐤ ᑳ ᑮ ᑲᓇᐄᐧᖨᒥᑯᔮᕽ᙮

ᓇᒨᖬ ᑭᐣᐄᐧᐢᐠ ᑳ ᐊᑎ ᓂᓯᑐᐦᑕᒫᐣ ᐋᑲᖭᓰᒧᐃᐧᐣ᙮

4. ᐄ ᑮᒨᑖᐱᔮᐣ

ᒋᑰᒋ! ᑮᐢᐱᐣ ᐄ ᐱᒥᖭᔭᐣ, ᑖᐱᐢᑰᐨ ᐱᖩᓰᐢ, ᐃᑯᑏ ᐃᐢᐱᒥᕽ ᐅᐦᒋ ᑲᑮ ᐚᐸᐦᑏᐣ ᐊᓂᐦᐃ ᐚᐢᑲᐦᐃᑲᓇ ᐃᑕ ᑳ ᑮ ᑲᓇᐄᐧᖨᒥᑲᐃᐧᔮᕽ ᐃᐢᐲ ᐅᐦᐱᒦ ᑳ ᑮ ᓂᑕᐃᐧ ᐊᔭᒥᐦᒋᑮᔮᕽ᙮ ᑭᑲ ᐚᐸᐦᑏᐣ ᓃᓯ ᑭᓀᑲᒥᑲᐧ ᐃᑲᐧ ᐊᓂᑕ ᐋᐱᐦᑕᐚᖨᕽ ᐄ ᐚᓂᐢᑰᐢᑏᑭ, ᐱᔭᑲᐧᐣ ᐊᓂᒪ ᐋᑲᖭᓰᒧᐃᐧᐣ ᒪᓯᓂᐲᐦᐃᑲᓂᐢ “*H*” ᑭᑲ ᐃᓯᓃᐣ᙮ ᐱᔭᑳᐧᖨᕽ ᑭᓀᑲᒥᑯᕽ ᐃᐢᑮᐧᓯᓴᐠ ᑮ ᑲᓇᐄᐧᖨᒫᐊᐧᐠ, ᐃᑲᐧ ᐊᓂᒪ ᑯᑕᐠ ᑭᓀᑲᒥᑯᕽ ᓈᐲᓯᓴᐠ ᑮ ᑲᓇᐄᐧᖨᒫᐊᐧᐠ, ᐃᑲᐧ ᐊᓂᑕ ᐋᓂᐢᑮᑳᑲᓂᕽ ᑲᓈᒋᐦᒋᑮᐃᐧᑲᒥᑲᐧ ᑮ ᐊᐢᑏᐊᐧ᙮

ᒫᑲ ᒦᓇ ᐆᒪ ᓂᑮ ᐱᔭᑲᐧᐦᑲᒥᑭᓯᐣ ᐃᐢᐲ ᑳ ᑮ ᒥᐢᑲᒫᐣ ᐸᐦᑖᐦᑕᐄᐧᐃᐧᐣ ᐃᑕ ᐅᐦᒋ ᐃᐢᐱᒥᐦᑕᑯᕽ ᑕ ᐃᑐᐦᑏᔮᐣ᙮ ᐃᑯᑏ ᐃᐢᐱᒥᐦᑕᑯᕽ ᓂᑮ ᐱᒥᑖᒋᒧᐣ ᐄ ᓂᑕᐃᐧ ᑲᓇᐚᐸᒪᑳᐧᐤ ᐃᐢᑮᐧᓯᓴᐠ ᐅᑲᓈᒋᐦᒋᑮᐃᐧᑲᒥᑯᐚᕽ, ᐊᐧᐦᐚ! ᑲᐧᔭᐢᐠ ᓂᑮ ᒥᖭᐧᐱᓯᓂᐣ᙮

ᐃᑳᐧᓂ ᐃᑯᓯ ᓂᑮ ᐊᖨᑕᐦᑲᒥᑭᓯᐣ, ᒫᑲ ᐱᔭᑳᐧᐤ ᐄ ᑮᓴᐦᑲᒥᑭᓯᔮᐣ, ᐄ ᐲ ᓂᐦᑖᐦᑕᐄᐧᔮᐣ, ᑳ ᒧᐢᑎᓂᐟ ᐱᔭᐠ ᓂᐄᐧᒌᐚᑲᐣ᙮ ᓂᑮ ᑲᑮᐧᒋᒥᐠ ᑖᓂᓯ ᐆᒪ ᑳ ᐃᑕᐦᑲᒥᑭᓯᐊᐧᐠ᙮ ᓂᐄᐧᐦᑕᒪᐚᐤ ᐄ ᑮ ᓂᑕᐃᐧ ᑮᒨᑖᐸᒪᑳᐧᐤ ᐃᐢᑮᐧᓯᓴᐠ ᐄ ᒦᑳᐧ ᓰᐲᑭᓇᐢᑏᒋᐠ᙮ ᓂᑎᑎᐠ ᑭᑕ ᐄᐧᒌᐃᐧᐟ ᑮᐦᑖᐧᑦ ᐃᑯᓯ ᐃᑑᑕᒫᓂ᙮

ᐃᑯᓯ ᒫᓂ ᒫᑲ ᓂᑮ ᐲ ᐄᐧᒌᐃᐧᐠ ᑮᐦᑖᐧᑦ ᑳ ᓂᑕᐃᐧ ᑮᒨᑖᐸᒪᑳᐧᐤ ᐃᐢᑮᐧᓯᓴᐠ᙮ ᑲᐧᔭᐢᐠ ᓂᑮ ᒥᖭᐧᐱᓯᓂᓈᐣ᙮

ᐃᑲᐧ ᐃᐢᐲ ᑳ ᐴᓂ ᑭᑖᐱᒫᔮᐦᑳᐧᐤ ᐃᐢᑮᐧᓯᓴᐠ ᓂᑮ ᐊᑎ ᓂᐦᑖᐦᑕᐋᐧᓈᐣ ᐃᐢᐱᒥᐦᑕᑯᕽ ᐅᐦᒋ, ᐄᐧᔦ ᓃᑳᐣ ᓂᐄᐧᒌᐋᐧᑲᐣ᙮ ᑮᑕᐦᑕᐄᐧ ᑳ ᐲᐦᑕᐊᐧᐠ ᐊᓇ ᓈᐲᐤ ᑳ ᑮ ᑲᓇᐄᐧᔦᒥᑯᔮᕽ, ᐄ ᒪᑏᐧ ᑏᐲᐧᐟ᙮ ᑮᓯᐢᑲᐤ ᓂᑮ ᑳᓲᐸᔦᐦᐅᐣ ᐊᐊᐧᓲᐃᐧᐋᐧᐃᐧᑲᓂᐦᑕᑯᕽ᙮

“ᑖᓂᓯ ᐆᒪ ᐄ ᐃᑕᐦᑲᒥᑭᓯᔭᐣ?” ᐃᓯ ᑏᐹᐧᑏᐤ ᐊᐊᐧ ᓈᐲᐤ ᓂᐄᐧᒌᐋᐧᑲᓇ᙮

“ᓇᒨᔦ ᑮᑲᐧᐩ᙮ ᐄ ᓂᑕᐋᐧᐲᓂᑭᔮᐣ ᐆᒪ ᒪᐦᑎ ᑮᑲᐧᐩ ᐃᐢᐱᒥᐦᑕᑯᕽ ᐊᐢᑏᐤ,” ᑳ ᐃᑏᐧᐟ ᓂᐄᐧᒌᐋᐧᑲᐣ᙮

“ᓇᒪ ᑮᑲᐧᐩ ᐃᑯᑕ ᐊᐢᑏᐤ,” ᑳ ᐃᑏᐧᐟ ᐊᓇ ᓈᐲᐤ᙮ “ᑯᑕᐠ ᒌ ᐊᐃᐧᔭᐠ ᐃᐢᐱᒥᐦᑕᑯᕽ ᐊᔮᐤ?” ᑳ ᐃᓯ ᑲᑮᐧᒋᒫᐟ ᓂᐄᐧᒌᐋᐧᑲᓇ᙮

“ᓇᒨᔦ᙮ ᓂᐱᔭᑯᐣ ᐊᓂᒪ,” ᑳ ᒪᑏᐧ ᐃᑏᐧᐟ ᓂᐄᐧᒌᐋᐧᑲᐣ, ᐄᑳ ᐄ ᒥᓯᒥᐟ᙮ ᐃᑲᐧ ᓵᑭᐢᑎᑳᐧᓃᐤ ᐊᐊᐧ ᓈᐲᐤ ᐄ ᓂᑕᐃᐧ ᑭᐦᒋᓈᐦᐅᐟ, ᒫᑲ ᓇᒫᐧᐨ ᓂᑮ ᐅᐦᒋ ᐋᐧᐸᒥᐠ᙮

ᐃᑳᐧᓂ ᐊᑎ ᓯᐲᐧᐦᑏᐊᐧᐠ ᐃᑲᐧ ᐊᒋᔦᐤ ᓂᐲᐦᐅᐣ, ᒫᑲ ᐲᔦᐢᐠ ᓂᐲ ᓂᐦᑖᐦᑕᐋᐧᐣ ᓃᐢᑕ᙮

ᑮᐦᒑᐧᑦ ᑳ ᑯᒋᐦᒑᔮᕽ ᑕ ᐃᐢᑳᐧᐦᑕᐄᐧᔮᕽ ᐃᐢᐱᒥᐦᑕᐠ ᓂᒥᐢᑮᓈᐣ ᐄ ᑭᐳ ᓴᑲᐦᐃᑳᑎᐠ ᓂᐳᐦᒑᐦᐄᐧᐃᐧᓂᓈᐣ᙮ ᐄᐧᐢᐱᓇᐨ!

5. ᒥᐢᑕᑎᒨᐣ

ᐅᐦᐱᒦ ᑭᐢᑭᓈᐧᐦᐊᒫᑐᐃᐧᑲᒥᑯᕽ ᑮ ᐊᐢᑏᐤ ᒦᓂᓯᐦᑳᐤ ᐃᑯᑕ ᒫᓇ ᑮ ᐅᐦᒋ ᒪᐃᐧᓱᐊᐧᐠ ᐅᑭᐢᑭᓈᐧᐦᐊᒫᑮᐊᐧᐠ ᐄᐧᓴᑭᐱᒋᑳᐧᓴ, ᐄ ᐋᐦᐊᓴᒥᑯᔮᐦᑳᐧᐤ ᐃᐢᐲ ᑳ ᐊᑎᐦᑏᑭ᙮ ᒫᑲ ᒫᓇ ᒥᐦᒌᑖᐧᐤ ᓂᑮ ᓂᑕᐃᐧ ᑭᒧᑎᓈᐣ᙮

ᐃᔭᑯᐦᒋ ᐄᑐᑮ ᐱᔭᑳᐧᐤ ᐃᑯᑕ ᒦᓂᓯᐦᑳᕽ ᑳ ᑮ ᑭᑏᕀᒥᐦᐟ ᐱᔭᐠ ᒥᐢᑕᑎᒼ, ᐄᑲ ᑭᑕ ᑭᒧᑎᔮᕽ ᐄᐧᓴᑭᐱᒋᑳᐧᓴ, ᐄᑐᑮ, ᒫᑲ ᓇᒪ ᓈᓂᑕᐤ᙮

ᐱᔭᑳᐧᐤ ᐄ ᐅᑖᑯᓯᐠ, ᓂᑮ ᓂᑕᐃᐧ ᑭᒧᑎᓈᐣ ᐃᔭᑯᓂ ᐄᐧᓴᑭᐱᒋᑳᐧᓴ᙮ ᑭᔮᒼ ᐊᓇ ᒥᐢᑕᑎᒼ᙮ ᓂᑮ ᓰᐸᐦᑕᐋᐧᓈᐣ ᒦᓂᑲᐣ ᐃᑲᐧ ᐹᐦ ᐱᔭᐠ ᒥᐢᑎᐠ ᓂᑮ ᐃᐢᑳᐧᐦᑕᐋᐧᑖᓈᐣ᙮ ᓇᒫᐧᐨ ᓈᓂᑕᐤ ᐃᑕ ᓂᑮ ᐅᐦᒋ ᐋᐧᐸᒫᓈᐣ ᐊᓇ ᒥᐢᑕᑎᒼ᙮

ᐃᑳᐧᓂ ᐆᒪ ᐄ ᐊᑯᓯᔮᕽ ᒥᐢᑎᑯᕽ ᐄ ᒫᐦ ᒨᒥᓂᔮᕽ, ᑮᑕᐦᑕᐄᐧ ᑳ ᐲᐦᑕᐊᐧᑳᐧᐤ ᓂᐄᐧᒌᐋᐧᑲᓇᐠ᙮

“ᒫᑲᐊᐧ! ᐃᑲᐧ ᑕᐸᓰᑖᐣ!” ᐄ ᒪᑏᐧ ᐃᑏᐧᒋᐠ᙮ ᓂᐲᐦᑕᐋᐧᐊᐧᐠ ᐄ ᓯᐲᐧᐹᐦᑖᒋᐠ᙮

“ᐊᐦᐴ ᐄᑐᑮ ᐱᔭᐠ ᓈᐲᐤ ᑳ ᑭᑏᕀᒥᑯᔮᕽ,” ᓂᑎᑏᕀᐦᑏᐣ᙮ “ᒥᓴᐋᐧᐨ ᐃᐢᐱᒥᕽ ᒥᐢᑎᑯᕽ ᓂᑕᑯᓵᐣ, ᓇᒫᐧᐨ ᓂᑲ ᐋᐧᐸᒥᐠ,” ᓂᑎᑖᐧᐣ᙮ ᓂᑖᐦᑲᒥ ᒨᒥᓈᐣ᙮

ᐃᑳᐧᓂ ᐆᒪ ᐊᐧᑎᐦᑲᐧᓂᕽ ᐅᐦᒋ ᓂᑎᓯ ᑲᑮᐧ ᐅᐦᒋᐱᑏᐣ ᐄᐧᓴᑭᐱᒋᑳᐧᐢ ᑳ ᓵᒥᓇᒫᐣ ᑮᑲᐧᐩ ᐄ ᓵᐳᐲᐠ! ᑮᑕᐦᑕᐄᐧ ᑳ ᑭᑐᐟ ᒥᐢᑕᑎᒼ᙮ “ᓂᐦᐃᐦᐃᐦᐄ!” ᓂᑯᐢᑯᒥᐠ!

ᒥᑐᓂ ᐄ ᓂᐦᒋᐸᐦᑭᓯᓂᔮᐣ ᒥᐢᑎᑯᕽ ᐅᐦᒋ ᐃᕀᑯᕽ ᐄ ᑯᐢᑯᒥᐟ! ᐅᑯᐟ ᐄᓴ ᐄ ᑮ ᑲᑮᐧ ᒨᒥᓂᔮᐣ!

6. ᑳ ᒪᑯᓰᑮᓯᑳᐠ

ᐃᐢᐲ ᑳ ᑮ ᐊᐋᐧᓯᓰᐃᐧᔮᐣ ᓃᐢᑕ ᓂᑮ ᑳᐧᓯᐦᐃᑲᐃᐧᐣ ᐅᐦᐱᒦ ᓃᑭᕽ ᐅᐦᒋ ᑕ ᓂᑕᐃᐧ ᐊᔭᒥᐦᒋᑮᔮᐣ, ᑭᐢᑕᐱᓈᓂᕽ ᓂᑮ ᓂᑕᐃᐧ ᐊᔭᒥᐦᒋᑳᐣ, ᒥᐦᒌᑖᐧᐤ ᒫᓇ ᓂᑮ ᑲᐢᑮᐩᐦᑏᐣ ᓃᑭ᙮ ᐃᑲᐧ ᐆᒪ, ᐋ ᐲ ᒪᑯᓰᑮᓯᑳᐠ ᓂᐄᐧ ᐋᑐᑏᐣ ᑖᓂᓯ ᒫᓇ ᑳ ᑮ ᐃᑕᐦᑲᒥᑲᕽ ᐃᐢᐲ ᑳ ᒪᑯᓰᑮᓯᑳᐠ ᐃᑯᑕ ᑭᐢᑭᓈᐧᐦᐋᒫᑐᐃᐧᑲᒥᑯᕽ᙮

ᐋᑎᐦᐟ ᒫᓇ ᐊᐋᐧᓯᓴᐠ ᑮ ᐲ ᓈᑎᑎᓴᐦᐅᑯᐊᐧᐠ ᐅᓃᑭᐦᐃᑯᐋᐧᐊᐧ ᑕ ᑮᐋᐧᒋᐠ, ᑕ ᓂᑕᐃᐧ ᐋᐧᒋ ᒪᑯᓰᑮᓯᑲᓂᒫᒋᐠ ᐅᐋᐧᐦᑰᒪᑲᓂᐋᐧᐊᐧ᙮ ᓇᒫᐧᐨ ᒫᓇ ᓃᔭᐩᓈᐣ᙮ ᓃᑳᐣ ᓂᐢᑏᐢ ᐃᑲᐧ ᓂᒥᓴᐠ ᐃᑲᐧ ᓂᓰᒥᓴᐠ (ᒦᐧᐢᑕᐢ ᐄᐧᔭᐩᐋᐧᐤ ᑳ ᑮ ᐲ ᐊᔭᒥᐦᒋᑮᒋᐠ) ᓂᑮ ᑭᓵᒐᓈᐣ, ᐅᓵᑦ ᐋ ᑮ ᒥᐦᒌᑎᔮᕽ, ᐅᓵᑦ ᑮ ᒥᐢᑕᑭᓱᐤ ᐆᓱᑖᐹᓈᐢᐠ, ᓇᒫᐧᐨ ᑮ ᐃᐢᐸᐩᐦᐃᑯᐊᐧᐠ ᓂᓃᑭᐦᐃᑲᐧᐠ ᑕ ᑎᐸᐦᐊᐦᑳᐧᐤ ᑕ ᑮᐋᐧᔮᕽ ᓃᐢᑖᓈᐣ᙮ ᐃᑳᐧᓂ ᐃᑯᑕ ᑭᐢᑭᓈᐧᐦᐋᒫᑐᐃᐧᑲᒥᑯᕽ ᓂᑮ ᒪᑯᓰ ᑮᓯᑲᓂᓯᓈᐣ᙮

ᑮ ᓈᐦ ᓂᑐᒫᐊᐧᐠ ᒫᓇ ᐊᓂᑭ ᐊᐋᐧᓯᓴᐠ ᑳ ᑮ ᐲ ᓈᑎᑎᓴᐦᐅᐦᒋᐠ᙮ ᐋᑕ ᒫᓇ ᓂᑮ ᓂᑐᐦᑏᐣ ᓈᓂᑕᐃᐧᓯ ᓃᐢᑖᓈᐣ ᓂᑐᒥᑲᐃᐧᔮᐦᑭ, ᒫᑲ ᓇᒪ ᐋᐧᐦᑳᐨ ᐃᑯᓯ ᑮ ᐃᐢᐸᐩᐣ᙮ ᐱᔭᑳᐧᐤ ᒫᑲ, ᐋ ᐴᓂ ᐋᐱᐦᑖ ᑮᓯᑳᐠ, ᓂᐲᐦᑏᐣ ᓂᒥᐢ ᐋ ᒪᑏᐧ ᓂᑐᒥᐦᐟ᙮

ᑲᐧᔭᐢᐠ ᓂᑮ ᑭᓯᐋᐧᓯᐣ, ᐃᑲᐧ ᐲᐩᐢᐠ ᓂᑮ ᒫᑐᐣ᙮ ᐄᐧᔭᐩ ᐳᑯ ᓂᒥᐢ ᐋ ᐲ ᓈᑎᑎᓴᐦᐅᐦᐟ: ᒥᐢᑕᐦᐃ ᓂᑮ ᐸᑳᐧᑏᐣ᙮

ᐃᐢᐲ ᑳ ᓂᑕᐃᐧ ᐅᑖᑲᐧᓂ ᒦᒋᓱᔮᕽ, ᐊᐄᐧᓇ ᒫᑲ ᑳ ᐋᐧᐸᒪᐠ? ᓂᒥᐢ! ᑖᐳᑳᓂ ᓂᓈᒋᐸᐦᐋᐧᐤ᙮ ᓂᑲᑮᐧᒋᒫᐤ ᑖᓂᐦᑭ ᐄᑳ ᑳ ᑮ ᑮᐄᐧᐟ᙮ ᓂᑮ ᐄᐧᐦᑕᒫᐠ ᑏᐱᔭᐩᕽ ᐄ ᑮ ᓂᑐᒥᐦᐟ ᑕ ᓂᑕᐃᐧ ᐋᐧᒋᐩᒫᐟ ᐅᐄᐧᒌᐋᐧᑲᓇ ᐅᓃᑭᐦᐃᑯᐩᐊᐧ᙮

ᐃᑳᐧᓂ ᐅᓵᑦ ᐳᑯ ᑲᐦᑭᐩᔭᐤ ᐊᐋᐧᓯᓴᐠ ᑮ ᑮᐄᐧᐊᐧᐠ, ᐋᑎᐦᐟ ᐳᑯ ᓃᔭᐩᓈᐣ ᓂᑭᓵᒐᓈᐣ᙮ ᐃᐢᐲ ᑳ ᑭᐦᒋ ᑎᐱᐢᑳᐠ, ᐄ ᒪᐧᐩ ᒪᑯᓰᑮᓯᑳᐠ, ᓂᑮ ᐴᓯᓈᐣ ᐴᓱᑖᐹᓈᐢᑯᕽ ᐄ ᓂᑕᐃᐧ ᑳᐦ ᑲᓇᐋᐧᐸᐦᑕᒫᕽ

ᒪᑯᓰ ᑮᓯᑲᓂ ᐚᓴᐢᑯᒌᓂᑲᓂᕽ ᐆᑏᓈᕽ᙮ ᓂᑮ ᒨᒋᑭᓃᐣ᙮ ᐃᑿ ᑳ ᑕᑯᓯᓂᔮᕽ ᑭᐢᑭᓌᐦᐊᒫᑐᐏᑲᒥᑯᕽ ᓂᑮ ᐊᑯᑖᓈᓇᐠ ᓂᑕᓯᑲᓂᓈᓇᐠ᙮

ᐃᐢᐲ ᑳ ᒪᑯᓰᑮᓯᑳᐠ, ᓂᑕᓯᑲᓂᓂᓈᕽ ᓂᑮ ᒥᐢᑮᓈᐣ ᒦᖨᑯᐏᓂᕽ, ᐃᑿ ᓰᐏᒌᓴᐠ᙮ ᑲᐲ ᐄ ᑮᑭᓰᐸᔩᐠ ᓂᑮ ᒦᑕᐚᑳᓈᐣ ᓂᑐᐢᑭ ᒦᑕᐚᑲᓂᓈᓇ᙮ ᐃᑿ ᑳ ᐋᐱᐦᑖ ᑮᓯᑳᐠ ᓂᑮ ᒥᓯ ᒦᒋᓱᓈᐣ᙮ ᐃᐢᐲ ᑳ ᐴᓂ ᐋᐱᐦᑖ ᑮᓯᑳᐠ ᓂᑮ ᓛᒪᐏᐦᐃᑐᓈᐣ ᑕ ᓈᐦ ᓂᑲᒨᔮᕽ᙮ ᐃᑿ ᑮᑕᐦᑕᐑ ᒫᓇ ᑳ ᐲ ᑕᑯᓯᕽ ᐑᓴᐦᑮᒑᕽ, ᐄ ᒫᐦ ᒦᖨᑯᔮᕽ ᒦᖨᑯᐏᓂᕽ᙮

7. ᑭᓃᑳᓃᐢᑲᐚᐘᐠ ᑭᑎᖨᓃᒪᐠ

ᐃᐢᐲ ᑳ ᑮ ᐊᑎ ᐴᓂᐸᖨᐠ ᓂᑕᔭᒥᐦᒋᑮᐏᓈᐣ ᓂᑮ ᓛᒪᐏᐦᐃᑐᓈᐣ ᓛᓇ᙮ ᑲᐦᑭᖭᐤ ᐅᑭᐢᑭᓌᐦᐊᒫᑲᓇᐠ ᒦᑕᐑᐏᑲᒥᑯᕽ ᑮ ᐃᑐᐦᑏᐘᐠ᙮

ᐅᑭᐢᑭᓌᐦᐊᒫᑮᐘᐠ ᐃᑿ ᐅᑭᑏᖨᒫᐘᓱᐘᐠ ᓈᐦ ᓂᑐᒦᐘᐠ ᐅᑭᐢᑭᓌᐦᐊᒫᑲᓇ ᑕᐦᑐ ᐃᑕᑭᓱᐏᓂᕽ ᐅᐦᒋ ᐄ ᒫᒦᖭᒋᐠ ᐃᔭᑯᓂ ᑳ ᓃᑳᓃᖨᐟ ᐅᑕᔭᒥᐦᒋᑮᐏᓂᐚᐘ ᐅᑕᐏᐦᐅᐑᐏᓇ: ᑲᐢᑭᐦᑕᒫᑮᐏᐣ ᒪᓯᓇᐦᐃᑲᓃᑭᓇ: ᐃᑿ ᒪᓯᓇᐦᐃᑲᐣ ᐃᑿ *cowboy* ᐊᐢᑐᑎᓇ ᑮ ᐅᑕᐦᐃᑮᐘᐠ ᐃᔭᑯᓂᐠ᙮

ᐋᐢᑲᐤ ᒫᓇ ᓃᐢᑕ ᓂᑮ ᓂᑐᒥᑲᐏᐣ ᐊᖨᐢᐠ ᐄ ᑮ ᐊᑎ ᓇᑭᖭᐢᑳᑕᒫᐣ ᐊᔭᒥᐦᒋᑮᐏᐣ ᐃᑿ ᒦᓇ ᐋᐢᑲᐤ ᐄ ᑮ ᒥᖪ ᓈᐲᓯᓯᐏᔮᐣ᙮

(*Heh, heh,* ᑮᐢᐱᐣ ᐳᑯ ᑮ ᑭᐢᑮᖨᐦᑕᐦᒁᐤ! ᒪᑗᐣ ᒌ ᑮ ᐅᐦᒋ ᑭᐢᑮᖨᐦᑕᒷᐠ ᐊᐑᓇ ᑳ ᑮ ᑭᒧᑎᐟ ᑏ ᐃᑿ ᓰᐏᐦᑲᓯᑲᓂᓴᐠ ᐅᑭᐢᑭᓌᐦᐊᒫᑮᐘᖩᐧᐲᐏᑲᒥᑯᕽ ᐅᐦᒋ? ᐊᓂᑭ ᓰᐏᐦᑲᓯᑲᓂᓴᐠ ᑮ ᐑᐦᑭᒋᓯᐘᐠ!)

ᑳ ᐚᒋᖩᒫᔮᐦᒁᐤ ᐅᑭᐢᑭᓌᐦᐊᒫᑮᐘᐠ ᑮ ᐃᑏᐧᐘᐠ “ᑭᒪᒥᐦᒋᐦᐃᓈᐣ” ᐃᑿ ᒦᓇ “ᑭᒪᒥᐦᒋᐦᐚᐘᐠ ᑭᑕᖨᓯᑎᓃᒪᐠ᙮”

ᐄ ᑮ ᑲᑹ ᑕᑲᐦᑭᒥᑯᔮᐦᒀᐤ ᐊᓂᑭ᙮ ᓇᒨᔭ ᑮ ᐅᐦᒋ ᑭᐢᑮᔪᐦᑕᒪᐧᐠ ᐄ ᒫᒋ ᐃᑗᒋᐠ᙮ ᓅᐢᑖᓈᐣ ᒦᓇ ᓂᑮ ᒥᔪᐦᑏᓈᐣ ᐃᔭᑯᓂ᙮

8. ᐸᑿᓂᑕ ᐃᑗᐏᐣ

ᐃᐢᐲ ᑳ ᑮ ᐊᔭᒥᐦᒋᑮᔮᐣ ᓂᑮ ᓂᐦᑖ ᐊᑐᐢᑳᑏᐣ ᓂᑭᐢᑭᓈᐦᐋᒫᑮᐊᐧᑐᑕᒫᑲᐏᐣ᙮ ᐃᑿ ᒫᓇ ᑳᐏ ᑳ ᒦᔥᑲᐏᔮᐣ ᓂᑐᐢᑮᐏᐣ ᒥᐦᒌᑛᐤ ᒫᓇ ᓂᑭᐢᑭᓈᐦᐋᒫᑮᒪᐠ ᓂᑮ ᐃᑎᑿᐠ᙮ ᐄ ᐋᑲᔮᓰᒧᒋᐠ: *"Excellent work, Solomon! You are a true credit to your race."* ᓂᑮ ᒥᔪᐦᑏᐣ ᒫᓇ ᐃᔭᑯ᙮ ᒫᑲ ᐃᐢᐲ ᑳ ᐊᑎ ᑮᓱᐦᐱᑮᔮᐣ ᓂᑮ ᓂᓯᑕᐑᓃᐣ ᐃᔭᑯ ᓇᐊᐧ- ᐹᑯ ᐄ ᓂᐦᑖᑕᐐᐦᐃᑲᐐᔮᐣ᙮ ᐃᑿ ᒦᓇ ᑳ ᐊᑎ ᑮᓯ ᐅᐦᐱᑮᔮᐣ, ᐃᐢᐲ ᑳ ᐚᐸᒪᐠ ᐃᔥᓂᐤ ᐄ ᑲᐢᑭᐦᑕᒫᓱᐟ ᑮᑲᐧᐩ ᑳ ᓲᐦᑲᓂᔥᐠ, ᒫᓇ ᓂᑮ ᐃᑖᐧᐣ: *"Not bad for an Indian."*

5

ᓃᑭᕽ ᑳ ᓃᐱᕽ

1. ᑳ ᐃᐢᐱᑎᓯᒋᐠ ᐃᓲᐦᒋᑮᐏᐣ

ᑲᔫᐢ ᒫᓇ ᒥᐦᒌᑘᐤ ᓂᑮ ᓂᑕᐏᒥᓈᓈᐣ ᓇᑕᒥᕽ ᐃᑕ ᐅᐦᒋ ᑳ ᑮ ᐑᑭᔮᕽ᙮ ᓃᔭ, ᓃᑎᓵᓇᐠ, ᓂᑳᐏᐩ ᐃᑲᐧ ᐱᔭᐠ ᓅᐦᑯᒼ ᓂᑮ ᐆᓯᓈᐣ ᒫᓇ ᒌᒫᓂᕽ ᓇᑕᒥᕽ ᐄ ᐃᓯᒋᒦᔮᕽ ᑕ ᓂᑕᐏᒥᓃᔮᕽ ᓄᐦᒋᒥᕽ ᐃᑕ ᐄ ᐃᐢᐸᑎᓈᐠ᙮ ᓂᑮ ᑯᐢᐱᓈᐣ ᒫᓇ ᐃᑲᐧ ᓂᑮ ᒫᐦ ᒪᐏᓱᓈᐣ᙮ ᓇᒨᔭ ᒫᓇ ᑭᓃᐧᐢᐠ ᓵᓴᐩ ᑳ ᐃᐢᑲᑏᔨᐦᑕᒫᕽ ᑕ ᒪᐏᓱᔮᕽ, ᓃᔭ, ᓂᐢᑏᐢ ᐃᑲᐧ ᐱᔭᐠ ᓂᓰᒥᐢ᙮ ᓂᑮ ᒫᐦ ᒫᒋ ᒦᑕᐚᓈᐣ ᐄᐢᑳᐧ ᐄ ᒪᐏᓱᒋᐠ ᓂᑳᐏᐩ, ᓅᐦᑯᒼ ᐃᑲᐧ ᓂᓰᒥᓴᐠ, ᐊᓂᑭ ᐃᐢᑮᐧᓯᓴᐠ᙮ ᒥᑐᓂ ᒫᓇ ᑲᐲ ᑮᓯᐠ ᐄ ᒫᐦ ᒦᑕᐑᔮᕽ᙮ ᐲᔨᐢᐠ ᑳ ᐊᑎ ᐅᑖᑯᓯᐠ ᓂᑏᐹᐧᑎᑯᓈᐣ ᓂᑳᐏᐩ, ᐃᑲᐧ ᑳ ᑕᑯᐸᐦᑖᔮᕽ ᓂᑎᑎᑯᓈᐣ ᑕ ᓇᔭᐧᐦᑖᔮᕽ ᒦᓂᓴ ᓈᓯᐲᑎᒥᕽ ᐃᓯ᙮ ᒥᑐᓂ ᒫᓇ ᒥᐢᑕᐦᐃ ᒥᐢᒋᑯᐘᒋᓴ ᐄ ᑮ ᓵᐦ ᓵᑲᐢᑭᓈᐦᑖᒋᐠ ᐃᔨᓂᒥᓇ ᐅᐦᒋ᙮ ᑮ ᑯᓯᑲᐧᓇ ᒫᓇ ᐊᓂᐦᐃ ᒦᓂᓴ ᐃᑲᐧ ᐚᐦᔭᐤ ᑕ ᐃᓯ ᓇᔭᐦᑖᔮᕽ ᓈᓯᐲᑎᒥᕽ ᐃᓯ, ᒫᑲ ᓇᒨᔭ ᓈᓂᑖᐤ ᓂᑮ ᐃᑏᔨᐦᑏᓈᐣ ᐊᔨᐢᐠ ᐃᑯᓯ ᒫᓇ ᑲᐲ ᐄ ᑮ ᐃᓯ ᐊᑐᐢᑮᐦᐃᑲᐏᔮᕽ ᓃᔭᓈᐣ ᓈᐲᓯᓴᐠ᙮

2. ᓇᑳᐧᑎᓱᐃᐧᐣ ᐃᑲᐧ ᒫᑎᓇᒫᑮᐃᐧᐣ

ᓂᑭᐢᑭᓯᐣ ᑳ ᑮ ᐊᐋᐧᓯᓰᐃᐧᔮᕽ ᓂᑮ ᓂᑐᒥᑲᐃᐧᓈᐣ ᓃᖪ ᒦᓇ ᓂᐢᑏᐢ ᑕᓂᑕᐃᐧ ᓇᑳᐧᑎᓱᔮᕽ᙮ ᐱᔭᐠ ᐊᐊᐧ ᓂᐋᐧᐦᑰᒫᑲᓂᓈᐣ ᐄ ᑮ ᓂᐸᐦᐋᐧᐟ ᒨᓴᐧ ᐃᑲᐧ ᐋᐧᐦᖪᐤ ᓄᐦᒋᒥᕽ ᓴᑳᕽ ᐄ ᑮ ᓇᑲᑖᐟ ᐄ ᑮ ᐲ ᓈᑖᐟ ᐅᐋᐧᐦᑰᒫᑲᓇ ᑕᓇᑳᐧᑎᓱᖨᐟ, ᐃᑯᓯ ᒫᓇ ᑲᔮᐢ ᐅᒫᒌᐊᐧᐠ ᐄ ᑮ ᐃᑑᑕᐦᑳᐧᐤ᙮ ᑕᐦᑐ ᐄᐧᑎᓵᓃᐦᑐᐃᐧᓂᕽ ᐅᐦᒋ ᓂᑐᒦᐤ ᑲᓇᑮ ᐱᔭᐠ ᓈᐲᓯᓴ ᑕᓂᑕᐃᐧ ᓇᑳᐧᑎᓱᖨᐟ᙮ ᓂᐢᑏᐢ ᑮ ᐄᐧᓵᒫᐤ ᓂᐄᐧᑎᓵᓃᐦᑐᐃᐧᓂᓈᕽ ᐅᐦᒋ ᐃᑲᐧ ᓃᐢᑕ ᓂᑮ ᐄᐧᓵᒥᑲᐃᐧᐣ ᑕᓈᑕᒪᐊᐧᐠ ᒨᓯ ᐃᐧᔮᐢ ᐱᔭᐠ ᓄᐦᑯᑦ ᑳ ᐱᔭᑯᐄᐧᑭᐟ᙮ ᐄᐧᐸᐨ ᐄ ᑮᑭᓰᐹᔮᐠ ᓂᑮ ᓯᐲᐧᐦᑖᓈᐣ, ᓃᖪᓈᐣ ᓈᐲᓯᓴᐠ ᒦᓇ ᓈᐲᐊᐧᐠ᙮ ᑭᐣᐄᐧᐢᐠ ᓄᐦᒋᒥᕽ ᓴᑳᕽ ᓂᑮ ᐱᒧᐦᑖᓈᐣ᙮ ᓂᑮ ᒨᒋᑭᐦᑖᓈᐣ, ᐄ ᐋᐦᐊᒋᒧᒋᐠ ᓈᐲᐊᐧᐠ ᒦᓇ ᐄ ᓈᐦ ᓇᓅᖪᒋᐦᐃᑯᔮᐦᑳᐧᐤ᙮ ᐲᖨᐢᐠ ᓂᑕᑯᐦᑖᓈᐣ ᒥᓇᐦᐅᐃᐧᓂᕽ᙮ ᓈᐲᐊᐧᐠ ᑮ ᒫᐦ ᒪᓂᓵᐋᐧᑏᐊᐧᐠ ᐊᓂᐦᐃ ᒨᓴᐧ ᐃᑲᐧ ᓂᑮ ᐋᐦᐊᓯᐊᐧᑖᓈᐣ ᒨᓯ ᐃᐧᔮᐢ ᓂᒪᐢᑭᒧᑎᓈᕽ᙮ ᑳᐃᐧ ᓂᑮ ᑮᐋᐧᓈᐣ᙮ ᐃᐢᐲ ᑳ ᑕᑯᐦᑏᔮᕽ ᓂᑲᐲᓰᐃᐧᓂᓈᕽ ᓂᑮ ᐄᐧᐦᑯᐦᑳᓈᐣ᙮ ᐊᓇ ᓄᐦᑯᑦ ᑳ ᑮ ᐲᑕᒪᐊᐧᐠ ᐃᐧᔮᐢ ᓂᑮ ᑮᓯᓴᒫᐠ ᒨᓯ ᐃᐧᔮᐢ, ᐄ ᑮ ᓇᐊᐧᒌᐢᑕᒪᐃᐧᐟ᙮ ᐊᐧᐦᐋᐧ! ᑲᐧᔭᐢᐠ ᓂᑮ ᐄᐧᐦᑭᐢᑏᐣ ᐃᔭᑯ ᒨᓯ ᐃᐧᔮᐢ! ᑲᐧᔭᐢᐠ ᒦᓇ ᓂᑮ ᒨᒋᑭᐦᑖᐣ ᐃᑯᐢᐲ ᑳ ᑮ ᓂᑕᐃᐧ ᓇᑳᐧᑎᓱᔮᕽ᙮

3. ᑭᓰᐋᐧᑎᓯᐃᐧᐣ

ᑲᔮᐢ ᑳ ᑮ ᐊᐋᐧᓯᓰᐃᐧᔮᕽ ᓂᑮ ᐄᐧᒋᐦᐃᓈᐣ ᓄᐦᑖᐄᐧᐸᐣ ᑕ ᓂᑯᐦᑕᐋᐧᐟ ᐊᑖᐄᐧᐃᐧᑭᒫᐊᐧ᙮ ᐅᓵᑦ ᐳᑯ ᑲᐲ ᓃᐱᐣ ᓂᑮ ᓂᑯᐦᑖᓈᐣ ᓇᑕᒥᕽ ᓃᑭᓈᕽ ᐅᐦᒋ᙮ ᓄᐦᑖᐄᐧᐸᐣ ᑮ ᑳᐦ ᑮᐢᑲᑕᐦᐋᐧᐦᑎᑮᐧᐤ ᐃᑲᐧ ᓃᖪᓈᐣ ᓂᑮ ᓈᓯᐲᔮᐊᐧᑖᓈᐣ ᐊᓂᐦᐃ ᒥᐦᑕ᙮ ᓂᑮ ᓲᐦᑭ ᐊᑐᐢᑳᓈᐣ ᒫᓇ᙮ ᐲᖨᐢᐠ ᒥᐦᒌᐟ ᒥᐦᑕ ᓂᑮ ᐋᐊᐧᑖᓈᐣ ᐃᑲᐧ ᒥᐦᑐᐟ ᓂᑮ ᐅᓲᐦᑖᓈᐣ᙮ ᓃᐢᑖᐤ ᓂᑮ ᐲ ᐄᐧᒋᐦᐃᑯᓈᐣ ᑕ ᐱᒥᑖᐲᐸᐦᑖᐧᐟ ᐅᑑᐟ ᐅᐦᒋ, ᑕ ᓴᑲᐦᐱᑕᕽ ᐊᓂᒪ ᒥᐦᑐᐟ ᐅᑑᑎᕽ᙮ ᓂᑮ ᐃᑎᑲᐃᐧᓈᐣ ᑕ ᐴᓯᔮᕽ ᐆᓯᕽ ᒫᑲ ᓂᑮ ᐊᑳᐋᐧᑏᓈᐣ ᑕᐦᑯᐦᐨ ᒥᐦᑐᑎᕽ ᑕ ᐴᓯᔮᕽ᙮ ᑮ ᐹᐦᐱᓯᐤ ᓄᐦᑖᐄᐧᐸᓂᓈᐣ ᒫᑲ

ᓂᑮ ᐸᑭᑎᓂᑯᓈᐣ ᑕᐦᑯᐦᐨ ᒥᐦᑐᑎᕽ ᑕᐴᓯᔮᕽ᙮ ᐊᐧᐦᐋᐧ! ᑲᐧᔭᐢᐠ ᑮ ᒎᒋᑲᐣ!

4. ᑭᐢᑏᔨᐦᑕᒧᐃᐧᐣ

ᐃᐢᐲ ᑳ ᑮ ᐊᐋᐧᓯᓰᐃᐧᔮᕽ ᓃᔪ ᐃᑲᐧ ᓂᒥᐢ ᓂᑮ ᑲᓈᒋᐦᑖᓈᐣ ᔨᑲᐧᐦᐊᐢᑳᐣ ᐊᑳᒥᕽ ᐃᑕ ᐅᐦᒋ ᑳ ᑮ ᐄᐧᑭᔮᕽ᙮ ᒌᒫᓂᕽ ᓂᑮ ᐴᓯᓈᐣ ᐄ ᐋᓱᐊᐧᐦᐊᒫᕽ ᓰᐱᕀ᙮ ᑮ ᒥᔪ ᑮᓯᑳᐤ᙮

ᓂᑮ ᒫᒋ ᑲᓈᒋᐦᑖᓈᐣ ᔨᑲᐧᐦᐊᐢᑳᐣ᙮ ᑲᐲ ᑮᓯᐠ ᓂᑮ ᑲᓈᒋᐦᒋᑳᓈᐣ᙮ ᑮᑕᐦᑕᐄᐧ, ᐄ ᐴᓂ ᐋᐱᐦᑖ ᑮᓯᑳᐠ, ᑳ ᐊᑎ ᓰᐦᑭᔭᐄᐧᐠ ᐃᑲᐧ ᐄ ᐲᑖᓇᐢᑳᐧᐠ᙮ ᑲᐧᔭᐢᐠ ᑮ ᑲᐢᑭᑏᐋᐧᓇᐢᑳᐧᐤ ᐃᑲᐧ ᒦᓇ ᑲᐧᔭᐢᐠ ᑮ ᓰᐦᑭᔭᐄᐧᐤ! ᐱᔨᓯᐊᐧᐠ ᑮ ᑳᐦ ᑭᑐᐊᐧᐠ ᐃᑲᐧ ᑮ ᐋᐧᐦ ᐋᐧᓴᐢᑯᑏᐸᔭᐣ!

ᒫᑲ ᒦᓇ ᓃᔪ ᓂᑮ ᓅᐦᑏ ᒫᔨᔨᐦᑏᐣ ᐆᒪ ᑳ ᐃᓯ ᑮᓯᑳᐠ, ᓂᑮ ᑲᐢᑭᒫᐤ ᓂᒥᐢ ᑭᑕ ᑲᑮᐧ ᐋᓱᐊᐧᐦᐊᒫᕽ ᑭᔮᑦ ᐆᒪ ᑳ ᐃᓯ ᑮᓯᑳᐠ᙮ ᐃᑳᐧᓂ ᓂᑮ ᐴᓯᓈᐣ᙮ ᐊᐧᐦᐋᐧ! ᑲᐧᔭᐢᐠ ᑮ ᒫᐦ ᒥᓯ ᒪᒪᐦᑳᐦᐊᐣ ᒫᑲ ᑭᔮᐱᐨ ᓂᐱᒥᐢᑳᓈᐣ, ᐄ ᓇᓂᒪᐦᐊᒫᕽ! ᑲᐧᔭᐢᐠ ᓂᒫᐦ ᒫᑲᐧᐦᐃᑯᓈᐣ ᔮᑎᐣ ᐃᔨᑯᕽ ᐄ ᒫᐦ ᒥᓯ ᒪᒪᐦᑳᐦᐊᕽ ᒫᑲ ᐲᔨᐢᐠ ᓂᒥᓴᑳᓈᐣ ᓅᑭᓈᕽ᙮ ᓂᑮ ᒫᐦ ᒪᒥᐦᒋᐦᐃᓱᓈᐣ ᑳ ᑮ ᐃᓯ ᒫᔨᔨᐦᒋᑮᔮᕽ᙮ ᒫᑲ ᓅᐦᑖᐄᐧᓈᐣ ᓂᑮ ᑭᐦᑳᒥᑯᓈᐣ, ᐄ ᑮ ᐃᑎᑯᔮᕽ ᑕ ᑮ ᑭᐢᑏᔨᐦᑕᒪᕽ ᐊᓂᒪ ᑳ ᑮ ᐃᓯ ᑮᓯᑳᐠ, ᓇᒎᔪ ᐸᑲᐧᓂᑕ ᑕ ᑮ ᐴᓯᔮᕽ ᐃᐢᐲ ᑳ ᓰᐦᑭᔭᐄᐧᐠ ᒦᓇ ᑳ ᒫᐦ ᒥᓯ ᑮᐢᑎᕽ᙮

5. 1969 ᐊᐢᑮᐃᐧᐣ ᑳ ᑮ ᐊᑭᐦᑏᐠ

1969 ᐊᐢᑮᐃᐧᐣ ᑳ ᑮ ᐊᑭᐦᑏᐠ: ᓈᐲᐤ ᑮ ᐱᒧᐦᑏᐤ ᑎᐱᐢᑳᐃᐧ ᐲᓯᒧᕽ, ᑮ ᒫᒪᐃᐧᐦᐃᑐᓈᓂᐃᐧᐣ ᑭᑕ ᑭᑐᐦᒋᑳᓂᐃᐧᐠ *Woodstock*ᐃᕽ, ᐃᑲᐧ

ᑮᐄᐧᑎᓄᕽ, ᓃᔦ ᓂᔮᓇᓄᓵᐟ ᓂᑮ ᐃᑕᐦᑐᐱᐳᓈᐣ ᐄ ᐄᐧᒋᐦᐊᑳᐧᐤ ᓂᐢᑏᐢ ᐃᑲᐧ ᓂᓲᒥᓯᐸᐣ ᐃᑲᐧ ᓄᐦᑖᐄᐧᐸᐣ ᑭᑕ ᐋᐧᐢᑲᐦᐃᑲᓂᐦᑮᔫᕽ ᐋᒪᒋᐄᐧᐢᐱᒧᐃᐧᓂᕽ᙮

ᑕᐦᑐ ᑮᑭᓲᐸᔫᐤ ᒫᓇ ᓂᑮ ᐴᓯᓈᐣ ᓇᑕᒥᕽ ᐄ ᓂᑕᐃᐧ ᑮᐢᑲᑕᐦᐋᐦᑎᑮᐧᔫᕽ᙮ ᓂᑮ ᓃᒫᓈᐣ ᒫᓇ ᐃᑯᑏ ᐅᐦᐱᒦ ᑕ ᐋᐱᐦᑖ ᑮᓯᑲᓂ ᒦᒋᓱᔫᕽ᙮ ᐃᐢᐲ ᑳ ᒥᓵᑳᔫᕽ ᓂᑮ ᑯᐢᐱᓈᐣ ᐄ ᓂᑐᓇᐋᐧᔭᐦᑳᐧᐤ ᒥᓇᐦᐃᑲᐧᐠ ᐄ ᑲᐧᔭᐢᑯᓯᒋᐠ ᐃᑲᐧ ᐃᔭᑯᓂᐠ ᓂᑮ ᑮᐢᑲᑕᐦᐋᐧᓈᓇᐠ᙮ ᓂᑮ ᒪᓇᐦᑲᐧᑕᑕᐦᐋᐧᓈᓇᐠ ᒥᓇᐦᐃᑲᐧᐠ ᐃᑲᐧ ᓂᑮ ᓈᓯᐲᑕᐦᐋᓈᓇᐠ ᒥᐢᑎᑲᐧᐠ, ᐋᐧᓴᑳᐨ ᐄ ᐊᐦᔦᔮᐦᑳᐧᐤ᙮

ᒦᐧᐢᑕᐢ, ᑳ ᑮᓯ ᑮᐢᑲᑕᐦᐋᐦᑎᑮᐧᔫᕽ ᓃᐢᑖᐸᐣ ᓂᑮ ᐱ ᐄᐧᒋᐦᐃᑯᓈᐣ, ᐄ ᓴᑲᐦᐱᑖᐟ ᒥᐢᑎᑲᐧ ᐅᒎᑎᕽ ᐃᑯᓯ ᐄ ᐃᓯ ᐅᑖᐲᐟ ᐃᑏ ᑳ ᑮ ᐄᐧ ᐋᐧᐢᑲᐦᐃᑲᓂᐦᑮᔫᕽ᙮ ᓂᒋᐋᐧᒥᐸᐣ ᓂᑮ ᐱ ᐄᐧᒋᐦᐃᑯᓈᐣ ᑭᑕ ᑯᐢᐱᐦᑕᑖᔫᕽ ᒥᐢᑎᑲᐧ᙮ ᓃᐢᑖᐸᐣ ᑮ ᐅᔦᐢᑖᐤ ᒥᐢᑎᑲᐧ ᐃᑕ ᑳ ᐄᐧ ᐋᐧᐢᑲᐦᐃᑲᓂᐦᑮᔫᕽ ᐃᑲᐧ ᐃᑯᑕ ᐅᐦᒋ ᓃᔦᓈᐣ ᓈᐲᓯᓴᐠ ᑳ ᑮ ᐊᑎ ᐋᐧᐢᑲᐦᐃᑲᓂᐦᑮᔫᕽ᙮

ᐅᓵᐨ ᐳᑯ ᑲᐲ ᓃᐱᐣ ᓂᑮ ᐅᑕᒥᔦᓈᐣ ᐃᔭᑯ᙮ ᐃᐢᐲ ᑮ ᐃᐦᑭᐣ ᑳᐃᐧ ᑭᑕ ᓂᑕᐃᐧ ᐊᔭᒥᐦᒋᑮᔫᕽ ᑭᐢᑕᐱᓈᓂᕽ ᐋᐱᐦᑕᐃᐧᔦᑯᕽ ᐳᑯ ᐄ ᑮ ᑮᓯ ᐊᐢᑖᔫᕽ ᐊᐸᐦᑳᐧᐣ᙮ ᑳ ᐊᑎ ᐅᐦᐸᐦᐅᔫᕽ ᐅᐱᒥᔦᐤ ᓃᓵᐧᐤ ᐋᐧᐢᑳᑯᒋᐣ ᓂᐋᐧᐢᑲᐦᐃᑲᓂᓯᓈᐣ ᑭᑕ ᐋᐧᐸᐦᑕᒫᕽ ᑳ ᑮ ᐃᓯ ᐊᑐᐢᑮᔫᕽ᙮ ᐄ ᑮ ᐋᐧᐸᒥᑯᔫᕽ ᐄᑐᑮ ᐄ ᑮ ᐋᐧᐢᑲᐦᐃᑲᓂᐦᑮᔫᕽ ᐃᐢᐲ ᒫᓇ ᑳ ᑮ ᑖᐦ ᑏᐧᐦᐅᐟ᙮

ᐃᑯᐢᐲ 1969 ᓂᐢᑕᐨ ᑳ ᑮ ᑮᐄᐧᔫᐣ ᐊᐢᐱᐣ ᐃᐢᐲ ᑳ ᑮ ᑳᐧᓯᐦᐃᑲᐃᐧᔫᐣ ᑭᑕ ᓂᑕᐃᐧ ᐊᔭᒥᐦᒋᑮᔭᐣ ᐅᐦᐱᒦ, ᓃᑏ ᑭᐢᑕᐱᓈᓂᕽ᙮ ᓂᑮ ᒪᒥᐦᒋᐦᐅᐣ ᐊᔦᐢᐠ ᓄᐦᑖᐄᐧᐸᐣ, ᓂᑳᐄᐧᐸᐣ, ᐃᑲᐧ ᓂᓲᒥᓴᐠ ᐃᑯᑕ ᐄ ᐄᐧᑭᒋᐠ, ᐊᓂᒪ ᐋᐧᐢᑲᐦᐃᑲᓂᐢ ᑳ ᑮ ᐅᓲᐦᑖᔫᕽ᙮

ᐃᑯᐢᐲ ᒫᓇ ᐊᐃᐧᔭᐠ ᑳ ᑮ ᐋᐧᐢᑲᐦᐃᑲᓂᐦᑮᐟ ᑲᐦᑭᖬᐤ ᐊᖨᓯᑎᓂᐊᐧᐠ ᑮ ᐲ ᐄᐧᒋᐦᐅᐄᐧᐋᐧᐠ᙮ ᓄᐦᑖᐄᐧᐸᐣ ᐄᑐᑮ ᐄ ᑮ ᐃᑖᐟ ᓇᒨᖬ ᑲᑖ-ᑕ ᐲ ᐄᐧᒋᐦᐃᑯᔮᐦᑳᐧᐤ ᐊᖨᐢᐠ ᐄ ᓂᑕᐄᐧᖨᒥᑯᔮᕽ ᓃᖬᓈᐣ ᓈᐲᓯᓴᐠ ᐳᑯ ᑭᑕ ᐋᐧᐢᑲᐦᐃᑲᓂᐦᑮᔮᕽ᙮ ᐃᑯᓯ ᑭᑕ ᐊᑎ ᑭᐢᑮᖨᐦᑕᒫᕽ ᐃᔭᑯ ᑮᑲᐧᐩ᙮ ᑖᐲᐧ ᒫᓂ ᒫᑲ: ᓂᐢᑏᐢ ᐃᑲᐧ ᓂᓰᒥᓯᐸᐣ ᑮ ᒥᐢᑎᑯᓈᐲᐃᐧᐊᐧᐠ ᐃᑲᐧ ᓃᖬ ᓂᑐᐦᐱᑭᐦᑖᐣ ᐃᑏᐧᐃᐧᓇ ᒪᓯᓇᐦᐃᑲᓂᕽ᙮

6
ᐄ ᐊᔭᐦᒋᑎᓈᐃᐧᔮᕽ ᓂᑕᐢᑮᓈᕽ

1. *Canada, oh Canada*, **150 ᐊᐢᑮᐃᐧᓇ**

Canada, oh Canada, ᒥᑖᑕᐦᑐᒥᑕᓇᐤ ᒦᓇ ᓂᔮᓇᓄᒥᑕᓇᐤ ᐊᐢᑮᐃᐧᓇ
ᐄ ᑭᑎᓂᐦᒋᐠ ᐃᔨᓂᐊᐧᐠ
ᐄ ᐅᔭᓯᐋᐧᑕᒋᐠ ᐄᑳ ᑭᑕ ᐱᒥᑎᓴᐦᐊᐦᑳᐧᐤ ᐃᔨᓂᐃᐧᓰᐦᒋᑮᐃᐧᓇ:
ᓇᑳᐧᑎᓱᐃᐧᓇ, ᐹᐧᑎᓯᒧᐃᐧᓇ, ᒪᑐᑎᓵᓇ;
ᒪᓯᓇᐦᐃᑲᓃᑭᓄᐢ ᐳᑯ ᑕ ᐊᔮᐟ ᑮᐢᐱᐣ ᑕ ᓇᑲᑕᕽ ᐃᐢᑯᓂᑲᐣ –
ᑕ ᓂᑐᓇᕽ ᐊᑐᐢᑮᐃᐧᐣ –
ᐋᑕ ᓃᐢᑖᓈᐣ ᓂᑮ ᓂᑕᐃᐧ ᓅᑎᓂᑳᓈᐣ ᐃᐢᐲ ᑳ ᓅᑎᓂᑐᓈᓄᐃᐧᐠ᙮
ᒫᑲ ᓃᑳᐣ ᐳᑯ ᑕ ᐸᑭᑎᓇᒫᕽ ᓂᑎᐢᑯᓂᑲᓇᑮᐦᑖᓱᐃᐧᓂᓈᓇ,
ᐃᑲᐧ ᐃᐢᐲ ᑳ ᐲ ᑮᐄᐧᔮᕽ ᓇᒫᐧᐨ ᓂᒦᔨᑲᐃᐧᓈᐣ
ᓯᒫᑲᓂᓯᐦᑳᐣ ᒥᔪ ᑑᑖᑮᐃᐧᓇ,
ᓇᒫᐧᐨ ᓂᑲᑮ ᑮᐋᐧᓈᐣ: ᓇᒪᒦ ᓂᑮ ᐸᑭᑎᓃᓈᐣ
ᓂᑎᐢᑯᓂᑲᓇᑮᐦᑖᓱᐃᐧᓂᓈᓇ᙮
Canada, oh Canada, ᒥᑖᑕᐦᑐᒥᑕᓇᐤ ᒦᓇ ᓂᔮᓇᓄᒥᑕᓇᐤ ᐊᐢᑮᐃᐧᓇ
ᐄ ᒦᐢᒋᐦᐃᐄᐧᔮᐣ: ᓃᑳᐣ ᑭᒦᐢᒋᐦᐋᐊᐧᐠ ᐸᐢᑳᐧᐃᐧ ᒧᐢᑐᓴᐧᐠ,

ᐃᑲᐧ ᐊᐋᐧᓯᓴᐠ ᑭᑮ ᑳᐧᓯᐦᐋᐊᐧᐠ ᐅᐦᐱᒦ ᑕ ᓂᑕᐃᐧ ᑭᐢᑭᓇᐧᐦᐊᒫᑯᒋᐠ
ᐊᔭᒥᐦᐃᑭᒫᐊᐧ
ᐃᑕ ᑳ ᑮ ᓅᒥᐦᐃᔮᕽ ᐃᐢᐲ ᑳ ᐲᑭᐢᑮᐧᔮᕽ ᓂᐲᑭᐢᑮᐧᐃᐧᓂᓈᓇ᙮
ᐃᑯᓰᓯ ᓂᑮ ᑭᐱᐦᑎᓂᑲᐃᐧᓈᐣ ᐄᑳ ᑭᑕ ᑭᐢᑮᔦᐦᑕᒫᕽ
ᓂᑎᔦᓂᐃᐧ ᐃᓰᐦᒋᑮᐃᐧᓇ ᒦᓇ ᓂᑳᑮᓯᒧᐃᐧᓂᓈᓇ
ᑳ ᑮ ᐋᓂᐢᑰ ᑭᐢᑮᔦᐦᑕᒫᕽ ᐋᒐᔦᐦᑮᐃᐧᓂᕽ ᐅᐦᒋ:
ᐋᒐᔦᐦᑮᐃᐧᓇ ᑳ ᑮ ᑭᐢᑭᓇᐧᐦᐊᒫᑯᔮᕽ ᑭᑕ ᐃᓯ ᐱᒫᑎᓯᔮᕽ ᐆᑕ ᐊᐢᑮᕽ᙮
ᐅᐦᐱᒦ ᑭᐢᑭᓇᐧᐦᐋᒫᑐᐃᐧᑲᒥᑯᕽ ᐃᑕ ᐊᐋᐧᓯᓴᐠ ᑳ ᑮ ᓈᐦ ᓅᒥᐦᐃᐦᒋᐠ ᐃᑲᐧ
ᑳ ᑮ ᐋᐦᐅᑎᐦᑎᓂᐦᒋᐠ;
ᐊᐋᐧᓯᒦ ᑭᐦᒋ ᒥᑖᑕᐦᑐᒥᑕᓇᐤ ᑮ ᐴᓂ ᐱᒫᑎᓯᐊᐧᐠ – ᒥᐦᒌᐟ ᓇᒫᐧᐨ
ᑭᐢᑮᔦᐦᑖᑲᐧᐣ ᐃᑕ ᑳ ᑮ ᓇᐦᐊᐦᔦᐦᒋᐠ᙮
ᑳ ᑮᓯ ᐊᔭᒥᐦᒋᑮᔮᕽ ᓂᑮ ᐋᐧᐦ ᐊᐧᓂᐦᐅᓈᐣ, ᑲᐲ ᐊᔦᐢᐠ
ᐄ ᑮ ᑭᑏᔦᒥᑲᐃᐧᔮᕽ ᓇᒫᐧᐨ ᓂᑮ ᑭᐢᑮᔦᐦᑏᓈᐣ ᑖᓂᓯ
ᑭᑕ ᐃᓯ ᐸᒥᐦᐃᓱᔮᕽ᙮
ᒥᐦᒌᐟ ᓂᑮ ᓂᓯᐊᐧᓈᑕᐦᑳᒥᑭᓯᓈᐣ ᐃᑯᓯ ᑭᐸᐦᐅᑐᐃᐧᑲᒥᑯᕽ ᑭᑕ ᐊᔮᔮᕽ:
ᑭᑕ ᑭᐸᐦᐅᑲᐃᐧᔮᕽ ᓇᒪᒌ ᒫᑲ ᐳᑯ ᑳ ᑭᐢᑮᔦᐦᑕᒫᕽ᙮
ᒥᐦᒌᐟ ᒥᓂᐦᑮᐧᐃᐧᐣ ᐃᑲᐧ ᒪᒋ ᒪᐢᑭᐦᑭᔭ ᑮ ᓂᓯᐊᐧᓈᒋᐦᐃᑯᐊᐧᐠ ᐃᑲᐧ ᑳᑭᑮ
ᓈᐦ ᓅᑎᓂᑮᐢᑯᐊᐧᐠ᙮
Canada, oh Canada, ᒥᑖᑕᐦᑐᒥᑕᓇᐤ ᒦᓇ ᓂᔮᓇᓄᒥᑕᓇᐤ ᐊᐢᑮᐃᐧᓇ
ᐄ ᐱ ᐊᔭᐦᒋᑎᓃᐃᐧᔮᕽ ᓂᑕᐢᑮᓈᕽ᙮

2. ᒨᔭ ᓃᔭ *Indian*

ᑲᔮᐢ ᒫᓇ ᑳ ᑮ ᐊᐋᐧᓯᓰᐃᐧᔮᐣ ᐆᑏ ᒫᓇ ᓂᑮ ᓂᑕᐃᐧ ᐊᔭᒥᐦᒋᑳᓈᐣ ᑭᐢᑕᐱᓈᓂᕽ ᐃᑯᑏ ᒫᓇ ᐄ ᓂᑕᐃᐧ ᑭᐢᑭᓇᐧᐦᐊᒫᑯᓯᔮᕽ᙮ ᑕᐦᑐ ᐊᐢᑭᐩ ᒫᓇ ᑖᑲᐧᑭ ᐲᓯᑦ ᑳ ᑮ ᒫᒋᐦᑖᔮᕽ ᐄ ᑮ ᓂᑕᐃᐧ ᑳᐦ ᑭᐢᑭᓇᐧᐦᐊᒫᑯᓯᔮᕽ ᐃᑯᑕ ᐆᒪ *residential schools* ᑳ ᑮ ᐃᒋᑳᑏᑭ, ᐃᑯᑏ ᑳ ᑮ ᐃᑐᐦᑏᔮᐣ, ᐋᐦ, *Prince Albert Indian Student Residences* ᑮ ᐃᓯᔦᐦᑳᑏᐤ ᐃᔭᑯ ᐋᓂᒪ᙮ ᐃᑲᐧ ᐃᑯᑕ ᒫᓇ ᒥᐢᑕᐦᐃ ᒫᓇ ᐊᐋᐧᓯᓴᐠ ᑮ ᑭᑎᒫᑭᓯᐊᐧᐠ ᒥᐢᑕᐦᐃ ᒫᓇ ᑮ ᒫᐦ ᒪᐄᐧᐦᑳᑏᐊᐧᐠ ᐅᓃᑭᐦᐃᑯᐋᐧᐊᐧ᙮

ᐊᔭ, ᒦᓇ ᒥᐢᑕᐦᐃ ᒦᓇ ᒫᓇ ᓂᑮ ᒨᒋᑭᐦᑖᓈᐣ ᒫᓇ ᑕᐦᑖᐧᐤ ᑳ ᒫᑎᓈᐃᐧ ᑮᓯᑳᐠ, ᐃᑯᐢᐲ ᒫᓇ ᓂᑮ ᑲᓇᐋᐧᐸᐦᑏᓈᐣ, ᐋᐦ, ᒋᑳᐢᑏᐸᖨᐦᒋᑲᓇ, *picture shows* ᓂᑮ ᐃᓯᖨᐦᑳᑏᓈᐣ ᒫᓇ᙮ ᐃᔭᑯᓂ ᒫᓇ, ᒥᑐᓂ ᒫᓇ ᓂᑮ ᒫᐦ ᒨᒋᑭᐦᑖᓈᐣ ᑳ ᐴᓂ ᐋᐧᐸᐦᑕᒫᕽ ᐄᐧᖬ ᐊᖨᐢᐠ ᒫᓇ ᐄ ᓂᑕᐃᐧ ᒦᑕᐄᐧᔮᕽ ᐊᐧᖬᐄᐧᑎᒥᕽ ᑖᐱᐢᑰᐨ ᒫᓇ ᓃᖬᓈᐣ, ᐋᐦ, *Pirates* ᒫᓇ ᓂᑮ ᒦᑕᐋᐧᓈᐣ ᐃᑲᐧ ᒦᓇ *Cowboys and Indians*. ᐃᑯᓯ ᒫᓇ ᑳ ᑮ ᐃᓯ ᒦᑕᐄᐧᔮᕽ, ᐃᑲᐧ ᐆᒪ ᑳ ᑮ ᐲ ᐃᓯ ᐅᐦᐱᑭᔮᕽ ᐆᒪ ᒥᑐᓂ ᒫᓇ, ᐋᐦ …, ᓂᑮ ᐄᐧᓃᖨᒥᓱᓈᐣ, ᒨᖬ ᓃᖬᓈᐣ ᓃᐦᐃᖬᐊᐧᐠ ᑕ ᑮ ᐃᓯ ᐱᒫᑎᓯᔮᕽ ᐄ ᐃᑎᑲᐃᐧᔮᕽ ᒫᓇ᙮ ᐃᑯᓯ ᒫᓇ ᑳ ᑮ ᐃᓯ ᐅᐦᐱᑭᐦᐃᑲᐃᐧᔮᕽ ᐄᑯᑕ ᑭᐢᑭᓈᐧᐦᐊᒫᑐᐃᐧᑲᒥᑯᕽ᙮

ᒫᑲ ᐱᔭᑳᐧᐤ ᐆᒪ ᐄ ᑮ ᓂᑕᐃᐧ ᑲᓇᐋᐧᐸᐦᑕᒫᕽ *Cowboys and Indians* ᒋᑳᐢᑏᐸᖨᐦᒋᑲᐣ, *John Wayne* ᐃᑯᑕ ᒦᓇ ᑳ ᑮ ᐊᔮᐟ, ᐄ ᑮ ᓅᑯᓯᐟ, ᓂᑮ ᒌᐦᑭᓃᐣ, ᐃᔭᑳᐧᓂᒪ ᓂᑮ ᒌᐦᑳᐸᐦᑏᐣ, ᓂᒥᖩᐧᖨᐦᑏᐣ ᑕ ᐋᐧᐸᐦᑕᒫᐣ, *John Wayne* ᑕ ᑲᓇᐋᐧᐸᒪᐠ᙮ ᐃᑲᐧ ᒫᓇ ᑳ ᑮ ᐴᓂ ᐋᐧᐸᐦᑕᒫᕽ ᐃᔭᑯᓂ ᐊᔭ ᒫᓇ ᓂᑮ ᓂᑕᐃᐧ ᒦᑕᐋᐧᓈᐣ *Cowboys and Indians* ᒫᑲ ᒫᓇ ᐄ ᑮ ᒫᐊᐧᓴᑯᓂᑐᔮᕽ᙮ ᐋᐦ, ᐱᔭᑳᐧᖨᕽ ᐃᑕ *Indians* ᐃᑲᐧ ᐱᔭᑳᐧᖨᕽ ᑯᑕᐠ *Cowboys*; ᐃᑲᐧ ᒫᓇ ᓃᖬ ᑲᐲ ᒫᓇ ᓃᖬ ᐃᐢᑭᐧᔮᓂᕽ ᑳ ᑮ ᐅᑎᓂᑲᐃᐧᔮᐣ᙮ ᐃᑲᐧ ᑮᑕᐦᑕᐄᐧ ᐆᒪ ᐆᑕ ᐱᔭᐠ ᑮᓯᑳᐤ ᓂᑮ ᐊᑎ ᐅᑎᓂᑲᐃᐧᐣ, *Indians* ᐄᓴ ᓃᖬ ᑕ ᐊᔮᔮᐣ᙮ ᐋᐦ, ᓇᒨᖬ ᓂᑮ ᒌᐦᑮᖨᐦᑏᐣ, ᓇᒨᖬ ᓃᖬ *Indian* ᓂᑮ ᓅᐦᑏ ᐃᑕᑭᓱᐣ ᐃᑯᑕ᙮

“ᒨᖬ ᓃᖬ *Indian*,” ᓂᑮ ᐃᑖᐧᐣ᙮ “ᓇᒨᖬ ᓂᐄᐧ*Indian*ᐃᐃᐧᐣ!” ᐄ ᐃᑏᐧᔮᐣ᙮

“ᐁ+,” ᐃᑏᐧᐤ ᐆᑕ ᐱᔭᐠ ᓈᐲᐤ ᑳ ᑮ ᑲᓇᐄᐧᖨᒥᑯᔮᕽ, *supervisor* ᑳ ᑮ ᐃᑎᐦᐟ; “ᐁ+, ᑖᐲᐧ ᑭᑭᑎᒫᑭᓯᐣ ᐃᑯᓯ ᐄ ᐃᑏᖨᐦᑕᒪᐣ᙮ *Indian* ᐊᖨᐢᐠ ᐆᒪ ᑮᖬ ᑕ ᑮ ᐃᑏᖨᒥᓱᔭᐣ ᐃᑯᓯ ᐃᓯ ᐄ ᐃᑕᑭᓱᔭᐣ,” ᓂᑮ ᐃᑎᑲᐃᐧᐣ᙮

ᐃᑯᓯ

3. ᐋᐦᑮᒑᑊ ᐃᔨᓂᐘᐠ, ᒋᑳᐢᑏᐸᔨᐦᒋᑲᐣ ᐃᔨᓂᐘᐠ

"ᐁ! ᐑᐸᐨ ᐑ ᓇᓈᐢᑯᒧᐑᑮᓯᑳᐤ!

ᐃᑯᐢᐲ ᑲ ᐑᒋ ᒪᔭᐚᑕᒫᔭᐦᑾᐤ ᑭᐚᐦᑰᒪᑲᓂᓇᐘᐠ ᓴᐑᔨᐦᑐᐏᓇ ᑳ ᐲ ᐚᐸᐦᑕᒪᕽ ᑭᐱᒫᑎᓯᐏᓂᓈᕽ᙮

ᑖᓂᐦᑭ ᒫᑲ ᐄᑳ ᑲ ᑖᐷ ᐃᑕᐦᑲᒥᑭᓯᔭᐣ?

ᐄᐦᐄ, ᑖᐱᐢᑰᐨ ᐊᓂᑭ ᐅᐲᑕᑐᐑᐘᐠ ᓂᐢᑕᐟ ᑳ ᑮ ᓇᓈᐢᑯᒧᐑᑮᓯᑳᐠ ᑲᔮᐢ᙮

ᑖᓂᓯ ᒫᑲ? ᑭᑎᓯ ᑲᑹᒋᒧᐣ᙮

ᐑᐦᒐᓯᐣ!

ᐊᑐᐢᑮᐦᐃᐠ *Reel Injuns*!

ᑭᔮᐱᐨ ᒌ ᐱᒪᐦᑲᒥᑭᓯᐘᐠ? ᑭᑎᓯ ᑲᑹᒋᒧᐣ᙮

ᐄᐦᐄ! ᐲ ᓰᐑᐱᑕᒪᐏᓈᐣ ᐃᑿ ᑲ ᑮ ᐃᑎᓴᐦᐊᒫᑎᓈᐣ *Reel Injuns*!

ᒫᐘᒋ ᐑᐦᑕᑭᓱᐘᐠ ᑏᐱᔮᕽ ᓇᓈᑐᕽ *Reel Injuns da Rez* ᐅᐦᒋ, ᐊᐦᐴ ᒦᓇ *da Hood* ᐅᐦᒋ᙮

ᐃᑿ ᓇᐘᐨ ᒥᐢᑕᑭᓱᐘᐠ *Reel Injuns* ᑳ ᐘᐑᓰᐦᐅᒋᐠ᙮

ᐃᑿ ᑮᐢᐱᐣ ᓇᒨᔭ ᓈᓂᑕᐤ ᑕ ᒥᐢᑕᐦᐃ ᒦᐢᑎᓂᑮᔭᐣ ᑭᑲ ᑮ ᐃᑎᓴᐦᐊᒫᑎᓈᐣ *Reel Injuns* ᑭᔮᐱᐨ ᐄ ᐲᑭᐢᑹᒋᐠ *Injun*!

ᐄᐦᐄ! ᒋᑰᒋ!

Reel Injuns ᐄ ᐚᐑᓲᐦᐅᒋᐠ ᐄ ᓃᒥᓂᑮᒋᐠ ᑭᓇᓈᐢᑯᒧᐃᐧᓂ ᒦᒋᓲᐃᐧᓂᕽ ᐄ ᐲᑭᐢᑮᐧᒋᐠ ᐊᓂᒪ ᑳᔮᐢ ᐲᑭᐢᑮᐧᐃᐧᐣ *Injun* ᑳ ᐃᑖᐧᓂᐃᐧᐠ!

ᓲᐄᐧᐱᒋᑮ ᓲᒫᐠ *REE-LIN-JUNS*.

ᐃᑲᐧ ᑲ ᒍᐢᒋ ᒦᖬᑯᓯᐃᐧᐣ ᑮᑲᐧᐩ᙮

ᒋᑰᒋ, ᐋᐧᐸᒥᐢᑳᐧᐃᐧ ᑭᐋᐧᐦᑰᒫᑲᓇᐠ, ᒦᓇ ᑭᓯᐋᐧᐠ ᑳ ᐄᐧᑭᒋᐠ ᑮᑑᑏᒪᐠ: ᐄ ᓇᑐᒪᒋᐠ *Reel Injuns* ᑮᑭᐋᐧᕽ ᑕ ᑭᐦᒋᓈᐦᐅᐊᐧᐠ ᐄᑳ ᑮᖬ ᐄ*racist*ᐅᐃᐧᔭᐣ!

4. ᑳ ᐸᐹᒥ ᐊᑖᐄᐧᔭᐣ ᐃᐢᐲ ᑳ ᐄᐧᐢᑲᐧᐢᑏᐃᐧᓈᑯᓯᔭᐣ

ᐱᔭᑳᐧᐤ ᐄ ᑮ ᓂᑕᐃᐧ ᐸᐹᒥ ᐊᑖᐄᐧᔮᐣ ᐃᐢᐲ ᑳ ᑮ ᒫᑎᓈᐃᐧᑮᓯᑳᐠ᙮ ᐊᔮᓂᓴ ᐄ ᑮ ᓅᐦᑏ ᐊᑖᐄᐧᔮᐣ᙮ ᐊᑖᐃᐧᑲᒥᑯᕽ ᓂᑮ ᐃᓯ ᐸᒥᐦᒋᑳᐣ᙮ ᓂᑮ ᑲᐹᐣ ᐅᑖᐹᓈᐢᑯᕽ ᐅᐦᒋ ᐃᑲᐧ ᓂᑮ ᐲᐦᑐᑳᐣ ᐊᑖᐃᐧᑲᒥᑯᕽ᙮ ᐅᑎᓂᑮᐃᐧ ᐋᐧᐊᐧᒋᑲᐣ ᓂᑮ ᓇᐊᐧᓲᓃᐣ ᐃᑲᐧ ᓂᑮ ᐊᑎ ᐸᐹᒥ ᐊᑖᐋᐧᐣ ᐊᔮᓂᓴ᙮

ᐸᐱᔮᐦᑕᐠ ᓂᑮ ᖬᐦᑯᐄᐧᐱᓃᐣ ᐅᑎᓂᑮᐃᐧ ᐋᐧᐊᐧᒋᑲᐣ᙮ ᐊᔮᓂᓴ ᓂᑮ ᓈᑏᐣ᙮ ᓂᑮ ᓇᐊᐧᓲᓈᐤ ᐄ ᓲᐱᐦᑯᓯᐟ ᒥᑖᐢ᙮ ᓂᑮ ᓇᐊᐧᓲᓈᐊᐧᐠ ᐄ ᑲᐢᑭᑏᓯᒋᐠ ᐊᓯᑲᓇᐠ ᐃᑲᐧ ᒦᓇ ᐋᐧᑎᐦᐟ ᐄ ᓲᐱᐦᑯᓯᒋᐠ᙮ ᓂᑮ ᐴᓯᐦᐋᐧᐊᐧᐠ ᐅᑎᓂᑮᐃᐧ ᐋᐧᐊᐧᒋᑲᓂᕽ᙮ ᓂᑮ ᓇᐊᐧᓲᓂᐣ ᐄ ᒥǂᑳᐧᐠ ᐸᐸᑭᐊᐧᔮᐣ ᐃᑲᐧ ᒥᐢᑯᑖᑲᐩ ᐄ ᓲᐱᐦᑯᒥǂᑳᐧᐠ᙮ ᐃᔭᑯᓂ ᒦᓇ ᓂᐴᓯᐦᑖᐣ ᐅᑎᓂᑮᐃᐧ ᐋᐧᐊᐧᒋᑲᓂᕽ᙮

ᒥᐧᐦᒋ ᐄ ᐄᐧ ᓇᐊᐧᓲᓇᑳᐧᐤ ᑖᐱᐢᑳᑲᓇᐠ ᐄ ᐋᐧᐱᐢᑭᓯᒋᐠ ᑳ ᐋᐧᐸᒪᐠ ᐊᑖᐃᐧᑲᒥᐠ ᓲᒫᑲᓂᐢ ᐄ ᑳᐦ ᑮᒨᑖᐸᒥᐟ᙮ ᓂᐸᑭᑎᓈᐋᐧᐠ ᑖᐱᐢᑳᑲᓇᐠ, ᓇᒨᖬ ᑲᑖᐨ ᓂᐄᐧ ᐅᑎᓈᐊᐧᐠ᙮

ᒦᒋᐃᐧᓇ ᓂᑮ ᐊᑎ ᓈᑏᐤ᙮ ᐃᑯᑏ ᓂᑮ ᐃᓯ ᐱᒥᑎᓴᐦᐅᐠ ᐊᓇ ᐊᑖᐃᐧᑲᒥᐠ ᓯᒫᑲᓂᐢ᙮ ᑲᐲ ᓂᑮ ᐱᒥᑎᓴᐦᐅᐠ ᐊᐊᐧ ᐊᑖᐃᐧᑲᒥᐠ ᓯᒫᑲᓂᐢ᙮

ᓂᑮ ᓇᐊᐧᓲᓃᐤ ᐋᐧᐊᐧ, ᓇᐸᑖᑲᐧ, ᑳ ᑳᐢᐹᐧᐠ ᒦᓂᐢ, ᓇᓈᑐᕽ ᑯᑕᑲ ᒦᓂᓴ, ᐃᑲᐧ ᓃᐱᖬ᙮ ᓂᑮ ᓇᐊᐧᓲᓈᐊᐧᐠ ᐲᓲᐧᐦᑲᓯᑲᓇᐠ ᒦᓇ ᑯᐦᑰᓯᐄᐧᖬᐤ᙮ ᐋᐦᒋ ᐳᑯ ᓂᑮ ᐱᒥᑎᓴᐦᐅᐠ ᐊᐊᐧ ᐊᑖᐃᐧᑲᒥᐠ ᓯᒫᑲᓂᐢ᙮

ᓂᑮ ᑭᓱᐋᐧᐦᐃᐠ!

ᓲᐢᑳᐧᐨ ᐳᑯ ᑮᑲᐧᐩ ᓂᑮ ᐊᑎ ᐊᓱᐊᐧᑖᐤ ᓂᑐᑎᓂᑮᐃᐧ ᐋᐊᐧᒋᑲᓂᕽ᙮ ᒥᑐᓂ ᐄ ᑮ ᓵᑲᐢᑭᓈᐦᑖᖬᐤ ᓂᑐᑎᓂᑮᐃᐧ ᐋᐊᐧᒋᑲᐤ᙮ ᐃᑯᓯ ᓂᑮ ᓇᑲᑏᐤ ᐃᑯᑕ᙮

ᓇᒨᖬ ᑲᑖᐨ ᑮᑲᐧᐩ ᓂᑮ ᐊᑖᐋᐧᐤ ᐃᑯᑕ ᐅᐦᒋ᙮ ᓂᑮ ᐊᐧᖬᐋᐧᐤ ᐃᑲᐧ ᓂᑮ ᐸᒥᐦᒋᑳᐤ ᑯᑕᑭᕽ ᐊᑖᐃᐧᑲᒥᑯᕽ ᐃᓯ᙮

ᒥᓴᐋᐧᐨ ᒥᐦᒌᑎᓈᐧ ᐊᑖᐃᐧᑲᒥᑲᐧ᙮

5. **ᐋᐧᓂᐢᑰ ᑭᐢᑭᓇᐧᐦᐊᒫᑮᐃᐧᐤ**

ᐱᖬᑳᐧᐝ ᐄ ᓃᐲᕽ ᓂᑮ ᓂᑕᐃᐧ ᐸᐹᒥᐢᑳᓈᐤ ᒫᒥᕽ ᐋᒪᒋᐄᐧᐢᐱᒧᐃᐧᓂᕽ ᐅᐦᒋ, ᐄ ᐱᒥᑎᓴᐦᐊᒫᕽ ᒫᐦᑖᐃᐧᓲᐱᐩ᙮ ᓂᑮ ᒌᒫᐊᐧᐠ ᓂᑑᑏᒪᐠ᙮ ᓂᑮ ᐊᑎ ᑲᐲᓯᓈᐤ ᐹᐃᐧᐢᒋᑯᓯᕽ ᓂᐢᑕᶜ ᑳ ᑎᐱᐢᑳᐠ ᐃᑲᐧ ᐄ ᐊᑎ ᐋᐧᐸᕽ ᑮᐦᑖᐧᶜ ᓂᑮ ᐴᓯᓈᐤ, ᐄ ᐋᓱᐊᐧᐦᐊᒫᕽ ᓵᑲᐦᐃᑲᓂᓲᐢ᙮ ᐲᖬᐢᐠ ᐊᐧᐹᓯᕽ ᓂᑮ ᑕᑯᒋᒫᓈᐤ, ᑳ ᒫᖬᒋᐊᐧᓯᐠ ᐃᓯᖬᐦᑳᑏᐝ ᐊᓂᒪ ᐊᐧᐹᐢ᙮ ᑮᑕᐦᑕᐄᐧ ᑳ ᒪᑏᐧ ᑏᐲᐧᒋᐠ ᓂᑑᑏᒪᐠ᙮ “ᐅᐦᒋᐢᑎᐤ ᑮᑑᑎᓇᐝ!”

ᓂᑮ ᐃᑖᐱᐤ ᒧᐢᑎᑕᑯᕽ, ᐊᐧᐦᐋᐧ! ᑖᐲᐧ ᒫᓂ ᒫᑲ, ᓂᑮ ᐅᐦᒋᐢᑎᓂᓯᓈᐤ᙮

“ᐊᐦᐋᐝ, ᒌᐢᑲᐧ᙮ ᑭᑲ ᓲᐢᑭᐱᑏᓇᐝ ᒌᒫᐤ ᒥᓂᐢᒋᑯᓯᕽ ᒥᓴᑳᖬᐦᑭ,” ᓂᑮ ᐃᑖᐊᐧᐠ᙮

ᐃᐢᐲ ᑳ ᒥᐢᑳᐧᔮᕽ ᒥᓂᐢᒋᑯᓯᕽ ᓂᑮ ᓰᐢᑭᐱᑏᓈᐣ ᒌᒫᐣ ᐃᑲᐧ ᓂᑮ ᑲᐧᑕᐱᓃᓈᐣ᙮ ᓂᑮ ᐃᑖᐊᐧᐠ ᓂᑑᑏᒪᐠ ᑕᑯᑖᐄᐧᒋᐠ ᐃᑲᐧ ᓃᔮ ᓂᑮ ᑯᐢᐱᐣ ᐄ ᓂᑐᓇᐊᐧᐠ ᐱᑭᐤ ᒥᓇᐦᐃᑯᕽ᙮ ᓂᑮ ᒥᐢᑲᐋᐧᐤ᙮

ᐃᐢᐲ ᑳ ᐲ ᓈᓯᐲᐦᑏᔮᐣ ᑮ ᑕᑲᐦᑭ ᑲᐧᐦᑯᑏᐤ ᑯᑕᐋᐧᐣ᙮ ᐃᑯᑕ ᓂᑮ ᐊᑎ ᑎᐦᑭᓵᐧᐤ ᐊᓇ ᒥᓇᐦᐃᐠ ᐱᑭᐤ᙮ ᑳ ᑮ ᑮᓯ ᑎᐦᑭᓱᐟ ᐊᓇ ᐱᑭᐤ ᓂᑮ ᐊᑎ ᒦᓴᐦᐋᐣ ᓂᒌᒫᓂᒥᓈᐣ ᐃᔭᑯ ᐱᑭᐤ ᐄ ᐋᐸᒋᐦᐊᐠ᙮ ᓂᑭᑖᐸᒥᑲᐧᐠ ᓂᑑᑏᒪᐠ ᑖᐱᐢᑰᐨ ᓇᐊᐧᐨ ᐳᑯ ᐄ ᐋᐣᐄᐧᐦᑕᐦᑳᐧᐤ ᐆᒪ ᑳ ᐃᑕᐦᑲᒥᑭᓯᔮᐣ᙮ ᓂᐲᐦᐅᓈᐣ ᑕ ᐹᓯᐟ ᐊᓇ ᐱᑭᐤ, ᐲᔨᐢᐠ ᐹᓯᐤ ᐃᑲᐧ ᑮᐦᑖᐧᑦ ᓂᐴᓯᓈᐣ᙮ ᑳ ᒪᑏᐧ ᑏᐲᐧᒋᐠ ᓂᑑᑏᒪᐠ᙮

“ᓇᒎᔮ ᐊᐊᐧᓯᒦ ᐅᐦᒋᐢᑎᐣ! ᐊᐧᐦᐋᐧ! ᑖᓂᓯ ᐆᒪ ᐄ ᐃᓯ ᑭᐢᑮᔨᐦᑕᒫᐣ ᑕ ᒦᓴᐦᐊᒪᐣ ᒌᒫᐣ?”

“ᑳᔮᐢ ᐃᔨᓂᐤ ᒪᒪᐦᑖᐃᐧᓯᐃᐧᐣ ᐊᓂᒪ᙮ ᑳᔮᐢ ᐃᔨᓂᐤ ᐄ ᑮ ᑭᐢᑭᓇᐧᐦᐊᒪᐃᐧᐟ: ᓄᐦᑖᐄᐧᐸᐣ᙮”

6. ᐋᐦᑲᒥ ᓃᐦᐃᔭᐄᐧᑖᐣ

ᐋᐦᑲᒥ ᓃᐦᐃᔭᐄᐧᑖᐣ:
ᑭᐲᑭᐢᑮᐧᐃᐧᓂᓈᕽ ᐊᐢᑏᐤ ᑭᓂᓯᑐᐦᑕᒧᐃᐧᓂᓇᐤ᙮
ᐋᐦᑲᒥ ᓃᐦᐃᔭᐄᐧᑖᐣ:
ᑭᐲᑭᐢᑮᐧᐃᐧᓂᓈᕽ ᐊᐢᑏᐤ ᑭᓂᓯᑕᐄᐧᔨᒥᑐᐃᐧᓂᓇᐤ᙮
ᐋᐦᑲᒥ ᓃᐦᐃᔭᐄᐧᑖᐣ:
ᑭᐲᑭᐢᑮᐧᐃᐧᓂᓈᕽ ᐊᐢᑏᐤ ᑭᐱᒫᑎᓯᐃᐧᓂᓇᐤ᙮
ᐋᐦᑲᒥ ᓃᐦᐃᔭᐄᐧᑖᐣ:
ᑭᐲᑭᐢᑮᐧᐃᐧᓂᓈᕽ ᐊᐢᑏᐤ ᑭᓃᐦᐃᔮᐃᐧᐃᐧᓂᓇᐤ᙮

7
ᑖᐲᐧᐃᐧᐣ ᓃᑳᐣ ᐄ ᒪᐧᔩ ᒦᓄᓯᐦᑕᒫᕽ ᒥᔭ ᐄᐧᒌᐦᑐᐃᐧᐣ

1. ᑖᐲᐧᐃᐧᐣ

ᑖᐲᐧᐃᐧᐣ: ᐊᐚᓯᓴᐠ ᑮ ᓯᐲᐧᐦᑕᐦᐚᐊᐧᐠ;
ᑖᐲᐧᐃᐧᐣ: ᐅᓃᑭᐦᐃᑯᒫᐊᐧᐠ ᑮ ᒪᐢᑳᒫᐊᐧᐠ ᐅᑕᐚᓯᒥᓯᐚᐊᐧ;
ᑖᐲᐧᐃᐧᐣ: ᐚᑎᐦᐟ ᐊᐚᓯᓴᐠ ᓇᒫᐧᐨ ᑮ ᐅᐦᒋ ᑮᐄᐧᐊᐧᐠ;
ᑖᐲᐧᐃᐧᐣ: ᐊᐚᓯᓴᐠ ᑭᓇᓅᔭᒋᐦᐚᐊᐧᐠ ᐃᐢᐲ ᑳ ᑮ ᐲᑭᐢᑮᐧᒋᐠ
ᐅᐲᑭᐢᑮᐧᐃᐧᓂᐚᐊᐧ;
ᑖᐲᐧᐃᐧᐣ: ᐚᑎᐦᐟ ᐊᐚᓯᓴᐠ ᑮ ᐅᑎᐦᑎᓈᐊᐧᐠ;
ᑖᐲᐧᐃᐧᐣ: ᐚᑎᐦᐟ ᐊᐚᓯᓴᐠ ᑮ ᓂᐸᐦᐚᐊᐧᐠ;
ᑖᐲᐧᐃᐧᐣ: ᐊᐚᓯᓴᐠ ᑮ ᐊᐧᓂᐦᑖᐊᐧᐠ ᐅᐲᑭᐢᑮᐧᐃᐧᓂᐚᐊᐧ;
ᑖᐲᐧᐃᐧᐣ: ᐊᐚᓯᓴᐠ ᑮ ᐊᐧᓂᐦᑖᐊᐧᐠ ᐅᑎᓲᐦᒋᑮᐃᐧᓂᐚᐊᐧ;
ᑖᐲᐧᐃᐧᐣ: ᓇᒫᐧᐨ ᐚᐦᑰᐄᐧᒋᐦᐃᐄᐧᐃᐧᐣ ᑕ ᑮ ᐃᐢᐸᔮᐣ ᐹᑎᒫ
ᓇᐢᑮᐧᐊᐧᓲᐦᑖᑖᐧᐃᐧ ᐊᔕᒥᐦᐃᑭᒫᐊᐧᐠ ᒦᓇ ᐅᑭᒫᐊᐧᐠ ᐅᑭᒫᓈᕽ ᐅᐦᒋ
ᐆᐦᐅ ᑖᐲᐧᐃᐧᓇᕽ

2. ᑭᔮᐢᑭᐃᐧᐣ

ᐊᔭᓴᐢᑏᐊᐧ ᑭᔮᐢᑭᐃᐧᐣ
ᐃᐢᐲ ᐊᐊᐧᓯᒦ ᐊᐋᐧᓯᓴᐠ
ᐄ ᒥᐢᑲᐃᐧᐦᒋᐠ ᐋᐧᑎᐦᑳᓂᕽ
ᐅᐢᑲᓂᐋᐧᐊᐧ ᐄ ᐊᓴᐢᑏᔨᑭ᙮

3. ᓇᒨᔭ ᐋᐦᑮᑖᑊ *Indian*

Solomon ᓂᑎᓯᔨᐦᑳᓱᐣ᙮ ᐋᒪᒋᐄᐧᐢᐱᒧᐃᐧᓃᕽ ᐅᐦᒋ ᓃᔭ᙮ *William John Ratt* (ᐅᓱᐊᐧᔩᑭᐢ) ᑮ ᐃᑖᐤ ᓅᐦᑖᐄᐧᐸᐣ, ᐅᐦᑖᐄᐧᐸᓇ *Patrick* (ᐅᐢᑳᑖᐢᐠ) ᑮ ᐃᑎᒫᐊᐧ, ᐋᒪᒋᐄᐧᐢᐱᒧᐃᐧᓂᕽ ᐅᐦᒋ᙮ *Alice Emily Ratt* (ᐸᐦᑲᕽ) ᑮ ᐃᑖᐤ ᓂᑳᐄᐧᐸᐣ, ᐅᑳᐄᐧᐸᓇ *Maggie McKenzie* ᑮ ᐃᑎᒫᐊᐧ, ᒥᐢᑕᐦᐃ ᓵᑲᐦᐃᑲᓂᕽ ᐅᐦᒋ᙮

4. ᑭᐱᐦᑐᐄᐧᐃᐧᐣ

ᑭᑮ ᑲᑮᐧ ᑭᐱᐦᑐᐄᐧᓂᑯᓇᐊᐧᐠ:
ᑮ ᓂᓯᐊᐧᓈᒋᐦᑖᐊᐧᐠ ᑭᐋᐧᐦᑰᐦᑐᐃᐧᓂᓇᐤ;
ᑮ ᓂᓯᐊᐧᓈᒋᐦᑖᐊᐧᐠ ᑭᐲᑭᐢᑮᐧᐃᐧᓂᓇᐤ;
ᑮ ᓂᓯᐊᐧᓈᒋᐦᑖᐊᐧᐠ ᑭᑎᓲᐦᒋᑮᐃᐧᓂᓇᐤ;
ᑮ ᓂᓯᐊᐧᓈᒋᐦᑖᐊᐧᐠ ᑭᑕᐦᒐᐦᑯᐃᐧᓂᓇᐤ᙮
ᐋᐧᑎᐦᐟ ᑭᑮ ᓂᓯᐊᐧᓈᒋᐦᐃᓱᓇᐤ;
ᐋᐧᑎᐦᐟ ᑭᑮ ᐴᓂ ᐲᑭᐢᑳᐧᓇᐤ ᑭᐲᑭᐢᑮᐧᐃᐧᓂᓇᐤ;
ᐋᐧᑎᐦᐟ ᑭᑮ ᐊᐧᓂᐦᐅᓇᐤ
ᑳ ᐲᐦᑖᑲᐧᕽ ᑭᐱᐦᑐᐄᐧᐃᐧᓂᕽ᙮
ᒫᑲ ᑮᑕᐦᑕᐄᐧ
ᐊᐱᐢᒋ ᐲᑭᐢᑮᐧᐃᐧᓂᐢ ᑮᒦᐧᐤ
“ᑭᒥᐢᑳᑯᓇᐊᐧᐠ᙮”
ᑮᑕᐦᑕᐄᐧ
ᑳ ᐲᐦᑖᑲᐧᕽ ᑭᐱᐦᑐᐄᐧᐃᐧᐣ
ᑳ ᑭᓲᐄᐧᐠ᙮

5. ᐄ ᓂᓯᐚᓈᒋᐦᑖᔭᕽ ᑭᐲᑭᐢᑹᐏᓂᓇᐤ

ᑖᓂᐦᑭ ᐆᒪ ᑭᐲᑭᐢᑹᐏᓂᓇᐤ ᑳ ᐊᑎ ᐘᓂᐦᑖᔭᕽ?
ᐑᔮ ᑮᔮᓇᐤ ᐄ ᐃᑑᑖᓱᔭᕽ:
ᑕᐦᑣᐤ ᐄᑳ ᑳ ᓃᐦᐃᔮᐑᒥᑎᑐᔭᕽ;
ᑕᐦᑣᐤ ᐄᑳ ᑳ ᓃᐦᐃᔮᐑᔭᕽ ᐃᐢᐲ ᑳ ᒫᒪᐏᐦᐃᑐᔭᕽ;
ᑕᐦᑣᐤ ᐄᑳ ᑳ ᓃᐦᐃᔮᐑᔭᕽ ᐃᐢᐲ ᑳ ᒫᒪᐘᐱᔭᕽ;
ᑕᐦᑣᐤ ᐄᑳ ᑳ ᓃᐦᐃᔮᐑᔭᕽ ᐃᐢᐲ ᑳ ᑭᐢᑭᓌᐦᐊᒫᑮᔭᕽ;
ᑕᐦᑣᐤ ᐄᑳ ᑳ ᓃᐦᐃᔮᐑᔭᕽ ᐃᐢᐲ ᑳ ᐋᒐᔮᐦᑮᔭᕽ;
ᑕᐦᑣᐤ ᐄᑳ ᑳ ᓃᐦᐃᔮᐑᔭᕽ ᐃᐢᐲ ᑳ ᑳᑮᓯᒧᔭᕽ;
ᑕᐦᑣᐤ ᑳ ᑭᑎᒫᑭᒫᔭᕽ ᐅᐢᑳᔭ ᑳ ᑲᑹ ᓃᐦᐃᔮᐑᐟ:
“ᑭᒨᓂᔮᐏᐦᑖᑯᓯᐣ ᒫᓇ,” ᐄ ᐃᓯ ᓇᓅᔮᒋᒫᔭᕽ.
ᐃᑯᓯ ᑭᑎᓯ ᓂᓯᐚᓈᒋᐦᑖᓇᐤ ᑭᐲᑭᐢᑹᐏᓂᓇᐤ:
ᒥᑐᓂ ᑖᐱᐢᑰ- ᐄ ᐊᑎ ᓂᓯᐚᓈᒋᐦᐃᓲᒪᑲᕽ ᑭᐲᐱᐢᑹᐏᓂᓇᐤ.

6. ᑖᓂᐑ ᓵᑭᐦᐃᐑᐏᐣ?

ᒌᐢᐟ! ᒫᒥᑐᓃᔩᐦᑕ ᐆᐦᐅ:
ᐆᒪ:
ᐄ ᑎᐱᐢᑳᐠ ᑮᑭᐚᕽ:
ᑭᐴᓃᓈᐚᐤ ᑯᑕᐚᓈᐱᐢᑯᐢ;
ᑭᓵᐢᑲᐦᐄᓈᐚᐤ ᐚᓯᐢᑯᒌᓂᑲᓂᐢ;
ᑭᑕᓈᐢᑳᓈᐚᐤ ᐃᑿ ᑭᑕᑿᓇᐦᐆᓈᐚᐤ
ᐅᐲᐘᔭᑯ‴ ᐅᐦᒋ;
ᒫᒋ ᐋᒐᔮᐦᑮᐤ ᑭᑳᐏᐩ.
ᐆᐦᐆ ᒪᑗ ᑭᑐᐤ ᐘᔮᐑᑎᒥᕽ;
ᑯᑕᐚᓈᐱᐢᐠ ᒪᑗᐦᑲᐦᑏᐤ;
ᐚᓯᐢᑯᒌᓂᑲᓂᐢ ᒋᑳᐢᑏᐸᔩᐤ;
ᑭᑳᐏᐩ ᐸᐱᔮᐦᑕᐠ ᐋᒐᔮᐦᑮᐤ.
ᑭᑕᑎ ᓂᐹᐣ.
ᐊᐦᐴ ᐆᒪ:

ᐁ ᑎᐱᐢᑳᐠ ᐊᔭᒥᐦᐋᐃᐧ ᑭᐢᑭᓇᐧᐦᐊᒫᑐᐃᐧᑲᒥᑯᕽ:
ᑭᓃᐱᑏᑳᐸᐃᐧᓈᐋᐧᐤ ᑭᑕ ᐅᑎᓇᒫᓱᔦᐠ ᐱᐢᑭᑎᐢ (*dog biscuit*);
ᑭᑕᔭᒥᐦᐋᓈᐋᐧᐤ;
ᑭᑲᐃᐧᓯᒧᓈᐋᐧᐤ;
ᐋᐢᑕᐄᐧᐦᐃᑳᑏᐤ᙮
ᑭᓄᐧᐣᐠ ᑭᑲᓇᐋᐧᐸᐦᑌᐣ ᒋᑳᐢᑌᓯᓂᐃᐧᓇ ᑕᐦᑖᐧᐤ ᓴᐦᑫᐸᔫᐣ ᑳ ᐱᒪᑯᒥᕽ
ᐊᐧᔭᐄᐧᑎᒥᕽ᙮
ᐱᔫᐣᐠ ᑭᓂᐹᐣ᙮

8
ᐄ ᑮᐐᐦᑐᑕᐦᐃᑐᔭ᙮

1. ᐊᐢᑭᕀ ᑭᑐᐦᑖᐸᒥᐦᐃᑯᓇᐤ

ᐊᐢᑭᕀ ᑭᑐᐦᑖᐸᒥᐦᐃᑯᓇᐤ;
ᖫᑎᐣ ᑭᑐᐦᑖᖭᐦᖭᐦᐃᑯᓇᐤ;
ᐃᐢᑯᑏᐤ ᑭᑐᐦᑖᑮᓲᐏᐦᐃᑯᓇᐤ;
ᓂᐱᕀ ᑭᑐᐦᑖᒥᓂᐦᑹᓇᐤ;
ᑭᐲᑭᐢᑹᐏᓂᓇᐘ, ᑭᑖᒐᖫᐦᑮᐏᓂᓇᐘ, ᑭᐚᐦᑰᒥᑐᐏᓂᓇᐘ,
ᑭᒫᒪᐏᐦᐃᑐᐏᓂᓇᐘ
ᑲᐦᑭᖬᐤ ᐆᐦᐅ ᑭᑐᐦᑖᐸᒥᐦᐃᑯᓇᐤ, ᑲᐦᑭᖬᐤ ᑭᐱᒫᒋᐦᐃᑯᓇᐤ᙮

2. ᐋᓂᐢᑰᐦᑐᐏᐣ

ᐃᔭᑯ ᐆᒪ ᐋᓂᐢᑰᐦᑐᐏᐣ:

ᐱᒥᑎᓴᐦᐊᒪᓂ ᒥᖪ ᒦᐢᑲᓇᐤ ᑭᑲ ᐐᒌᐏᑯᐣ ᑲᐦᑭᖬᐤ
ᑭᐦᒋ ᑭᐢᑭᓇᐧᐦᐊᒫᑮᐏᓇ:

ᓰᐲᖨᐦᑕᒧᐃᐧᐣ, ᑭᓰᐋᐧᑎᓯᐃᐧᐣ, ᓰᐱᖬᐄᐧᓯᐃᐧᐣ, ᓵᑭᐦᐃᑐᐃᐧᐣ, ᓲᐦᑭᓯᐃᐧᐣ, ᓰᐱᐦᑯᓯᐃᐧᐣ, ᓇᓈᐢᑯᒧᐃᐧᐣ, ᑲᓈᒋᐦᐅᐃᐧᐣ, ᒥᖩᐧᖨᐦᑕᒧᐃᐧᐣ, ᑭᐢᑏᖨᐦᑕᒧᐃᐧᐣ, ᑖᐳᐊᐧᑮᖨᐦᑕᒧᐃᐧᐣ, ᓇᓇᐦᐃᐦᑕᒧᐃᐧᐣ, ᒫᑎᓇᒫᑐᐃᐧᐣ, ᒪᓈᒋᐦᐃᑐᐃᐧᐣ, ᐸᑯᓰᖨᐦᑖᑯᓯᐃᐧᐣ, ᑕᐸᐦᑏᖨᒥᓱᐃᐧᐣ᙮

3. ᓂᓇᓈᐢᑯᒧᐣ

ᐊᓄᐦᐨ ᐃᑲᐧ ᑕᐦᑐ ᑮᓯᑳᐤ:

ᓂᓇᓈᐢᑯᒧᐣ ᐁ ᒥᖩᐧᔮᒋᐠ ᓂᒐᐋᐧᓯᒥᓴᐠ ᐃᑲᐧ ᓅᓯᓯᒪᐠ; ᓂᓇᓈᐢᑯᒧᐣ ᐄᑳ ᐊᐊᐧᓯᒦ ᐄ ᐋᐧᐸᒋᐦᑖᔮᐣ ᒥᓂᐦᑮᐧᐃᐧᐣ ᐃᑲᐧ ᒪᒋ ᒪᐢᑭᐦᑭᔭ; ᓂᓇᓈᐢᑯᒧᐣ ᐄ ᑲᐢᑭᐦᑖᔮᐣ ᑕ ᑲᓇᐋᐧᐸᐦᑕᒫᐣ ᐊᐢᑭᐩ ᑖᐱᐢᑰᐨ ᐊᐋᐧᓯᐢ: ᐃᑕ ᑲᐦᑭᖬᐤ ᑮᑲᐧᐩ ᐄ ᒫᒪᐢᑳᑖᐸᐦᑕᒫᐣ ᑲᐦᑭᖬᐤ ᑮᑲᐧᐩ ᐄ ᒥᖪᓈᑲᐧᕽ᙮

ᒥᖪ ᓇᓈᐢᑯᒧᐃᐧᑮᓯᑲᓂᓯᐠ ᑕᐦᑐ ᑮᓯᑳᐤ

4. ᑳ ᐆᐦᑖᐄᐧᒫᐃᐧ ᑮᓯᑳᐠ

ᐃᐢᐲ ᑳ ᑮ ᐊᐋᐧᓯᓰᐃᐧᔮᐣ ᑲᐲ ᒫᓇ ᓂᑮ ᐄᐧᒌᐋᐧᐤ ᓅᐦᑖᐄᐧᐸᐣ ᑳ ᐸᐹᒪᐦᑲᒥᑭᓯᐟ᙮ ᓂᑮ ᐄᐧᒌᐋᐧᐤ ᑳ ᓂᑕᐃᐧ ᑖᐸᑮᐧᐟ ᐃᑲᐧ ᒦᓇ ᑳ ᑮ ᓈᑕᑮᐧᐟ; ᓂᑮ ᐄᐧᒌᐋᐧᐤ ᑳ ᑮ ᓂᑕᐃᐧ ᐸᑭᑕᐦᐋᐧᐟ ᐃᑲᐧ ᒦᓇ ᑳ ᑮ ᓈᑕᖬᐲᐟ; ᓂᑮ ᐄᐧᒌᐋᐧᐤ ᑳ ᑮ ᓂᑕᐃᐧ ᐊᐧᓂᐦᐃᑮᐟ ᐃᑲᐧ ᒦᓇ ᑳ ᑮ ᓂᑕᐃᐧ ᓈᒋᐊᐧᓂᐦᐃᑲᓃᐟ; ᓂᑮ ᐄᐧᒌᐋᐧᐤ ᑳ ᑮ ᓈᒋᓂᐦᑑᔮᕽ ᐃᑲᐧ ᑳ ᓂᑕᐃᐧᒥᓃᐟ᙮ ᑲᐦᑭᖬᐤ ᐃᔭᑯᓂ ᑮᑲᐧᔭ ᓂᑮ ᐊᑎ ᑭᐢᑮᖨᐦᑑᐣ, ᐄ ᑮ ᑭᐢᑭᓇᐧᐋᐧᐸᒪᐠ ᓅᐦᑖᐄᐧᐸᐣ᙮ ᐃᑲᐧ ᐃᐢᐲ ᑳ ᑮ ᒫᒋ ᐊᔭᒥᐦᒋᑮᔮᐣ ᑖᐱᐢᑰᐨ ᐄᑳ ᑮᑲᐧᐩ ᐄ ᑭᐢᑮᖨᐦᑕᒫᐣ ᓂᑮ ᐃᓯ ᐸᒥᐦᐃᑲᐧᐠ ᐅᑭᐢᑭᓇᐧᐦᐊᒫᑮᐊᐧᐠ, ᐄ ᑮ ᑲᑮᐧ ᓃᐲᐃᐧᐦᐃᒋᐠ ᑳ ᑮ ᐱ ᐃᓯ ᓃᐦᐃᖬᐃᐧ ᐱᒫᑎᓯᔮᐣ᙮

ᐊᓄᐦᐨ ᐆᒪ ᑮᖬᓇᐤ ᑳ ᐊᑎ ᑭᐢᑭᓇᐧᐦᐊᒫᑮᔭᕽ ᑲᓇᐋᐧᐸᐦᑏᑖᐣ ᐃᑐᐃᐧᕽ ᑭᐢᑮᖨᐦᑕᒧᐃᐧᐣ ᐊᐋᐧᓯᐢ ᑳ ᐲᑖᐟ ᐅᑭᐢᑭᓇᐧᐦᐊᒫᑐᐃᐧᓂᕽ ᐃᑲᐧ ᐃᑯᑕ ᐅᐦᒋ ᐊᑎ ᑕᑲᐧᐢᑖᑖᐣ ᑯᑕᑲ ᑭᐢᑮᖨᐦᑕᒧᐃᐧᓇ᙮

ᑏᓂᑭ ᓄᐦᑖᐑᐸᐤ.

5. ᓇᐦᐄᐎᐤ

ᐅᑭᐢᑭᓊᐦᐊᒫᑲᓇᐠ ᓂᑳᐦ ᑲᑮᐢᑭᒫᐗᐠ, ᐊᓂᑭ ᑳ ᓄᐦᑏ ᓃᐦᐃᔦᐄᐧᒋᐠ:

ᓄᐦᑖᐑᐸᐤ ᓂᑮ ᑭᐢᑭᓊᐦᐊᒫᐠ ᑕ ᐃᓯ ᑖᐸᑸᔮᐤ. ᓂᑮ ᒦᔦᐠ ᐋᐸᒋᐦᒋᑲᓇ ᑕ ᐅᐦᒋ ᑖᐸᑿᑮᔮᐤ: ᒌᑲᐦᐃᑲᓂᐢ ᑕ ᑮᐢᑲᑕᐦᐗᑿ° ᒥᐢᒋᑯᓴᐠ, ᑖᐸᑿᓂᔮᐱᐩ, ᐃᑾ ᒎᐦᑯᒫᐤ ᑕ ᒪᓂᓵᒫᐤ ᒥᐢᒋᑯᓴ ᑕ ᓯᐦᑐᐢᑲᐦᐊᒫᐤ ᑖᐸᑿᐤ. ᓂᑮ ᑭᐢᑭᓄᐦᑕᐦᐃᐠ ᐃᑕ ᑕ ᒥᐢᑳᒫᐤ ᐚᐳᓱ ᒦᐢᑲᓈᓴ ᐃᑾ ᒦᓇ ᑕ ᐃᓯ ᓂᓯᑕᐎᓇᒫᐤ ᐃᔭᑯᓂ. ᓂᑮ ᑭᐢᑭᓊᐦᐊᒫᐠ ᑕ ᐃᓯ ᐅᔫᐢᑖᔮᐤ ᑖᐸᑿᓂᔮᐱᐩ ᐃᑾ ᑖᓂᓯ ᑕ ᐃᓯ ᐊᑯᑖᔮᐤ ᐚᐳᓱ ᒦᐢᑲᓈᓯᕽ.

ᓂᐢᑕᐨ ᑳ ᐊᑯᑖᔮᐤ ᐚᐳᓱ ᑖᐸᑿᐤ ᓂᑮ ᒪᒫᔫᐤ, ᒫᑲ ᒥᐦᒉᑗ° ᑳ ᐊᑎ ᑖᐦ ᑖᐸᑹᔮᐤ ᓂᑮ ᐊᑎ ᓇᐦᐋᐤ. ᒫᑲ ᐊᓄᐦ- ᓂᒫᔫᐤ ᐊᔦᐢᐠ ᑲᔮᐢ ᐊᐢᐱᐤ ᑳ ᑮ ᑖᐸᑹᔮᐤ. ᑲᐲ ᒫᓇ ᐳᑯ ᑕ ᑖᐦ ᑖᐸᑹᔮᐤ ᑮᐢᐱᐤ ᓂᓄᐦᑏ ᓇᐦᐋᐤ.

ᐃᑯᓯ ᐊᓂᒪ ᑲᐦᑭᔫ° ᑮᑾᐩ: ᑮᐢᐱᐤ ᓄᐦᑏ ᓇᐦᐄᔮᓂ ᐅᐦᒋᑕ° ᐳᑯ ᑲᐲ ᑕ ᐱᒥ ᐊᑐᐢᑳᑕᒫᐤ.

6. ᑭᐢᑮᔦᐦᑕᒍᐎᐤ

ᓂᑲ ᑮ ᒪᓯᓇᐦᐃᑳᐤ
    ᐋᑳᔫᓰᒍᐎᐤ ᒦᓇ ᓃᐦᐃᔪᐗᓯᓇᐦᐃᑮᐎᐤ
ᒫᑲ ᓇᒎᔫ ᓂᑲ ᑮ ᐸᑭᑕᐦᐚᐤ
    ᐊᐦᐴ ᓇᒎᔫ ᓂᑲ ᑮ ᐗᓂᐦᐃᑳᐤ
    ᑖᐱᐢᒎ- ᑮᔫ.

ᑳ ᐲ ᐃᓯ ᑭᐢᑭᓯᔮᐣ

ᓂᑲ ᑮ ᑭᐢᑭᓈᐦᐊᒫᑳᐣ
ᓇᓈᑐˣ ᒪᓯᓇᐦᐃᑮᐃᐧᐣ
ᒦᓇ ᑖᓂᓯ ᑕ ᐃᓯ ᑭᐢᑭᓈᐦᐊᒫᑲᓂᐃᐧᐠ
ᒫᑲ ᓇᒫᐧ⁻ ᓂᑲ ᑮ ᒫᒑᐣ
ᓇᒫᐧ⁻ ᓂᑲ ᑮ ᒫᑖᐦᐋᐧᐤ ᒨᓴᐧ
ᓵᐳ ᓴᑳˣ ᐊᐦᐴ ᐋᑲᒥ ᒪᐢᑮᑯˣ
ᑖᐱᐢᑰ⁻ ᑮᔦ×

ᓂᑕᐢᐲᔑᒧᐣ ᒪᓯᓇᐦᐃᑲᓇ ᑕ ᐄᐧᒋᐦᐃᑰᔮᐣ
ᑳ ᐃᓯ ᑲᐢᑭᐦᑖᔮᐣ;
ᑮᔦ ᐄᐧᔦ, ᑭᑕᐢᐲᔑᒧᐣ ᑭᑭᐢᑭᓯᐃᐧᐣ
ᑳ ᐱ ᐃᓯ ᑭᐢᑭᓈᐦᐊᒫᐢᑳᐧᐤ
ᑭᑖᓂᐢᑰ ᐋᐧᐦᑰᒫᑲᓂᓇᐊᐧᐠ×

7. ᑭᐢᑮᔑᐦᑕᒧᐃᐧᐣ ᐅᐦᒋ

ᑭᔮᑦ ᐋᑕ ᐄ ᒥᔦᐧᓯᑭ ᐃᑏᐧᐃᐧᓇ ᒦᓇ ᐲᑭᐢᑮᐧᐃᐧᓇ ᐊᐱᓰᐢ ᐳᑯ ᐃᑯᑕ ᑳ ᐊᐢᑏᑭ ᐃᔑᓂᐤ ᑭᐢᑮᔑᐦᑕᒧᐃᐧᓇ, ᐃᔑᓅᓯᐃᐧᓇ, ᐃᑲᐧ ᒫᒥᑐᓅᔑᐦᒋᑮᐃᐧᓇ, ᓇᐊᐧ⁻ ᒥᐢᑕᐦᐃ ᑭᐢᑮᔑᐦᑕᒧᐃᐧᐣ ᐊᐢᑏᐤ ᐋᒐᔦᐧᐦᑮᐃᐧᓂˣ, ᐋᒋᒧᐃᐧᓂˣ, ᐃᑲᐧ ᓂᑲᒧᐃᐧᓂˣ ᐃᑯᑕ ᑳ ᐃᓯ ᒫᒪᐃᐧᓇᒫˣ ᑲᐦᑭᔦᐤ ᑭᑭᐢᑮᔑᐦᑕᒧᐃᐧᓂᓇᐊᐧ×

ᐃᑯᑕ ᑲ ᒥᐢᑮᓇᐤ ᑲᐦᑭᔦᐤ ᑮᑲᐧ+ ᑳ ᐅᐦᒋ ᑭᐢᑮᔑᒥᒋᔭˣ, ᐃᑕ ᑳ ᐅᐦᒋ ᓅᐦᐃᔦᐋᐧᑎᓯᔭˣ, ᓇᓈᑐˣ ᐃᑏᔑᐦᒋᑮᐃᐧᓇ, ᓇᓈᑐˣ ᐃᑏᔑᐦᑕᒪᐃᐧᓇ, ᓇᓈᑐˣ ᒨᓯᐦᑖᐃᐧᓇ, ᐃᑲᐧ ᓇᓈᑐˣ ᐋᒋᒥᒋᐃᐧᓇ ᑳ ᐲ ᐃᓯ ᐃᑕᐦᑲᒥᑭᓯᔮˣ ᑕ ᐅᐦᐱᓇᒫˣ ᑭᐢᑭᓈᐦᐊᒫᑐᐃᐧᓇ ᐃᑲᐧ ᓅᐦᐃᔦᐃᐧᓰᐦᒋᑮᐃᐧᓇ ᐃᑲᐧ ᓇᓈᑐˣ ᐃᓰᐦᒋᑮᐃᐧᓇ×

Basil H. Johnston

8. ᓂᑐᐦᑕ!

ᑳᐃᐧᔭ ᓇᑲᑕ ᐃᔨᓂᐚᑎᓯᐃᐧᐣ:
ᑲᐲ ᑲ ᐄᐧᒌᐃᐧᑯᐣ;
ᑲᐲ ᑲ ᐄᐧᒋᐦᐃᑯᐣ᙮
ᑏᐱᔭᕽ ᐊᒋᔭᐤ ᓇᑲᑕ ᐊᐧᓃᐃᐧᑐᐃᐧᐣ:
ᑳᑭᑐ!
ᓂᑐᐦᑕ!
ᑭᐱᐦᑐᐄᐧᐃᐧᓂᕽ ᑲ ᐲᐦᑕᐋᐧᐊᐧᐠ ᑭᑖᓂᐢᑰ ᐋᐧᐦᑰᒫᑲᓂᓇᐊᐧᐠ
ᐄ ᐋᒐᔮᐦᑳᑎᑯᔮᐦᑳᐧᐤ᙮
ᑳᒫᐧᑕᐣ᙮

ᐋᒐᔮᐦᑮᐃᐧᓇ

9
ᓃᐦᐃᖬᐤ ᑭᐢᑭᓇᐧᐦᐊᒫᑮᐃᐧᐣ: ᓂᐢᑕᑦ ᒫᒥᑐᓃᖨᐦᒋᑮᐃᐧᐣ

1. ᒑᓂᓯ ᒫᓇ ᑳ ᑮ ᐃᓯ ᑭᐢᑭᓇᐧᐦᐊᒫᐦᒋᐠ ᐊᐚᓯᓴᐠ ᑲᔮᐢ?

ᑲᔮᐢ ᒫᓇ, ᐄ ᒪᐧᖩ ᑳᐧᓯᐦᐃᐦᒋᐠ ᐊᐚᓯᓴᐠ ᐅᐦᐱᒦ ᑭᑕ ᓂᑕᐃᐧ ᐊᔭᒥᐦᒋᑮᒋᐠ ᐃᑲᐧ ᐄ ᒪᐧᖩ ᑭᐢᑭᓇᐧᐦᐊᒫᐦᒋᐠ ᑭᐢᑭᓇᐧᐦᐊᒫᑐᐃᐧᑲᒥᑯᕽ, ᐄ ᒪᐧᖩ ᐃᐦᑕᑯᐦᑭ ᑭᐢᑭᓇᐧᐦᐊᒫᑐᐃᐧᑲᒥᑲᐧ, ᑮ ᑳᐦ ᑭᐢᑭᓇᐧᐦᐊᒪᐚᐊᐧᐠ ᐊᐚᓯᓴᐠ ᑳ ᒦᑳᐧ ᐱᒪᐦᑲᒥᑭᓯᒋᐠ ᑕᐦᑐ ᑮᓯᑳᐤ᙮

ᑲᐦᑭᖬᐤ ᑮᑲᐧᐩ ᑮ ᑭᐢᑭᓇᐧᐦᐊᒪᐚᐊᐧᐠ: ᓈᐲᓯᓴᐠ ᑮ ᐸᐹᒥ ᐄᐧᒌᐄᐧᐊᐧᐠ ᐅᐦᑖᐄᐧᒥᐚᐊᐧ ᐄ ᐄᐧᒋᐦᐚᒋᐠ ᑮᑲᐧᔭ ᑳ ᐊᑐᐢᑳᑕᒥᖨᐟ᙮ ᐃᑯᓰᓯ ᐄᐧᖬᐚᐤ ᑮ ᐊᑎ ᑭᐢᑮᖨᐦᑕᒪᐧᐠ ᒑᓂᓯ ᑭᑕ ᐃᓯ ᐱᒫᒋᐦᐃᓱᒋᐠ᙮ ᑮ ᑭᐢᑭᓇᐚᐸᐦᒋᑮᐊᐧᐠ ᒑᓂᓯ ᑭᑕ ᐃᓯ ᓅᒋᐦᒋᑮᒋᐠ, ᑭᑕ ᐃᓯ ᒫᒌᒋᐠ, ᑭᑕ ᐃᓯ ᓈᒋᓂᐦᑏᒋᐠ ᐃᑲᐧ ᑭᑕ ᓂᑯᐦᑏᒋᐠ, ᑭᑕ ᐃᓯ ᓅᒋᑭᓄᓰᐄᐧᒋᐠ, ᑭᑕ ᐃᓯ ᐅᓰᐦᒌᒋᐠ ᒌᒫᓇ ᐃᑲᐧ ᐋᐧᐢᑲᐦᐃᑲᓇ; ᑭᑕ ᐃᓯ ᐅᓰᐦᐋᒋᐠ ᐊᓵᒪ, ᐊᐳᔭ, ᐋᐦᒑᐱᔭ, ᐃᑲᐧ ᐊᑲᐢᑲᐧ᙮

ᐃᑿ ᐃᐢᑹᓯᓴᐠ ᑮ ᐸᐹᒥ ᐐᒌᐐᐘᐠ ᐅᑳᐐᒥᐚᐘ ᐄ ᐐᒋᐦᐋᒋᐠ ᑮᑿᔭ ᑳ ᐊᑐᐢᑳᑕᒥᖨᐟ᙮ ᐃᑯᓰᓯ ᐐᖬᐚᐤ ᑮ ᐊᑎ ᑭᐢᑮᖨᐦᑕᒷᐠ ᑖᓂᓯ ᑭᑕ ᐃᓯ ᐱᒫᒋᐦᐃᓱᒋᐠ᙮ ᑮ ᑭᐢᑭᓇᐚᐸᐦᒋᑮᐘᐠ ᑖᓂᓯ ᑭᑕ ᐃᓯ ᐱᒥᓇᐘᓱᒋᐠ, ᑭᑕ ᐃᓯ ᐹᐦᑮᑭᓂᐦᑮᒋᐠ, ᑭᑕ ᐃᓯ ᒦᑭᓯᐦᑳᒋᑮᒋᐠ, ᑭᑕ ᐃᓯ ᒪᐢᑭᓯᓂᐦᑮᒋᐠ, ᑭᑕ ᐅᓰᐦᑖᒋᐠ ᒦᑭᐚᐦᐸ, ᐊᔮᓂᓴ, ᑎᐦᑭᓈᑲᓇ ᐃᑿ ᑭᑕ ᐃᓯ ᒪᐏᓱᒋᐠ ᐃᑿ ᑭᑕ ᒪᓈᐦᐅᒋᐠ ᒪᐢᑭᐦᑭᔭ᙮ ᒦᓇ ᑭᐢᑭᓇᐚᐸᐦᑮᐘᐠ ᑖᓂᓯ ᑭᑕ ᐃᓯ ᐐᒋᐦᐅᐐᒋᐠ ᐃᐢᐲ ᐅᐢᑲᐚᓯᓴ ᑳ ᓂᐦᑖᐐᑭᖨᐟ᙮

ᑲᐦᑭᖬᐤ ᑮᑿᐩ ᑮ ᑭᐢᑭᓌᐦᐊᒪᐚᐘᐠ ᑳ ᑮᓯᑳᖨᐠ᙮ ᐃᑿ ᑳ ᑎᐱᐢᑳᖨᐠ ᑮ ᑭᐢᑭᓌᐦᐊᒪᐚᐘᐠ ᑖᓂᓯ ᑭᑕ ᐃᓯ ᐐᒋ ᐱᒫᑎᓰᒪᒋᐠ ᐐᒋ ᐊᖨᓯᑎᓃᒥᐚᐘ, ᐋᒐᖪᐦᑮᐏᓇ ᐅᐦᒋ ᑮ ᑭᐢᑭᓇᐘᐦᐊᒪᐚᐘᐠ ᐃᔭᑹᖨᐤ ᑭᐢᑭᓌᐦᐊᒫᑮᐏᐣ᙮ ᑳ ᐱᐳᓂᖨᐠ ᒫᓇ ᑳ ᑮ ᐋᒐᖪᐦᑳᓂᐏᐠ᙮

ᐃᐢᐲ ᑳ ᑮ ᒁᓯᐦᐃᐦᒋᐠ ᐊᐚᓯᓴᐠ ᐅᐦᐱᒦ ᑭᑕ ᓂᑕᐏ ᐊᔭᒥᐦᒋᑮᒋᐠ ᓇᒨᖬ ᐊᐘᓯᒦ ᐆᐦᐅ ᑭᐢᑭᓌᐦᐊᒫᑮᐏᓇ ᑮ ᐅᐦᒋ ᑭᐢᑭᓌᐦᐊᒧᐚᐘᐠ᙮ ᓇᒨᖬ ᐊᐘᓯᒦ ᑮ ᐲᐦᑕᒷᐠ ᐋᒐᖪᐦᑮᐏᓇ ᐐᖬ ᐊᖨᐢᐠ ᑳ ᐱᐳᕽ ᐳᑯ ᑳ ᑮ ᐋᒐᖪᐦᑳᓂᐏᐠ ᐃᑿ ᐃᑯᐢᐲ ᐚᐦᖬᐤ ᐅᐦᐱᒦ ᑮ ᐊᔮᐘᐠ ᐊᐚᓯᓴᐠ᙮

ᒫᑲ ᐆᐦᐅ ᐋᒐᖪᐦᑮᐏᓇ ᑮ ᒥᖪ ᐋᐸᑕᓌ ᑭᑕ ᑭᐢᑭᓌᐦᐊᒫᑮᒪᑲᐦᑭ᙮ ᐊᓄᐦᐨ ᐆᒪ ᒥᐦᒌᐟ ᐊᖨᓯᑎᓂᐘᐠ ᓇᒹᐨ ᑭᐢᑮᖨᐦᑕᒷᐠ ᐆᐦᐅ ᐋᒐᖪᐦᑮᐏᓇ᙮ ᐃᑿ ᐋᑎᐦᐟ ᐃᖨᓂᐘᐠ ᐃᑗᐘᐠ ᐄᑳ ᑭᑕᑮ ᐋᒐᖪᐦᑮᒋᐠ ᐐᖬ ᓇᒨᖬ ᐐᖬᐚᐤ ᐅᑖᒐᖪᐦᑮᐘᐠ, ᐃᑯᓯ ᐄ ᐃᑏᖨᒥᓱᒋᐠ᙮ ᒫᑲ ᑲᔮᐢ ᐅᓃᑭᐦᐃᑯᒫᐘᐠ ᒫᓇ ᑳ ᑮ ᐋᒐᖪᐦᑮᒋᐠ, ᓇᒨᖬ ᑲᑖᐨ ᑮ ᐲᐦᐄᐘᐠ ᐅᑖᒐᖪᐦᑮᐘ, ᑭᑕᑮ ᐃᐢᑲᒋᐲᐦᐄᐘᐠ ᐃᔭᑯᓂ ᐊᐏᔭ᙮

ᐃᑿ ᑲᔮᐢ ᑳ ᐱᐳᕽ ᒫᓇ ᑮ ᐋᒐᖪᑳᓂᐏᐣ᙮ ᒫᑲ ᐊᓄᐦᐨ ᒥᐢᑕᐦᐃ ᐘᓂᐦᑖᓂᐏᐣ ᑭᐲᑭᐢᑹᐏᓂᓇᐤ, ᐅᐦᒋᑕᐤ ᐳᑯ ᐳᑮᐢᐲ ᑭᑕᑮ ᐋᒐᖪᐦᑮᔭᕽ ᐊᐏᑳᒦ ᑭᑲ ᐘᓂᐦᑖᓇᐤ ᑲᐦᑭᖬᐤ ᑭᑭᐢᑭᓌᐦᐊᒫᑮᐏᓂᓇᐘ᙮

2. ᑮᑳᐧ+ ᑭᐄᐧᐦᑖᒫᑯᓇᐤ ᐋᒐᖫᐦᑲᓇ? ᒋᐦᒋᐱᐢᒋᑳᐧᐣ

ᑖᓂᓯ ᒫᑲ ᑲᖭᐢ ᐄ ᑮ ᐃᑖᐸᑕᐦᑭ ᐋᒐᖫᐦᑲᓇ?

ᐃᐢᐲ ᒫᓇ ᑳ ᑮ ᐱᐳᕽ ᐅᓃᑭᐦᐃᑯᒫᐊᐧᐠ ᒫᓇ ᑮ ᒫᐦ ᒫᒋ ᐋᒐᖫᐦᑮᐊᐧᐠ, ᐄ ᐅᑕᒥᐦᐋᒋᐠ ᐅᒐᐋᐧᓯᒥᓯᐋᐧᐊᐧ ᐃᐢᐲ ᑳ ᐱᐦᒑ ᑎᐱᐢᑳᐧᖬᐠ᙮ ᓂᐢᑕᑦ ᑳ ᒥᐢᐳᐠ ᒫᓇ ᑳ ᑮ ᒫᒋ ᐋᒐᖫᐦᑳᓄᐃᐧᐠ᙮

ᓂᑭᐢᑭᓯᐣ ᑳ ᑮ ᐊᐋᐧᓯᓰᐃᐧᖭᐣ: ᐃᑯᑕ ᓂᐋᐧᐢᑲᐦᐃᑲᓂᓯᓈᓂᕽ ᓂᓃᑭᐦᐃᑯᓈᓇᐠ ᑮ ᒥᓯ ᐴᓇᒪᐧᐠ ᑯᑕᐋᐧᓈᐱᐢᐠ, ᑮ ᓴᐢᑲᐦᐊᒪᐧᐠ ᐋᐧᓯᐢᑯᒌᓂᑲᓂᓴ, ᓂᑮ ᑮᓰᓯᒥᑯᓈᓇᐠ, ᐃᑲᐧ ᑮ ᒫᒋ ᐋᒐᖫᐦᑮᐊᐧᐠ᙮ ᐄᐧᓴᐦᑮᒑᐦᑲᐧ ᓃᑳᐣ ᑳ ᑮ ᐋᒋᒫᒋᐠ᙮

ᑖᐱᐢᑰᐨ ᒫᓇ ᑏᐱᖬᕽ ᐄ ᐅᑕᒦᐦᐋᐊᐧᓯᒋᐠ ᐃᐢᐲ ᑳ ᐋᒐᖫᐦᑮᒋᐠ, ᐄᐧᖬ ᒫᓇ ᐄ ᐊᐧᐃᐧᔭᓰᐦᑖᑲᐧᐦᑭ ᐊᓂᐦᐃ ᐋᒐᖫᐦᑮᐃᐧᓇ, ᐃᖬᑯᕽ ᐄ ᑳᐦ ᑲᑮᐹᑎᓯᐟ ᐄᐧᓴᐦᑮᒑᕽ᙮ ᓇᒎᖬ ᒫᑲ ᐊᓂᒪ ᐃᔭᑯᐦᒋ ᐳᑯ: ᑮ ᑭᐢᑭᓇᐧᐦᐊᒫᑮᒪᑲᓇ: ᐊᓂᐦᐃ ᐋᒐᖫᐦᑮᐃᐧᓇ᙮ ᐃᔭᑯᓂ ᐆᐦᐅ ᐋᒐᖫᐦᑮᐃᐧᓇ ᐄ ᐅᐦᒋ ᑭᐢᑭᓇᐧᐦᐊᒫᑮᒋᐠ ᑖᓂᓯ ᑭᑕ ᐃᓯ ᐱᒫᑎᓯᒋᐠ ᐆᑕ ᐊᐢᑮᕽ ᑳᑭᑮ ᑳ ᐱᒥᐸᖬᐠ᙮

ᒫᒥᐢᑰᑏᑖᐣ ᓂᐢᑕᑦ ᐊᓂᒪ ᐄᐧᓴᐦᑮᒑᕽ ᐋᒐᖫᐦᑮᐃᐧᐣ, "ᒋᐦᒋᐱᐢᒋᑳᐧᐣ" ᑳ ᐃᒋᑳᑏᐠ᙮ ᐃᑯᑕ ᐋᒐᖫᐦᑲᓂᕽ ᑭᑲᑮ ᒥᐢᑮᓇᐤ ᑲᐦᑭᖬᐤ ᑭᐢᑭᓇᐧᐦᐊᒫᑮᐃᐧᓇ ᐋᐧᓴᑳᑦ ᐱᒫᑎᓯᐃᐧᐣ ᐅᐦᒋ:

1. ᓃᐊᐧᔭᐠ ᐃᓯ ᑕᐸᓰᐊᐧᐠ ᐄᐧᓴᐦᑮᒑᕽ ᐃᑲᐧ ᐅᓰᒥᓴ,
   ᐃᐢᐲ ᑳ ᑕᐸᓰᐦᐋᒋᐠ ᒋᐦᒋᐱᐢᒋᑳᐧᓇ:

2. ᑭᐋᐧᐸᒫᓇᐊᐧᐠ ᑲᐦᑭᖬᐤ ᐃᑐᐃᐧᕽ ᐱᓯᐢᑭᐊᐧᐠ:
   ᑳ ᐱᒍᐦᑏᒋᐠ, ᑳ ᐸᑳᓯᒍᒋᐠ, ᑳ ᐱᒥᖭᒋᐠ,
   ᑳ ᐱᒥᑖᒋᒍᒋᐠ;

3. ᑳ ᐊᑎ ᐃᓯ ᐱᒫᑎᓯᓈᓂᐏᐠ: ᐅᐢᑲᐚᓯᓯᐏᐣ,
ᐅᐢᑳᔨᐏᐣ, ᑮᓱᐦᐱᑭᐦᐅᐏᐣ, ᐃᑲᐧ ᑭᓯᔭᔭᐏᐣ;

4. ᓂᔪ ᐃᑐᐏᕽ ᑳ ᐃᐦᑖᓄᐏᐠ: ᐊᔩᓯᑎᓃᐏᐣ,
ᐱᓯᐢᑭᐏᐣ, ᐅᐢᑭᐦᑏᐸᑭᐏᐣ, ᐃᑲᐧ ᐊᓯᓃᐏᐣ;

5. ᓂᔪ ᐊᔮᑮᐦᐃᐏᐣ: ᐊᐢᑭᐩ, ᐃᐢᑯᑏᐤ, ᓂᐱᐩ,
ᔩᐦᔩᐏᐣ;

6. ᓂᔪ ᑮᑲᐧᔭ ᐅᐦᒋᑕᐤ ᐳᑯ ᑕ ᐃᐦᑕᑯᐦᑭ
ᑕᒥᔦ ᐱᒫᑎᓯᓈᓂᐏᐠ: ᑲᓇᐑᔨᒥᑯᓯᐏᐣ,
ᐱᒫᒋᐦᐃᐑᐏᐣ, ᐅᐦᐱᑭᐏᐣ, ᐃᑲᐧ ᒥᓯᐑᔮᐏᐣ;

7. ᓂᔪ ᐃᓯ ᐊᔮᐏᓇ: ᒎᓯᐦᑖᐏᐣ, ᓲᐦᑳᑎᓯᐏᐣ,
ᒫᒥᑐᓃᔨᐦᑕᒧᐏᐣ, ᐃᑲᐧ ᐊᐦᑫᐦᑯᐏᐣ᙮

ᐃᑲᐧ ᐅᑕᐸᔫᐏᓂᐚᐤ ᐄ ᐚᑐᑕᐦᑳᐧᐤ ᑖᓂᓯ ᑳ ᐲ ᐃᓯ ᐱᒎᑏᐦᐅᒋᐠ ᓃᐦᐃᔭᐘᐠ: ᓵᑳᐢᑏᓄᕽ ᐅᐦᒋ, ᓵᐚᓄᕽ ᐃᓯ, ᐸᐦᑭᓯᒧᑖᕽ ᐃᓯ, ᑮᐚᑎᓄᕽ ᐃᓯ ᐃᑲᐧ ᑲᐏ ᓵᑳᐢᑏᓄᕽ ᑕᑯᐸᐦᑖᐘᐠ᙮ ᑲᐱ ᐆᑕ ᑭᑮ ᐊᔮᓇᐤ!

ᑮᐢᐱᐣ ᐄᑳ ᐊᐘᓯᒦ ᐋᑫᔦᐦᑮᔭᐦᑭ ᑭᑲ ᐘᓂᐦᑖᓇᐤ ᐆᐦᐅ ᑭᐢᑭᓌᐦᐊᒫᑮᐏᓇ᙮

10
ᒋᐦᒋᐱᐢᒋᑳᐧᐣ

ᑲᔮᐢ ᐄᓴ, ᑮ ᐱᔭᑳᐧᐦᑲᒥᑭᓯᐊᐧᐠ ᐊᐊᐧ ᐱᔭᐠ ᓈᐲᐤ ᐃᑲᐧ ᐄᐧᐊᐧ ᐃᑲᐧ ᒦᓇ ᓃᓱ ᐅᒐᐋᐧᓯᒥᓯᐋᐧᐊᐧ, ᓃᓱ ᓈᐲᓯᓴ, ᐱᔭᐠ ᓈᐲᓯᐢ ᒥᑐᓂ ᐄ ᐊᑎ ᐅᐢᑭᓃᑮᓯᐃᐧᐟ ᐃᑲᐧ ᐊᓇ ᑯᑕᐠ ᓈᐲᓯᐢ ᑲᒋᐢᑲᐤ ᐄ ᑲᐢᑭᐦᑖᐟ ᑕ ᐱᒧᐦᑏᐟ᙮ ᐄ ᑮ ᐱᔭᑯᐦᐱᑭᐦᐋᐊᐧᓱᒋᐠ ᐄᓴ ᐆᑯ ᐆᑏ ᐱᑲᐧᑕᐢᑲᒥᑳᕽ, ᐆᑏ ᑲᓈᑕᐢᑮᕽ᙮ ᑮ ᒥᖪ ᐄᐧᒑᔮᒥᑐᐊᐧᐠ ᐄᓴ: ᑕᐦᑐ ᑮᓯᑳᐤ ᑮ ᑯᐢᐱᐤ ᐊᐊᐧ ᓈᐲᐤ, ᐄ ᒫᐦ ᒫᒋᐟ ᐃᑲᐧ ᓇᒫᐧᐨ ᒫᐧᓯ ᑮ ᑮᐧᑕ ᒦᒋᓱᐊᐧᐠ ᐄᐧᖬ ᐃᖨᑯᕽ ᐄ ᑮ ᓂᐦᑖ ᒫᒋᐟ᙮

ᑮ ᒌᐦᑮᖨᐦᑕᑦ ᐅᐱᒫᑎᓯᐃᐧᐣ, ᐄ ᑮ ᒥᖪ ᐄᐧᒑᔮᒪᐟ ᐄᐧᐊᐧ ᐃᑲᐧ ᐅᒐᐋᐧᓯᒥᓴ᙮

ᑮᑕᐦᑕᐄᐧ ᐊᑎ ᐃᐢᐸᖨᐣ ᐄ ᐊᑎ ᒦᐢᒋᐦᐋᐊᐧᓱᐟ ᐃᑕ ᑳ ᑮ ᐄᐧᑭᒋᐠ᙮ ᐅᐦᒋᑕᐤ ᐳᑯ ᓇᐊᐧᐨ ᐋᐧᐦᖬᐤ ᑕ ᓈᐦ ᓂᑕᐃᐧ ᒫᒋᐟ᙮ ᐋᐢᑲᐤ ᒫᓇ ᐱᔭᐠ ᑎᐱᐢᑲᓂᓯᐤ᙮ ᐃᑯᓯ ᐊᖨᐦᑭᐣ ᑭᐣᐄᐧᓲᐢ ᐃᑲᐧ᙮

ᑳ ᐲ ᑮᐄᐧᐟ ᒥᐢᑲᐄᐧᐤ ᐄᐧᐊᐧ ᐄ ᐊᐧᐄᐧᓲᐦᐅᖨᐟ ᐃᑲᐧ ᐄ ᓲᐦᑮᐧᐢᑎᑳᐧᓃᖨᐟ ᑖᐱᐢᑰᐨ ᐄᓴ ᐄ ᑮ ᐸᐹᓯᐸᖨᐦᐅᖨᐟ᙮ ᒫᐦᒪᐢᑳᑏᖨᐦᑕᑦ ᑳ ᐃᑕᐦᑲᒥᑭᓯᖨᐟ᙮

ᑭᐢᑮᖨᐦᑕᑦ ᐄᐧᖬ ᐄ ᐊᑎ ᐲᑐᓯᔭᔮᖨᐟ᙮ ᐃᑕ ᒫᓇ ᑳ ᑮ ᓇᐦᐄᖨᐦᑕᒥᖨᐟ ᓇᐊᐧᐨ ᐃᑲᐧ ᑯᑕᐠ ᑮᑲᐧᐩ ᐄ ᐅᑕᒦᖨᐦᑕᒥᖨᐟ᙮ ᐅᐢᑮᓯᑯᖨᖬᐊᐧ ᓇᐊᐧᐨ ᐳᑯ ᑮ ᑮᐢᑮᐧᔮᑲᐧᓂᖨᖬᐊᐧ᙮ ᐄ ᐅᑕᒦᖨᐦᑕᒥᖨᐟ᙮ ᐅᐢᑮᓯᑯᖨᖬᐊᐧ ᓇᐊᐧᐨ ᐳᑯ ᑮ ᑮᐢᑮᐧᔮᑲᐧᓂᖨᖬᐊᐧ᙮

ᑮ ᐊᔭᐱᐤ ᐱᔭᑳᐧᐤ ᐄ ᑲᓇᐋᐧᐸᒫᐟ ᐅᑌᐋᐧᓯᒥᓴ ᐄ ᒦᑕᐄᐧᖨᐟ, ᑳ ᐱᓯᐢᑳᐸᒫᐟ ᐄᐧᐊᐧ ᐄ ᐊᑎ ᐊᐧᐄᐧᓲᐦᐅᖨᐟ ᐄ ᐄᐧ ᓈᒋᓂᐦᑏᖨᐟ ᑭᐦᒋᐋᐧᐠ ᓵᑲᓯᕽ᙮ ᐃᑯᓯ ᐋᐦᐃᑑᑕᒥᖨᐊᐧ ᐋᑕ ᓇᒨᖬ ᑲᑖᐨ ᑕ ᓈᒋᓂᐦᑖᓄᐃᐧᖨᐠ᙮

ᓇᒨᖬ ᓈᓂᑕᐤ ᐃᑏᐧᐤ ᐊᐊᐧ ᓈᐲᐤ, ᒫᑲ ᐃᑕᓱᐄᐧᐤ ᐄ ᐄᐧ ᓂᑕᐋᐧᐲᓂᑮᐟ ᑖᓂᐦᑯᒪ ᑳ ᐃᑕᐦᑲᒥᑭᓯᖨᐟ, ᑕᐄᐧᒋᐦᐋᐟ ᑮᐢᐱᐣ ᐃᐢᐸᖨᐦᐃᑯᒋ᙮ ᐃᑯᓯ ᐱᔭᑳᐧᐤ ᓯᐲᐧᐦᑏᐤ, ᐋᐦᑮᑖᐠ ᐄ ᓂᑕᐃᐧ ᒫᒌᐟ᙮ ᑳᓲᐤ ᓵᑲᓯᕽ ᒌᑭ ᒦᐢᑲᓈᓯᕽ ᐃᑕ ᒫᓇ ᑳ ᐱᒧᐦᑏᖨᐟ᙮

“ᒪᐦᑎ ᑳ ᐃᑑᑕᕽ,” ᐃᑏᖨᐦᑕᑦ᙮

ᐋᐧᐸᒦᐤ ᐄ ᐲ ᐋᐢᑕᒧᐦᑏᖨᐟ᙮ ᒥᑐᓂ ᐸᐹᓱᐦᑏᖨᐊᐧ ᐃᐢᐲ ᑳ ᐊᑎ ᐱᒥᑎᓴᐦᐋᐧᐟ, ᑳᐦ ᑳᓲᐸᖨᐦᐅᐤ ᓵᑲᓯᕽ ᐃᐢᐲ ᑳ ᓂᓯᐦᑳᒋ ᐱᒧᐦᑏᖨᐟ᙮

ᐋᐧᐸᒦᐤ ᐄ ᓇᑮᖨᐟ ᐸᐢᑳᐧᒌᕽ᙮ ᑕᓱᐸᖨᐦᐃᓯᐤ ᐃᑲᐧ ᐅᒋᐦᒋᓴ ᐋᐸᒋᐦᑖᐤ ᑕ ᓲᑲᐦᐅᓱᐟ᙮ ᐅᑎᓈᑦ ᒥᐢᒋᑯᐢ ᒧᐦᒋᕽ ᐅᐦᒋ ᐃᑲᐧ ᐹᐦ ᐸᐊᐧᐦᐊᑦ ᐸᐢᑳᐧᒋᐩ᙮

ᐴᑦ! ᐴᑦ! – ᐴᑦ! ᐴᑦ!

ᓂᓈᐲᑦ, ᑳ ᓵᑭᐦᐊᐠ, ᓂᑕᑯᐦᑖᐣ!”

ᐃᑯᑕ ᐅᐦᒋ ᐸᐢᑳᐧᒌᕽ ᑳ ᐲ ᐊᐧᖬᐄᐧᔮᐦᑕᐄᐧᖨᐟ ᒥᐦᒌᐟ ᑭᓃᐱᑲᐧ᙮ ᑮ ᑯᐢᑖᓯᓇᑦ ᐊᐊᐧ ᓈᐲᐤ᙮ ᒥᓯᐄᐧ ᐅᒥᔭᐃᐧᖨᕽ ᐱᒫᐦᑕᐄᐧᖨᐊᐧ ᐊᓂᐦᐃ ᑭᓃᐱᑲᐧ᙮

ᓇᒫᐧᐨ ᓈᓂᑕᐤ ᐃᑑᑕᒼ ᒫᑲ ᐃᑯᑕ ᐅᐦᒋ ᑭᓯᐃᐧ ᓯᐲᐧᐦᑏᐤ᙮ ᐱᔭᐠ ᑎᐱᐢᑲᓂᓯᐤ᙮

ᑮᐦᑖᐧᒼ ᑳ ᐋᐧᐸᓂᔨᐠ ᑭᐣᐄᐧᐢᐠ ᐱᒧᐦᑏᐤ ᒥᐦᒌᐟ ᐱᓯᐢᑭᐊᐧ ᒥᔮᐢᑲᐄᐧᐤ ᒫᑲ ᐲᔨᐢᐠ ᓂᐸᐦᐄᐤ ᒨᓴᐧ᙮ ᓇᒫᐧᐨ ᐊᐦᐴ ᑮ ᐅᐦᒋ ᐸᐦᑯᓃᐤ ᐃᑯᓯ ᑳ ᐊᑎ ᑮᐄᐧᐟ᙮ ᒪᐦᑲᑖᒧᐤ, ᑖᐱᐢᑰᐨ ᐄ ᑲᑳᐧᑕᑭ ᓃᐢᑐᓯᐟ, ᐲᐦᑐᑮᐤ ᐄᐧᑭᕽ᙮

“ᓂᑮ ᓂᐸᐦᐋᐤ ᒨᓴᐧ,” ᐃᑏᐤ ᐄᐧᐊᐧ, “ᒫᑲ ᐅᓵᒼ ᓂᑖᐦᑯᓯᐣ ᑕᓇᑳᐧᑎᓯᔮᐣ᙮ ᑮᔭ ᐳᑯ ᑕᓈᑕᒪᐣ ᐃᐧᔮᐢ᙮”

ᐄᐧᐦᑕᒪᐄᐧᐤ ᐃᑕ ᑳ ᑮ ᓇᑲᑖᐟ ᐊᓂᐦᐃ ᒨᓴᐧ, ᐋᐧᐦᔭᐤ ᐅᑲᐲᓰᐃᐧᓂᐋᐧᕽ ᐅᐦᒋ, ᐃᑲᐧ ᐅᐦᒋᑕᐤ ᐳᑯ ᓰᒫᐠ ᑕ ᓯᐲᐧᐦᑏᔭᐟ ᑮᐢᐱᐣ ᓄᐦᑏ ᐲ ᑮᐄᐧᔭᒋ ᐄ ᒪᐧᔩ ᐸᐦᑭᓯᒧᔭᐠ᙮ ᓇᐊᐧᐨ ᐳᑯ ᓇᒫᐧᐨ ᓄᐦᑏ ᓯᐲᐧᐦᑏᐤ ᐊᐊᐧ ᐃᐢᑮᐧᐤ᙮

“ᒪᐦᑎ ᓃᑳᐣ ᓂᑲ ᓈᒋᓂᐦᑖᐣ!”

“ᓇᒪ! ᓰᒫᐠ ᓯᐲᐧᐦᑏ!”

ᓴᑲᒧᑏᔭᓃᐄᐧᐤ ᐊᐊᐧ ᐃᐢᑮᐧᐤ ᐃᐢᐲ ᑳ ᐊᑎ ᓯᐲᐧᐦᑏᐟ ᐃᑲᐧ ᐄ ᒪᐧᔩ ᓯᐲᐧᐦᑏᐟ ᑲᑮᐧ ᑮᒧᒋ ᐸᑭᑎᓇᒼ ᒪᐢᑭᓯᓂᔮᐱᐢ ᑯᑕᐋᐧᓂᕽ ᐃᑯᓯ ᓇᐊᐧᐨ ᐄᐧᐸᐨ ᑕ ᑕᑯᓯᕽ᙮ ᒫᑲ ᐊᐊᐧ ᓈᐲᐤ ᐋᐧᐸᒦᐤ ᐃᑯᑕ ᐄ ᐸᑭᒋᐄᐧᐱᓇᒥᔭᐟ ᒪᐢᑭᓯᓂᔮᐱᐢ᙮ ᐅᑎᓇᒼ ᐊᓂᒦᔭᐤ ᒪᐢᑭᓯᓂᔮᐱᐢ ᐃᑲᐧ ᓵᐳᐸᑖᐤ ᒦᓇ ᐊᑎ ᓰᐲᑭᐱᑕᒼ ᐃᑯᓯ ᓇᐊᐧᐨ ᑭᐣᐄᐧᐢᐠ ᑕ ᐱᒧᐦᑏᔭᐟ ᐊᓂᐦᐃ ᐃᐢᑮᐧᐊᐧ᙮

ᑕᐦᑯᐦᑕᐢᑖᐤ ᒪᐢᑭᓯᓂᔮᐱᐩ ᓃᐲᕽ ᐊᓂᑕ ᒧᐦᒌᕽ᙮ ᑮᓯᐢᑲᐤ ᐲᐦᑐᑮᐤ ᒦᑭᐋᐧᐦᐱᕽ ᐄ ᓂᑕᐃᐧ ᐳᐢᑎᐢᑲᕽ ᐄᐧᐊᐧ ᐅᑕᔮᓂᓴ, ᐄ ᐃᐢᑮᐧᐃᐧᓰᐦᐅᐟ᙮ ᑕᐦᑯᓇᒼ ᒧᐦᑯᒫᐣ᙮ ᐃᐢᐸᐦᑖᐤ ᓴᑳᕽ ᐃᑏ ᑳ ᑮ ᐋᐧᐸᒫᐟ ᐄᐧᐊᐧ ᐄ ᒦᑕᐋᐧᑳᑖᔭᐟ ᑭᓃᐱᑲᐧ, ᐃᑲᐧ ᑖᐱᐢᑰᐨ ᐄᐧᐊᐧ, ᐹᐦ ᐹᐋᐧᐦᐊᒼ ᐸᐢᑳᐧᒋᐩ᙮

ᐴᒼ! ᐴᒼ – ᐴᒼ ᐴᒼ!

ᓂᓈᐲᑦ, ᑳ ᓵᑭᐦᐊᐠ, ᓂᑕᑯᐦᑖᐣ!”

ᑖᐲᐧ ᒫᓂ ᒫᑲ, ᑖᐱᐢᑰᐨ ᓂᐢᑕᑦ ᐲ ᐊᐧᖫᐄᐧᔭᐦᑕᐄᐧᐊᐧᐠ ᐊᓂᑭ ᑭᓃᐱᑲᐧᐠ ᐸᐢᑳᐧᒌᕽ ᐅᐦᒋ᙮ ᒪᔭᐤ ᑳ ᐲ ᐃᑐᐦᑏᖧᐟ ᑮᐢᑭᑲᐧᔭᐄᐧᓵᐋᐧᑏᐤ᙮ ᑮᑳᐨ ᑲᐦᑭᖫᐤ ᒦᐢᒋᐦᐄᐤ᙮ ᐱᔭᐠ ᐳᑯ ᐸᐢᐲᐦᐄᐤ, ᐊᓂᐦᐃ ᐄ ᐊᐱᓰᓯᓯᖫᐟ, ᐃᑲᐧ ᐃᑯᑕ ᐅᖫᓯᐄᐧᐤ᙮

“ᐃᐢᐲ ᐊᑎ ᒥᐦᒌᑎᑖᐧᐃᐧ ᐃᖧᓂᐊᐧᐠ ᐆᑕ ᐊᐢᑮᕽ ᓇᒫᐧᐨ ᑲ ᑲᐢᑭᐦᑖᐣ ᑕ ᐊᐧᓈᐦᐅᐃᐧᔭᐣ᙮ ᑲᐲ ᑭᑲ ᐊᐱᓰᓯᓯᐣ ᐃᑲᐧ ᑕ ᐄᐧᐦᒐᓯᐣ ᑕ ᓂᐸᐦᐃᑲᐃᐧᔭᐣ᙮” ᑳ ᐴᓂ ᐄᐧᐦᑕᕽ ᐆᒪ ᒨᓴᐦᑭᓃᐤ ᐊᓂᐦᐃ ᑳ ᑮ ᓂᐸᐦᐋᐟ ᑭᓃᐱᑲᐧ ᐃᑲᐧ ᑮᐄᐧᐸᐦᑖᐤ, ᐄ ᓂᑕᐃᐧ ᑲᐧᔮᑎᓯᐟ, ᒪᐧᖬ ᑕᑯᓯᓂᖧᒥ ᐄᐧᐊᐧ᙮

ᓂᑐᒦᐤ ᐅᑯᓯᓴ ᐃᑲᐧ ᐄᐧᐦᑕᒪᐄᐧᐤ ᐄ ᒫᖧᐸᖧᐦᐃᑯᒋᐠ᙮

“ᐋᐦᑯᓯᐤ ᑭᑳᐄᐧᐋᐧᐤ,” ᐃᑏᐤ᙮ “ᓂᐄᐧ ᒪᐢᑭᐦᑭᐋᐧᐴᐢᑕᒪᐋᐧᐤ ᑕ ᓇᓈᑕᐃᐧᐦᐊᕽ ᒫᑲ ᑮᐢᐱᐣ ᑭᐲᐦᑏᓈᐋᐧᐤ ᐄᑳ ᐄ ᒥᓂᐦᑮᐧᐟ, ᐆᑕ ᐅᐦᒋ ᑕᐸᓰᐠ! ᐆᐦᐅ ᓂᖩ ᑮᑲᐧᔭ ᑲ ᒦᖧᑎᓈᐋᐧᐤ ᑕ ᐸᐢᐲᐦᐃᑯᖨᐠ ᐃᐢᐲ ᐊᑎ ᑯᐢᑖᒋᖨᑯ: ᐆᒪ ᐅᐢᑳᒋᐠ ᐋᐸᑕᐣ ᑭᐦᒋ ᐅᑳᐄᐧᒥᓇᑲᓯᔭᐠ ᑕ ᐅᐦᐱᑭᒋᐠ; ᐆᒪ ᐋᐱᐦᐟ ᐋᐸᑕᐣ ᐊᓯᓂᐩ ᐊᐧᒋᔭ ᑕ ᐅᐦᐱᑭᑭ; ᐊᐊᐧ ᐳᓵᑲᐣ ᑲ ᑲᐧᐦᑯᑏᐦᑳᑳᐣ; ᐃᑲᐧ ᐆᒪ ᐊᒥᐢᑯᐄᐧᐱᐟ ᑲᑮ ᐅᐦᒋ ᐅᓰᐦᑖᐣ ᓰᐱᐩ᙮”

“ᐃᑲᐧ ᐳᑯ ᑕ ᑳᓰᒎᖨᐠ ᐋᐧᑎᐦᑳᓂᕽ ᑕ ᓂᑐᐦᑕᒦᐠ᙮ ᑮᐢᐱᐣ ᑭᑳᐄᐧᐋᐧᐤ ᐄᑳ ᒥᓂᐦᑮᐧᒋ ᒪᐢᑭᐦᑮᐋᐧᐳᐩ ᓰᒫᐠ ᐆᑕ ᐅᐦᒋ ᑕᐸᓰᐠ ᓇᒨᖫ ᐊᖧᐢᐠ ᐊᐊᐧᓯᒦ ᐃᔭᑯ ᑭᑳᐄᐧᐋᐧᐤ᙮ ᒥᖩ ᐱᒎᑏᐦᐅᐠ ᓂᑯᓯᓴᐠ! ᑖᐱᑲ ᑕ ᒥᖩᐸᖧᐦᐃᑯᖨᐠ ᑭᔮᑦ ᐆᑕ ᒦᑳᐧᐨ ᐄ ᒫᖧᐸᖧᐦᐃᑯᔮᕽ᙮ ᐃᐢᐲ ᐆᑏ ᓃᑳᐣ ᓄᐦᑏ ᐋᐧᐸᒥᖨᑯ ᐃᐢᐱᒥᕽ ᑮᐄᐧᑎᓄᕽ ᐃᓯ ᐃᑖᐱᐠ, ᐃᑯᑕ ᓂᑲ ᐊᒌᔭᐣ ᑭᐦᒋᐋᐧᐠ ᐄᑳ ᑳ ᐊᐦᒌᐟ ᐊᒑᐦᑯᐢ ᐊᖧᐢᐠ ᐄᐧᖫ ᓂᑲ ᓈᑲᑏᖧᒥᐠ᙮”

ᓈᐲᐤ ᑳᑏᐤ ᐅᑯᓯᓴ ᐋᐧᑎᐦᑳᓂᕽ ᐃᑲᐧ ᐊᑲᐧᓇᐦᐊᑦ ᐃᔭᑮᐧᔨᐤ ᐊᑯ‴ ᐅᐦᒋ᙮ ᐃᑏᐤ ᐅᑖᐸᒋᐦᒋᑲᓇ ᐄᑳ ᓈᓂᑕᐤ ᑕ ᐄᐧᐦᑕᒪᐋᐧᔨᐟ ᐊᓂᐦᐃ ᐃᐢᑮᐧᐊᐧ᙮ ᐱᐦᑕᐤ ᐱᔭᐠ ᐊᓯᓃᐢ ᐊᐧᓂᐦᐅᐤ ᓰᐹ ᐊᑯᐦᐱᕽ ᓇᒫᐧᐨ ᐅᐦᒋ ᐲᐦᑕᐄᐧᐤ᙮ ᐃᑯᑕ ᐅᐦᒋ ᐊᑎ ᐸᐦᑮᐧᓯᑲᓈᐳᐦᑳᑮᐤ ᐊᓂᐦᐃ ᑭᓃᐱᑲᐧ ᑳ ᑮ ᓂᐸᐦᐋᐧᐟ᙮

ᓇᒨᔭ ᐅᓵᑦ ᑭᐣᐄᐧᐢᐠ ᑳ ᑕᑯᐸᐦᑖᔨᐟ ᐄᐧᐊᐧ, ᐄ ᐹᐦᑲᐧᑖᒧᔨᐟ ᐃᑲᐧ ᐄ ᐊᐲᐧᓯᔨᐟ᙮ ᐸᑭᒋᐄᐧᐱᓇᑦ ᐅᓇᔭᐦᒋᑲᐣ ᐃᑲᐧ ᓴᑳᕽ ᐊᑎ ᑲᑮᐧ ᐃᐢᐸᐦᑖᐤ, ᒫᑲ ᑏᐹᐧᑎᐠ ᐅᓈᐲᒪ᙮

“ᐋᐢᑕᑦ ᓃᐊᐧ, ᐊᐱ, ᒫᐢᑰᐨ ᑭᓄᐦᑏᐦᑲᑖᐣ᙮ ᓇ, ᒦᒋ ᐆᒪ ᐸᐦᑮᐧᓯᑲᓈᐳᐩ,” ᐃᑏᐧᐤ ᓈᐲᐤ᙮ ᓈᐦ ᓂᓯᐦᑳᐨ ᑯᑕᐋᐧᓂᕽ ᐃᑐᐦᑏᐤ ᐃᐢᑮᐧᐤ ᐃᑲᐧ ᓇᐦᐊᐱᐤ᙮ ᐊᑎ ᒦᒋᐤ ᐸᐦᑮᐧᓯᑲᓈᐳᐩ᙮

“Mmm, ᑮᑳᐧᐩ ᐆᒪ ᑳ ᐄᐧᐦᑲᓯᐠ?”

“ᐅᒥᐢᑰᑦ ᐊᓇ ᑭᓈᐲᑦ ᑭᓃᐱᐠ,” ᐃᑏᐧᐤ ᐊᐊᐧ ᓈᐲᐤ ᐄ ᑭᓯᐋᐧᐦᐃᑯᐟ᙮ “ᐄ ᐸᐦᑮᐧᓯᑲᓈᐳᐦᑮᐢᑕᒫᑖᐣ ᐆᒪ!”

“ᓇᒨᔭ ᑖᐲᐧ!” ᐃᑏᐧᐤ ᐊᐊᐧ ᐃᐢᑮᐧᐤ ᐄ ᐃᐢᐸᐦᑖᐟ ᓴᑳᕽ ᐃᑕ ᑳ ᑮ ᐊᔮᔨᐟ ᑭᓃᐱᑲᐧ᙮

ᐃᑯᑕ ᑳ ᑕᑯᐸᐦᑖᐟ ᐹᐦ ᐹᐊᐧᐦᐊᑦ ᐸᐢᑳᐧᒋᐩ᙮

ᐴᑦ! ᐴᑦ! – ᐴᑦ! ᐴᑦ!

“ᓂᓈᐲᑦ, ᑳ ᓵᑭᐦᐊᐠ, ᓂᑕᑯᐦᑖᐣ!” ᒫᑲ ᓇᒫᐧᐨ ᐊᐃᐧᔭ ᐲ ᐃᑐᐦᑏᔨᐊᐧ᙮

ᐴᑦ! ᐴᑦ! – ᐴᑦ! ᐴᑦ!

“ᓂᓈᐲᑦ, ᓂᑕᑯᐦᑖᐣ!” ᑮᔭᐱᐨ ᓇᒫᐧᐨ ᐊᐃᐧᔭ ᐲ ᐃᑐᐦᑏᔨᐊᐧ᙮

ᐆᑦ! ᐆᑦ! – ᐆᑦ! ᐆᑦ!

“ᓂᓈᐲᑦ, ᑳ ᒥᖪᓯᐟ, ᓂᑕᑯᐦᑖᐣ!” ᒥᑐᓂ ᐊᑎ ᐊᐧᐋᐧᓃᖬᒧᐤ, ᐄ ᒫᑐᐟ. ᑮᐦᑖᐧᑦ ᑯᒥᐦᑖᐤ.

ᐆᑦ! ᐆᑦ! – ᐆᑦ! ᐆᑦ!

“ᓂᓈᐲᑦ, ᑳ ᓵᑭᐦᐊᐠ, ᓂᑕᑯᐦᑖᐣ! ᐋᐢᑕᑦ!”

ᓈᐦ ᓂᓯᐦᑳᐨ ᑳ ᐲ ᐊᐧᖬᐄᐧᔭᐦᑕᐄᐧᖬᐟ ᐱᔭᐠ ᑭᓃᐱᑯᓯᓴ, ᐄ ᐊᐱᓰᓯᓯᖬᐟ.

“ᑖᓂᐄᐧᐦᑳᐠ ᒫᑲ ᑯᑕᑲᐠ?!”

“ᐊᐃᐧᔭᐠ ᐊᓇ ᑮ ᐲ ᐃᑐᐦᑏᐤ ᑲᐦᑭᖬᐤ ᐄ ᓂᐸᐦᐋᐧᐟ,” ᐃᑏᐧᐤ ᐊᓇ ᑭᓃᐱᑯᓯᐢ. ᑲᐧᔭᐢᐠ ᑭᓱᐋᐧᓯᐤ ᐊᓇ ᐃᐢᑮᐧᐤ. ᐃᐢᐸᐦᑖᐤ ᒦᑭᐋᐧᐦᐱᕽ ᐄ ᑲᑳᐧᑕᑭ ᖬᐄᐧᓯᐟ.

ᐃᑲᐧ ᒦᑭᐋᐧᐦᐱᕽ ᑮ ᒪᒪᓃᐤ ᐄᓴ ᐊᐊᐧ ᓈᐲᐤ: ᐊᖬᐱᔭ ᑮ ᐊᐦᖭᐤ ᐃᐢᑳᐧᐦᑏᒥᕽ ᐃᑲᐧ ᐃᑯᑕ ᓃᐸᐃᐧᐤ, ᐄ ᒥᒋᒥᓇᕽ ᒌᑲᐦᐃᑲᐣ, ᐄ ᐱᐦᐋᐟ ᐄᐧᐊᐧ. ᐲ ᐱᒧᐦᑏᖬᐊᐧ, ᐄ ᑭᓱᐋᐧᓯᖬᐟ, ᒫᑲ ᐊᖬᐲᕽ ᐅᐢᑎᑳᐧᐣ ᐅᑕᐦᐋᐧᖬᐤ, ᑭᓰ ᑏᐲᐧᐤ! ᓰᒫᐠ ᓈᐲᐤ ᑮᐢᑭᑲᐧᔭᐄᐧᓵᐋᐧᑏᐤ ᒌᑲᐦᐃᑲᐣ ᐅᐦᒋ. ᐃᐢᐲ ᐄ ᐊᑎ ᐸᐦᑭᐦᑎᕽ ᒥᐢᑎᑳᐧᐣ ᒧᐦᒋᕽ ᐃᓯ ᑏᐹᐧᑕᑦ ᐅᒥᔭᐤ.

“ᐅᑎᐦᑎᐣ! ᓂᐸᐦ! ᓃᖬ ᓂᑲ ᓇᐊᐧᓵᐧᑎᒫᐊᐧᐠ ᐅᒐᐋᐧᓯᒥᓴ.”

ᐋᑕ ᐊᖬᐲᕽ ᐄ ᐅᑕᐦᐋᐧᒪᑲᕽ ᒥᔭᐤ ᐅᑎᐦᑎᓃᐤ ᓈᐲᐊᐧ ᐃᑲᐧ ᑭᐣᐄᐧᐢᐠ ᒫᓯᐦᐃᑐᐊᐧᐠ, ᒥᑐᓂ ᒥᓯᐄᐧ ᐲᐦᒑᖬᕽ ᒦᑭᐋᐧᐦᐱᕽ ᐄ ᑖᐦ ᑎᐦᑎᐲᒋᐠ, ᓵᑳᐢᑏᓅᕽ ᐅᐦᒋ ᐃᐢᑯ ᐹᐦᑭᓯᒨᓅᕽ; ᑮᐄᐧᑎᓅᕽ ᐅᐦᒋ ᐃᐢᑯ ᓵᐊᐧᓅᕽ. ᐲᖬᐢᐠ ᐃᐢᐱᒥᕽ ᐃᓯ ᐊᑎ ᐃᐢᐸᖬᐊᐧᐠ ᐃᖬᑯᕽ ᒎᐦᑭ ᐄ ᒫᓯᐦᐃᑐᒋᐠ, ᐲᖬᐢᐠ ᐃᑯᑏ ᐃᐢᐱᒥᕽ ᐊᑎ ᐊᑖᐦᑯᓯᐃᐧᐊᐧᐠ.

ᐊᐦᔫ ᐊᓄᐦᐨ ᑭᔮᐱᐨ ᑲᑮ ᐚᐸᒫᓇᐘᐠ: ᓈᐲᐤ ᐊᓇ ᐅᒦᑲᑖ᙮ ᐃᑲᐧ ᒥᔭᐘ ᑳ ᓇᐘᔮᐧᑎᑯᐟ, ᐊᓂᑭ ᐊᑎᒫᑖᐦᑲᐧᐠ, ᓇᒫᐧᐨ ᑲᐢᑭᐦᑖᐤ ᑕ ᐅᑎᐦᑎᓂᑯᐟ ᐊᐧᔨᐢᐠ ᐊᓇ ᐄᑳ ᑳ ᐚᐦᒌᐟ ᐊᑖᐦᑯᐢ ᐄ ᓈᑲᑖᐄᐧᔨᒥᑯᐟ᙮

11
ᐄᐧᓴᐦᑮᒫᕽ ᑕᐸᓰᐤ

ᐊᐢᐱᐣ ᑳ ᐊᑎ ᐊᑖᐦᑯᐏᒋᐠ ᐅᐦᑖᐑᒫᐤ ᐄᑲᐧ ᐅᒥᔭᐤ ᐊᓇ ᐅᑳᐑᒫᐤ᙮ ᐃᑲᐧ ᒦᑭᐚᐦᐱᕽ ᐊᓂᒪ ᒥᐢᑎᑳᐧᐣ, ᒋᐦᒋᐱᐢᒋᑳᐧᐣ ᐊᐘ, ᐊᑎ ᑖᐦ ᑎᐦᑎᐲᐸᔨᐤ ᐄ ᑳᐦ ᑲᑮᐧᒋᒫᐟ ᐋᐸᒋᐦᒋᑲᓂᓴ ᑖᓂᑏ ᐄ ᑮ ᐃᑐᐦᑏᔨᐟ ᐅᑕᐚᓯᒥᓴ᙮ ᓇᒫᐧᐨ ᑯᑕᐠ ᐊᐏᔭᐠ ᐲᑭᐢᑮᐧᐤ, ᐊᐘ ᐳᑯ ᐊᓯᓃᐢ ᐄᑳ ᐄ ᑮ ᐅᐦᒋ ᐲᐦᑕᐚᐟ ᐊᓂᐦᐃ ᓈᐲᐘ ᑳ ᑮ ᐃᑏᐧᔨᐟ᙮

ᐊᓯᓃᐢ ᐑᐦᑕᒪᐑᐤ ᒋᐦᒋᐱᐢᒋᑳᐧᓇ ᐊᓂᐦᐃ ᓈᐲᐘ ᐄ ᑮ ᑳᑖᔨᐟ ᓈᐲᓯᓴ ᐚᑎᐦᑳᓂᕽ ᓰᐹ ᐊᑯᐦᐱᕽ᙮ ᒋᐦᒋᐱᐢᒋᑳᐧᐣ ᓰᒫᐠ ᐊᑎ ᓇᐚᓵᐧᑏᐤ!

ᑲᐧᔭᐢᐠ ᓲᐦᑮᐸᔨᐤ ᒋᐦᒋᐱᐢᒋᑳᐧᐣ ᐄ ᓇᐚᓵᐧᑖᐟ ᓈᐲᓯᓴ᙮ ᐚᐸᒦᐤ ᐚᐦᔭᐤ ᐃᑲᐧ ᑏᐲᐧᐤ᙮

“ᑖᓂᑏ, ᑖᓂᑏ ᑲᑮ ᐃᓯ ᑕᐸᓵᓈᐚᐤ? ᑭᑲ ᓂᐸᐦᐃᑎᓈᐚᐤ!”

ᐊᓂᑭ ᓈᐲᓯᓴᐠ ᐲᐦᑖᐑᐘᐠ ᒋᐦᒋᐱᐢᒋᑳᐧᓇ ᒫᑲ ᐊᓇ ᐅᐢᑏᓯᒫᐤ ᑭᐢᑭᓯᐤ ᐅᐦᑖᐑᐚᐘ ᑳ ᑮ ᐃᑏᐧᔨᐟ ᐄᑳ ᐊᐘᓯᒦ ᐆᐦᐅ ᐅᑳᐑᐚᐘ, ᓇᐘᐨ ᐊᑎ ᓲᐦᑳᓃᐸᐦᑖᐤ᙮

ᓇᐊᐧᐨ ᑭᓯᐋᐧᐠ ᐲᐦᑖᑲᐧᓂᔨᐤ ᐅᑭᑐᐃᐧᓂᔨᐤ ᐅᑳᐄᐧᐊᐧ᙮ ᑭᐢᑭᓯᐤ ᐊᓂᐦᐃ ᒦᑭᐃᐧᓇ ᑳ ᑮ ᒦᔨᑯᐟ ᐅᐦᑖᐃᐧᔭ ᐃᑲᐧ ᐸᑭᑎᓃᐤ ᐅᓰᒥᓴ ᐃᑲᐧ ᐅᑖᕽ ᐃᓯ ᐱᒧᓯᓃᐤ ᐅᐢᑳᒋᐠ᙮ ᓰᒫᐠ ᐃᑯᑕ ᐅᐦᒋ ᐅᐦᐱᑭᔨᐊᐧ ᑭᐦᒋ ᐅᑳᐄᐧᒥᓇᑲᓯᔭᐠ, ᓵᐊᐧᓄᕽ ᐅᐦᒋ ᐃᐢᑯ ᑮᐄᐧᑎᓄᕽ ᐄ ᐅᐦᐱᑭᒋᐠ᙮ ᑭᐳᐢᑳᑯᐤ ᐆᐦᐅ ᒋᐦᒋᐱᐢᒋᑳᐧᐣ, ᓇᒫᐧᐨ ᒥᐢᑲᑦ ᐃᑕ ᑕ ᑕᐋᐧᔨᐠ᙮

ᐃᑯᓰᓯ ᒥᓯᐄᐧ ᐃᑯᑕ ᑖᐦ ᑎᐦᑎᐲᐤ ᒫᑲ ᐊᓂᐦᐃ ᑭᐦᒋ ᐅᑳᐄᐧᒥᓇᑲᓯᔭ ᐅᐦᐱᑭᔨᐊᐧ ᑭᐦᒋᑲᒫᕽ ᐅᐦᒋ ᐃᐢᑯ ᑯᑕᐠ ᑭᐦᒋᑲᒫᕽ᙮ ᑮᑕᐦᑕᐄᐧ ᑳ ᐲᐦᑕᕽ ᑮᑲᐧᐩ ᑭᐦᒋ ᐅᑳᐄᐧᒥᓇᑲᓰᕽ, ᑖᐱᐢᑰᐨ ᐊᐃᐧᔭ ᐄ ᑲᐢᐹᐦᒋᑮᔨᐟ, ᓇᑐᐦᑕᑦ᙮ ᑮᑕᐦᑕᐄᐧ ᑳ ᐋᐧᐸᒫᐟ ᑭᐦᒋ ᒧᐦᑑᐊᐧ ᐄ ᐲ ᑖᐃᐧᓯᔨᐟ ᑭᐦᒋ ᐅᑳᐄᐧᒥᓇᑲᓰᕽ ᐅᐦᒋ᙮ ᑖᐲᐧ ᐳᑳᓂ ᓈᒋᐸᐦᑖᐧᐤ ᐊᓂᒪ ᐃᑕ ᑳ ᑕᐋᐧᑕᕽ ᒦᐢᑲᓈᐢ ᐊᓇ ᑭᐦᒋ ᒧᐦᑑᐤ, ᒥᑐᓂ ᐄ ᐊᑎ ᓇᐸᑭᐢᑲᐋᐧᐟ, ᑭᓯᐠ ᐄ ᐃᐧᔭᐦᑳᐧᑖᐟ, ᐃᔭᑯᓂ, ᐃᑲᐧ ᐊᑎ ᓇᐊᐧᓵᐧᑑᐤ ᓈᐲᓯᓴ᙮

ᒋᐦᒋᐱᐢᒋᑳᐧᐣ ᐊᑎ ᐱᒥᐸᐦᑖᐤ, ᐋᐧᐸᒦᐤ ᓈᐲᓯᓴ ᐋᐧᐦᔭᐄᐧᐢ᙮ ᐃᑲᐧ ᒦᓇ ᑏᐲᐧᐤ᙮

“ᑖᓂᑏ, ᑖᓂᑏ ᑲᑮ ᐃᓯ ᑕᐸᓵᓈᐋᐧᐤ? ᑭᑲ ᓂᐸᐦᐃᑎᓈᐋᐧᐤ!”

“ᓇᒨᔭᓇ ᑭᑲᐄᐧᓇᐤ!” ᐃᑏᐧᐤ ᐅᓰᒥᒫᐤ᙮ ᓈᐲᓯᓴᐠ ᐊᑎ ᓲᐦᑭᐸᐦᑖᐊᐧᐠ ᐄᐧᓵᐦᑮᒑᕽ ᐄ ᓇᔮᐦᔭᐟ ᐅᓰᒥᓴ᙮

ᓇᐊᐧᐨ ᑭᓯᐋᐧᐠ ᐲᐦᑕᒪᐧᐠ ᐅᑳᐄᐧᐋᐧᐊᐧ ᐅᐲᐦᑖᑯᓯᓂᔨᐤ᙮ ᐄᐧᓵᐦᑮᒑᕽ ᐅᑎᓇᑦ ᑯᑕᐠ ᑮᑲᐧᐩ ᑳ ᑮ ᒦᔨᑯᐟ ᐅᐦᑖᐃᐧᔭ ᐃᑲᐧ ᐸᑭᑎᓃᐤ ᐅᓰᒥᓴ ᐅᑖᕽ ᐃᓯ ᐱᒧᓯᓃᐤ ᐋᐱᐦᐟ, ᓰᒫᐠ ᐃᑯᑕ ᐅᐦᒋ ᐅᐦᐱᐸᔨᓇᐧ ᐊᓯᓂᐩ ᐊᐧᒋᔭ ᐄ ᓇᑭᐢᑳᑯᐟ ᒋᐦᒋᐱᐢᒋᑳᐧᐣ᙮ ᑮᐦᑖᐧᑦ ᓇᑭᓈᐤ ᒋᐦᒋᐱᐢᒋᑳᐧᐣ, ᓇᒫᐧᐨ ᑮ ᒥᐢᑲᑦ ᓈᓂᑕᐃᐧᑕ ᑕ ᑕᐋᐧᔨᐠ᙮

ᑭᔮᑦ ᒥᓯᐄᐧ ᐃᑕ ᐄ ᐃᓯ ᑖᐦ ᑎᐦᑎᐲᐟ᙮ ᑮᑕᐦᑕᐄᐧ ᑳ ᐲᐦᑕᕽ ᑮᑲᐧᐩ ᑖᐱᐢᑰᐨ ᐊᐃᐧᔭ ᐄ ᑲᐢᐹᐦᒋᑮᔨᐟ ᐊᓯᓂᐩ ᐊᐧᒌᕽ᙮ ᑭᐱᐦᒌᐤ᙮ ᐋᐧᐸᒦᐤ ᑭᐦᒋ ᐊᒥᐢᑲᐧ ᐄ ᐲ ᑕᐢᑲᒧᐦᑏᔨᐟ ᐊᓯᓂᐩ ᐊᐧᒌᕽ᙮ ᑖᐲᐧ ᐳᑳᓂ

ᐃᐢᐸᐦᑖᐤ ᒦᐢᑳᓈᓯᕽ, ᐃᑕ ᑳ ᑕᐢᑕᐚᒋᑮᔨᐟ ᑭᐦᒋ ᐊᒥᐢᑾ, ᐄ ᓂᐸᐦᐃ ᓇᐸᑭᐢᑲᐚᐟ, ᐃᔨᑯᕽ ᐄ ᓇᓂᐦᑭᓯᐟ ᑕᓇᐘᔖᑖᐟ ᓈᐲᓯᓴ᙮

ᒋᐦᒋᐱᐢᒋᒀᐤ ᐊᑎ ᐱᒥᐸᐦᑖᐤ, ᐚᐸᒦᐤ ᓈᐲᓯᓴ ᐚᐦᔮᐑᐣ᙮ ᐃᑾ ᒦᓇ ᑏᐶᐤ᙮

“ᑖᓂᑏ, ᑖᓂᑏ ᑲᑮ ᐃᓯ ᑕᐸᓵᓈᐚᐤ? ᑭᑲ ᓂᐸᐦᐃᑎᓈᐚᐤ!”

“ᓇᒨᔭᓇ ᑭᑳᐑᓇᐤ!” ᐃᑗᐤ ᐅᓰᒥᒫᐤ᙮ ᓈᐲᓯᓴᐠ ᐊᑎ ᒨᐦᑭᐸᐦᑖᐘᐠ ᐑᓴᐦᑮᒫᕽ ᐄ ᓇᔭᐦᔫᐟ ᐅᓰᒥᓴ᙮

ᓇᐘᐨ ᑭᓯᐚᐠ ᐲᐦᑕᒷᐠ ᐅᑳᐑᐚᐘ ᐅᐱᐦᑖᑯᓯᓂᔨᐤ᙮ ᐑᓴᐦᑮᒫᕽ ᐅᑎᓇᑦ ᑯᑕᐠ ᑮᑾᐩ ᑳ ᑮ ᒦᔨᑯᐟ ᐅᐦᑖᐏᔭ ᐃᑾ ᐸᑭᑎᓃᐤ ᐅᓰᒥᓴ᙮ ᐅᑖᕽ ᐃᓯ ᐱᒧᓯᓃᐤ ᐳᓵᑲᓇ᙮ ᓰᒫᐠ ᐃᑯᑕ ᐅᐦᒋ ᑾᐦᑯᑏᐤ ᐃᐢᑯᑏᐤ ᐄ ᓇᑭᐢᑳᑯᐟ ᒋᐦᒋᐱᐢᒋᒀᐤ᙮ ᑮᐦᑣᑦ ᓇᑭᓈᐤ ᒋᐦᒋᐱᐢᒋᒀᐤ᙮ ᓇᒹᐨ ᑮ ᒥᐢᑲᑦ ᓈᓂᑕᐏᑕ ᑕ ᑕᐚᔨᐠ᙮

ᑭᔫᑦ ᒥᓯᐑ ᐃᑕ ᐄ ᐃᓯ ᑖᐦ ᑎᐦᑎᐲᐟ᙮ ᐅᐦᒋᑕᐤ ᐳᑯ ᑕ ᑕᐢᑲᒥᐢᑲᕽ ᐊᓂᒦᔨᐤ ᐃᐢᑯᑏᐤ ᑕᓇᐘᔖᑖᐟ ᓈᐲᓯᓴ᙮

ᒋᐦᒋᐱᐢᒋᒀᐤ ᐊᑎ ᐱᒥᐹᑖᐤ, ᐚᐸᒦᐤ ᓈᐲᓯᓴ ᐚᐦᔮᐑᐣ᙮ ᐃᑾ ᒦᓇ ᑏᐶᐤ᙮

“ᑖᓂᑏ, ᑖᓂᑏ ᑲᑮ ᐃᓯ ᑕᐸᓵᓈᐚᐤ? ᑭᑲ ᓂᐸᐦᐃᑎᓈᐚᐤ!”

“ᓇᒨᔭᓇ ᑭᑳᐑᓇᐤ!” ᐃᑗᐤ ᐅᓰᒥᒫᐤ᙮ ᓈᐲᓯᓴᐠ ᐊᑎ ᒨᐦᑭᐸᐦᑖᐘᐠ ᐑᓴᐦᑮᒫᕽ ᐄ ᓇᔮᐦᔫᐟ ᐅᓰᒥᓴ᙮

ᓇᐘᐨ ᑭᓯᐚᐠ ᐲᐦᑕᒷᐠ ᐅᑳᐑᐚᐘ ᐅᐲᐦᑖᑯᓯᓂᔨᐤ᙮ ᐑᓴᐦᑮᒫᕽ ᑲᒀᑕᑭ ᓃᐢᑐᓯᐤ ᐊᔨᐢᐠ ᐄ ᐹᐦ ᐱᒥᐸᐦᑖᐟ ᐃᑾ ᐄ ᓇᔮᐦᔫᐟ ᐅᓰᒥᓴ᙮ ᐅᑎᓇᑦ ᐃᐢᑶᔮᓂᕽ ᑮᑾᐩ ᑳ ᑮ ᒦᔨᑯᐟ ᐅᐦᑖᐏᔭ, ᐊᒥᐢᑯᐑᐱᐟ, ᒫᑲ ᐄ ᒷᔩ ᐸᑭᑎᓈᐟ ᐅᓰᒥᓴ, ᑭᒥᐢᑭᓇᑦᐃᔭᑸᔨᐤ ᓃᑳᓂᕽ ᐃᓯ᙮ ᓰᒫᐠ

ᐃᑯᑕ ᐅᐦᒋ ᐅᐦᐱᐸᖨᐣ ᓰᐱᐩ, ᐄ ᓇᑭᐢᑳᑯᒋᐠ, ᐄ ᒥᒋᒧᓯᐦᑳᐧᐤ᙮ ᐃᑲᐧ ᐊᓇ ᒋᐦᒋᐱᐢᒋᑳᐧᐣ ᓇᒨᖬ ᐅᓵᑦ ᐋᐧᐦᖭᐤ ᐄ ᐲ ᓅᑯᓯᐟ᙮

ᑲᐧᔭᐢᐠ ᒋᐦᒋᐱᐢᒋᑳᐧᐣ ᒥᖩᐧᖨᐦᑕᑦ ᐄ ᐋᐧᐸᒫᐟ ᓈᐲᓯᓴ ᐄ ᒥᒋᒧᓯᓂᖨᐟ, ᐄᐧᐸᐨ ᑕ ᑲᐦᒋᑎᓈᐟ᙮ ᒥᑐᓂ ᐊᑎ ᐊᐧᐋᐧᓃᖨᐦᑕᒪᐧᐠ ᓈᐲᓯᓴᐠ, ᒥᐧᐦᒋ ᑮᑳᐨ ᐄ ᐸᑭᒦᒋᐠ ᐃᐢᐲ ᑳ ᐲᐦᑕᐋᐧᒋᐠ ᐊᐃᐧᔭ ᐄ ᐲᑭᐢᑳᐧᑎᑯᒋᐠ ᓰᐲᕽ ᐅᐦᒋ᙮

“ᑭᑲ ᐋᓯᐊᐧᑳᒦᐦᐅᖨᑎᓈᐋᐧᐤ ᓅᓯᓯᒪᐠ,” ᐃᑏᐧᐤ ᐄᓴ ᐊᐊᐧ ᑭᓰᑎᓂᐤ ᒨᐢᑲᐦᐅᓯᐤ᙮ “ᓂᐢᐱᐢᑲᐧᓂᕽ ᑖᐦᑯᐢᑮᐠ ᐃᑲᐧ ᑭᑲ ᐋᓯᐊᐧᐦᐅᖨᑎᓈᐋᐧᐤ᙮ ᒫᑲ ᐱᔮᐦᑕᐠ ᑖᐦᑯᐢᑮᐠ ᐊᖨᐢᐠ ᐄ ᐄᐧᓴᑮᖨᐦᑕᒫᐣ ᓂᑲᐧᔭᐤ᙮” ᓇᐦᐃᐦᑕᐄᐧᐊᐧᐠ ᐊᓂᐦᐃ ᐃᑲᐧ ᐋᓯᐊᐧᐦᐅᖨᑯᐊᐧᐠ ᐊᓂᐦᐃ ᑭᓰᑎᓂᐤ ᒨᐢᑲᐦᐅᓯᐊᐧ᙮

ᒋᐦᒋᐱᐢᒋᑳᐧᐣ ᓂᑐᒦᐤ ᒨᐢᑲᐦᐅᓯᐊᐧ ᐄ ᑲᑮᐧ ᑲᐢᑭᒫᐟ ᑕ ᐋᓯᐊᐧᖩᐦᐃᑯᐟ ᒫᑲ ᐊᓇ ᒨᐢᑲᐦᐅᓯᐤ ᓇᒫᐧᐨ ᓅᐦᑏ ᐋᓯᐊᐧᐦᐅᖩᐤ᙮ ᒫᑲ ᒥᐢᑕᐦᐃ ᒫᐦ ᒪᒥᐦᒋᒦᐤ ᐲᖨᐢᐠ ᑏᐲᖨᒧᐤ ᐊᐊᐧ ᒨᐢᑲᐦᐅᓯᐤ ᑕ ᐋᓯᐊᐧᐦᐅᖭᐟ ᒋᐦᒋᐱᐢᒋᑳᐧᓇ᙮ ᐄᐧᐦᑕᒪᐄᐧᐤ ᒫᑲ ᐄᑳ ᑕ ᑖᐦᑯᐢᑳᑕᒥᖨᐟ ᐅᑲᐧᔭᐤ᙮ ᑮᑳᐨ ᐄ ᒥᓵᑲᒋᐠ ᑳ ᐊᑎ ᑳᐦ ᑳᐧᐢᑯᐦᑎᐸᖨᐦᐅᐟ ᒋᐦᒋᐱᐢᒋᑳᐧᐣ, ᐄ ᐱᐢᑎᐢᑲᐋᐧᐟ ᒨᐢᑲᐦᐅᓯᐊᐧ ᐅᑲᐧᔮᖨᕽ, ᑳ ᐸᑲᐢᑕᐄᐧᐦᐃᑯᐟ᙮

ᒪᔭᐤ ᐄᐧᓴᐦᑮᒑᕽ ᐄ ᐋᐧᐸᒫᐟ ᓂᐲᕽ ᒋᐦᒋᐱᐢᒋᑲᐧᓇ ᐱᒧᓯᓈᑏᐤ ᐊᓯᓂᔭ ᐄ ᐋᐸᒋᐦᐋᐟ, ᐃᑲᐧ ᐃᑏᐧᐤ: “ᐆᑕ ᐅᐦᒋ ᓇᒦᐤ ᑭᑲ ᐃᑎᑲᐃᐧᐣ, ᑕ ᒧᐃᐧᐢᑳᐧᐤ ᐆᑯ ᐃᖨᓂᐊᐧᐠ ᑳ ᐄᐧ ᐊᔮᒋᐠ ᐆᑏ ᓃᑳᐣ᙮”

ᐃᑯᓯ ᐋᓂᒪ ᐄᓴ᙮ ᓃᐢᑐᓯᐊᐧᐠ ᓈᐲᓯᓴᐠ᙮ ᐊᖩᐧᐱᐊᐧᐠ ᐋᐧᓴᑳᑦ ᓰᐲᕽ ᑲᐲ ᑮᓯᐠ, ᒥᑐᓂ ᐃᐢᑯ ᐄ ᑎᐱᐢᑳᖨᐠ᙮ ᐃᐢᐱᒥᕽ ᐊᖨᑖᐱᐊᐧᐠ, ᐄ ᑲᓇᐋᐧᐸᒫᒋᐠ ᐅᐦᑖᐄᐧᐋᐧᐊᐧ, ᐊᓂᐦᐃ ᐅᒦᑲᑖᐦᑲᐧ᙮

12
ᐐᓴᐦᑮᒑᕽ ᐃᑲᐧ ᐐᒥᓰᓯᐩ

ᐆᑕ ᐋᒐᖫᐦᑮᐎᓂᕽ ᑭᐢᑭᓇᐧᐦᐊᒫᑮᐎᐣ ᐊᐢᑏᐤ ᑖᓂᓯ ᐄᑳ ᑭᑕ ᐃᑕᐦᑲᒥᑭᓯᔮᕽ ᐃᐢᐲ ᑭᒪᓈᑎᓯᒫᑲᓂᓇᐗᐠ ᐐᑕᐱᒥᑯᔭᐦᑳᐧᐎ: ᐅᓯᓴ ᐐᓴᐦᑮᒑᕽ ᐆᑕ ᑲᑮᐧ ᓂᐸᐦᐃᑯᐤ᙮ ᐆᑕ ᒦᓇ ᐋᒐᖫᐦᑮᐎᓂᕽ ᑭᐢᑭᓇᐧᐦᐊᒫᑮᐎᐣ ᐊᐢᑏᐤ ᑖᓃᓯ ᑭᑕ ᐅᓰᐦᐃᐦᒋᐠ ᐊᐦᒑᐱᔭᐠ ᐃᑲᐧ ᐊᑲᐢᑲᐧᐠ᙮

ᐃᑲᐧ ᐆᑯ ᓈᐲᓯᓴᐠ ᐸᐹᒧᐦᑏᐦᐅᐗᐠ; ᒥᐢᑕᐦᐃ ᐄ ᑲᑳᐧᑕᑭᐦᑖᒋᐠ᙮ ᐃᑯᐢᐲ ᑮ ᓯᐲᐧᐦᑏᐗᐠ ᐅᓰᒥᓴ ᐄ ᐐᒌᐗᐟ ᐐᓴᐦᑮᒑᕽ᙮ ᒫᑲ ᑮᐧᑕᑏ ᐃᓯ ᐅᑕᒥᐦᐄᐤ᙮ ᐲᖨᐢᐠ ᒪᓈᐦᐅᐤ ᒥᐢᑳᐧᐲᒪᑯᐦᐸᑲᐧ ᐃᑲᐧ ᐐᐐᑭᓇᑦ ᐃᔭᑯᓂ᙮ ᑳᐧᐢᑮᐧᓂᑐᐚᓇ ᐄ ᐅᓰᐦᑕᒪᐚᐟ ᐅᓰᒥᓴ᙮ ᐃᑯᓯ ᐄ ᐃᓯ ᐅᑕᒥᐦᐚᐟ᙮ ᐃᔭᑯᓂ ᑕ ᒦᑕᐚᑮᖨᐟ᙮

ᐃᑯᑕ ᐙᓴᑳᑦ ᓰᐲᕽ ᒫᐦ ᒦᑕᐚᑮᐗᐠ ᐊᓂᐦᐃ ᑳᐧᐢᑮᐧᓂᑐᐚᓇ, ᐄ ᐋᐦᐅᐦᐱᐐᐱᓈᒋᐠ ᐃᑲᐧ ᐄ ᓈᐦ ᓇᐗᑎᓈᒋᐠ᙮ ᑮᑕᐦᑕᐐ ᑳ ᐲᐦᑕᐚᒋᐠ ᐊᐎᔭ ᐄ ᐲ ᓇᑕᐦᐊᒥᖨᐟ ᓰᐱᐩ᙮ ᓇᑕᒥᕽ ᐃᑖᐱᐗᐠ᙮ ᐙᐸᒦᐗᐠ ᐊᐎᔭ ᐄ ᐲ ᐃᓯᒋᒦᖨᐟ, ᐹᐢᑲᐨ ᒫᓇ ᐄ ᐸᑲᒪᐦᐊᒥᖨᐟ ᐋᖩᑕᐤ ᐅᑑᑎᖨᕽ ᐃᑯᓯ ᒫᓇ ᑳ ᓯᐲᐧᑯᑏᖨᐠ ᐅᑑᐟ᙮ ᑲᓇᐙᐸᒦᐗᐠ ᐄᓴ ᐆᑯ

ᓈᐲᓯᓴᐠ ᐊᓂᐦᐃ ᐊᔭᐦᒋᑎᓂᐊᐧ ᐃᑯᑕ ᐆᓯᕽ ᑳ ᐴᓯᔨᐟ᙮ ᑮᓵᐢᑕᐤ ᐱᔭᑲᐧᐣ ᐄᐧᔭᐋᐧᐤ ᑳ ᐃᓯ ᓈᑯᓯᒋᐠ ᐄ ᐃᓯᓈᑯᓯᔨᐟ, ᒫᑲ ᓇᐊᐧᐨ ᒥᐢᑕᐦᐃ ᒦᔭᐄᐧᓯᔨᐊᐧ᙮

ᑭᐱᐦᒋᐸᔨᐤ ᐊᓂᒪ ᐆᓯ ᐊᑳᒥᕽ ᒥᓃᐋᐧᑎᒥᕽ ᐃᑕ ᑳ ᐊᔮᒋᐠ ᐆᑯ ᓈᐲᓯᓴᐠ᙮ ᑮᐦᑖᐧᒼ ᒫᒋ ᒫᐦ ᒦᑕᐋᐧᑳᑏᐊᐧᐠ ᐊᓂᐦᐃ ᑳᐧᐢᑮᐧᓂᑐᐋᐧᓇ᙮ ᐃᐢᐱᒥᕽ ᐄ ᐋᐦᐃᓯ ᐄᐧᐱᓈᒋᐠ ᐃᑲᐧ ᐄ ᓈᐦ ᓇᐊᐧᑎᓈᒋᐠ᙮ ᑮᑕᐦᑕᐄᐧ ᑳ ᐊᑎ ᐋᐧᐦ ᐋᐧᑳᑯᒋᕽ ᐊᓇ ᑳᐧᐢᑮᐧᓂᑐᐋᐧᐣ, ᒥᑐᓂ ᐆᓯᕽ ᐄ ᓂᑕᐃᐧ ᐸᐦᑭᓯᕽ᙮

“ᒪᐦᑎ ᒦᔨᐣ ᓂᑳᐧᐢᑮᐧᓂᑐᐋᐧᓂᓈᐣ,” ᐃᓯ ᑏᐲᐧᐤ ᐄᐧᓴᐦᑮᒑᕽ᙮ “ᐃᔭᑯ ᐊᓇ ᐳᑯ ᐄ ᐃᓯ ᐅᑕᒥᐦᐊᐠ ᓂᔩᒥᐢ᙮”

ᐊᓇ ᓈᐲᐤ ᐊᐦᔩᐤ ᐊᓂᐦᐃ ᑳᐧᐢᑮᐧᓂᑐᐋᐧᓇ ᐅᑖᐳᒥᕽ ᐃᑲᐧ ᐃᑎᓯᓇᒪᐄᐧᐤ ᐃᔭᑯᓂ ᐄᐧᓴᐦᑮᒑᐦᑲᐧ᙮

“ᐦᐋᐧᐤ, ᐲ ᓈᐢ ᐊᐊᐧ,” ᐃᑏᐧᐤ ᐊᐊᐧ ᐊᔭᐦᒋᑎᓂᐤ᙮ ᐄᐧᓴᐦᑮᒑᕽ ᐸᐦᑯᐲᐤ ᐄ ᓈᑖᐟ ᐊᓂᐦᐃ ᑳᐧᐢᑮᐧᓂᑐᐋᐧᓇ᙮ ᒥᐧᐦᒋ ᐄ ᐊᑎ ᐅᑎᓈᐟ ᑳᐧᐢᑮᐧᓂᑐᐋᐧᓇ ᑳ ᐴᓯᐄᐧᐸᐦᐃᑯᐟ ᐊᓂᐦᐃ ᐊᔭᐦᒋᑎᓂᐊᐧ ᐅᑑᑎᔨᕽ᙮ ᓰᒫᐠ ᐸᑲᒪᐦᐊᒼ ᐅᑑᐟ ᐊᐊᐧ ᑭᓰᑎᓂᐤ ᐃᑯᓯ ᐄ ᐊᑎ ᓯᐲᐧᒋᒦᐟ᙮ ᐃᑯᓯ ᐄ ᐃᓯ ᑳᐧᓯᐦᐃᐦᐟ ᐄᐧᓴᐦᑮᒑᕽ᙮ ᐃᑳᐧᓂ ᐄ ᓇᑲᑕᐦᐅᐦᐟ ᐊᐊᐧ ᐅᓰᒥᒫᐤ᙮

“ᓂᐢᑏᓰ!” ᐃᓯ ᑏᐲᐧᐤ ᐊᐊᐧ ᓈᐲᓯᐢ᙮ “ᑭᔮᒼ! ᓂᑲ ᒪᐦᐃᐦᑲᓂᐃᐧᐣ! ᐊ ᐆᐧ ᐆ ᐆ ᐆ,” ᐄ ᐊᑎ ᐆᔦᐟ᙮

“ᓂᔩᒦ! ᑳᐃᐧᔭ ᐸᐦᑯᐲᐦᑲᐣ ᐃᐢᐲ ᓇᐊᐧᓵᐧᑕᑖᐧᐃᐧ ᒨᓴᐧᐠ! ᑭᑲ ᓂᐢᑖᐸᐋᐧᐣ,” ᐃᓯ ᑏᐲᐧᐤ ᐄᐧᓴᐦᑮᒑᕽ᙮

ᐄᐧᓴᐦᑮᒑᕽ ᐋᐧᐸᒦᐤ ᒪᐦᐃᐦᑲᓂᓴ ᒍᐦᒋᒥᕽ ᐄ ᐃᐢᐸᐦᑖᔨᐟ᙮ ᒥᐢᑕᐦᐃ ᒫᑐᐤ ᐄᐧᓴᐦᑮᒑᕽ ᐄ ᒪᐃᐧᐦᑳᑖᐟ ᐅᔩᒥᓴ᙮ ᑭᐣᐄᐧᐢᐠ ᒫᑐᐤ᙮ ᐲᔨᐢᐠ ᐊᑎ ᓃᐢᑐᓯᐤ ᐃᑲᐧ ᐊᑎ ᓂᐹᐤ᙮

ᑮᑕᐦᑕᐚ ᒥᓴᑳᐘᐠ ᐃᑕ ᐑᒥᓲᓱᐩ – ᐃᔭᑯ ᒫᓂ ᒫᑲ ᐊᐘ ᒪᒋ ᑭᓲᑎᓂᐤ – ᑳ ᐑᑭᐟ᙮ ᓲᐢᑭᐱᑕᑦ ᐅᒎᐟ ᐃᑲᐧ ᐊᑎ ᑿᑕᐱᓇᑦ᙮ ᐃᑯᑕ ᓰᐹ ᐆᓯᕽ ᐊᐦᔫᐤ ᐑᓴᐦᑮᒫᐦᑿ, ᑮᔮᐱ⁻ ᐄ ᓂᐹᔫᐟ᙮ ᑯᐢᐱᐤ᙮ ᐃᐢᐲ ᑳ ᑕᑯᐦᑏᐟ ᐑᑭᕽ ᓂᑐᒦᐤ ᐅᑖᓂᓴ, ᓃᓯ ᐅᑖᓂᓯᐤ᙮

“ᐦᐋᐤ ᓂᑖᓂᓴᐠ! ᓂᐲᓯᐚᐤ ᐊᐏᔭᐠ ᑭᑕ ᐅᓈᐲᒥᔮᐠ,” ᐃᑏᐤ ᐅᑖᓂᓴ᙮ “ᓂᔮ, ᓂᑕᐏ ᐚᐸᒥᕽ, ᓰᐹ ᓂᑑᑎᕽ ᐊᐢᐱᐣ ᐄ ᓇᑲᑕᐠ, ᐄ ᓂᐹᐟ᙮”

ᐃᒀᓂ ᐅᒥᓯᒫᐤ ᓈᓯᐲᐤ ᐄ ᓂᑕᐚᐲᓇᐚᐟ ᐆᐦᐅ ᐊᐏᔭ᙮ ᐚᐸᒦᐤ ᐃᑯᑕ ᓰᐹ ᐆᓯᕽ ᐑᓴᐦᑮᒫᐦᑿ᙮

ᑭᑎᒫᑭᓈᑯᓯᐤ ᐊᐘ ᐑᓴᐦᑮᒫᕽ ᐄ ᒥᓯ ᐹᑲᒫᐱᐟ᙮ ᒥᑐᓂ ᒪᒋᓇᐚᐤ ᐊᐘ ᐅᒥᓯᒫᐤ ᐃᔭᑯᓂ᙮ ᐋᑕᐚᔫᒦᐤ᙮ ᑳᐏ ᑯᐢᐱᐤ ᐄ ᑭᓱᐏ ᐊᔭᒥᐦᐋᐟ ᐅᐦᑖᐏᔭ᙮

“ᓇᒨᔭ ᓂᑲᑮ ᐅᓈᐲᒥᐣ ᐊᓇ ᐅᐢᑭᓃᑮᐢ! ᐅᒫᑦ ᒪᒋᓈᑯᓯᐤ,” ᐃᑏᐧᐤ ᐊᐘ ᐅᒥᓯᒫᐤ᙮

ᐃᒀᓂ ᐅᓲᒥᒫᐤ ᐊᑎ ᓈᓯᐲᐤ, ᐄ ᓂᑕᐚᐱᓇᐚᐟ ᐆᐦᐅ ᐅᐢᑭᓃᑮᓴ᙮ ᑭᑎᒫᑭᓇᐚᐤ᙮ ᐃᑯᑕ ᐊᑎ ᑳᓲᐦᑹᓃᐤ, ᒥᑐᓂ ᐄ ᐊᑎ ᒥᔦᓈᑯᓯᔫᐟ᙮ ᓂᑐᒦᐤ ᑕ ᐑᒌᐏᑯᐟ ᐑᑭᐚᕽ ᐃᓯ᙮ ᐃᑯᑕ ᐸᒥᐦᐚᐤ, ᐄ ᐊᑎ ᐑᑭᒫᐟ ᐑᓴᐦᑮᒫᐦᑿ᙮

ᐃᑲᐧ ᐊᐘ ᐅᒥᓯᒫᐤ ᐊᑳᐚᑏᐤ ᐆᐦᐅ ᐅᐢᑭᓃᑮᓴ ᐊᔫᐢᐠ ᐄ ᒥᔦᓈᑯᓯᔫᐟ᙮ ᒫᑲ ᑕᐦᑣᐤ ᑳ ᓈᑖᐟ ᐋᑕᐚᔫᒥᐠ᙮ ᑲᐦᑹᔫᒦᐤ ᐅᓲᒥᓴ᙮ ᐊᓇ ᑭᓲᑎᓂᐤ ᐸᒀᑏᐤ ᐅᓇᐦᐊᐦᑭᓲᒪ ᐃᒀᓂ ᐄ ᐅᔫᔫᐦᑕᕽ ᑖᓂᓯ ᓈᓂᑕᐤ ᑕᑮ ᐃᓯ ᓂᐸᐦᐚᐟ᙮

ᐱᔭᐠ ᑮᓯᑳᐤ ᐄᓴ ᐑᓴᐦᑮᒫᕽ ᑮ ᓄᐦᑏ ᐊᐦᒫᐲᐦᑮᐤ᙮

“ᑖᐱᑲ ᐊᐧᐢᑲᐧᔭᐠ ᐆᑕ ᐄ ᐃᐦᑕᑯᒋᐠ ᑕ ᐊᐦᒫᐲᐦᑳᑮᔮᐣ,” ᐃᑏᐤ ᐄᐧᓴᐦᑮᒫᕽ ᐄᐧᐊᐧ᙮

“ᓂᑭᐢᑮᔭᐦᑏᐣ ᐃᑕ ᑳ ᒥᐦᒌᑎᒋᐠ ᐊᐧᐢᑲᐧᔭᐠ,” ᐃᑏᐧᐤ ᐄᐧᒥᓲᓱᐩ᙮ “ᐃᑯᑕ ᓂᒋ ᐋᐧᐸᐦᑭ ᑲ ᐃᑕᐦᐅᔭᑎᐣ᙮”

ᑳ ᐋᐧᐸᓂᔭᐠ ᐄᐧᓴᐦᑮᒫᕽ ᐃᑲᐧ ᐅᓯᓴ ᐃᓯᒋᒦᐊᐧᐠ ᐃᑕ ᑳ ᐃᑏᐧᔭᐟ ᐅᓯᓴ ᐄ ᒥᐦᒌᑎᔭᐟ ᐊᐧᐢᑲᐧᔭ᙮ ᐃᐢᐱ ᑳ ᐊᑎ ᒥᓴᑳᒋᐠ ᐋᐧᐸᐦᑕᑦ ᐄᐧᓴᐦᑮᒫᕽ ᑖᐲᐧ ᒫᓂ ᒫᑲ ᐄᓴ ᐄ ᒥᐦᒌᑎᔭᐟ ᐊᐧᐢᑲᐧᔭ ᐃᑯᑕ᙮ ᒪᔭᐤ ᑳ ᑲᐹᐟ ᐄᐧᓴᐦᑮᒫᕽ ᐊᑎ ᓯᐲᐧᒋᒦᔭᐊᐧ ᐅᓯᓴ, ᐄ ᑎᐲᐧᔭᐟ᙮

“ᐦᐋᐤ ᓂᐳᐋᐧᑲᐣ! ᑭᑕᓴᒥᑎᐣ ᐊᐊᐧ ᓈᐲᐤ ᑭᑕ ᒍᐊᐧᐟ!” ᐃᓯ ᑎᐲᐧᐤ ᐄᐧᒥᓲᓱᐩ, ᐄ ᓂᑐᒫᐟ ᐅᐳᐋᐧᑲᓇ᙮ ᑳ ᒪᑖᐃᐧᓯᔭᐟ ᐋᐧᐸᐢᑲᐧ᙮

ᐄᐧᓴᐦᑮᒫᕽ ᓂᐸᐦᐄᐤ ᐋᐧᐸᐢᑲᐧ᙮ ᑮᐢᑭᑲᐧᔭᐄᐧᓵᐋᐧᑏᐤ ᐃᑲᐧ ᑕᐦᑯᓇᑦ ᐅᐢᑎᑳᐧᓂᔭᐤ ᑭᓯᐠ ᐊᐧᐢᑲᐧᔭ ᐄ ᐄᐧ ᐊᐦᒫᐹᐦᑕᑯᐦᑳᑮᐟ᙮ ᐋᓯᐢᑲᐄᐧᐤ ᐆᐦᐅ ᑭᓰᑎᓂᐊᐧ ᐃᑲᐧ ᐄᐧᑭᔭᕽ ᐊᑯᑖᐤ ᐊᓂᒪ ᒥᐢᑎᑳᐧᐣ᙮ ᐃᐢᐲ ᑳ ᒥᓴᑳᐟ ᐊᐊᐧ ᐄᐧᒥᓲᓱᐩ ᐋᐧᐸᐦᑕᑦ ᐅᐳᐋᐧᑲᓇ ᐋᐧᐸᐢᑲᐧ ᐅᐢᑎᑳᐧᓂᔭᐤ ᐄ ᐊᑯᑏᔭᐠ ᐄᐧᑭᕽ᙮

“ᐋᐧᐦ, ᓂᐳᐋᐧᑲᐣ!” ᑳ ᐃᓯ ᒪᐃᐧᐦᑳᑖᐟ ᐄᓴ ᐅᐳᐋᐧᑲᓇ ᐊᐊᐧ ᑭᓰᑎᓂᐤ᙮

ᐸᐱᔮᐦᑕᐠ ᐊᑎ ᐅᔭᐦᑯᑕᑦ ᐊᐦᒫᐹᐦᑎᐠ ᐄᐧᓴᐦᑮᒫᕽ ᐊᐧᐢᑲᐧᔮᐦᑎᐠ ᐄ ᐋᐧᐸᒋᐦᑖᐟ᙮

“ᑖᐱᑲ ᒎᓴᐧᐠ ᐆᑕ ᐄ ᐃᐦᑕᑯᒋᐠ ᑕ ᐅᑎᓇᒫᐣ ᒌᐢᑕᑏᔮᐱᐩ ᑕ ᑮᓯ ᐊᐦᒫᐲᐦᑳᑮᔮᐣ,” ᐃᑏᐤ ᐄᐧᓴᐦᑮᒫᕽ ᐄᐧᐊᐧ᙮

“ᓂᑭᐢᑮᔭᐦᑏᐣ ᐃᑕ ᑳ ᐊᔮᒋᐠ ᒎᓴᐧᐠ,” ᐃᑏᐧᐤ ᐄᐧᒥᓲᓱᐩ᙮ “ᐃᑯᑕ ᓂᒋ ᐋᐧᐸᐦᑭ ᑲ ᐃᑕᐦᐅᔭᑎᐣ᙮”

ᑳ ᐋᐧᐸᓂᔨᐠ ᐄᐧᓴᐦᑮᒑᕽ ᐃᑲᐧ ᐅᓯᓴ ᐃᓯᒋᒦᐊᐧᐠ ᐃᑕ ᑳ ᐃᑏᐧᔨᐟ ᐅᓯᓴ ᐄ ᐊᔮᔨᐟ ᒨᓴᐧ᙮ ᐃᐢᐲ ᑳ ᐊᑎ ᒥᓴᑳᒥᐠ, ᑲᐹᐸᔨᐦᐅᐤ ᐄᐧᓴᐦᑮᒑᕽ᙮ ᒪᔭᐤ ᑳ ᑲᐹᐟ ᐊᑎ ᓯᐲᐧᒋᒦᔨᐊᐧ ᐅᓯᓴ, ᐄ ᑏᐲᐧᔨᐟ᙮

“ᐦᐋᐧᐤ ᓂᐸᐋᐧᑲᐣ! ᑭᑕᓴᒥᑎᐣ ᐊᐊᐧ ᓈᐲᐤ ᑭᑕ ᒧᐊᐧᐟ!” ᐃᓯ ᑏᐲᐧᐤ ᐄᐧᒥᓲᓱᐩ, ᐄ ᓂᑐᒫᐟ ᐅᐸᐋᐧᑲᓇ᙮ ᑳ ᐲ ᒪᑖᐃᐧᓯᔨᐟ ᒨᓴᐧ᙮

ᐄᐧᓴᐦᑮᒑᕽ ᓂᐸᐦᐄᐤ ᒨᓴᐧ ᐃᑲᐧ ᒪᓈᐦᐅᐤ ᒌᐢᑕᑏᔮᐱᔭ᙮ ᑮᐢᑭᑲᐧᔭᐄᐧᓵᐋᐧᑏᐤ ᐃᑲᐧ ᑕᐦᑯᓇᑦ ᐅᐢᑎᑳᐧᓂᔨᐤ ᑭᓯᐠ ᒌᐢᑕᑏᔮᐱᔭ ᐄ ᐄᐧ ᐊᐦᒑᐹᐦᑕᑯᐦᑳᑮᐟ᙮ ᐋᓯᐢᑲᐄᐧᐤ ᐆᐦᐅ ᑭᓲᑎᓂᐊᐧ ᐃᑲᐧ ᐄᐧᑭᔨᕽ ᐊᑯᑖᐤ ᐊᓂᒪ ᒥᐢᑎᑳᐧᐣ᙮ ᐃᐢᐲ ᑳ ᒥᓴᑳᐟ ᐊᐊᐧ ᐄᐧᒥᓲᓱᐩ ᐋᐧᐸᐦᑕᑦ ᐅᐸᐋᐧᑲᓇ ᒨᓴᐧ ᐅᐢᑎᑳᐧᓂᔨᐤ ᐄ ᐊᑯᑏᔨᐠ ᐄᐧᑭᕽ᙮

“ᐋᐧᐦ, ᓂᐸᐋᐧᑲᐣ!” ᑳ ᐃᓯ ᒪᐃᐧᐦᑳᑖᐟ ᐄᓴ ᐅᐸᐋᐧᑲᓇ ᐊᐊᐧ ᑭᓲᑎᓂᐤ᙮

ᑮᓯᐦᐄᐤ ᐊᐦᒑᐱᔭ ᐄᐧᓴᐦᑮᒑᕽ᙮ ᐊᑲᐢᑲᐧ ᐃᑲᐧ ᐸᑯ ᑭᑕ ᐅᓲᐦᐋᐧᐟ᙮

“ᑖᐱᑲ ᓃᐱᓯᔭᐠ ᐆᑕ ᐄ ᐃᐦᑕᑯᒋᐠ ᑕ ᐊᑲᐢᑯᐦᑳᑮᔮᐣ,” ᐃᑏᐤ ᐄᐧᓴᐦᑮᒑᕽ ᐄᐧᐊᐧ᙮

“ᓂᑭᐢᑮᔨᐦᑏᐣ ᐃᑕ ᑳ ᒥᐦᒌᑎᒋᐠ ᓃᐱᓯᔭᐠ,” ᐃᑏᐧᐤ ᐄᐧᒥᓲᓱᐩ᙮ “ᐃᑯᑕ ᓂᒋ ᐋᐧᐸᐦᑭ ᑲ ᐃᑕᐦᐅᔨᑎᐣ᙮”

ᑳ ᐋᐧᐸᓂᔨᐠ ᐄᐧᓴᐦᑮᒑᕽ ᐃᑲᐧ ᐅᓯᓴ ᐃᓯᒋᒦᐊᐧᐠ ᐃᑕ ᑳ ᐃᑏᐧᔨᐟ ᐅᓯᓴ ᐄ ᒥᐦᒌᑎᔨᐟ ᓃᐱᓯᔭ᙮ ᐃᐢᐲ ᑳ ᐊᑎ ᒥᓴᑳᒥᐠ ᐃᑯᑕ, ᑖᐲᐧ ᒫᓂ ᒫᑲ ᒥᐦᒌᑎᔨᐊᐧ ᓃᐱᓯᔭ᙮ ᒪᔭᐤ ᑳ ᑲᐹᐟ ᐄᐧᓴᐦᑮᒑᕽ ᐊᑎ ᓯᐲᐧᒋᒦᔨᐊᐧ ᐅᓯᓴ, ᐄ ᑏᐲᐧᔨᐟ᙮

“ᐦᐋᐧᐤ ᓂᐸᐋᐧᑲᐣ! ᑭᑕᓴᒥᑎᐣ ᐊᐊᐧ ᓈᐲᐤ ᑭᑕ ᒧᐊᐧᐟ!” ᐃᓯ ᑏᐲᐧᐤ ᐄᐧᒥᓲᓱᐩ, ᐄ ᓂᑐᒫᐟ ᐅᐸᐋᐧᑲᓇ᙮ ᑳ ᒪᑖᐃᐧᓯᔨᐟ ᑭᓃᐱᑲᐧ᙮

ᐐᓴᐦᑮᒑᕽ ᓂᐸᐦᐄᐤ ᑭᓃᐱᑿ᙮ ᑮᐢᑭᑿᔭᐐᓵᐚᑏᐤ ᐃᑿ ᑕᐦᑯᓇᑦ ᐅᐢᑎᒀᓂᔨᐤ ᑭᓯᐠ ᓃᐱᓯᔭ ᑳ ᐐ ᐊᑲᐢᑯᐦᑳᑮᐟ᙮ ᐚᓯᐢᑲᐐᐤ ᐆᐦᐅ ᑭᓰᑎᓂᐘ ᐃᑿ ᐐᑭᔨᕽ ᐊᑯᑖᐤ ᐊᓂᒦᔨᐤ ᑭᓃᐱᑯᐢᑎᒀᐣ᙮ ᐃᐢᐲ ᑳ ᒥᓴᑳᐟ ᐊᐘ ᐐᒥᓲᓱᐩ ᐚᐸᐦᑕᑦ ᐅᐳᐚᑲᓇ ᑭᓃᐱᑿ ᐅᐢᑎᒀᓂᔨᐤ ᐄ ᐊᑯᑏᔨᐠ ᐐᑭᕽ᙮

“ᐚᐦ, ᓂᐳᐚᑲᐣ!” ᑳ ᐃᓯ ᒪᐏᐦᑳᑖᐟ ᐄᓴ ᐅᐳᐚᑲᓇ ᐊᐘ ᑭᓰᑎᓂᐤ᙮

ᐊᑎ ᑮᓯ ᐅᔨᓵᐚᑏᐤ ᐊᑲᐢᑿ ᐐᓴᐦᑮᒑᕽ᙮ ᑕᐦᑯᐱᑕᑦ ᒎᐦᑯᒫᓇᑐᓵᐱᐢᑿ ᐱᔭᒀᔨᕽ ᑭᓯᐸᓅᕽ, ᐃᑿ ᑯᑕᑭᕽ ᒫᐢᑭᓵᐚᒦᓯᐤ, ᑏᐱᔭᕽ ᐊᐱᓲᐢ᙮

“ᑖᐱᑲ ᒦᑿᓂᓴᐠ ᑭᑕ ᐊᐢᑖᐐᓵᐣ ᐆᑯ ᐊᑲᐢᑿᐠ,” ᐃᑏᐤ ᐐᓴᐦᑮᒑᕽ ᐐᐘ᙮

“ᓂᑭᐢᑮᔨᐦᑏᐣ ᐃᑕ ᑳ ᒥᐦᒌᑎᒋᐠ ᒦᑿᓂᓴᐠ,” ᐃᑘᐤ ᐐᒥᓲᓱᐩ᙮ “ᐃᑯᑕ ᓂᒋ ᐚᐸᐦᑭ ᑲ ᐃᑕᐦᐅᔨᑎᐣ᙮”

ᑳ ᐚᐸᓂᔨᐠ ᐐᓴᐦᑮᒑᕽ ᐃᑿ ᐅᓯᓴ ᐃᓯᒋᒦᐘᐠ ᐃᑕ ᑳ ᐃᑘᔨᐟ ᐅᓯᓴ ᐄ ᒥᐦᒌᑎᔨᐟ ᒦᑿᓂᓴ᙮ ᐃᐢᐲ ᑳ ᐊᑎ ᒥᓵᑲᒋᐠ ᐃᑯᑕ, ᒫᓂ ᒫᑲ ᒥᐦᒌᑎᔨᐘ ᒦᑿᓂᓴ, ᒥᓯᐐᐢᑲᒥᐠ ᐃᑯᑕ ᓈᑕᑳᑦ ᐄ ᐱᒥᓯᓂᔨᐟ᙮ ᒪᔭᐤ ᑳ ᑲᐹᐟ ᐐᓴᐦᑮᒑᕽ ᐊᑎ ᓯᐲᐧᒋᒦᔨᐘ ᐅᓯᓴ, ᐄ ᑏᐲᐧᔨᐟ᙮

“ᐦᐚᐤ ᓂᐳᐚᑲᐣ! ᑭᑕᓴᒥᑎᐣ ᐊᐘ ᓈᐲᐤ ᑭᑕ ᒍᐘᐟ!” ᐃᓯ ᑏᐲᐧᐤ ᐐᒥᓲᓱᐩ, ᐄ ᓂᑐᒫᐟ ᐅᐳᐚᑲᓇ᙮ ᑳ ᑘᐦᐅᔨᐟ ᒥᑭᓯᐘ᙮

ᐐᓴᐦᑮᒑᕽ ᓂᐸᐦᐄᐤ ᒥᑭᓯᐘ᙮ ᑮᐢᑭᑿᔭᐐᓵᐚᑏᐤ ᐃᑿ ᑕᐦᑯᓇᑦ ᐅᐢᑎᒀᓂᔨᐤ᙮ ᒎᓴᐦᑭᓃᐤ ᒥᐦᒌᐟ ᒦᑿᓂᓴ ᑕ ᐊᐢᑖᐐᐟ᙮ ᐚᓯᐢᑲᐐᐤ ᐆᐦᐅ ᑭᓰᑎᓂᐘ ᐃᑿ ᐐᑭᔨᕽ ᐊᑯᑖᐤ ᐊᓂᒪ ᒥᑭᓯᐤ ᒥᐢᑎᒀᐣ᙮ ᐃᐢᐲ ᑳ ᒥᓴᑳᐟ ᐊᐘ ᐐᒥᓲᓱᐩ ᐚᐸᐦᑕᑦ ᐅᐳᐚᑲᓇ ᒥᑭᓯᐘ ᐅᐢᑎᒀᓂᔨᐤ ᐄ ᐊᑯᑏᔨᐠ ᐐᑭᕽ᙮

“ᐋᐧ", ᓂᐸᐋᐧᑲᐣ!” ᑳ ᐃᓯ ᒪᐃᐧᐦᑳᑖᐟ ᐄᓴ ᐅᐸᐋᐧᑲᓇ ᐊᐊᐧ ᑭᓰᑎᓂᐤ᙮

ᐃᑳᐧᓂ ᑮᓯᐦᐄᐤ ᐊᐦᓛᐱᔭ ᐃᑲᐧ ᐊᑲᐢᑲᐧ ᐄᐧᓴᐦᑮᓛᕽ᙮

“ᑖᐲᐧ ᑫᐦᒋ,” ᐃᑏᐧᐤ ᐄᐧᒥᓰᓯᐩ᙮ “ᐋᐧᐸᐦᑫ ᓂᒋ ᑫᑲ ᓂᑕᐃᐧ ᒫᓛᓇᐤ᙮” ᒫᑲ ᒦᓇ ᐄᑐᑮ ᐄᒥᐢᑮᐧᔮᐦᑕᕽ ᑕᓂᓯᐊᐧᓈᒋᐦᐋᐧᐟ ᐄᐧᓴᐦᑮᓛᐦᑲᐧ᙮

ᐃᑳᐧᓂ ᑳ ᑮᑭᓰᐹᔭᔦᐠ ᓂᑕᐃᐧ ᒫᒌᐊᐧᐠ᙮ ᑲᐲ ᑮᓯᐠ ᓅᒋᐦᒋᑮᐊᐧᐠ᙮ ᑮ ᐊᑎ ᐄᐧᐹᒋ ᑮᓯᑲᔦᐤ᙮ ᒥᑐᓂ ᐄ ᓵᐳᐲᔦᑭ ᐅᓚᔫᓂᓯᐋᐧᐊᐧ᙮ ᐲᔦᐢᐠ ᐄ ᐊᑎ ᐅᑖᑯᓯᓂᔦᐠ ᐃᐢᐲ ᑳ ᓂᐸᐦᐋᒋᐠ ᒎᓴᐧ᙮

“ᐅᐦᒋᑕᐤ ᐳᑯ ᑭᑕ ᑲᐲᓯᔫᕽ ᐅᔫᑦ ᐊᑎ ᑎᐸᐢᑳᐤ,” ᐃᑏᐧᐤ ᐄᐧᒥᓰᓯᐩ᙮ “ᑭᑕ ᐹᓴᒪᕽ ᐳᑯ ᑭᓚᔫᓂᓯᓇᐊᐧ ᐊᑳᐧᐋᐧᓂᓯᕽ᙮”

ᐃᑳᐧᓂ ᐊᑯᑖᐊᐧᐠ ᐅᓚᔫᓂᓯᐋᐧᐊᐧ ᐊᑳᐧᐋᐧᓂᓯᕽ, ᐄ ᐄᐧ ᐹᓴᐦᑳᐧᐤ᙮ ᐊᑎ ᑲᐃᐧᓯᒍᐊᐧᐠ᙮ ᒪᔭᐤ ᐄ ᓂᐹᔦᐟ ᑭᓰᑎᓂᐊᐧ ᓂᐦᑎᓇᑦ ᐅᑖᔫᓂᓴ ᐄᐧᓴᐦᑮᓛᕽ, ᐄ ᐊᐢᐸᐢᑮᐧᓯᒍᓂᐦᑳᑮᐟ᙮

ᐃᑲᐧ ᑭᓰᑎᓂᐤ ᐊᐧᓂᐢᑳᐤ, ᐄ ᑮᐢᑮᐧᐦᑲᐧᒥᐦᑳᔦᐟ ᐄ ᓈᑕᕽ ᐊᔫᓂᓴ᙮ ᐅᑎᓇᑦ ᐊᔫᓂᓴ ᐃᑲᐧ ᒪᒍᐢᑏᐦᐊᑦ᙮

“ᐦᐄ, ᑮᑳᐧᐩ ᐆᒪ ᑳ ᑮᓯᑏᐠ?” ᐃᓯ ᑏᐲᐧᐤ᙮

“ᑭᑖᔫᓂᓴ ᐊᓂᐦᐃ! ᑮᔦ ᐊᓂᐦᐃ ᑭᑖᔫᓂᓴ! ᓃᔦ ᐄᐧᔦ ᓂᑕᐢᐸᐢᑮᐧᓯᒍᐣ ᓂᑖᔫᓂᓴ,” ᐃᑏᐤ ᐄᐧᓴᐦᑮᓛᕽ ᐅᓯᓴ᙮ “ᐃᑯᓯ ᐊᔦᐢᐠ ᐄ ᑮ ᐄᐧ ᐃᒎᑕᐃᐧᔭᐣ!”

ᐃᑳᐧᓂ ᒍᓰᐢᑲᑏᑳᐸᐃᐧᐤ ᐊᐊᐧ ᑭᓰᑎᓂᐤ᙮ ᒥᑐᓂ ᐊᑎ ᑲᐊᐧᒋᐤ᙮

“ᐋ", ᑭᔫᑦ ᓂᑲ ᒎᓯᐃᐧᐣ,” ᐃᑏᐧᐤ᙮ ᒫᑲ ᓇᒫᐧ- ᑲᐢᑫᐦᑖᐤ ᑭᑕ ᒎᓯᐃᐧᐟ᙮

ᑳ ᐲ ᐃᓯ ᑭᐢᑭᓯᔮᐣ

ᓂᑐᑕᐟ ᑭᓯᓈᐤ ᐄᐧᓴᐦᑮᒫᕽ, ᑕ ᐋᐦᑲᐧᒋᔮᐟ ᐅᓯᓴ᙮ ᐃᑳᐧᓂ ᐃᑯᓯ ᐃᓯ ᓂᐸᐦᐄᐤ ᒪᒋ ᑭᓰᑎᓂᐊᐧ, ᐄᐧᒥᓰᓯᔭ᙮

13
ᖬᐢᑭᐲᐤ

ᐆᒪ ᐋᒐᖫᐦᑮᐃᐧᐣ ᑭᑭᐢᑭᓇᐦᐊᒫᑯᓇᐤ ᑭᑕ ᓈᑲᑏᖬᐦᑕᒫᕽ
ᐄᑳ ᐊᔭᐦᒋᑎᓂᐤ ᑭᑕ ᐑᐦᑕᒪᐚᔭᕽ ᑭᐦᒋ ᐃᓲᐦᒋᑮᐃᐧᐣ
ᑭᐢᑮᖬᐦᑕᒍᐃᐧᐣ᙮ ᐃᒁ ᒦᓇ ᑭᐑᐦᑕᒫᑯᓇᐤ ᐄ ᒥᖭᐧᓯᐠ
ᑭᑕ ᐚᐦ ᐑᒋᐦᐃᑐᒋᐠ ᐊᖬᓯᑎᓂᐘᐠ᙮

ᑮ ᐲᐦᑕᐨ ᐄᓴ ᐑᓴᐦᑮᒫᕽ ᐄ ᑮ ᓂᐸᐦᐃᒥᐦᐟ ᐅᓰᒥᓴ ᒪᐦᐃᐦᑲᓇ᙮ ᐃᒁᓂ ᐄᓴ ᑳ ᓯᐺᐦᑏᐟ ᐑᓴᐦᑮᒫᕽ᙮ ᑭᐣᐑᐢᐠ ᑮ ᐱᒧᐦᑏᐤ᙮ ᑮᑕᐦᑕᐑ ᐅᑎᐦᑕᐑᐤ ᐅᑮᐢᑭᒪᓇᓯᐘ ᓂᐲᕽ ᐄ ᐊᖬᑖᐱᖬᐟ᙮

“ᑮᒁᐩ ᐆᒪ ᑳ ᑭᑖᐸᐦᑕᒪᐣ ᓂᓲᒦ?” ᐃᑗᐤ ᐑᓴᐦᑮᒫᕽ᙮

“ᐋᐦᑿᐠ ᐆᑯ ᐄ ᒪᑗ ᒦᑕᐚᑮᒋᐠ ᒪᐦᐃᐦᑲᓂ ᐅᓯᐩ,” ᐃᑗᐤ ᐊᐘ ᐅᑮᐢᑭᒪᓇᓯᐤ᙮

ᑭᓯᐚᓯᐤ ᐑᓴᐦᑮᒫᕽ ᐑᖭ ᐄ ᑭᐢᑮᖬᐦᑕᕽ ᐅᓰᒥᓴ ᐄ ᑮ ᓂᐸᐦᐃᑯᖬᐟ ᐋᐦᑿ᙮ ᓂᒥᑖᐘᐦᐊᐨ ᐑᓴᐦᑮᒫᕽ ᐄ ᓈᑕᕽ ᒪᐦᐃᐦᑲᓄᓯᐩ᙮ ᐊᑎ ᓈᐦ ᓂᐸᐦᐄᐤ ᐋᐦᑿ, ᐄ ᑖᐦ ᑕᐦᑲᒫᐟ ᐊᑲᐢᑿ ᐅᐦᒋ᙮ ᑮᑳ- ᐃᔭᐏᐢ

ᐄ ᒦᐢᒥᐦᐋᐧᐟ᙮ ᐸᐢᐲᐦᐄᐤ ᒫᑲ ᐊᓂᐦᐃ ᐅᑭᒫᐊᐧ, ᒌᒥᓯᑲᐧᓇᔭ᙮ ᐃᑲᐧ ᐅᑎᓇᒼ ᒪᐦᐃᐦᑲᓄᓯᐩ᙮ ᑳᐃᐧ ᐱᒫᒥᐦᐄᐤ ᐅᓰᒥᓴ ᒪᐦᐃᐦᑲᓇ᙮

ᐃᑳᐧᓂ ᐄᓴ ᐄᐧᓴᐦᑮᒑᕽ ᑳ ᐸᐱᒧᐦᑏᐟ᙮ ᑮᑕᐦᑕᐄᐧ ᑳ ᐋᐧᐸᒫᐟ ᐊᔩᑭᓴ ᐄ ᑳᐧᐢᑯᐦᑎᔩᐟ᙮ᑳᐧᐢᑯᑎᔩᐟ᙮

“ᐄ ᓂᑕᐃᐧ ᓂᐱᐢᑮᔮᐣ, ᐄ ᓂᑕᐃᐧ ᓂᐱᐢᑮᔮᐣ, ᐄ ᓂᑕᐃᐧ ᓂᐱᐢᑮᔮᐣ,” ᐄ ᐃᓯ ᓂᑲᒧᐟ ᐄᓴ ᐊᔩᑭᐢ᙮

“ᐄᐩ! ᓄᐦᑰ, ᑖᓂᑏ ᐆᒪ ᐄ ᐃᑐᐦᑏᔭᐣ,” ᐃᑏᐤ ᐄᓴ ᐄᐧᓴᐦᑮᒑᕽ ᐊᓂᐦᐃ ᐊᔩᑭᓴ᙮

“ᐆᑏ ᐆᒪ᙮ ᐄᐧᓴᐦᑮᒑᕽ ᐄᓴ ᐄ ᑮ ᑲᑮᐧ ᓂᐸᐦᐋᐟ ᒌᒥᓯᑲᐧᓇᔭ ᐃᑲᐧ ᓃᔭ ᐳᑯ ᑕ ᑲᐢᑭᐦᑖᔭᐣ ᐊᓇ ᑕ ᓇᓈᑕᐃᐧᐦᐊᐠ,” ᐃᑏᐧᐤ ᐄᓴ ᐊᔩᑭᐢ᙮

“ᑖᓂᓯ ᒫᑲ ᒫᓇ ᑳ ᐃᑑᑕᒪᐣ ᐃᐢᐱ ᑳ ᓂᐱᐢᑮᔭᐣ?” ᑳ ᐃᑏᐧᐟ ᐄᐧᓴᐦᑮᒑᕽ᙮

ᐄᐧᐦᑕᒪᐄᐧᐤ ᐊᔩᑭᐢ ᐄᐧᓴᐦᑮᒑᐦᑲᐧ ᑖᓂᓯ ᒫᓇ ᑳ ᐃᑕᐦᑲᒥᑭᓯᐟ ᐃᐢᐲ ᑳ ᓂᐱᐢᑮᐟ᙮ ᐃᑲᐧ ᒪᔭᐤ ᑳ ᑮᓯ ᐄᐧᐦᑕᒪᐋᐧᐟ ᑳ ᓂᐸᐦᐃᑯᐟ ᐄᐧᓴᐦᑮᒑᐦᑲᐧ᙮ ᐃᑲᐧ ᐃᑯᑕ ᐄᐧᓴᐦᑮᒑᕽ ᐸᐦᑯᓃᐤ ᐊᓂᐦᐃ ᐊᔩᑭᓴ ᐃᑲᐧ ᐄ ᐊᑎ ᑭᑭᐢᑲᕽ ᐊᓂᒦᔫᐤ ᐊᔩᑭᓴᔮᐣ ᐃᑯᑕ ᐅᐦᒋ ᐊᑎ ᑳᐧᐢᑯᐦᑎᐤ᙮

“ᐄ ᓂᑕᐃᐧ ᓂᐱᐢᑮᔮᐣ, ᐄ ᓂᑕᐃᐧ ᓂᐱᐢᑮᔮᐣ, ᐄ ᓂᑕᐃᐧ ᓂᐱᐢᑮᔮᐣ,” ᐄ ᐃᑏᐧᐟ ᐊᐢᐱᐣ ᐄ ᑳᐧᐦᒋ ᑳᐧᐢᑯᐦᑎᐟ᙮ ᐄ ᓈᑖᐟ ᐊᓂᐦᐃ ᒌᒥᓯᑲᐧᓇᔭ᙮ ᐃᑯᑕ ᐄᐧᑭᔩᕽ ᑳ ᑕᑯᐦᑏᐟ᙮

“ᓂᐲ ᓇᓈᑕᐃᐧᐦᐅᐋᐧᐣ ᐆᒪ᙮ ᐊᐊᐧᐢ! ᑲᐦᑭᔭᐤ ᐳᑯ ᐊᐃᐧᔭᑲᐠ ᑕ ᐊᐧᔭᐄᐧᒋᐠ ᐆᑕ ᐅᐦᒋ ᒦᑭᐋᐧᐦᐱᕽ ᐃᑲᐧ ᐃᑯᐢᐲ ᓂᑲ ᓇᓈᑕᐃᐧᐦᐋᐤ ᐊᐊᐧ᙮”

ᐃᑳᐧᓂ ᐃᑯᑕ ᐅᐦᒋ ᑲᐦᑭᔭᐤ ᐊᐧᔭᐄᐧᐊᐧᐠ᙮

ᐚᐚᑯᐦᑏᐤ ᐃᑯᑕ ᐄ ᑳᐦ ᑲᓇᐚᐸᒫᐟ ᐆᐦᐅ ᒌᒥᓯᑿᓇᔭ ᐃᑕ ᐄᓴ ᐊᑲᐢᒁᐦᑎᑿ ᐄ ᐊᔮᔨᐟ ᐅᓰᔨᕽ᙮ ᐃᑯᑕ ᑖᐳᒁᓂ ᐊᑲᐢᑿ ᑳ ᐅᑎᓈᐟ ᑮᐦᑤᐨ ᐄ ᑖᐦ ᑕᐦᑲᒫᐟ ᐊᓂᐦᐃ, ᐄ ᓂᐸᐦᐚᐟ᙮ ᒪᔭᐤ ᑳ ᓂᐸᐦᐚᐟ ᐃᑯᑕ ᐅᐦᒋ ᐄ ᐲ ᔨᐢᑭᐲᔨᐠ᙮ ᐃᑯᑕ ᐅᐦᒋ ᓂᐱᐩ ᐄ ᐲᒋᐸᔨᔨᐠ, ᐊᓂᑕ ᐅᐦᒋ ᐅᓰᔨᕽ᙮ ᒥᑐᓂ ᑮ ᐊᑎ ᔨᐢᑭᐲᐤ᙮ ᐑᓴᐦᑮᒑᕽ ᑮ ᐊᑎ ᓯᐿᐸᐦᑖᐤ ᐃᑯᑕ ᐅᐦᒋ, ᐃᐢᐸᑎᓈᕽ ᐄ ᐃᐢᐸᐦᑖᐟ᙮

ᓂᑐᒦᐤ ᑲᐦᑭᔭᐤ ᐱᓯᐢᑭᐘ᙮

“ᐋᐢᑕᒥᐠ! ᐑᒋᐦᐃᐠ! ᒥᐦᑐᐟ ᐳᑯ ᑕ ᐅᓰᐦᑖᔭᕽ,” ᐄ ᐃᑖᐟ᙮ ᑲᐦᑭᔭᐤ ᐆᑯ ᐱᓯᐢᑭᐘᐠ ᐲ ᐃᐢᐸᐦᑖᐘᐠ ᐄ ᐲ ᐑᒋᐦᐆᐑᒋᐠ ᒥᐦᑐᐟ ᑭᑕ ᐅᓰᐦᑖᒋᐠ᙮ ᐃᒁᓂ ᐃᑯᑕ ᒥᑐᓂ ᒥᓯᐑᐢᑲᒥᐠ ᐄ ᑮ ᔨᐢᑭᐲᐠ ᐃᑿ ᐃᑯᑕ ᒥᐦᑐᑎᕽ ᐹᐦ ᐴᓯᐸᐦᑖᐘᐠ ᐊᓂᑭ ᐱᓯᐢᑭᐘᐠ᙮

ᐃᒁᓂ ᐃᑯᑕ ᐅᐦᒋ ᐸᐹᒫᐦᐅᑯᐘᐠ᙮ ᑭᐣᐑᐢᐠ ᐆᒪ ᐃᑯᑕ ᑳ ᐸᐹᒫᐦᐅᑯᒋᐠ᙮ ᓇᒹᐨ ᓈᓂᑕᐤ ᐃᑕ ᐊᐢᑭᐩ ᐅᐦᒋ ᐚᐸᐦᑕᒷᐠ᙮

ᑮᑕᐦᑕᐑ ᐑᓴᐦᑮᒑᕽ ᑳ ᐃᑜᐟ, “ᐊᐏᔭᐠ ᐳᑯ ᐅᐦᒋᑕᐤ ᑭᑕ ᑰᑮᐟ ᑕ ᓈᑕᕽ ᐊᐢᑭᐩ᙮ ᓂᑮ ᐘᓂᑭᐢᑭᓯᐣ ᐊᐢᑭᐩ ᑕ ᐲ ᐃᑐᐦᑕᑖᔮᐣ᙮”

ᒹᑿ ᐑᔭ ᓃᑲᐣ ᑳ ᐲᑭᐢᑹᐟ: “ᐊᐦᐋᐤ ᓃᔭ ᓂᑲ ᑰᑳᐣ᙮ ᓂᓂᐦᑖ ᑰᑳᐣ ᐆᒪ᙮”

ᐃᒁᓂ, ᐊᐢᐱᐣ ᑳ ᑰᑮᐟ᙮

ᒥᑐᓂ ᑭᐣᐑᓰᐢ ᐃᑯᑕ ᑳ ᑰᑮᐟ᙮ ᑮᑕᐦᑜ ᑳ ᐲᑯᐲᐟ, ᐄ ᑮ ᓂᐢᑖᐹᐑᐟ ᐄᓴ᙮ ᐑᓴᐦᑮᒑᕽ ᐅᑎᓃᐤ ᐅᓰᒥᓴ᙮ ᐴᑖᑏᐤ᙮ ᑳᐑ ᐄ ᐱᒫᒋᐦᐋᐟ᙮ ᑳᐑ ᐊᐦᔩᐤ ᐊᓂᑕ ᒥᐦᑐᑎᕽ᙮

“ᐋᐑᓇ ᐃᑿ?” ᐃᑜᐤ ᐑᓴᐦᑮᒑᕽ᙮

ᐃᑲᐧ ᓂᑭᐠ ᐃᑲᐧ ᐋᐧᐢᑕ ᑳ ᐱᑭᐢᑮᐧᐟ᙮ "ᓃᔭ ᐃᑲᐧ ᓂᑲ ᑰᑳᐣ᙮ ᓂᓂᐦᑖ ᑰᑳᐣ ᐆᒪ," ᐃᑏᐧᐤ᙮

ᐃᑳᐧᓂ ᐃᑯᑕ ᐊᓇ ᑳ ᑰᑮᐟ᙮ ᑭᐣᐋᐧᓲᐢ ᐋᐧᐢᑕ ᐃᑯᑏ ᐊᔫᐤ, ᐊᑖᒥᐲᕽ᙮ ᐃᑳᐧᓂ ᑮᑕᐦᑕᐋᐧ ᑳ ᐲᑯᐲᐟ ᐃᑯᑕ ᐋᐧᐢᑕ ᐋ ᓂᐢᑖᐹᐋᐧᐟ᙮ ᐋᐧᓴᐦᑮᒑᕽ ᐅᑎᓃᐤ ᐊᓂᐦᐃ ᐊᓂᑕ ᓂᑭᑲᐧ᙮ ᐴᑖᑏᐤ ᐃᑲᐧ ᒦᓇ ᐱᒑᒥᐦᐋᐤ ᑮᐦᑖᐧᑦ ᐊᐦᔮᐤ ᐊᓂᑕ ᒥᐦᑐᑎᕽ᙮

"ᐊᐋᐧᓇ ᐆᒪ ᐃᑲᐧ?" ᐃᑏᐧᐤ ᐋᐧᓴᐦᑮᒑᕽ

ᐊᒥᐢᐠ ᐊᐊᐧ ᑳ ᐃᑏᐧᐟ "ᓃᔭ ᓂᓂᐦᑖ ᑰᑳᐣ᙮ ᓂᑲ ᑰᑳᐣ᙮"

ᐃᑳᐧᓂ ᐋᐧᐢᑕ ᐊᒥᐢᐠ ᐊᐊᐧ ᑳ ᑰᑮᐟ᙮ ᐊᐩ ᑭᐣᐋᐧᓲᐢ ᐃᑲᐧ ᓇᐊᐧᐨ ᐊᐊᐧ ᐊᒥᐢᐠ ᐊᑖᒥᐲᕽ ᐊᔫᐤ᙮ ᑮᑕᐦᑕᐋᐧ ᐳᑯ ᑳ ᐲᑯᐲᐟ ᐋᐧᐢᑕ ᐋ ᓂᐢᑖᐹᐋᐧᐟ᙮ ᐃᑳᐧᓂ ᐅᑎᓃᐤ ᐋᐧᓴᐦᑮᒑᕽ᙮ ᐴᑖᑏᐤ ᐃᑲᐧ ᑮᐦᑖᐧᑦ ᐱᒑᒥᐦᐋᐤ ᐊᐦᔮᐤ ᑳᐃᐧ ᒥᐦᑐᑎᕽ᙮

ᐃᑲᐧ ᐊᓇ ᐊᐧᒐᐢᑯᐢ ᑳ ᐃᑏᐧᐟ "ᓅᐢᑕ ᐆᒪ ᓂᓂᐦᑖ ᑰᑳᐣ᙮ ᒪᐦᑎ ᓃᔭ ᐃᑲᐧ᙮"

ᐊᐢᐱᐣ ᑳ ᑰᑮᐟ ᐊᐊᐧ ᐊᐧᒐᐢᑯᐢ᙮ ᒥᑐᓂ ᑭᐣᐋᐧᓲᐢ ᐃᑯᑏ ᐃᑲᐧ ᐋᐧᔭ ᐊᑖᒥᐲᕽ ᑳ ᐊᔫᐟ᙮ ᑮᑕᐦᑕᐋᐧ ᐳᑯ ᑳ ᐲᑯᐲᐟ᙮

ᐅᒥᐦᒌᓯᕽ ᐋᓴ ᐃᑯᑕ ᐊᐢᑭᐩ ᐊᐢᑏᔮᐤ ᐃᑲᐧ ᒦᓇ ᐋᐧᐱᑎᕽ᙮ ᐃᑲᐧ ᐋᐧᔭ ᐋᐧᓴᐦᑮᒑᕽ ᐅᑎᓇᑦ ᐃᑲᐧ ᓇᐦᐊᐢᑖᐤ ᒥᐦᑐᑎᕽ᙮

"ᐦᐋᐧᐤ ᑮᐦᑖᐧᑦ ᑰᑮ᙮ ᑮᔮᐱᐨ ᒥᐢᑕᐦᐃ ᐊᐢᑭᐩ ᑭᓂᑕᐋᐧᔭᐦᑏᓇᐤ᙮"

ᐃᑲᐧ ᐊᓇ ᐊᐧᒐᐢᑯᐢ ᑮᐦᑖᐧᑦ ᑰᑮᐤ᙮ ᐊᐩ, ᑭᐣᐋᐧᓲᐢ ᐊᔫᐤ ᐃᑯᑕ ᐊᑖᒥᐲᕽ᙮ ᑮᑕᐦᑕᐋᐧ ᐳᑯ ᑳ ᐲᑯᐲᐟ᙮ ᐃᑲᐧ ᒦᓇ ᑮᐦᑖᐧᑦ ᐊᐢᑭᐩ ᐊᐢᑏᔮᐤ ᐅᒥᐦᒌᓯᔮᕽ᙮ ᐅᑎᓇᑦ ᐋᐧᓴᐦᑮᒑᕽ ᐃᑲᐧ ᐊᐢᑭᐩ ᒥᐦᑐᑎᕽ ᓇᐦᐊᐢᑖᐤ᙮

ᐃᑲᐧ ᒦᓇ ᑮᐦᑖᐧᒼ ᑰᑮᐤ ᐊᐊᐧ ᐊᐧᒐᐢᑯᐢ᙮ ᓃᓵᐧᐤ ᑭᔮᐱᐨ ᐄ ᑮ ᑰᑮᐟ᙮ ᐃᑲᐧ ᒥᑐᓂ ᒥᐢᑕᐦᐃ ᐊᐢᑭᐩ ᐹᐦ ᐲᑖᐤ᙮ ᒫᒪᐃᐧ ᓃᐋᐧᐤ ᐄ ᑮ ᑰᑮᐟ᙮ ᐲᖬᐢᐠ ᓇᐦᐄᖬᑯᕽ ᐊᐢᑭᐩ ᐊᔮᐊᐧᐠ᙮

ᐃᑲᐧ ᐑᓴᐦᑮᒑᕽ ᐊᑎ ᐹᐦ ᐴᑖᑕᒼ ᐊᓂᒦᖪᐤ ᐊᐢᑭᐩ᙮ ᑭᐣᐋᐧᐢᐠ ᐹᐦ ᐴᑖᑕᒼ ᐊᐢᑭᐩ, ᐄ ᒥᓯᓯᐦᑖᐟ᙮ ᐃᑲᐧ ᐃᐢᐲ ᐄ ᐃᑏᖬᐦᑕᕽ ᓇᐦᐄᖬᑯᕽ ᐄ ᒥᓵᖬᐠ ᐊᑐᑏᐤ ᐅᓰᒥᓴ ᒪᐦᐃᐦᑲᓇ ᑭᑕ ᐋᐧᐢᑳᐸᐦᑖᖬᐟ᙮ ᐱᔭᐠ ᑎᐱᐢᑲᓂᓯᐤ ᐊᐊᐧ ᒪᐦᐃᐦᑲᐣ᙮

“ᐅᓵᒼ ᐊᐱᓵᓯᐣ ᐊᐢᑭᐩ,” ᑳ ᐃᑏᐧᐟ ᐑᓴᐦᑮᒑᕽ᙮

ᑮᐦᑖᐧᒼ ᐄ ᒫᒋ ᐴᑖᑕᕽ ᐊᐢᑭᐩ᙮ ᑭᐣᐋᐧᓰᐢ ᐴᑖᑕᒼ᙮ ᐃᑲᐧ ᒦᓇ ᓯᐲᐧᑎᓴᐦᐄᐧᐤ ᐅᓰᒥᓴ ᒪᐦᐃᐦᑲᓇ᙮ ᓃᓯ ᑎᐱᐢᑲᓂᓯᖬᐊᐧ ᐃᑲᐧ, ᑭᔮᐱᐨ ᐅᓵᒼ ᐊᐱᓵᓯᐣ ᐊᐢᑭᐩ᙮

ᑮᐦᑖᐧᒼ ᒫᒋ ᐴᑖᑕᒼ ᐊᐢᑭᐩ ᐑᓴᐦᑮᒑᕽ᙮ ᑭᐣᐋᐧᐢᐠ ᐴᑖᑕᒼ᙮ ᐃᑲᐧ ᒦᓇ ᓯᐲᐧᑎᓴᐦᐄᐧᐤ ᒪᐦᐃᐦᑲᓇ᙮ ᑭᐣᐋᐧᓰᐢ ᐃᑲᐧ, ᒫᑲ ᐲᖬᐢᐠ ᑮᐦᑖᐧᒼ ᑕᑯᐸᐦᑖᖬᐊᐧ᙮ ᑮᐦᑖᐧᒼ ᐑᓴᐦᑮᒑᕽ ᐴᑖᑕᒼ ᐊᐢᑭᐩ, ᓇᐊᐧᐨ ᐄ ᐄᐧ ᒥᓯᓯᐦᑖᐟ᙮ ᐃᑲᐧ ᒦᓇ ᓯᐲᐧᑎᓴᐦᐄᐧᐤ ᐅᓰᒥᓴ᙮

ᒥᑐᓂ ᑭᐣᐋᐧᐢᐠ ᑮ ᐲᐦᐄᐊᐧᐠ ᒫᑲ ᓇᒨᖬ ᐅᐦᒋ ᑕᑯᐸᐦᑖᖬᐊᐧ᙮

“ᐃᑳᐧᓂ ᓇᐦᐄᖬᑯᕽ ᒥᓵᐤ ᐊᐢᑭᐩ,” ᑮ ᐃᑏᐧᐤ ᐑᓴᐦᑮᒑᕽ, ᐄ ᐊᑎ ᓯᐲᐧᐦᑏᐟ᙮

ᐃᑯᓯ ᐱᑕᒫ ᐃᑲᐧ ᐊᓂᒪ᙮

14
ᐅᐸᓴᑳᐧᐱᓯᒧᐊᐧᐠ

ᐆᒪ ᐋᒋᒧᐃᐧᐣ ᑭᐄᐧᐦᑕᒫᑯᓇᐤ ᑕ ᐊᓰᐧᔦᐦᑕᒫᕽ ᐃᐢᐲ
ᐊᐃᐧᔭᐠ ᐃᑏᐧᒋ ᐄ ᐄᐧ ᒦᔦᑯᔭᕽ ᑮᑲᐧᐩ᙮

ᐱᔭᑳᐧᐤ ᐄᓴ ᐄᐧᓴᐦᑮᒑᕽ ᑮ ᐸᐱᒧᐦᑏᐤ ᐋᐧᓴᑳᐨ ᓵᑲᐦᐃᑲᓂᕽ᙮ ᑮᑕᐦᑕᐄᐧ ᐄᓴ ᑳ ᐋᐧᐸᒫᐟ ᓰᓰᐸ ᐃᑲᐧ ᓂᐢᑲ ᐄ ᐊᑲᐧᒧᔦᐟ ᓈᑕᑳᐨ᙮ ᑮᓯᐢᑲᐤ ᑳᓰᐸᔦᐦᐅᐤ᙮

“ᑖᓂᓯ ᐆᒪ ᐆᑯ ᑕ ᑮ ᐃᓯ ᓂᐸᐦᐊᑳᐧᐤ?” ᐃᑏᔦᐦᑕᐨ᙮

ᒫᑲ ᒦᓇ ᐄᓴ ᐄ ᓄᐦᑏᐦᑲᑏᐟ᙮ ᐊᑎ ᑮᒨᒋ ᐸᓯᑰᐤ, ᐄ ᐊᑎ ᓯᐲᐧᐦᑏᐟ ᐃᑯᑕ ᐅᐦᒋ᙮ ᐲᔦᐢᐠ ᒪᐢᑮᑯᕽ ᑳ ᑕᑯᐦᑏᐟ᙮

“ᐃᔭᑯᓂ ᓂᑲ ᐋᐧᐸᒋᐦᑖᐣ,” ᐃᑏᔦᐦᑕᐨ, ᐄ ᐊᑎ ᒫᐦ ᒨᓴᐦᑭᓇᕽ ᐊᐢᑭᔭ, ᐄ ᐊᓯᐊᐧᑖᐟ ᐅᒪᐢᑭᒧᑎᕽ᙮ ᓵᑲᐢᑭᓇᐦᑖᐤ ᐅᒪᐢᑭᒧᐟ᙮ ᑳᐃᐧ ᓵᑲᐦᐃᑲᓂᕽ ᐃᑐᐦᑏᐤ ᐄ ᐋᐧᐦ ᐋᐧᓴᑳᒦᐟ ᐃᑯᑕ ᐃᑕ ᑭᓯᐋᐧᐠ ᑳ ᐊᑲᐧᒧᔦᐟ ᓰᓰᐸ ᐃᑲᐧ ᓂᐢᑲ᙮ ᐃᑯᑕ ᐄᓴ ᐋᐧᐦ ᐋᐧᓴᑳᒦᐤ, ᐄ ᐱᒧᐊᐧᑖᐟ ᐅᒪᐢᑭᒧᐟ᙮ ᑮᑕᐦᑕᐄᐧ ᐱᓯᐢᑳᐸᒥᐠ ᓰᓰᐸ ᐃᑲᐧ ᓂᐢᑲ᙮

“ᒌᐢᐟ! ᑭᐢᑏᓯᓇᐤ!” ᐃᑏᐧᐊᐧᐠ᙮ “ᑮᑳᐧᐩ ᐊᐊᐧ ᑳ ᓇᔭᐦᑕᕽ?”

“ᒪᐦᑎ ᓂᑲ ᑲᑮᐧᒋᒫᐤ,” ᐃᑏᐧᐤ ᐊᐊᐧ ᐱᔭᐠ ᓰᓰᑊ᙮

“ᐋᐦᐋᐤ,” ᐃᑏᐧᐊᐧᐠ᙮

“ᓂᐢᑏᓲ, ᑮᑳᐧᐩ ᑳ ᓇᔭᐦᑕᒪᐣ?”

ᐋᐦᒋ ᐳᑯ ᐸᐱᒧᐦᑏᐤ ᐑᓴᐦᑫᒑᕽ, ᐋᐦᑮᑖᑊ ᐄᑳ ᐄ ᐲᐦᑕᐚᐟ᙮

ᓵᓴᐩ ᒦᓇ ᓰᓰᑊ ᑳ ᐲᑭᐢᑮᐧᐟ᙮

“ᓂᐢᑏᓲ, ᑮᑳᐧᐩ ᑳ ᓇᔭᐦᑕᒪᐣ?” ᑳ ᐃᑏᐧᐟ᙮

ᐋᐦᒋ ᐳᑯ ᐸᐱᒧᐦᑏᐤ ᐑᓴᐦᑫᒑᕽ᙮ ᐲᔦᐢᐠ ᓃᐚᐤ ᑳ ᑲᑮᐧᒋᒥᑯᐟ ᓇᐢᑮᐧᐊᐧᓯᐦᐄᐤ ᐊᓂᐦᐃ ᓰᓰᐸ᙮

“ᓂᓂᑲᒧᓇ ᐆᐦᐅ,” ᐃᑏᐤ ᐑᓴᐦᑫᒑᕽ᙮

“ᒪᐦᑎ ᒫᑲ ᓂᑲᒧᐢᑕᐃᐧᓈᐣ,” ᐃᑏᐧᐤ ᓰᓰᑊ᙮

“ᓇᒪ! ᐅᐢᑭ ᓂᑲᒧᓇ ᐆᐦᐅ ᐄ ᑮ ᒦᔦᑲᐃᐧᔮᐣ᙮ ᓇᒨᔦ ᐸᑲᐧᓂᑕ ᐳᑮᑏ ᓂᑲᑮ ᓂᑲᒧᐣ,” ᐃᑏᐧᐤ ᐑᓴᐦᑫᒑᕽ᙮

“ᑖᓂᓯ ᒫᑲ ᑕᑮ ᐃᑑᑕᒪᕽ ᑕ ᓂᑲᒧᐢᑕᐃᐧᔮᕽ?” ᐃᑏᐧᐤ ᓰᓰᑊ᙮

ᐃᑳᐧᓂ ᐄᐧᐦᑕᒪᐄᐧᐤ ᑲᐦᑭᔦᐤ ᓰᓰᐸ ᐃᑲᐧ ᓂᐢᑲ ᑖᓂᓯ ᑭᑕ ᐃᑑᑕᒥᔦᐟ ᑮᐢᐱᐣ ᓅᐦᑏ ᐄᐧᐦᑕᒪᐄᐧᐤ ᐊᓂᐦᐃ ᐅᐢᑭ ᓂᑲᒧᓇ᙮ ᐊᑎ ᓰᐦᑭᒫᐊᐧᓲᐤ ᐑᓴᐦᑫᒑᕽ᙮

“ᐅᑖᕽ ᐊᐢᑭᐩ ᐆᒪ ᓂᑮ ᐊᓲᑕᒫᑳᐣ ᑕ ᓃᒥᐦᐃᐃᐧᔮᐣ ᐊᓄᐦ-ᑳ ᐊᐢᑮᐃᐧᐠ᙮ ᐃᑲᐧ ᐄᑮᐧᔦ- ᐊᓄᐦᒋᐦᑮ ᐄ ᒦᔦᑲᐄᐧᔮᐣ ᐅᐢᑭ ᓂᑲᒧᓇ, ᐃᔭᑯᓂ ᐆᐦᐅ ᑳ ᐱᒧᐋᐧᑖᔮᐣ᙮ ᓂᑮ ᓰᐦᑭᒥᑲᐃᐧᐣ ᐆᒪ ᑖᓂᓯ

ᑕ ᐃᓯ ᓃᒥᐦᐃᐄᐧᔮᐣ ᐃᐢᐲ ᓂᑲᒨᔭᓂ᙮ ᐅᐦᒋᑕᐤ ᐳᑯ ᑕ ᐅᓰᐦᑖᓂᐃᐧᐠ ᓃᒥᐃᐧᑲᒥᐠ ᓇᐦᐄᐧᔭᑯᕽ ᐄ ᐃᐢᐲᐦᒑᐠ ᐃᑲᐧ ᐱᔭᐠ ᐃᐢᑳᐧᐦᒌᒥᐢ ᓵᐊᐧᓄᕽ ᑕ ᐃᑕᒧᐠ᙮ ᐃᑲᐧ ᐃᐢᐲ ᓯᐲᐧᓯᒧᓈᓄᐃᐧᑭ ᐅᐦᒋᑕᐤ ᐳᑯ ᐊᓂᑭ ᐅᓃᒥᐊᐧᐠ ᑭᑕ ᐸᓴᑳᐧᐱᒋᐠ, ᑕ ᐲᐦᑐᑮ ᐸᓴᑳᐧᐱᓯᒧᒋᐠ ᓃᒥᐃᐧᑲᒥᑯᕽ᙮ ᑮᐢᐱᐣ ᓇᒨᔭ ᐊᐃᐧᔭᐠ ᓄᐦᑏ ᐸᓴᑳᐧᐱᓯᒧᐤ ᐆᑕ ᐅᐦᒋ ᑕ ᓯᐲᐧᐦᑏᐤ ᓰᒫᐠ!”

ᐃᑯᓰᓯ ᑲᑮᐧ ᐸᐦᑲᒋᒦᐤ ᐆᐦᐅ ᓰᓰᐸ ᐃᑲᐧ ᓂᐢᑲ᙮

ᑲᐦᑭᔭᐤ ᐆᑯ ᓰᓰᐸᐠ ᐃᑲᐧ ᓂᐢᑲᐠ ᓄᐦᑏ ᐸᓴᑳᐧᐱᓯᒧᐊᐧᐠ, ᐄ ᓄᐦᑏ ᐲᐦᑕᐦᑳᐧᐤ ᐊᓂᐦᐃ ᐅᐢᑭ ᓂᑲᒧᓇ᙮ ᑲᐦᑭᔭᐤ ᐃᑯᑕ ᑭᓵᒌᐊᐧᐠ᙮ ᐊᑎ ᐅᓰᐦᑖᐊᐧᐠ ᐊᓂᒦᔨᐤ ᓃᒥᐃᐧᑲᒥᐠ᙮ ᐃᐢᐲ ᑳ ᑮᓯᐦᑖᒋᐠ ᓃᒥᐃᐧᑲᒥᐠ ᐊᑎ ᐊᐧᐄᐧᓰᐦᐄᐤ ᐅᓰᒥᓴ ᐄᐧᓴᐦᑮᒑᕽ᙮ ᐄ ᓵᐦ ᓯᓯᐲᑲᐦᐋᐧᐟ ᐊᓂᐦᐃ ᓰᓰᐸ ᐃᑲᐧ ᓂᐢᑲ᙮ ᐊᓄᐦᐨ ᐊᓂᑭ ᓰᓰᐸᐠ ᐃᑲᐧ ᓂᐢᑲᐠ ᑳ ᐃᓯᓈᑯᓯᒋᐠ ᐃᑯᐢᐲ ᐊᓂᒪ ᐅᐦᒋ, ᐃᐢᐲ ᑳ ᑮ ᐃᓯ ᓯᓯᐲᑲᐦᐅᑯᒋᐠ ᐄᐧᓴᐦᑮᒐᐦᑲᐧ᙮ ᑲᐧᔭᐢᐠ ᒫᐦ ᒥᔨᓈᑯᓰᐦᐄᐤ ᐅᓰᒥᓴ ᐄᐧᓴᐦᑮᒑᕽ᙮ ᒥᑐᓂ ᒌᐦᑮᔨᐦᑕᒪᐧᐠ ᐊᓂᑭ ᓰᓰᐸᐠ ᐃᑲᐧ ᓂᐢᑲᐠ ᐄ ᐃᓯ ᒫᐦ ᒥᔨᓈᑯᓯᒋᐠ᙮

ᐃᑳᐧᓂ ᑮᓯ ᐊᐧᐄᐧᓰᐦᐄᐤ ᐄᐧᓴᐦᑮᒑᕽ ᑳ ᐲᐦᑐᑮᐟ ᓃᒥᐃᐧᑲᒥᑯᕽ᙮ ᐃᑯᑕ ᑖᐋᐧᔨᕽ ᓃᒥᐃᐧᑲᒥᑯᕽ ᐊᐱᐤ ᐄᐧᓴᐦᑮᒑᕽ᙮ ᐊᑎ ᓯᐲᐧᐦᐊᑦ ᑭᓯᐠ ᐄ ᒪᑏᐧᐦᐋᐧᐟ ᒥᐢᑎᑲᐧᐢᑭᐦᑲᐧ᙮

“ᐦᐊᐩ ᔭ, ᐦᐊᐩ ᔭ ᐸᓴᑳᐧᐱᓯᒧᐃᐧᐣ ᓂᓂᑲᒧᐦᑖᐣ,” ᐃᓯ ᓂᑲᒧᐤ ᐄᐧᓴᐦᑮᒑᕽ᙮ “ᐦᐊᐩ ᔭ, ᐦᐊᐩ ᔭ ᐸᓴᑳᐧᐱᓯᒧᐃᐧᐣ ᓂᓂᑲᒧᐦᑖᐣ᙮”

ᐃᑳᐧᓂ ᐊᑎ ᐹᐦ ᐲᐦᑐᑮᓯᒧᐊᐧᐠ ᐆᑯ ᓰᓰᐸᐠ ᐃᑲᐧ ᓂᐢᑲᐠ, ᐹᐢᑲ-ᐄ ᓇᓇᒥᐢᑎᑳᐧᓃᓯᒧᒋᐠ, ᐄ ᐸᓴᑳᐧᐱᓯᒧᒋᐠ᙮ ᐃᑯᑕ ᐲᐦᒑᔨᕽ ᐊᐱᐤ ᐄᐧᓴᐦᑮᒑᕽ, ᑖᐋᐧᔨᕽ ᓃᒥᐃᐧᑲᒥᑯᕽ ᐄ ᐅᐦᒋ ᓂᑲᒧᐟ᙮

ᐃᑲᐧ ᐋᐧᐢᑳᓯᒧᐊᐧᐠ ᐆᑯ ᓰᓰᐸᐠ ᐃᑲᐧ ᓂᐢᑲᐠ᙮ ᑮᑕᐦᑕᐄᐧ ᒫᓇ ᐋᐦᐅᑎᐦᑎᓃᐤ ᐄᐧᓴᐦᑮᒑᕽ ᓰᓰᐸ ᐊᓂᐦᐃ ᓇᐊᐧᐨ ᑳ ᐄᐧᔨᓄᓯᔨᐟ᙮

ᑮᐢᑭᑮᐧᓃᐤ ᐃᑲᐧ ᐊᓯᐊᐧᒋᐄᐧᐱᓃᐤ ᐅᒪᐢᑭᒧᑎᕽ᙮ ᐋᐦᑲᒥ ᓂᑲᒧᐤ ᐃᑲᐧ ᐲᔨᐢᐠ ᐅᑎᓇᒫᓱᐤ ᒥᐦᑮᐟ ᓲᓱᐸ᙮

ᐃᑲᐧ ᐄᓴ ᐊᐊᐧ ᐱᔭᐠ ᓲᓲ', ᐊᐊᐧ ᓯᐦᑭ‴, ᐊᑎ ᒫᒥᑐᓃᔦᐦᑕᐨ ᑖᓂᐦᑭ ᒫᓇ ᐋᐢᑲᐤ ᐄᑳ ᑳ ᓂᑲᒧᔦᐟ ᐄᐧᓴᐦᑮᑳᐦᑲᐧ᙮ ᐃᑳᐧᓂ ᑮᒨᑖᐱᐤ᙮ ᑳ ᐋᐧᐸᒫᐟ ᐄᐧᓴᐦᑮᑳᐦᑲᐧ ᐄ ᐅᑎᐦᑎᓈᔦᐟ ᓲᓲᐸ᙮ ᓲᒫᐠ ᑏᐲᐧᐤ!

"ᑕᐸᓲᐠ ᓃᑎᓵᓇᐠ! ᐄᐧᓴᐦᑮᑳᕽ ᐊᐊᐧ ᑭᓂᐸᐦᐃᑯᓇᐤ," ᐃᓯ ᑏᐲᐧᐤ ᐊᐊᐧ ᓯᐦᑭ‴᙮

ᑲᐦᑭᔦᔭᐤ ᐊᑎ ᐋᐧᐦ ᐊᐧᔦᐄᐧᐸᐦᑖᐊᐧᐠ ᐊᓂᑭ ᓲᓲᐸᐠ ᐃᑲᐧ ᓂᐢᑲᐠ!

ᐃᑲᐧ ᐊᓇ ᓯᐦᑭ‴ ᐃᐢᑭᐧᔮᓂᕽ ᐄᐧᔦ ᑲᑮᐧ ᑕᐸᓲᐤ᙮ ᐄᐧᓴᐦᑮᑳᕽ ᑕᐦᑭᐢᑳᑏᐤ ᐊᓂᐦᐃ ᓯᐦᑭᐦᐸ ᒥᐧᐦᒋ ᐄ ᐊᑎ ᐊᐧᔦᐄᐧᐸᐦᑖᔦᐟ᙮ ᐅᓲᑲᓂᕽ ᑳ ᑕᐦᑭᐢᑳᑖᐟ! ᐃᔭᑯᐦᒋ ᐊᓄᐦ- ᓯᐦᑭ‴ ᑭᔮᐱ- ᑳ ᓇᐦᐃᐦᑖᐃᐧᐦᐃᑯᐟ ᑕ ᐱᒧᐦᑏᐟ ᐊᐢᑮᕽ: ᑭᔮᐱ- ᐄ ᒫᐢᑭᓯᐟ᙮

15
ᒫᐢᑭᑳᑏᐤ ᒪᐦᑮᓰᐢ

ᐆᒪ ᐋᒐᖫᐦᑮᐏᐣ ᑭᑭᐢᑭᓇᐧᐦᐊᒫᑯᓇᐤ: ᐄᑳ
ᑭᑕ ᑲᑮᐧ ᒌᓯᐦᐋᖩᐦᑳᐧᐤ ᑮᒋ ᐊᖨᓯᑎᓃᒥᓇᐘᐠ᙮

ᐃᑯᓯ ᐘᖬᐑᐤ ᐑᓴᐦᑮᒑᕽ, ᐄ ᐸᐦᐱᐟ, ᐄ ᒥᖩᐧᖨᐦᑕᕽ᙮

“ᒥᐢᑕᐦᐃ ᓂᑲ ᒦᒋᓱᐣ,” ᐄ ᐃᑏᖨᐦᑕᕽ᙮

ᐃᑯᓯ ᑲᐏᓇᑦ ᐅᓃᒥᐏᑲᒥᐠ᙮ ᒨᓴᐦᑭᓂᐦᑏᐤ ᐃᑲᐧ ᐊᑎ ᑯᑕᐑᐤ᙮ ᐋᑎᐦᐟ ᐊᓂᐦᐃ ᓰᓰᐸ ᐃᑲᐧ ᓂᐢᑲ ᐑ ᓇᐘᒌᐤ᙮ ᐋᑎᐦᐟ ᐚᐦ ᐑᐑᑭᓃᐤ ᓃᐲᕽ ᓃᑳᐣ ᐃᑲᐧ ᐃᑯᑕ ᐅᐦᒋ ᐊᓴᐢᑭᐩ ᐅᐦᒋ ᐑᐑᑭᓃᐤ᙮ ᐃᑲᐧ ᐊᑎ ᓰᑲᐧᐦᑯᓃᐤ, ᐊᑖᒥᕽ ᐃᐢᑯᑏᕽ ᐄ ᑮᓯᓵᐧᐟ᙮

ᐅᓵᑦ ᐄᓴ ᒥᐢᑕᐦᐃ ᑮ ᐴᓇᑦ, ᒥᑐᓂ ᐄ ᐊᑎ ᐊᐲᐧᓯᐟ᙮
ᐊᑎ ᓯᐲᐧᐦᑏᐤ᙮

“ᐱᑕᒫ ᓂᑲ ᐴᓂ ᐊᐲᐧᓯᐣ᙮ ᐃᑲᐧᖨᑯᕽ ᑭᑕ ᑮᓯᓱᐘᐠ ᓂᓰᓰᐱᒪᐠ ᐃᑲᐧ ᓂᓂᐢᑭᒪᐠ,” ᐄ ᐃᑏᖨᐦᑕᕽ᙮

ᓇᒨᔭ ᐅᓵᒼ ᐚᐦᔭᐤ ᑮ ᐃᑐᐦᑏᐤ ᐃᐢᐲ ᑳ ᐚᐸᒫᐟ ᒪᐦᑮᓰᓴ ᐄ ᒫᐢᑭᐸᔭᔮᐟ᙮ ᐄ ᐐᓴᑮᔭᐦᑕᒥᔭᐟ ᐄᓴ ᐅᐢᑳᑎᔭᐤ᙮ ᐐ ᑕᐸᓰᐦᐃᑯᐤ᙮

“ᒌᐢᑲᐧ, ᓂᓰᒼ!” ᐃᑏᐤ᙮

“ᐊᐘᐢ, ᓇᒨᔭ!” ᐃᑎᐠ᙮ “ᐅᓵᒼ ᒫᑲ ᒦᓇ ᓈᓂᑕᐤ ᑭᑲ ᐃᑑᑕᐏᐣ,” ᐃᑎᐠ᙮

“ᓇᒨᔭ!” ᐃᑏᐤ᙮ “ᐄ ᐐ ᐋᒋᒧᐢᑖᑖᐣ᙮ ᐄᐦ ᐆᒪ, ᑭᐚᐸᐦᑏᐣ ᒌ ᒥᐢᑕᐦᐃ ᓃᑏ ᑳ ᒪᑏᐧ ᑲᐢᑳᐸᐦᑏᐠ?”

“ᐄᐦᐄ,” ᐃᑎᐠ᙮

“ᐃᑯᑏ ᒥᐦᒌᐟ ᓂᑮ ᓂᐸᐦᐋᐘᐠ ᓂᐢᑳᐠ ᒦᓇ ᓰᓰᐸᐠ᙮ ᐃᑯᑏ ᐄ ᐱᒥᓇᐘᓰᔮᐣ ᐃᔭᑯᓂᐠ,” ᐄ ᐃᑖᐟ᙮ “ᒥᐢᑕᐦᐃ ᑭᑲ ᒌᒥᓯᓇᐤ,” ᐃᑏᐤ᙮ “ᒫᑲ ᐱᑕᒫ ᑭᑲ ᒪᐏᓃᐢᑳᑐᓇᐤ᙮ ᐆᒪ ᓵᑲᐦᐃᑲᐣ ᑭᑲ ᐚᐢᑳᐸᐦᑖᓇᐤ᙮ ᐊᓇ ᐸᐢᑭᔮᑮᒋ ᑭᑕ ᒧᐑᐤ ᐊᓂᐦᐃ ᓰᓰᐸ ᐃᑲᐧ ᓂᐢᑲ᙮”

“ᐦᐋ, ᓇᒨᔭ! ᓇᒪᒌ ᑭᐚᐸᒥᐣ ᐄᑳ ᑲᐧᔭᐢᐠ ᐄ ᑮ ᐱᒧᐦᑏᔮᐣ᙮ ᓂᐐᓴᑮᔭᐦᑏᐣ ᐆᒪ ᓂᐢᑳᐟ᙮ ᓂᒫᐢᑭᓯᑖᐣ ᐆᒪ!” ᐃᑏᐧᐤ ᒪᐦᑮᓰᐢ᙮

“ᐦᐋᐤ ᒌᐢᑲᐧ ᓂᓰᒼ᙮ ᐊᓯᓂᔭᐠ ᓂᐢᑳᑎᕽ ᓂᑲ ᑕᐦᑯᐱᑖᐘᐠ,” ᐃᑏᐧᐤ ᐐᓴᐦᑮᒑᕽ᙮

“ᐋᐦᐋᐤ,” ᐃᑏᐧᐤ ᒪᐦᑮᓰᐢ᙮

ᐊᓯᓂᔭ ᐅᑎᓃᐤ ᐐᓴᐦᑮᒑᕽ, ᐄ ᑕᐦᑯᐱᑖᐟ ᐅᐢᑳᑎᕽ᙮

“ᐦᐋᐤ, ᓂᓰᒼ, ᐃᑲᐧ!”

ᐃᑲᐧ ᓯᐲᐧᐸᐦᑖᐘᐠ᙮ ᓇᑲᒥᐸᐦᐄᐤ ᒪᐦᑮᓰᓴ ᐐᓴᐦᑮᒑᕽ᙮

“ᐦᐄ, ᐋᑕ ᒫᓇ ᒦᐦᑲᐃᐧᑮᐤ ᐊᐊᐧ ᒪᐦᑮᓰᐢ ᒫᑲ ᑭᔮᐱᐨ ᓂᓇᑲᒋᐸᐦᐋᐤ ᐋᑕ ᐄ ᑕᐦᑯᐱᑕᑳᐧᐤ ᐊᓯᓂᔭᐠ ᓂᐢᑳᑎᕽ! ᒦᐧᐢᑕᐢ ᓂᒋ ᐋᑎᐦᐟ ᓂᑲ ᐊᓴᒫᐤ ᓰᓰᐸ ᐃᑲᐧ ᓂᐢᑲ ᐃᐢᐲ ᑕᑯᐸᐦᑖᒋ,” ᐃᑏᐧᐤ ᐄᐧᓴᐦᑮᒑᕽ᙮

ᒪᔭᐤ ᐄ ᐊᐊᐧᓰᐄᐧᔭᐟ ᐄᐧᓴᐦᑮᒑᐦᑲᐧ ᑮᐄᐧᐸᔭᐤ ᐊᐊᐧ ᒪᐦᑮᓰᐢ᙮ ᓇᒨᔭ ᐄᓴ ᑮ ᐅᐦᒋ ᐄᐧᓴᑮᔭᐦᑕᑦ ᐅᐢᑳᐟ᙮ ᐆᑕ ᐆᒪ ᑳ ᐱᑭᐦᑏᔭᐠ ᐄ ᐃᐢᐸᐦᑖᐟ᙮ ᐃᐢᐲ ᑳ ᑕᑯᐦᑏᐟ ᓂᐢᑲ ᐃᑲᐧ ᓰᓰᐸ ᑳ ᐋᐧᐸᒫᐟ ᐄ ᑮᓯᓱᔭᐟ᙮ ᐅᑎᓅᐤ ᐃᑲᐧ ᐊᑎ ᒧᐄᐧᐤ᙮ ᐄᐧᓴᐦᑮᒑᐦᑲᐧ ᐄ ᑭᒧᑕᒪᐋᐧᐟ᙮ ᑭᑕᒦᐧᐤ ᑲᐦᑭᔭᐤ᙮ ᐅᓯᑎᔭᐊᐧ ᐳᑯ ᐆᐦᐅ ᓂᐢᑲ ᐃᑲᐧ ᓰᓰᐸ ᑳᐃᐧ ᐃᐢᑯᑏᕽ ᐊᐢᑖᐤ, ᑖᐱᐢᑰᐨ ᐄ ᓵᑭᓂᓯᑏᓯᓈᐟ ᓰᓰᐸ ᐃᑲᐧ ᓂᐢᑲ᙮

“ᑕ ᐋᐧᐸᐦᑕᕽ ᐄᐧᓴᐦᑮᒑᕽ,” ᐄ ᐃᑏᔭᐦᑕᕽ᙮ ᐃᑯᓯ ᑕᐸᓰᐤ᙮ “ᓂᑲ ᑭᓱᐋᐧᐦᐋᐤ,” ᐄ ᐃᑏᔭᒫᐟ ᐄᐧᓴᐦᑮᒑᐦᑲᐧ᙮

ᐃᑲᐧ ᐃᐢᐲ ᐄᐧᓴᐦᑮᒑᕽ ᑳ ᑕᑯᐸᐦᑖᐟ ᒥᐢᑕᐦᐃ ᑮ ᐊᐲᐧᓯᐤ ᐊᔭᐢᐠ ᒥᐢᑕᐦᐃ ᐄ ᑮ ᐱᒥᐹᐦᑖᐟ᙮

“ᐦᐄ, ᐋᐢᑏᐲᐧᓯᔮᓂ ᓂᑲ ᒦᒋᓱᐣ,” ᐄ ᐃᑏᔭᐦᑕᕽ, “ᐋᑎᐦᐟ ᓂᒋ ᓰᓰᐸ ᐃᑲᐧ ᓂᐢᑲ ᓂᑲ ᐊᓴᒫᐤ ᓂᓰᒥᐢ,” ᐃᑏᐤ ᒪᐦᑮᓰᓴ, “ᐃᐢᐲ ᑕᑯᐸᐦᑖᒋ,” ᐃᑏᔭᐦᑕᑦ᙮

ᓇᒨᔭ ᑭᐢᑮᔭᐦᑕᑦ ᓵᓴᐩ ᐄᓴ ᐄ ᑮ ᑭᑕᒫᐧᔭᐟ ᐅᓰᓰᐱᒪ ᐃᑲᐧ ᐅᓂᐢᑭᒪ᙮ ᐃᑯᓯ ᐃᑳᐧᓂ ᐅᑎᓇᑦ ᐆᒪ ᐅᓯᑎᔭᐤ ᓂᐢᑲ᙮ ᓇᒪ ᑮᑲᐧᐩ ᓂᐢᑲ!

“ᐦᐄ ᐦᐄ ᐦᐄ, ᓂᑐᓵᒥᐦᑲᓵᐧᐤ!” ᐃᑏᐧᐤ᙮

ᐲᔭᐢᐠ ᑲᐦᑭᔭᐤ ᓰᓰᐸ ᐃᑲᐧ ᓂᐢᑲ ᑲᑮᐧ ᐅᑎᓅᐤ᙮ ᒫᑲ ᑲᐦᑭᔭᐤ ᓇᒪ ᑮᑲᐧᐩ, ᐅᓯᑎᔭᐊᐧ ᐳᑯ᙮

“ᐦᐄ ᐦᐄ ᐦᐄ, ᒫᑲ ᒦᓇ ᐄᒥᑳᓂ ᐄ ᐊᐧᐃᐧᔭᓯᐦᐃᐟ ᒪᐦᑮᓲᐢ᙮ ᐄᐧᔮ ᐄᑐᑮ ᑳ ᑭᑕᒫᐧᐟ ᓂᓲᓲᐱᒪ ᐃᑲᐧ ᓂᓂᐢᑭᒪ! ᐃᑯᓯ ᐄᒥᑳᓂ ᑳ ᓅᐦᑏᐦᑲᑏᔮᐣ!” ᐃᑏᐧᐤ᙮

16
ᐄᐧᓴᐦᑮᒑᕽ ᐃᑲᐧ ᐅᑯᐢᑯᐦᐅᐄᐧᓴᐠ

ᐆᒪ ᐋᒐᖫᐦᑮᐃᐧᐣ ᑭᑭᐢᑭᓇᐧᐦᐊᒫᑯᓇᐤ: ᓈᑲᑏᖬᐦᑕ ᑭᓃᐦᐃᖬᐃᐧ ᐄᐧᐦᖪᐃᐧᐣ᙮

ᐱᖬᑳᐧᐤ ᐄᓴ ᐄᐧᓴᐦᑮᒑᕽ ᑮ ᐸᐱᒍᐦᑏᐤ᙮ ᑮᑕᐦᑕᐄᐧ ᐄᓴ ᐋᐧᐸᒦᐤ ᐱᖩᓯᓴ᙮

“ᐦᐅ! ᓂᓰᒥᑎᐠ!” ᐃᑏᐤ ᐄᓴ᙮ ᑲᓇᐋᐧᐸᒥᑯᐤ ᐆᐦᐅ ᐱᖩᓯᓴ᙮

“ᓂᓰᒥᑎᐠ, ᐱᖩᓯᓴᐠ, ᑖᓂᓯ ᑳ ᐃᑎᑲᐃᐧᖩᐠ?”

“ᓵᓴᐩ ᑭᐄᐧᐦᖬᓈᐣ, ᐱᖩᓯᓴᐠ, ᑳ ᐃᑏᐧᔭᐣ ᐃᑯᓯ ᑳ ᐃᑎᑲᐃᐧᔮᕽ᙮”

“ᓇᒪ! ᑲᐦᑭᖬᐤ ᐊᐃᐧᔭᐠ ᐊᐊᐧᓯᒦᐢ ᐄᐧᐦᖭᐤ᙮ ᑖᐱᐢᑰᐨ ᓃᖬ: ᐄᐧᓴᐦᑮᒑᕽ ᓂᑎᓯᖨᐦᑳᓱᐣ ᒫᑲ ᐅᐢᑏᓯᒫᐤ ᒦᓇ ᓂᑎᑎᑲᐃᐧᐣ᙮ ᐦᐋᐤ, ᑖᓂᓯ ᑮᖬᐋᐧᐤ ᑳ ᐃᑎᑲᐃᐧᖩᐠ᙮”

“ᓇᒨᖬ ᓂᑲᑮ ᐚ"ᑏᓈᐣ᙮ ᓂᓃᑭ"ᐃᑯᓈᓇᐠ ᐆᑯ ᓂᑮ ᐚ"ᑕᒫᑯᓈᓇᐠ ᐄᑳ ᑕ ᐐ"ᑕᒫᕽ ᑯᑕᐠ ᓂᐐ"ᖧᐃᐧᓂᓈᐣ ᐅᑯᐢᑯ"ᐅᐐᓴᐠ ᐄ ᐃᑎᑲᐃᐧᔮᕽ᙮”

“ᐅᑯᐢᑯ"ᐅᐐᓴᐠ! "ᐊ!” ᑳ ᐃᓯ ᐸ"ᐱ"ᐋᐧᐟ ᐄᓴ!

“ᐄᓴᐩ, ᐅᑯᐢᑯ"ᐅᐐᓴᐠ!”

“ᓂᑕᑭᓯᐩ, ᐅᑯᐢᑯ"ᐅᐐᓴᐠ,” ᐃᑏᐧᐤ ᐄᓴ ᐄ ᐊᑎ ᒦᓵᑖᐟ, ᐃᑲᐧ ᐊᓂ"ᐃ ᑳ ᐸᑕ"ᐋᐧᐟ, ᐅᑎᓃᐤ ᐄ ᐊᑎ ᑭᒥᓵ"ᐋᐧᑮᐟ!

“ᐅᑯᐢᑯ"ᐅᐐᓴᐠ! ᐅᓵᑦ ᑭᑕᐱᔩᓯᓯᓈᐋᐧᐤ ᑕ ᑯᐢᑯ"ᐅᐐᔩᐠ,” ᐃᑏᐧᐤ ᐄ ᐊᑎ ᓯᐲᐧ"ᑏᐟ᙮

ᐅᓃᑭ"ᐃᑯᒫᐊᐧᐠ ᑯᐢᑳᐧᐱᓯᓇᐧᐠ ᐃᐢᐲ ᑳ ᐲ ᑮᐄᐧᒥᐠ᙮

“ᐊᐄᐧᓇ ᐊᐊᐧ ᑳ ᐃᒎᑕᕽ! ᐊᐧ"ᐋᐧ! ᑲᐧᔭᐢᐠ ᑭᐄᐧ"ᒌᑭᓯᓈᐋᐧᐤ! ᐄᓴᐩ!” ᐃᑏᐧᐊᐧᐠ ᐄᓴ᙮

“ᐄᐧᓴ"ᑮᒫᕽ ᐊᓇ,” ᑳ ᐃᓯ ᒫᒍᐟ ᐄᓴ ᐱᔭᐠ ᐱᖩᓯᐢ᙮ “ᐄ ᐸ"ᑲᒋᒥᑯᔮᕽ ᑕ ᐐ"ᑕᒫᕽ ᑯᑕᐠ ᑭᐐ"ᖧᐃᐧᓂᓇᐤ᙮ ᒪᔭᐤ ᐅᑯᐢᑯ"ᐅᐐᓴᐠ ᐄ ᐃᑖᔮᕽ ᑳ ᒦᓵᑎᑯᔮᕽ!”

“"ᐊᐤ ᒌᐢᑲᐧ ᐄᐧᓴ"ᑮᒫᕽ!” ᐃᑏᐧᐤ ᐊᐊᐧ ᓅᔩ ᐱᖩᐤ᙮ ᓂᑐᒦᐤ ᐄᓴ ᑲ"ᑭᖬᐤ ᐅᒎᑏᒪ ᑕᒫᒪᐊᐧᐱᒥᐠ᙮ ᑮ ᓂᑕᐃᐧ ᐲ"ᐅᐊᐧᐠ ᐱᖩᐊᐧᐠ ᐋᐧᓴᑳᑦ ᔩᐲᕽ ᐃᑕ ᒫᓇ ᐄᐧᓴ"ᑮᒫ"ᑲᐧ ᑳ ᐋᐧᓯᐊᐧᑳᒦᑲᐧᐢᑯ"ᑎᖩᐟ᙮

ᑮᑕ"ᑕᐄᐧ ᑕᑯ"ᑏᐤ ᐊᐊᐧ ᓈᐲᐤ, ᑭᔮᐱ- ᐄ ᐸ"ᐱ"ᐋᐧᐟ ᐱᖩᓯᓴ᙮

“ᐅᑯᐢᑯ"ᐅᐐᓴᐠ! "ᐊ! ᐄᓴᐩ!” ᐋᐧᓴᑳᑦ ᔩᐲᕽ ᑕᑯ"ᑏᐤ᙮

“"ᐊ! ᒪ"ᑎ ᓂᑲ ᐋᐧᓯᐊᐧᑳᒦᑲᐧᐢᑯ"ᑎᐣ!”

ᓃᑳᐣ ᐄᓴ ᐊᓯᐦᑏᐤ ᐃᑲᐧ ᐃᑯᑏ ᐅᐦᒋ ᐲᒋᐸᐦᑖᐤ᙮ ᒥᐧᐦᒋ ᓰᐲᕽ ᐄ ᑕᑯᐸᐦᑖᐟ ᑳ ᓇᑮᐟ᙮

“ᑮᑳ-,” ᐃᑏᐧᐤ ᐄᓴ; ᑳ ᐋᐧᐸᒫᐟ ᐱᔭᐠ ᐱᔩᓯᓴ ᐄ ᐅᐦᐸᐦᐅᔩᐟ ᓴᑳᕽ ᐅᐦᒋ᙮ ᑮᐦᑖᐧᑦ ᐊᓯᐦᑏᐤ ᐃᑲᐧ ᒦᓇ ᐊᑎ ᓯᐲᐧᐸᐦᑖᐤ᙮

“ᑮᑳ-!” ᐃᑏᐧᐤ, ᐃᑲᐧ ᒦᓇ ᐄ ᓇᑮᐟ᙮ ᐋᐧᐸᒦᐤ ᓃᓱ ᐱᔩᓯᓴ ᐄ ᐅᐦᐸᐦᐅᔩᐟ ᓴᑳᕽ ᐅᐦᒋ᙮ ᑮᐦᑖᐧᑦ ᐊᓯᐦᑏᐤ, ᓇᐊᐧᐨ ᐃᑲᐧ ᐋᐧᐦᔭᐄᐧᐢ ᐅᐦᒋ ᐊᑎ ᓯᐲᐧᐸᐦᑖᐤ᙮

“ᑮᑳ-!” ᐃᑏᐧᐤ, ᐄ ᓇᑮᐟ ᐃᑲᐧ ᒦᓇ᙮ ᓂᐢᑐ ᐱᔩᓯᓴ ᐋᐧᐸᒦᐤ ᐄ ᐅᐦᐸᐦᐅᔩᐟ ᓴᑳᕽ ᐅᐦᒋ᙮ ᑮᐦᑖᐧᑦ ᐊᓯᐦᑏᐤ, ᓇᐊᐧᐨ ᐋᐧᐦᔭᐄᐧᐢ ᐅᐦᒋ ᐊᑎ ᓯᐲᐧᐸᐦᑖᐤ᙮ ᒥᐧᐦᒋ ᐄ ᐊᑎ ᑳᐧᐢᑯᐦᑎᐟ ᑳ ᓴᐢᒋ ᐅᐦᐸᐦᐅᒋᐠ ᒥᐦᒌᐟ ᐱᔩᐊᐧᐠ! ᐊᐧᐦᐋᐧ! ᑲᐧᔭᐢᐠ, ᑯᐢᑯᐃᐧᔩᐠ! ᒥᑐᓂ ᐄ ᐊᑎ ᐸᑲᐢᑕᐄᐧᓯᕽ ᓰᐲᕽ᙮

“ᐅᑯᐢᑯᐦᐅᐄᐧᓴᐠ, ᐅᑯᐢᑯᐦᐅᐄᐧᓴᐠ,” ᑳ ᐃᓯ ᐸᐦᐱᐦᐃᑯᐟ ᐄᓴ ᐊᓂᐦᐃ ᐅᑯᐢᑯᐦᐅᐄᐧᓴ!

ᐃᑳᐧᓂ ᐄ ᐃᐢᑳᐧᐦᒋᒥᐦᒋᐠ ᐅᑯᐢᑯᐦᐅᐄᐧᓴᐠ᙮

17
ᐑᓴᐦᑮᒑᕽ ᐃᑲᐧ ᑳ ᒪᓯᓈᓱᒋᐠ ᐊᐧᐢᑲᐧᔭᐠ

ᐆᒪ ᐋᒐᔫᐦᑮᐃᐧᐣ ᑭᑭᐢᑭᓇᐧᐦᐊᒫᑯᓇᐤ: ᓈᑲᑏᔨᐦᑕ ᑮᑳᐧᐩ ᑳ ᐸᑯᓰᔨᒧᔭᐣ᙮

ᓵᓴᐩ ᒦᓇ ᐑᓴᐦᑮᒑᕽ ᐸᐱᒧᐦᑏᐤ᙮ ᑮᑕᐦᑕᐑ ᐅᑎᐦᑕᐑᐤ ᒪᐢᑲᐧ ᐄ ᒨᒥᓃᔨᐟ ᐑᓴᑮᒥᓇ᙮ ᑳᓲᐸᔨᐦᐅᐤ ᓴᑳᓯᕽ ᐑᓴᐦᑮᒑᕽ ᐄ ᒫᒥᑐᓃᔨᐦᑕᕽ ᑖᓂᓯ ᐆᒪ ᑕᑮ ᐃᓯ ᓂᐸᐦᐋᐟ ᐆᐦᐅ ᐑᔭ ᒫᑲ ᒦᓇ ᐄ ᓅᐦᑏᐦᑲᑏᐟ᙮ ᑭᐢᑮᔨᐦᑕᑦ ᑖᓂᓯ ᑭᑕ ᐃᑑᑕᕽ!

ᐅᑎᓇᑦ ᐋᑎᐦᐟ ᐑᓴᑮᒥᓇ ᐃᑲᐧ ᐊᑎ ᐱᒧᐦᑏᐤ ᐃᑏ ᐃᓯ ᑳ ᐊᔮᔨᐟ ᐊᓂᐦᐃ ᒪᐢᑲᐧ᙮ ᐹᐦ ᐹᐢᑭᒌᓇᑦ ᐑᓴᑮᒥᓇ ᐅᐢᑮᓯᑯᕽ᙮ ᑕᐦᑖᐧᐤ ᑳ ᐹᐢᑭᒌᓇᕽ ᐑᓴᑮᒥᓇ ᐅᐢᑮᓯᑯᕽ ᒫᐦ ᒥᓯ ᑏᐲᐧ ᐸᐦᐱᐤ! ᐲᔨᐢᐠ ᐱᓯᐢᑳᐸᒥᐠ ᒪᐢᑲᐧ᙮

“ᑖᓂᓯ ᐆᒪ ᐄ ᐃᑕᐦᑲᒥᑭᓯᔭᐣ ᓂᐢᑏᓰ?” ᐃᓯ ᑲᑮᐧᒋᒥᐠ ᒪᐢᑲᐧ᙮

“ᐋᐦ, ᓂᓰᒦ! ᒌᐢᐟ! ᑭᐦᒋ ᑮᑳᐧᐩ ᐆᒪ᙮ ᑮᐢᐱᐣ ᐹᐢᑭᒌᓇᒪᓂ ᐆᐦᐅ ᐑᓴᑮᒥᓇ ᑭᐢᑮᓯᑯᕽ ᑭᑲ ᑲᑳᐧᑕᑭ ᒌᐦᑮᔨᐦᑏᐣ᙮ ᒥᑐᓂ ᐄ ᑕᑲᐦᑭᐢᑳᑯᔭᐣ

ᐃᔭᑯᐦᒋ ᑳ ᒥᓯ ᐸᐦᐱᔮᐣ ᑕᐦᑖᐧᐤ ᑳ ᐹᐢᑭᒦᓇᒫᐣ ᐆᐦᐅ ᓂᐢᑮᓯᑯᕽ᙮ ᒋᑰᒋ, ᑯᒋᐦᑖ!”

ᒪᐢᑲᐧ ᐅᑎᓇᑦ ᐋᐧᓴᑮᒥᓇ, ᓃᓱ ᐅᒋᐦᒋᔭ ᐄ ᐋᐸᒋᐦᑖᐟ᙮ ᐹᐢᑭᒦᓇᑦ ᐅᐢᑮᓯᑯᕽ᙮ ᐊᐧᐦᐋᐧ! ᐋᐧᓴᑭᐢᑳᑯᐤ᙮ ᒥᓯᐄᐧᑕ ᐃᐢᐸᐦᑖᐤ ᐄ ᒫᐦ ᒪᐃᐧᒧᐟ! ᓇᒨᔭ ᑮ ᐋᐧᐱᐤ᙮

“ᐊᔭᔮ! ᐊᔭᔮ!”

“ᐦᐋ ᓂᓰᑦ! ᐅᓵᑦ ᒥᐢᑕᐦᐃ ᑭᑮ ᐋᐸᒋᐦᑖᐣ! ᐄᐦ, ᓂᓰᒥᐢ, ᐆᑕ ᒥᐢᑎᑯᕽ ᐊᐢᑖ ᑭᐢᑎᑳᐧᐣ᙮ ᑭᑲ ᓇᓈᑕᐃᐧᐦᐃᑎᐣ!” ᐃᑏᐧᐤ ᐋᐧᓴᐦᑮᒫᕽ᙮

ᐃᑳᐧᓂ ᒥᐢᑎᑯᕽ ᐊᐢᑖᐤ ᐅᐢᑎᑳᐧᐣ ᐊᐊᐧ ᒪᐢᑲᐧ᙮ ᐋᐧᓴᐦᑮᒫᕽ ᐅᑎᓃᐤ ᐊᓯᓂᔭ ᐃᑲᐧ ᐸᑲᒥᐢᑎᑳᐧᓃᐦᐄᐤ ᒪᐢᑲᐧ, ᐄ ᓂᐸᐦᐋᐧᐟ᙮

ᐊᑎ ᑯᑕᐄᐧᐤ, ᐄ ᐄᐧ ᐱᒥᓇᐊᐧᓱᐟ, ᐄ ᐄᐧ ᒧᐋᐧᐟ ᐊᓂᐦᐃ ᒪᐢᑲᐧ᙮ ᒥᑐᓂ ᒥᓯ ᐴᓇᑦ, ᐄ ᒥᓯᐄᐧᐢᑲᓵᐧᐟ ᒪᐢᑲᐧ᙮ ᐃᐢᐲ ᑳ ᑮᓯᑏᐳᐟ ᓇᒨᔭ ᐄᓴ ᐅᓵᑦ ᑮ ᓄᐦᑏᐦᑲᑏᐤ᙮ ᓄᐦᑏ ᑭᑕᒦᐧᐤ ᐊᓂᐦᐃ ᒪᐢᑲᐧ ᒫᑲ ᓃᑳᐣ ᑭᑕ ᓄᐦᑏᐦᑲᑏᐟ ᒪᐧᔩ ᒧᐋᐧᒋ ᐃᔭᑯᓂ᙮

ᐋᐧᐸᒦᐤ ᐊᐧᐢᑲᐧᔭ ᐄ ᓃᓱᑳᐸᐃᐧᔭᐟ᙮ ᑖᐋᐧᔭᕽ ᐃᑯᑕ ᓂᑕᐃᐧ ᐱᒥᓯᐣ᙮

“ᐋᐢᑕᒥᐠ ᓂᓰᒥᑎᐠ! ᓇᐊᐧᐨ ᑭᓯᐋᐧᐠ ᐲ ᐃᓯᑳᐸᐃᐧᐠ᙮ ᐲ ᒥᒋᒥᓂᐠ,” ᐃᑏᐤ ᐊᓂᐦᐃ ᐊᐧᐢᑲᐧᔭ᙮ “ᑳᐃᐧᔭ ᐸᑭᑎᓂᐦᑮᐠ᙮ ᐹᑎᒫ ᑲᑳᐧᑕᑭ ᓄᐦᑏᐦᑲᑏᔭᓂ ᐃᑯᐢᐲ ᐳᑯ ᐸᑭᑎᓂᐦᑮᐠ᙮”

ᑖᐲᐧ ᒫᓂ ᒫᑲ ᑭᓯᐋᐧᐠ ᓇᐊᐧᐨ ᐄᐧᒋ ᑲᐸᐄᐧᐢᑖᑐᐋᐧᐠ ᐆᑯ ᐊᐧᐢᑲᐧᔭᐠ᙮ ᒥᒋᒧᐢᑲᐄᐧᐊᐧᐠ ᐋᐧᓴᐦᑮᒫᐦᑲᐧ᙮ ᑮᑕᐦᑕᐄᐧ ᑳ ᑏᐧᐦᐅᐟ ᐄᐧᐢᑲᒫᓂᐢ, ᐊᐧᑎᐦᑲᐧᓂᕽ ᐄ ᐊᔭᐱᐟ᙮ ᑳ ᐱᓯᐢᑲᐸᒫᐟ ᐋᐧᓴᐦᑮᒫᕽ᙮

“ᑲᑮᐸᑎᐢ ᐱᔭᓰᐢ!” ᐃᑏᐧᐤ ᐋᐧᓴᐦᑮᒫᕽ᙮ “ᑳᐃᐧᔭ ᐄᐧᐦᑕᒪᐃᐧᐠ ᐱᓯᓯᑭᐊᐧᐠ ᐄ ᑮᓯᑏᐳᔮᐣ ᐆᑕ᙮”

ᓇᒨᖭ ᐊᐦᐴ ᐃᑯᓯ ᑮ ᐅᐦᒋ ᐃᑏᖬᐦᑕᑦ ᑕ ᐃᑑᑕᕽ ᐊᐊᐧ ᐄᐧᐢᑲᒫᓂᐢ᙮ ᑖᐲᐧ ᐳᑳᓂ ᐃᑯᑕ ᐅᐦᒋ ᐅᐦᐸᐦᐅᐤ ᐄ ᓂᑕᐃᐧ ᐄᐧᐦᑕᒪᐊᐧᐟ ᐄᐧᒋ ᐱᓯᐢᑭᐊᐧ ᑭᑕ ᐲ ᒦᒋᓱᖬᐟ᙮ ᒥᐦᒌᐟ ᐱᓯᐢᑭᐊᐧᐠ ᐲ ᒦᒋᓱᐊᐧᐠ᙮ ᐲᖬᐢᐠ ᑭᑕᒦᐧᐊᐧᐠ ᐊᓂᐦᐃ ᒪᐢᑲᐧ, ᐅᐢᑲᓇ ᐳᑯ ᐄ ᐃᐢᑲᐧᐢᑕᐦᑳᐧᐤ᙮

ᐃᑲᐧ ᐊᐊᐧ ᐄᐧᓴᐦᑮᒫᕽ ᒥᑐᓂ ᓃᐢᑐᓯᐤ ᐅᓵᑦ ᒥᐢᑕᐦᐃ ᐄ ᑮ ᑲᑮᐧ ᑕᐦᒋᐸᖬᐦᐅᐟ ᒫᑲ ᓇᒫᐧᐨ ᑮ ᐅᐦᒋ ᑲᐢᑭᐦᑖᐤ᙮ ᑲᐧᔭᐢᐠ ᓲᐦᑭ ᑮ ᒥᒋᒥᓂᐠ ᐊᓂᐦᐃ ᐊᐧᐢᑲᐧᔭ᙮ ᐲᖬᐢᐠ ᐊᑎ ᓂᐹᐤ ᐃᖬᑯᕽ ᐄ ᑮ ᓃᐢᑐᓯᐟ᙮ ᒥᑐᓂ ᐄᑐᑮ ᑭᐣᐄᐧᐢᐠ ᑮ ᓂᐹᐤ᙮

ᐃᐢᐲ ᑳ ᑯᐢᑯᐸᖬᐟ ᑮ ᑕᐦᒋᐸᖬᐦᐅᐤ ᐃᑯᑕ ᐅᐦᒋ᙮ ᑮ ᑭᓱᐋᐧᐦᐃᑯᐤ ᐊᓂᐦᐃ ᐊᐧᐢᑲᐧᔭ᙮ ᓈᑕᑦ ᓃᐱᓯᔭ ᐄ ᐄᐧ ᐸᓴᐢᑏᐦᐋᐧᐟ ᐊᐧᐢᑲᐧᔭ᙮

ᑭᐣᐄᐧᐢᐠ ᑮ ᐸᓴᐢᑏᐦᐄᐧᐤ ᐊᓂᐦᐃ ᐊᐧᐢᑲᐧᔭ᙮ ᐲᖬᐢᐠ ᐄ ᐊᑎ ᒫᐦ ᒪᓯᓈᓱᖬᐟ᙮ ᐱᔭᑲᐧᐣ ᐃᑯᓯ ᐃᓯ ᒪᓯᓈᓱᐊᐧᐠ ᐊᐧᐢᑲᐧᔭᐠ ᐊᓄᐦᐨ᙮

18
ᐑᓴᐦᑮᒫᕽ ᐃᑿ ᐱᒋᑮᐢᑭᓰᓴ

ᐆᒪ ᐋᒪᔫᐦᑮᐃᐧᐣ ᑭᑭᐢᑭᓈᐦᐊᒫᑯᓇᐤ: ᑳᐃᐧᔭ ᒦᑕᐚᑮ ᑭᐦᒋ ᐃᓲᐦᒋᑮᐃᐧᐣ᙮

ᐱᔭᒀᐤ ᐄᓴ ᐑᓴᐦᑮᒫᕽ ᑮ ᐸᐱᒎᐦᑏᐤ᙮ ᑮᑕᐦᑕᐑ ᐄᓴ ᑳ ᐚᐸᒫᐟ ᐱᒋᑮᐢᑭᓰᓴ ᐄ ᒪᑘ ᒨᒋᑭᐦᑖᔩᐟ᙮ ᐄ ᐅᑎᓇᒥᔩᐟ ᒫᓇ ᐅᐢᑮᓯᑯᔩᐘ ᐃᑿ ᒫᓇ ᐄ ᐅᐦᐱᐚᐱᓇᒥᔩᐟ᙮ ᐃᑿ ᒫᓇ ᑳᐍ ᐅᐢᑮᓯᑯᔩᕽ ᐄ ᐲ ᐸᐦᑭᐦᑎᓂᔩᑭ᙮ ᒥᑐᓂ ᒫᓇ ᐄ ᑖᐦ ᑏᐲ ᐸᐦᐱᔩᐟ ᑕᐦᑖᐤ ᐃᑯᓯ ᑳ ᐃᐢᐸᔩᔩᐠ᙮ ᐦᐋᐤ, ᒪᒫᐦᑖᐏᓇᐑᐤ ᐆᐦᐅ᙮

"ᑖᐲ ᑭᒪᒫᐦᑖᐏᓯᓈᐚᐤ," ᐃᑏᐤ ᐑᓴᐦᑮᒫᕽ᙮ "ᒪᐦᑎ ᐃᔭᑯ ᑮᑿᐩ ᑭᐢᑭᓈᐦᐊᒪᐍᐠ᙮"

"ᐊᐘᐢ ᐑᓴᐦᑮᒫᕽ! ᑭᐦᒋ ᐃᓲᐦᒋᑮᐍᐣ ᐆᒪ! ᓇᒨᔭ ᑮᔭ ᐸᑿᓂᑕ ᑭᑲᑮ ᑭᐢᑭᓈᐦᐊᒫᑎᓈᐣ!" ᐃᑎᐠ᙮

ᐊᑎ ᓰᐲᐦᑏᐤ ᐑᓴᐦᑮᒫᕽ, ᓇᐘᐨ ᐳᑯ ᐄ ᑭᓱᐚᓯᐟ᙮ ᐃᒀᓂ ᓂᑕᐏ ᐋᐑᓰᐦᐃᓱᐤ᙮ ᑖᐱᐢᑰᐨ ᑭᓲᑎᓂᐤ ᐄ ᐃᓲᐦᐃᓱᐟ᙮ ᑮᐦᑗᐨ ᐃᑯᑕ

ᐲᒋ ᐱᒧᐦᑏᐤ ᐃᑕ ᑳ ᒦᑕᐑᔦᐟ ᐱᒋᑮᐢᑭᓰᓴ᙮ ᐹᐢᑲᐨ ᐄ ᐚᑯᐦᑏᐟ ᐆᒪ, ᑖᐱᐢᑰᐨ ᑭᓰᑎᓂᐤ᙮ ᐃᑿ ᒪᐏᒧᐤ᙮

“ᐊᔭᔮ! ᓂᐢᑎᒁᐣ!” ᐄ ᐃᑚᐟ᙮ ᐱᓯᐢᑳᐸᒥᐠ ᐊᓂᐦᐃ ᐱᒋᑮᐢᑭᓰᓴ, ᑭᑎᒫᑭᓈᑯᐤ ᐆᐦᐅ᙮

“ᐦᐋᐤ, ᒌᐢᑿ ᓂᒧᓰᐢ!” ᐃᑎᐠ᙮ “ᑭᑲ ᑭᐢᑭᓌᐦᐊᒫᑎᓈᐣ ᐆᒪ ᑭᑕ ᓇᓈᑕᐏᐦᐃᑯᔭᐣ᙮ ᑮᐢᐱᐣ ᐅᑎᓇᒪᓂ ᑭᐢᑮᓯᑿ ᐃᑿ ᐃᐢᐱᒥᕽ ᐃᓯ ᐑᐱᓇᒪᓂ ᐃᑿ ᑳᐏ ᑕ ᐸᐦᑭᐦᑎᐦᑭ ᑭᐢᑮᓯᑯᕽ ᓇᒨᔭ ᐊᐚᓯᒦ ᑭᑲ ᑏᐴᐢᑎᒁᓈᐣ,” ᐃᑎᐠ᙮

“ᐦᐋᐤ, ᒪᐦᑎ ᑭᐢᑭᓌᐦᐊᒪᐏᐣ ᓅᓯᓯᐢ,” ᐃᑚᐤ ᐑᓴᐦᑮᒑᕽ᙮

ᐊᐩ, ᐃᑯᓯ ᑳ ᐃᓯ ᑭᐢᑭᓌᐦᐊᒫᑯᐟ᙮ ᐃᐢᐱᒥᕽ ᐄ ᐋᐦᐃᓯ ᐑᐱᓇᕽ ᐅᐢᑮᓯᑿ ᐃᑿ ᒫᓇ ᑳᐏ ᐄ ᐲᐦᑑᑮ ᐸᐦᑭᐦᑎᓂᔦᑭ ᐅᐢᑎᒁᓂᕽ᙮

ᐊᐩ, ᒌᐦᑮᔦᐦᑕᐢ ᐑᓴᐦᑮᒑᕽ᙮

“ᐄᐦ, ᐅᐦᒋᑕᐤ ᐳᑯ ᐃᑯᓯ ᑕ ᐃᑑᑕᒪᐣ ᐃᐢᐲ ᑏᐴᐢᑎᒁᓃᔭᓂ,” ᐃᑚᐤ ᐊᐘ ᐱᔦᓰᐢ᙮ “ᑳᐏᔭ ᒫᑲ ᐸᑿᓂᑕ ᒦᑕᐚᑮ᙮”

“ᐊᐦ, ᓇᒨᔭ ᓈᓂᑕᐤ ᓅᓯᓯᐢ,” ᐃᑚᐤ ᐑᓴᐦᑮᒑᕽ᙮ “ᓇᒨᔭ ᓂᑲ ᒦᑕᐚᑳᐣ ᐃᔭᒁᓂᒪ᙮”

ᐃᑿ ᐃᑯᑕ ᐅᐦᒋ ᐊᑎ ᓯᐼᐦᑏᐤ ᐑᓴᐦᑮᒑᕽ, ᑭᔮᐱᐨ ᐄ ᐚᑯᐦᑏᐟ ᑖᐱᐢᑰᐨ ᑭᓰᑎᓂᐤ᙮ ᐃᑿ ᐚᐦᔦᐤ ᐃᑯᑕ ᐅᐦᒋ ᑳ ᓯᐼᐦᑏᐟ ᑳᐏ ᐑᓴᐦᑮᒑᕽ ᐃᓯᓈᑯᓯᐤ᙮

ᑿᔭᐢᐠ ᑮᑿᐩ ᑭᐦᒋ ᐃᓰᐦᒋᑮᐏᐣ ᐄ ᑮ ᑭᐢᑭᓌᐦᐊᒫᑯᐟ ᐱᔦᓰᓴ᙮ ᐃᐢᐲ ᑳ ᐚᐸᐦᑕᕽ ᓃᐱᓯᔭ, ᑖᐼ ᐳᑳᓂ ᒪᐏᒧᐤ, ᑖᐱᐢᑰᐨ ᐄ ᑏᐴᐢᑎᒁᓃᐟ᙮

“ᐊᔭᔮ! ᓂᐢᑎᒁᐣ! ᓂᑏᐴᐢᑎᒁᓈᐣ!” ᐃᑚᐤ᙮

ᐃᑳᐧᓂ ᐃᑯᑕ ᐅᐢᑮᓯᑲᐧ ᐅᑎᓇᐠ ᐃᐢᐱᒥᕽ ᐄ ᐃᓯ ᐄᐧᐱᓇᕽ᙮ ᑳᐃᐧ ᒫᓇ ᑳ ᐸᐦᑭᐦᑎᓂᔨᑭ ᐅᐢᑎᑳᐧᓂᕽ᙮

“ᐦᐊ ᐦᐊ ᐦᐊ, ᐊᐦ ᑖᐲᐧ ᐃᔭᑯ ᑭᐦᒋ ᐃᓲᐦᒋᑮᐃᐧᐤ ᒪᒫᐦᑖᐊᐧᐤ,” ᐃᑏᐧᐤ᙮ ᐃᑯᓯ ᐄ ᐊᑎ ᓯᐲᐧᐦᑏᐟ᙮

ᐃᑲᐧ ᒥᓇ ᑳ ᐋᐧᐸᐦᑕᕽ ᑯᑕᑲ ᓃᐱᓯᔭ᙮

“ᐊᔭᔮ! ᓂᐢᑎᑳᐧᐤ!” ᑳ ᐃᑏᐧᐟ᙮ ᐃᑲᐧ ᒥᓇ ᐅᑎᓇᐠ ᐅᐢᑮᓯᑲᐧ᙮ ᐃᐢᐱᒥᕽ ᐃᓯ ᐄᐧᐱᓇᐠ᙮ ᑳᐃᐧ ᐅᐢᑎᑳᐧᓂᕽ ᑳ ᐸᐦᑭᐦᑎᓂᔨᑭ᙮ ᐊᑎ ᐸᐱᒧᐦᑏᐤ᙮ ᑲᑳᐧᑕᑭ ᐄ ᒌᐦᑮᔨᐦᑕᕽ ᐆᒪ ᑭᐦᒋ ᐃᓲᐦᒋᑮᐃᐧᐤ ᑳ ᑮ ᑭᐢᑭᓇᐧᐦᐊᒫᐦᐟ᙮

ᐃᑲᐧ ᒥᓇ ᑳ ᐋᐧᐸᐦᑕᕽ ᑯᑕᑲ ᓃᐱᓯᔭ᙮

“ᐊᔭᔮ ᓂᑏᔨᐢᑎᑳᐧᓈᐤ!” ᑳ ᐃᓯ ᒪᐃᐧᒧᐟ᙮

ᐃᑳᐧᓂ ᐃᑯᑕ ᐅᑎᓇᐠ ᐃᑲᐧ ᒥᓇ ᐅᐢᑮᓯᑲᐧ᙮ ᐃᐢᐱᒥᕽ ᐃᓯ ᐄᐧᐱᓇᐠ᙮ ᑳᐃᐧ ᐸᐦᑭᐦᑎᓂᔨᐊᐧ ᐅᐢᑎᑳᐧᓂᕽ᙮

“ᐊᐧᐦᐋᐧ! ᒪᒫᐦᑖᐊᐧᐤ ᐊᓂᒪ ᑮᑲᐧᐩ᙮ ᑖᐲᐧ ᑭᐦᒋ ᑮᑲᐧᐩ!” ᐃᑏᐧᐤ᙮

ᐃᑳᐧᓂ ᐊᑎ ᐸᐱᒧᐦᑏᐤ᙮ ᐃᑲᐧ ᒥᓇ ᑳ ᐋᐧᐸᐦᑕᕽ ᓃᐱᓯᔭ᙮

“ᐊᔭᔮ! ᓂᐢᑎᑳᐧᐤ!” ᑳ ᐃᑏᐧᐟ᙮ ᐃᑳᐧᓂ ᐃᑯᑕ ᐅᐦᒋ ᑳ ᐅᑎᓇᕽ ᐅᐢᑮᓯᑲᐧ᙮ ᐃᐢᐱᒥᕽ ᐃᓯ ᐄᐧᐱᓇᐠ᙮

ᐊᐦ! ᐋᐧᐦ! ᐅᔮᐠ ᐋᐧᐦᔭᐤ ᐃᓯ ᐄᐧᐱᓇᐠ! ᐅᐦᐱᒦ ᐃᑕ ᑳ ᐸᐦᑭᐦᑎᓂᔨᑭ᙮ ᐃᑳᐧᓂ ᐄᑳ ᐄ ᑮ ᐋᐧᐱᐟ᙮

ᓂᑐᓇᐠ ᐊᓂᐦᐃ ᐊᓂᑕ ᐅᐢᑮᓯᑲᐧ, ᐄ ᐸᐹᒥᑖᒋᒧᐟ ᒧᐦᒋᕽ᙮ ᑮᑕᐦᑕᐄᐧ ᒫᓇ ᑳ ᒐᐦᑳᐸᐦᐅᑯᐟ ᐊᐃᐧᔭ᙮

"ᐊᔭᔮ!" ᐃᑏᐧᐤ᙮

ᐊᐩ, ᐃᑲᐧ ᐋᐦᒋ ᐸᑯ ᓂᑐᓇᑦ ᐆᐦᐅ ᐅᐢᑮᓯᑲᐧ ᐃᑯᑕ ᒍᐦᒋᕽ᙮ ᑮᐦᑖᐧᑦ ᑳ ᒐᐦᑳᐸᐦᐅᑯᐟ ᐊᐏᔭ᙮

"ᐊᔭᔮ!" ᐃᓯ ᒪᐏᒧᐤ᙮

ᓂᑐᓇᑦ ᐆᐦᐅ ᐅᐢᑮᓯᑲᐧ᙮

"ᑖᓂᐑᐦᐋ? ᑖᓂᐑᐦᐋ ᓂᐢᑮᓯᑲᐧ?" ᐃᑏᐧᐤ᙮ ᐃᑲᐧ ᒦᓇ ᑮᐦᑖᐧᑦ ᑳ ᒐᐦᑳᐸᐦᐅᑯᐟ ᐊᐏᔭ᙮

"ᐊᔭᔮ!" ᐃᑏᐧᐤ᙮

ᐃᑕ ᑳ ᒐᐦᑳᐸᐦᐅᐦᐟ ᒥᑐᓂ ᐄ ᐊᑎ ᑏᐹᐢᑎᑳᐧᓃᐟ᙮ ᐋᐦ ᑮᑕᐦᑕᐑ ᐸᑯ ᑳ ᐲᐦᑕᐚᐟ ᐆᐦᐅ ᐊᐏᔭ ᐃᑕ ᐄ ᐹᐦᐱᔩᐟ᙮ "ᐦᐄ ᐦᐄ ᐦᐄ ᐦᐄ ᐦᐄ ᐦᐄ!"

ᐃᐩ! ᓂᓯᑐᐦᑕᐑᐤ ᐃᔭᑯᓂ ᐆᐦᐅ! ᒪᐦᑮᓰᐢ ᐄᐢ ᒫᑲ ᒦᓇ ᐄ ᓇᓈᔦᒋᐦᐃᑯᐟ᙮

"ᐊᐦ, ᒦᐢᑲᐧ ᒪᐦᑮᓲᐢ, ᑭᑲ ᑭᐢᑭᓇᐧᐦᐋᒫᑎᐣ," ᐃᑏᐧᐤ᙮ ᐃᑲᐧ ᐃᑯᑕ ᐊᑎ ᐱᒥᑖᒋᒧᐤ᙮ ᒥᐢᑎᑲᐧ ᒥᐢᑲᐑᐤ ᐃᑯᑕ᙮

"ᐊᐑᓇ ᐆᒪ ᑮᔦ?" ᐃᑏᐤ᙮

"ᐘᐢᑲᐧᐩ ᐆᒪ ᓃᔦ," ᐃᑏᐧᐤ ᐊᐘ ᐘᐢᑲᐧᐩ᙮

"ᓇᒨᔦ ᑮᔦ ᑳ ᓂᑕᐑᔨᒥᑖᐣ," ᐃᑏᐧᐤ ᐑᓴᐦᑮᒫᕽ᙮ ᑮᑕᐦᑕᐑ ᑳ ᑖᐏᐢᑎᑳᐧᓃᓯᕽ᙮

"ᐊᐑᓇ ᑮᔦ?" ᐃᑏᐧᐤ᙮

"ᒦᑐᐢ ᐆᒪ ᓃᔭ," ᐃᑏᐧᐤ ᒦᑐᐢ᙮

"ᓇᒨᔭ ᑮᔭ ᑳ ᓂᑕᐄᐧᔨᒥᑖᐣ," ᐃᑏᐧᐤ ᐄᐧᓴᐦᑮᒑᕽ᙮ ᓯᐲᐧᑖᒋᒧᐤ᙮ ᑮᑕᐦᑕᐄᐧ ᑮᐦᑖᐧᐨ ᑳ ᑖᐃᐧᐢᑎᑳᐧᓃᓯᕽ᙮

"ᐊᐄᐧᓇ ᐆᒪ ᑮᔭ?" ᐃᑏᐧᐤ ᐄᐧᓴᐦᑮᒑᕽ᙮

"ᒥᓇᐦᐃᐠ ᐆᒪ ᓃᔭ," ᐃᑏᐧᐤ ᒥᓇᐦᐃᐠ᙮

"ᐦᐋᐧᐤ ᑮᔭ ᑳ ᓂᑕᐄᐧᔨᒥᑖᐣ," ᐃᑏᐧᐤ ᐄᐧᓴᐦᑮᒑᕽ᙮ "ᐱᑭᐤ ᓂᑲ ᐅᑎᓈᐤ ᐃᑯᑕ ᐅᐦᒋ᙮"

ᐃᑯᑕ ᐱᑭᐊᐧ ᐅᑎᓃᐤ ᒥᓇᐦᐃᑯᕽ ᐅᐦᒋ᙮ ᐃᑲᐧ ᒫᐦ ᒫᑲᐧᒦᐤ ᐃᑲᐧ ᐱᑎᑯᓃᐤ᙮ ᐋᐧᐃᐧᔨᔭᐢ ᐄᓴ ᐄ ᐅᓰᐦᑖᐟ᙮ ᐃᐢᐲ ᑳ ᑮᓯᐦᑖᐟ ᐄ ᐋᐧᐢᑳ ᐱᑎᑳᐧᔨᐠ ᑮᑲᐧᐩ ᐅᐢᑎᑳᐧᓂᕽ ᐊᐢᑖᐤ᙮ ᑯᑕᑲ ᐄᓴ ᐅᐢᑮᓯᑲᐧ ᐄ ᐅᓰᐦᑕᒫᓱᐟ᙮ ᑮᐦᑖᐧᐨ ᐋᐧᐱᐤ᙮

"ᐊᐦ, ᑖᓂᐋᐧ ᐊᓇ ᒪᐦᑮᓰᐢ," ᑳ ᐃᑏᐧᐟ᙮

ᐸᐱᒧᐦᑏᐤ, ᐄ ᓂᑐᓇᐋᐧᐟ ᐅᓰᒥᓴ ᒪᐦᑮᓰᓴ᙮ ᐃᐩ, ᐋᐧᐸᒦᐤ ᐃᑯᑏ ᐄ ᒪᑏᐧ ᓂᐹᔨᐟ᙮

"ᑖᓂᓯ ᒫᑲ ᐆᒪ ᑳᐃᐧ ᑕ ᐃᓯ ᑭᐢᑭᓇᐦᐊᒪᐊᐧᐠ ᐊᐊᐧ? ᑭᑕ ᑮ ᓂᐸᐦᐊᐠ ᒌ?" ᐃᑏᐧᐤ᙮ "ᐦᐋᐧᐤ ᓇᒫᐧ-! ᓇᐊᐧ- ᓈᓂᑕᐤ ᑕ ᐃᑑᑕᐊᐧᐠ᙮ ᐦᐋᐧᐤ, ᒪᐦᑎ ᓂᑲ ᐴᓃᐣ ᐃᑕ ᑳ ᓂᐹᐟ ᑭᑕ ᐋᐧᐢᑳ ᑲᐧᐦᑯᑏᐠ ᐃᑯᑕ ᐃᐢᑯᑏᐤ᙮ ᑭᑕ ᓂᐸᐦᐃᐦᑲᓱᐟ ᐊᐊᐧ ᒪᐦᑮᓰᐢ," ᐃᑏᐧᐤ᙮

ᐃᑳᐧᓂ ᐃᑯᑕ ᐴᓇᐨ᙮ ᐃᑯᑕ ᐄ ᑯᑕᐄᐧᐟ ᐋᐧᓴᑳᐨ ᐃᑕ ᑳ ᓂᐹᔨᐟ ᐆᐦᐅ ᐅᓰᒥᓴ ᒪᐦᑮᓰᓴ᙮ ᐃᑲᐧ ᐊᑎ ᑲᐧᐦᑯᑏᐤ ᐊᓂᒪ ᐃᐢᑯᑏᐤ ᐃᑯᑕ᙮ ᑮᑕᐦᑕᐄᐧ ᐳᑯ ᒪᐦᑮᓰᐢ ᑳ ᑯᐢᑯᐸᔨᐟ᙮ ᐋᐧᐸᐦᑕᐨ ᐃᐢᑯᑏᐤ ᒥᓯᐄᐧ ᐃᑏ ᐄ ᐋᐧᐢᑳ ᐸᓯᑏᔨᐠ ᐃᑕ ᑳ ᑮ ᓂᐹᐟ᙮

“ᐃᐩ, ᓇᒨᔭ ᓈᓂᑕᐤ,” ᐃᑏᔭᐦᑕᑦ᙮ ᑖᐿ ᐳᒁᓂ ᒁᐢᑯᐦᑎᐤ, ᐅᒥᓯ ᐃᓯ ᐃᑯᑕ ᐃᐢᐱᒥᕽ ᐃᓯ᙮ ᐄ ᐊᐘᓯᐐ ᒁᐢᑯᐦᑎᐟ ᐊᓂᒦᔦᐤ ᐃᐢᑯᑏᐤ᙮ ᐘᒋᐦᐲᐤ ᐊᔭᐢᐠ᙮ ᐃᑯᑕ ᐅᐦᒋ ᐊᑎ ᐸᐦᐱᐤ᙮ ᐃᑿ ᐅᓲᓯᕽ ᐳᑯ ᑳ ᐊᑎ ᐸᓯᓲᐟ᙮ ᐋᐦᒋ ᐳᑯ ᐃᑯᑕ ᐊᓄᐦᐨ ᑳ ᐚᐸᐦᑏᓇᐤ ᐄ ᐚᐱᐢᑳᔭᐠ ᐅᓰᐢ ᐊᐘ ᒪᐦᑮᓰᐢ᙮

19
ᐐᓴᐦᑮᒑᕽ ᐅᒥᑭᐩ ᒦᑭᐤ

ᐆᒪ ᐋᒐᖩᐦᑮᐏᐣ ᑭᑭᐢᑭᓇᐧᐦᐊᒫᑯᓇᐤ: ᓇᒎᖪ ᑲᐦᑭᖪᐤ ᑮᑲᐧᐩ ᑳ ᒥᐢᑲᒫᕽ ᑭᒦᐢᑳᓈᒥᓈᕽ ᐄ ᒦᖨᑯᔭᐦᑳᐧᐤ ᑭᒧᓲᒥᓇᐘᐠ᙮

ᐱᔭᑳᐧᐤ ᐃᓴ ᐐᓴᐦᑮᒑᕽ ᒥᐦᒌᐟ ᓰᓰᐸ ᑮ ᓂᐸᐦᐄᐢᑕᒫᓱᐤ᙮ ᑮ ᐲᐦᑭᓃᐤ ᐊᓂᐦᐃ ᓰᓰᐸ᙮ ᐃᑯᑕ ᑮ ᐊᑎ ᑯᑕᐐᐤ᙮

“ᐋᐦ, ᑲᐧᔭᐢᐠ ᓂᐐ ᒥᓯ ᒦᒋᓱᐣ,” ᐃᑏᖨᐦᑕᑦ᙮

ᐃᑳᐧᓂ ᐃᑯᑕ ᐅᐦᒋ ᐋᑎᐦᐟ ᐊᑎ ᓈᐦ ᓇᐘᒌᐤ᙮ ᒥᐢᒋᑯᓴ ᐄ ᐋᐸᒋᐦᑖᐟ ᑕ ᓇᐘᒌᐟ ᐃᑯᑕ ᑯᑕᐚᓂᕽ᙮ ᐃᑲᐧ ᐊᓂᐦᐃ ᓰᓰᐸ ᐋᑎᐦᐟ ᐄ ᐚᐦ ᐐᐐᑭᓈᐟ ᓃᐱᔭ ᐄ ᐋᐸᒋᐦᑖᐟ ᐃᑲᐧ ᒦᓇ ᐊᓯᐢᑭᐩ᙮ ᐃᑲᐧ ᓰᐦᑲᐧᐦᑭᓃᐤ, ᓰᐹ ᐃᐢᑯᑏᕽ ᐄ ᐊᐦᖪᐟ ᐃᔭᑯᓂ ᓰᓰᐸ᙮ ᐃᑳᐧᓂ ᐊᑎ ᑮᓯᓱᐘᐠ ᓰᓰᐸᐠ᙮ ᐐᓴᐦᑮᒑᕽ ᐹᐦ ᐲᐦᐅᐤ᙮ ᒥᑐᓂ ᐊᑎ ᐃᐢᑲᒋ ᐲᐦᐅᐤ᙮

“ᐋᐦ, ᒌᐢᑳᐧᐨ ᐱᑕᒫ ᓂᐄᐧ ᓂᐹᓯᐣ,” ᐃᑏᐧᐤ᙮ “ᒪᐦᑎ, ᑯᐦᒑᐠ!” ᐃᑏᐧᐤ, ᐄ ᐄᐧ ᐊᑐᑕᕽ ᐆᒪ ᐅᑯᐦᒑᐠ᙮

“ᑯᐦᒑᐠ! ᑯᐢᑯᓂᐦᑲᐣ ᐃᐢᐲ ᓰᓰᐸᐠ ᑮᓯᓱᑖᐧᐃᐧ!” ᐃᑏᐧᐤ ᐄᓴ᙮ ᐃᑳᐧᓂ ᐊᑎ ᓂᐹᐤ ᐃᑯᑕ᙮

ᑮᑕᐦᑕᐄᐧ ᐅᑯᐦᒑᐠ ᑳ ᐲᐦᑖᑲᐧᓂᔨᐠ “ᐴᐠ! ᐴᐠ!”

ᐋᐦᒋ ᐳᑯ ᐊᐊᐧ ᐄᐧᓴᐦᑮᒑᕽ ᑳ ᓈᐦ ᓂᐹᐟ᙮

“ᐴᐠ! ᐴᐠ!”

ᐋᐦᒋ ᐳᑯ ᐊᐊᐧ ᐄᐧᓴᐦᑮᒑᕽ ᑳ ᓈᐦ ᓂᐹᐟ ᐄᑳ ᐄ ᐱᐦᑕᕽ ᐅᑯᐦᒑᐠ᙮

ᑮᑕᐦᑕᐄᐧ ᐊᐊᐧ ᑳ ᐊᐧᓂᐢᑳᐟ᙮ ᑲᓇᐋᐧᐸᐦᑕᑦ ᐅᑯᑕᐋᐧᐣ᙮ ᐊᐧᐦᐋᐧ! ᐄ ᒦᐢᑖᐢᑲᓱᔨᐟ ᐃᓴ ᐆᐦᐅ ᓰᓰᐸ ᐅᓵᑦ ᑭᐣᐄᐧᐢᐠ ᐄ ᑮ ᓂᐹᐟ᙮ ᑲᐧᔭᐢᐠ ᑭᓱᐋᐧᐦᐃᐠ ᐅᑯᐦᒑᐠ᙮ ᐃᑳᐧᓂ ᐃᑯᑕ ᐅᐦᒋ ᑖᐳᑳᓂ ᐃᑯᑕ ᐃᐢᑯᑏᕽ ᐃᑎᓯᓇᑦ ᐅᑯᐦᒑᐠ᙮

“ᑭᑲ ᑭᐢᑭᓇᐧᐦᐊᒫᑎᐣ ᑮᔭ ᐄᑳ ᐄ ᓂᑐᐦᑕᐃᐧᔭᐣ,” ᐃᑏᐤ᙮

ᒥᑐᓂ ᐄ ᑮᓯᓴᕽ ᐅᑯᐦᒑᐠ᙮ ᐃᑯᑕ ᐅᐦᒋ ᐊᑎ ᓯᐲᐧᐦᑏᐤ᙮ ᑲᐧᔭᐢᐠ ᐄᐧᓴᑮᔨᐦᑕᑦ ᐅᑯᐦᒑᐠ ᐄᐧᔭ ᐄ ᐊᑎ ᐅᒥᑮᐟ᙮ ᑭᐣᐄᐧᐢᐠ ᐱᒧᐦᑏᐤ᙮ ᑲᐧᔭᐢᐠ ᐋᐧᐦ ᐄᐧᓴᑮᔨᐦᑕᑦ ᐅᑯᐦᒑᐠ᙮ ᐊᑎ ᒫᐦ ᒋᐦᒌᑭᓇᑦ ᐅᑯᐦᒑᐠ᙮ ᐲᔨᐢᐠ ᓯᔮᑮᐩ ᐃᓯᔭᔮᐤ᙮

ᐃᑳᐧᓂ ᒫᓂ ᒫᑲ ᑭᔮᐱᐨ ᐹᐦ ᐱᒧᐦᑏᐤ ᐊᐊᐧ᙮ ᐊᑎ ᑲᑳᐧᑕᑭ ᓅᐦᑏ ᒦᒋᓱᐤ᙮ ᑮᑕᐦᑕᐄᐧ ᑳ ᐋᐧᐸᒫᐟ ᐊᓯᓃᐋᐧᐦᑲᐧᓇ᙮ ᓇᐋᐧᑮᐤ ᐄ ᐄᐧ ᐅᑎᓈᐟ᙮

“ᑳᐃᐧᔭ ᒧᐃᐧᓈᐣ!” ᐃᑏᐧᐊᐧᐠ ᐆᑯ ᐊᓯᓃᐋᐧᐦᑲᐧᓇᐠ᙮

“ᑖᓂᓯ ᐐᔫᒪ ᑳ ᐃᑗᔩᐠ,” ᐃᑏᐤ᙮ “ᓂᓄᐦᑏᐦᑲᑖᐣ ᐆᒪ᙮”

ᒥᑐᓂ ᒥᐢᑕᐦᐃ ᒪᓈᐦᐅᐤ, ᐄ ᒧᐚᐟ᙮ ᒫᑲ ᑭᔮᐱᐨ ᓄᐦᑏᐦᑲᑏᐤ᙮ ᑮᑕᐦᑕᐐ ᑳ ᐚᐸᒫᐟ ᐅᑭᓂᔭ᙮ ᓇᐗᑮᐤ ᐄ ᐐ ᐅᑎᓈᐟ᙮

“ᑳᐏᔭ ᒧᐏᓈᐣ!” ᐃᑗᐘᐠ ᐆᑯ ᐅᑭᓂᔭᐠ᙮

“ᑖᓂᓯ ᐐᔫᒪ ᑳ ᐃᑗᔩᐠ,” ᐃᑏᐤ᙮ “ᓂᓄᐦᑏᐦᑲᑖᐣ ᐆᒪ᙮”

ᒥᑐᓂ ᒥᐢᑕᐦᐃ ᒪᓈᐦᐅᐤ, ᐄ ᒧᐚᐟ᙮ ᐊᑎ ᓯᐿᐦᑏᐤ᙮

ᑮᑕᐦᑕᐐ ᑳ ᐚᐸᒫᐟ ᐱᔩᐘ᙮ ᐅᑎᓃᐤ ᐅᑕᐦᒑᐱᔭ ᐃᑿ ᒹᐦᒋ ᑳ ᐊᑎ ᐱᒧᑕᐦᑹᐟ ᑳ ᒥᓯ ᐿᑭᑐᐟ᙮ ᐅᓴᐦᐐᐤ ᐊᓂᐦᐃ ᐱᔩᐘ᙮

ᐊᑎ ᐹᐦ ᐱᒧᐦᑏᐤ, ᐄ ᐹᐦ ᐿᑭᑐᐟ ᐊᔩᐢᐠ ᐊᓯᓃᐚᐦᑿᓇ ᐄ ᐿᑭᑎᐢᑳᑯᐟ ᐃᑿ ᐄ ᑭᔭᑭᑯᐦᒑᑮᐟ ᐊᔩᐢᐠ ᐅᑭᓂᔭ ᐄ ᑭᔭᑭᑯᐦᒑᑮᐢᑳᑯᐟ᙮ ᑲᒁᑕᑭ ᓄᐦᑏᐦᑲᑏᐤ᙮

ᑮᑕᐦᑕᐐ ᑳ ᐚᐸᐦᑕᕽ ᑮᑿᐩ ᒦᐢᑲᓈᕽ, ᑖᐱᐢᑰᐨ ᑳᐢᑮᐘᐠ ᐆᒪ ᐄ ᐃᓯᓈᑿᓂᔩᐠ᙮ ᐃᒁᓂ ᐊᑎ ᐅᑎᓇᒼ᙮

“ᐋᔩ, ᑖᐿ ᑭᐦᒋ! ᓂᒧᓲᒪᐠ ᐄ ᐊᓴᒥᒋᐠ ᐆᒪ ᑳᐢᑮᐘᐠ!” ᐄ ᐃᑗᐟ᙮ ᐅᑎᓇᒼ ᐃᑿ ᐊᑎ ᒦᒋᐤ ᐃᓴᑹᔨᐤ᙮ ᑮᑕᐦᑕᐐ ᐳᑯ ᑳ ᐲᐦᑕᐚᐟ ᐱᔩᓰᓴ᙮

“ᐐᓴᐦᑮᒑᕽ ᐅᒥᑭᐩ ᒦᒋᐤ! ᐐᓴᐦᑮᒑᕽ ᐅᒥᑭᐩ ᒦᒋᐤ!”

“ᐊᐩ ᐊᐘᐢ! ᓂᒧᓲᒼ ᐊᐘ ᐄ ᐲ ᐊᓴᒥᐟ ᐆᒦᔪᐤ ᑳᐢᑮᐘᐠ!”

“ᐐᓴᐦᑮᒑᕽ ᐅᒥᑭᐩ ᒦᒋᐤ! ᐐᓴᐦᑮᒑᕽ ᐅᒥᑭᐩ ᒦᒋᐤ!”

ᐊᑎ ᓂᑐᐦᑕᐄᐧᐤ ᐆᐦᐅ ᐱᔦᓰᓴ᙮ ᐸᓯᐤ ᐊᓂᒦᔦᐤ ᑳᐢᑮᐊᐧᐠ᙮ ᐃᔦᐤ! ᑖᐲᐧ ᒫᓂ ᒫᑲ ᐄᓴ ᐅᒥᑭᐩ ᐄ ᑮ ᒦᒋᐟ᙮ ᐋᐦ ᑭᔫᒥᐠ ᐆᐦᐅ ᐱᔦᓰᓴ᙮ ᐱᒧᓯᓈᑏᐤ ᒫᑲ ᐸᑕᐦᐋᐧᐤ᙮ ᐃᑯᑕ ᐊᐧᐢᑳᐧᕽ ᐊᓂᒪ ᑳ ᒥᒋᒧᐸᔦᔦᐠ ᐊᓂᒦᔦᐤ ᐅᒥᑭᐩ᙮

ᐃᑯᑕ ᐳᓵᑲᐣ ᐊᓄᐦ- ᑭᑎᓯ ᑭᐢᑮᔦᒫᓇᐤ ᐃᔦᑳᐧᓇ ᐊᐧᐢᑳᐧᕽ ᒫᓇ ᑳ ᐋᔦᐟ᙮ ᐃᔦᑯ ᒪᐢᑭᐦᑭᐩ ᒥᔦ̇ᐧᓯᐣ᙮

ᐃᑲᐧ ᒫᓇ ᑳ ᐊᐧᐸᐦᑕᒫᐣ ᐃᔦᑯ ᐃᑯᓯ ᒫᓇ "ᐄᐧᓴᐦᑮᒫᕽ ᐅᒥᑭᐩ" ᓂᑎᑏᔦᐦᑏᐣ᙮

20
ᐄᐧᓴᐦᑮᒑᕽ ᐱᒥᐦᐊᒧᐤ

ᐆᒪ ᐋᒐᖫᐦᑮᐃᐧᐣ ᑭᑭᐢᑭᓇᐧᐦᐊᒫᑯᓇᐤ: ᓇᐦᐄᖬᒥᓱᐤ᙮

ᐱᔭᑳᐧᐤ ᐄᓴ ᐄᐧᓴᐦᑮᒑᕽ ᑮ ᐹᐧᐦ ᐱᒧᐦᑏᐤ ᐋᐧᓴᑳᐨ ᓵᑲᐦᐃᑲᓂᕽ᙮ ᑳ ᐋᐧᐸᒫᐟ ᐄᓴ ᓂᐢᑲ ᐄ ᐋᐧᐦᐅᐦᐸᐦᐅᖬᐟ ᐃᑲᐧ ᒫᓇ ᑳᐃᐧ ᐄ ᑏᐧᐦᐅᖬᐟ᙮ ᒫᒪᐢᑳᑏᐤ᙮

“ᑖᓂᓯ ᐆᒪ ᐄ ᐃᑕᐦᑲᒥᑭᓯᔮᐠ, ᓂᓰᒥᑎᐠ?” ᐃᓯ ᑲᑮᐧᒋᒦᐤ ᐄᓴ ᐆᐦᐅ ᓂᐢᑲ᙮

“ᐃᔭᐤ, ᐄ ᑕᑳᐧᑭᐠ ᐆᒪ᙮ ᐋᐧᐸᐨ ᑕ ᐱᐳᐣ ᐃᑲᐧ ᑭᑕ ᑖᐦ ᑖᐦᑳᔮᐤ! ᐅᐦᒋᑕᐤ ᐳᑯ ᓵᐊᐧᓄᕽ ᑕ ᐃᓯ ᐱᒧᐦᑏᐦᐅᔮᕽ ᐄᑳ ᑭᑕ ᓂᐸᐦᐋᐧᐢᑲᒋᔮᕽ,” ᐃᑏᐧᐤ ᐄᓴ ᐊᐊᐧ ᐱᔭᐠ ᓂᐢᑲ᙮

“ᒪᐦᑎ ᓃᐢᑕ! ᑭᑲ ᐄᐧᒌᐃᐧᑎᓈᐋᐧᐤ!” ᐃᑏᐧᐤ ᐄᐧᓴᐦᑮᒑᕽ᙮

“ᒫᑲ ᐄᐧᖭ ᐄᑳ ᐄ ᐅᑕᐦᑕᐦᑲᐧᓂᔪᐣ!” ᐃᑏᐧᐤ ᐄᓴ ᐊᐊᐧ ᓂᐢᑲ᙮

“ᐦᐋ, ᑖᐲᐧ ᐄᐧᐢᐱᓇᐨ!”

“ᐦᐊᐤ ᒌᐢᑲᐧ, ᑭᑲ ᒫᒪᐃᐧ ᐄᐧᒋᐦᐃᑎᓈᐣ,” ᐃᑏᐧᐤ ᐊᐊᐧ ᓂᐢᑲ᙮ ᓂᑐᒦᐤ ᐅᐋᐧᐦᑰᒫᑲᓇ ᐃᑲᐧ ᐃᑏᐤ ᑕ ᑖᐦ ᑕᐦᑳᐧᒫᖨᐟ ᐄᐧᓴᐦᑮᒑᐦᑲᐧ ᐅᒥᔭᐃᐧᖨᕽ᙮ ᐆᑕ ᑖᐦ ᑕᐦᑳᐧᒥᐠ ᐆᐦᐅ ᓂᐢᑲ: ᐱᔭᐠ ᐅᐢᑎᑳᐧᓂᕽ, ᐃᑲᐧ ᐋᑎᐦᐟ ᐅᐢᐱᑐᓂᕽ, ᐃᑲᐧ ᒦᓇ ᑯᑕᑲᐠ ᐅᐢᑳᑎᕽ᙮ ᐃᑯᓯ ᐃᓯ ᑲᐢᑭᐦᑖᐊᐧᐠ ᑕ ᐱᒧᐦᑕᐦᐋᒋᐠ ᐅᐢᑏᓯᐋᐧᐊᐧ, ᐄᐧᓴᐦᑮᒑᐦᑲᐧ᙮ ᐃᐢᐱᒥᕽ ᐹᐢᑲᐨ ᐄ ᐃᑖᐱᖨᐟ ᐆᐦᐅ, ᐄ ᓵᓴᑭᒥᓯᓂᖨᐟ᙮

“ᑳᐃᐧᖬ ᐊᐧᐢᑲᐄᐧ ᓂᐢᑏᓯᒎ,” ᐃᑏᐤ ᐄᓴ ᐊᐊᐧ ᓂᐢᑲ ᐅᐢᑏᓴ᙮ “ᑭᑲ ᑭᒥᐢᑭᓂᑎᓈᐣ ᑮᐢᐱᐣ ᐊᐧᐢᑲᐄᐧᔭᓂ!”

“ᐦᐋᐤ, ᓇᒫᐧᐨ ᓂᑲ ᐊᐧᐢᑲᐋᐧᐣ,” ᐃᑏᐧᐤ ᐄᓴ ᐄᐧᓴᐦᑮᒑᕽ᙮ ᐃᑯᓯ ᐊᑎ ᓯᐲᐧᐱᖭᐊᐧᐠ ᐆᑯ ᓂᐢᑲᐠ, ᐄ ᑕᐦᑯᓈᒥᐠ ᐅᐢᑏᓯᐋᐧᐊᐧ᙮ ᒥᖩᐧᖨᐦᑕᑦ ᐄᐧᓴᐦᑮᒑᕽ ᐊᖨᐢᐠ ᐄᐧᐢᑕ ᓵᐊᐧᓄᕽ ᐄ ᐄᐧ ᐃᑐᐦᑏᐦᐅᐟ᙮

ᑮᑕᐦᑕᐄᐧ ᑳ ᐱᐦᑕᐋᐧᐟ ᐃᐢᑮᐧᐊᐧ ᐄ ᒪᑏᐧ ᒨᒥᑭᐦᑖᑯᓯᖨᐟ᙮ ᑭᓵᐢᑕᐤ ᐄ ᐸᑳᓯᒧᖨᐟ, ᐃᑏᖨᐦᑕᑦ᙮ ᓰᒫᐠ ᐊᐧᐢᑲᐄᐧᐤ, ᐄ ᑮᐧᐢᑭᐸᖨᐦᐅᐟ, ᐄ ᑲᑮᐧ ᐋᐧᐸᒫᐟ ᐊᓂᐦᐃ ᐃᐢᑮᐧᐊᐧ᙮ ᒪᔭᐤ ᑳ ᐊᐧᐢᑲᐄᐧᐟ, ᑳ ᑭᒥᐢᑭᓂᑯᐟ ᐊᓂᐦᐃ ᓂᐢᑲ᙮

ᒥᑐᓂ ᐄ ᐸᑲᐢᑕᐄᐧᓯᕽ ᐃᑕ ᐆᑯ ᐃᐢᑮᐧᐊᐧᐠ ᑳ ᐸᑳᓯᒧᖨᐟ᙮ ᑲᐧᔭᐢᐠ ᐸᐦᐱᐦᐃᐠ!

ᐃᑳᐧᓂ ᓇᒫᐧᐨ ᓵᐊᐧᓄᕽ ᐅᐦᒥ ᐃᑐᐦᑏᐦᐅᐤ ᐄᐧᓴᐦᑮᒑᕽ᙮ ᒫᑲ ᑭᖭᐱᐨ ᐆᑯ ᓂᐢᑲᐠ ᓵᐊᐧᓄᕽ ᐋᐦᐃᑐᐦᑏᐦᐅᐊᐧᐠ ᑕᐦᑐ ᑕᑳᐧᑭᐣ ᐃᑲᐧ ᑖᐱᐢᑰᐨ ᑭᖭᐱᐨ ᐄ ᒥᒋᒥᓈᒋᐠ ᐄᐧᓴᐦᑮᒑᐦᑲᐧ ᐄ ᐃᓯ ᐱᒥᖭᒋᐠ᙮

21
ᐑᓴᐦᑮᒑᕽ ᐃᑲᐧ ᐑᐦᑎᑯᐤ

ᐆᒪ ᐋᒐᖫᐦᑮᐏᐣ ᑭᑭᐢᑭᓇᐧᐦᐊᒫᑯᓇᐤ: ᓇᐦᐄᖬᒥᓱᐤ᙮

ᐱᔭᒁᐤ ᐄᓴ ᐑᓴᐦᑮᒑᕽ ᑮ ᐱᒧᐦᑏᐤ᙮ ᑮᑕᐦᑕᐑ ᐄᓴ ᑳ ᐚᐸᒫᐟ ᐑᐦᑎᑯᐘ᙮ ᑮᓯᐢᑲᐤ ᑳᓲᐸᖬᐦᐅᐤ, ᐊᖬᐢᐠ ᐄ ᑯᐢᑖᐟ ᐃᔭᑯᓂ᙮ ᐃᑯᓯ ᐃᑯᑕ ᓴᑳᓯᕽ ᐅᐦᒋ ᑲᓇᐚᐸᒦᐤ, ᐄ ᑲᑮᐧ ᐸᐢᐲᐦᐅᐟ᙮ ᑮᑕᐦᑕᐑ ᐳᑯ ᐑᐦᑎᑯᐤ ᑳ ᒪᑏᐧ ᐊᔭᒥᐟ᙮

“ᐑᓴᐦᐊᑮᒐᕽ, ᑭᐸᓵᐧᑎᑎᐣ᙮ ᐋᐢᑕᐨ! ᓂᓅᐦᑏ ᒦᒋᓱᐣ ᐆᒪ᙮”

ᐃᑯᓯ ᐑᓴᐦᑮᒑᕽ ᐊᑎ ᓈᑏᐤ ᐑᐦᑎᑯᐘ, ᐄ ᒫᐦ ᒫᒍᓯᐟ ᐹᐢᑲ⁻᙮ ᐄ ᒪᐏᐦᑳᑎᓱᐟ, ᐊᖬᐢᐠ ᐄ ᐑ ᒧᐏᐦᐟ᙮

“ᐑᓴᐦᑮᒑᕽ! ᓈᒋᓂᐦᑏ ᐃᑲᐧ ᑯᑕᐑ ᐃᑯᑕ ᐅᐦᒋ ᑭᑲ ᒧᐏᑎᐣ᙮”

ᐃᑯᓯ ᐑᓴᐦᑮᒑᕽ ᑯᐢᐱᐤ, ᐃᑯᑕ ᐅᐦᒋ, ᐄ ᓈᒋᓂᐦᑏᐟ᙮ ᑮᑕᐦᑕᐑ ᐳᑯ ᑳ ᐚᐸᒫᐟ ᓯᐦᑯᓴ᙮

“ᐋᐢᑕᐨ, ᓂᓰᒥᐢ!” ᐃᑏᐤ

ᐃᑿ ᐊᓇ ᓯᐦᑯᐢ,

“ᑮᒁᐩ? ᑮᒁᐩ ᐑᓴᐦᑮᒑᕽ?”

“ᒌᐢᑏ, ᓈᐦᐊ ᓃᑏ ᐐᐦᑎᑯᐤ᙮ ᐄ ᐐ ᒧᐏᐟ ᐊᓇ᙮ ᓂᔮ! ᐃᑯᑏ ᐃᐢᐸᐦᑖ᙮ ᓈᒋᐸᐦ! ᓯᐦᑳᐦᑕᐚᐢ ᐅᑯᐦᒑᑭᕽ ᐃᑯᑕ ᐅᐦᒋ ᑭᑕ ᓂᑕᐏ ᐸᐢᑮᐦᑕᒪᐣ ᐅᑏᐦᐃᔮᐱᐩ᙮”

ᐃᑿ ᐊᐘ ᓯᐦᑯᐢ:

“ᐄ᙮” ᐋᐣᐏᐦᑕᑦ, “ᐊᐘᐢ ᓂᑲ ᓂᐱᐣ!”

“ᓇᒨ ᐏᖬ, ᓯᐦᑯᐢ᙮ ᒥᓴᐚᐨ ᑳᐏ ᑭᑲ ᐱᒫᒥᐦᐃᑎᐣ᙮ ᐃᑿ ᑮᐢᐱᐣ ᐅᒥᓯ ᐃᑑᑕᒪᓂ ᑭᑲ ᐅᓲᐦᑕᒫᑎᐣ ᓇᐚᐨ ᑭᑕ ᒫᐘᒋ ᒥᖭᐧᓯᐠ ᑮᑕᐦᑕᐩ᙮”

ᒥᖬᐦᑕᑦ ᐊᐘ ᓯᐦᑯᐢ᙮ ᐊᑎ ᓈᒋᐸᐦᐄᐤ ᐐᐦᑎᑯᐘ᙮

ᐃᑯᓯ ᐊᐘ ᓯᐦᑯᐢ ᐃᐢᐹᐦᑖᐤ ᐃᑏ ᐐᐦᑎᑯᐘ ᑳ ᐊᔮᖪᐟ᙮ ᓂᑕᐏ ᓰᑯᐸᐦᑖᐤ ᐅᑯᐦᒑᑭᖬᐠ ᐃᑯᑕ ᐅᐦᒋ ᐃᐢᒁᐦᑕᐐᐤ, ᐄ ᓂᑕᐏ ᑖᐦ ᑕᐦᒁᒫᐟ ᐅᑏᐦᐃᔮᐲᕽ᙮ ᐃᑿ ᑮᑕᐦᑕᐐ ᐳᑯ ᑳ ᑏᐶᐟ ᐐᐦᑎᑯᐤ᙮

“ᐑᓴᐦᑮᒑᕽ ᑭᖪᐸ! ᓂᓄᐦᑏᐦᑲᑖᐣ ᐆᒪ᙮ ᐑᓴᐦᑮᒑᕽ ᑭᖪᐸ! ᓂᓄᐦᑏᐦᑲᑖᐣ ᐆᒪ!”

ᐃᒁᓂ ᑮᑕᐦᑕᐐ ᐳᑯ ᑳ ᐸᐦᑭᓯᕽ ᐊᐘ ᐐᐦᑎᑯᐤ, ᐄ ᓂᐱᐟ᙮

ᐑᓴᐦᑮᒑᕽ ᑿᔭᐢᐠ ᒥᖫᐧᖪᐦᑕᑦ᙮ ᓈᒋᐸᐦᐄᐤ ᐊᓂᐦᐃ ᐐᐦᑎᑯᐘ᙮ ᐃᑯᑕ ᐅᐦᒋ ᐸᐦᑯᓃᐤ, ᐄ ᐅᑎᓈᐟ ᐊᓂᐦᐃ ᓯᐦᑯᓴ᙮ ᐃᑿ ᐄᓴ ᐊᐘ ᓯᐦᑯᐢ ᐄ ᓂᐱᐟ, ᐄ ᑮ ᓂᐢᑖᐹᐐᐟ᙮

ᐃᑯᑕ ᐅᐦᒋ ᐚᓴᐦᑮᒫᕽ ᑳ ᐃᑐᐦᑕᐦᐚᐟ ᓵᑲᐦᐃᑲᓂᕽ, ᐄ ᓂᑕᐃᐧ ᓰᐲᑭᓈᐟ ᐊᓂᐦᐃ ᓯᐦᑯᓴ᙮ ᐄ ᐚᐦ ᐚᐢᑳᓈᐟ ᓂᐲᕽ᙮ ᐃᑲᐧ ᒫᓇ ᐄ ᐹᐦ ᐴᑖᑖᐟ, ᐄ ᑲᑮᐧ ᐱᒫᒋᐦᐚᐟ᙮ "ᐚ! ᑭᐣᐄᐧᐢᐠ ᐊᐊᐧ ᐃᑯᓯ ᐃᑑᑕᑦ᙮ ᐅᓰᓯᔮᐠ ᐄ ᒥᒋᒥᓈᐟ, ᐄ ᓰᐲᑭᓈᐟ ᐊᓂᐦᐃ ᓯᐦᑯᓴ᙮ ᐄ ᐹᐦ ᐴᑖᑖᐟ ᒫᓇ, ᐃᑲᐧ ᒫᓇ ᑮᐦᑖᐧᑦ ᐄ ᓰᐲᑭᓈᐟ᙮

ᑮᑕᐦᑕᐄᐧ ᑳᐃᐧ ᑳ ᐱᒫᑎᓯᔮᐟ ᐊᓂᐦᐃ ᓯᐦᑯᓴ᙮

“ᒌᐢᑏ, ᓂᓰᒥᐢ᙮ ᑲᓇᐚᐸᒥᓱ ᓂᐲᕽ!” ᐃᑏᐤ ᐅᓰᒥᓴ ᓯᐦᑯᓴ᙮

ᐊᐊᐧ ᓯᐦᑯᐢ ᑲᓇᐚᐸᒥᓱᐤ ᓂᐲᕽ᙮ ᐃᑯᑕ ᐚᐸᒥᓱᐤ, ᐄ ᐚᐱᐢᑭᓯᐟ᙮ ᑲᐧᔮᐢᐠ ᐄ ᒥᔦᐧᓈᑯᓯᐟ ᐊᓇ ᓯᐦᑯᐢ᙮ ᐃᑲᐧ ᐃᑕ ᑳ ᑮ ᒥᒋᒥᓂᑯᐟ ᐄ ᐚᓴᐦᑮᒫᐦᑲᐧ ᐚᓇᐢᑯᐨ ᐅᓰᕽ, ᐃᑯᑕ ᑲᐢᑭᑏᓯᐤ᙮

ᑭᔮᐱᐨ ᐚᓇᐢᑯᐨ ᐅᓰᕽ ᑲᐢᑭᑏᓯᐤ ᐊᓄᐦᐨ ᑳ ᑮᓯᑳᔮᐠ᙮

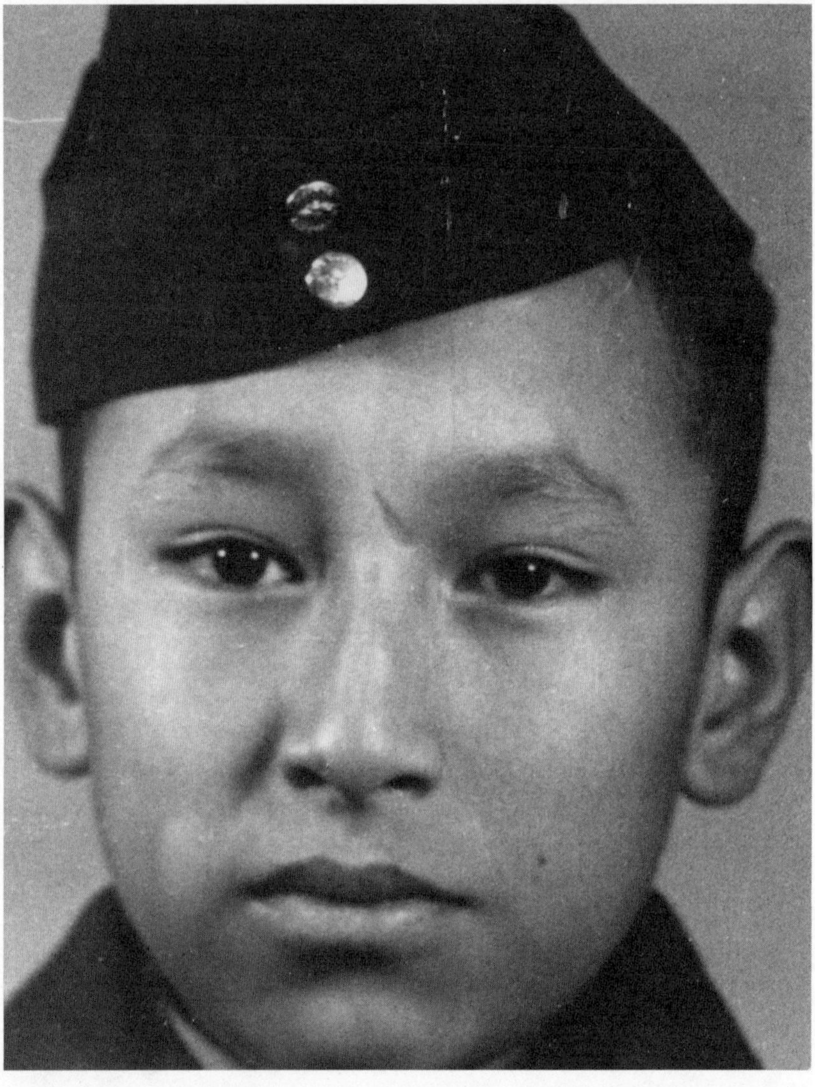

mitâtaht nistosâp kâ-kî-itahtopiponîyân,
î-kî-opimithâwi-simâkanisihkânisisiwiyân ikospî.

ᒥᑖᑕᐦᐟ ᓂᐢᑐᓵᑊ ᑳ ᑮ ᐃᑕᐦᑐᐱᐳᓃᔮᐣ, ᐄ ᑮ ᐅᐱᒥᖭᐎ ᓯᒫᑲᓂᓯᐦᑳᓂᓯᓯᐎᔮᐣ ᐃᑯᐢᐲ᙮ 1966

Solomon, age 13, in his cadet uniform, 1966.

Northern Saskatchewan Archive.

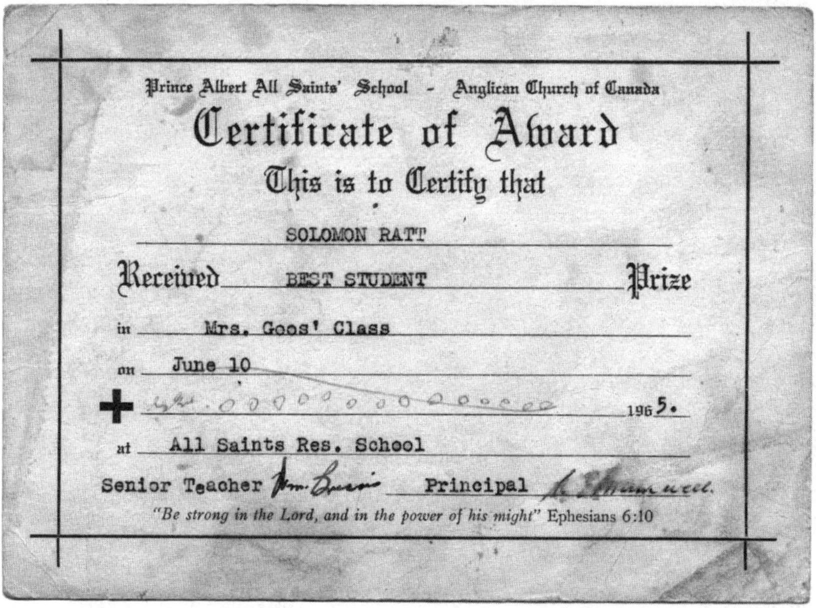

Prince Albert All Saints' School - Anglican Church of Canada

Certificate of Award

This is to Certify that

SOLOMON RATT

Received BEST STUDENT Prize

in Mrs. Goos' Class

on June 10

1965.

at All Saints Res. School

Senior Teacher Principal

"Be strong in the Lord, and in the power of his might" Ephesians 6:10

nikî-otahikân "mâwaci nihtâ-kiskinwahamâkosiw okiskinwahamâkan.

ᓂᑮ ᐅᑕᐦᐃᑳᐣ "ᒫᐘᒋ ᓂᐦᑖ ᑭᐢᑭᓌᐦᐊᒫᑯᓯᐤ ᐅᑭᐢᑭᓌᐦᐊᒫᑲᐣ᙮"

I won the best at being a student certificate. Certificate of Award from All Saints Residential School, June 10, 1965.

Courtesy of the author.

okimâwiwin otatoskîw: î-kî-âcimoyân kitohcikanihk. ikospî ohci nikî-atoskâtîn nîhithowîwin athisk mihcît kihtîyayak mâna î-kî-âcimostawicik.

ᐅᑭᒫᐃᐧᐃᐧᐣ ᐅᑕᑐᐢᑮᐤ: ᐄ ᑮ ᐋᒋᒧᔮᐣ ᑭᑐᐦᒋᑲᓂᕽ᙮ ᐃᑯᐢᐲ ᐅᐦᒋ ᓂᑮ ᐊᑐᐢᑳᑏᐣ ᓃᐦᐃᖬᐄᐧᐃᐧᐣᐊᖨᐢᐠ ᒥᐦᒌᐟ ᑭᐦᑏᔭᔭᐠ ᒫᓇ ᐄ ᑮ ᐋᒋᒧᐢᑕᐃᐧᒋᐠ᙮

Working as an information officer for the Department of Northern Saskatchewan doing canned radio broadcasts in Cree. This helped maintain his interest in the Cree language and Cree storytelling, as many of his radio programs were with Elders telling him stories, n.d.

Northern Saskatchewan Archives.

ispî kâ-kî-mâci-kiskinwahamâkîyân iyiniw kihci-kiskinwahamâtowikamikohk.

ᐃᐢᐲ ᑳ ᑮ ᒫᒋ ᑭᐢᑭᓌᐦᐊᒫᑮᔮᐣ ᐃᔨᓂᐤ ᑭᐦᒋ ᑭᐢᑭᓌᐦᐊᒫᑐᐏᑲᒥᑯᕽ᙮

Beginning as a sessional lecturer for SIFC (now FNUniv) in 1986. University of Regina classroom building.

Photo by Vivian Janvier, courtesy of the author.

ninîkihikwak ikwa nîtha.

ᓂᓃᑭᐦᐃᑲᐧᐠ ᐃᑲᐧ ᓃᖬ᙮

Solomon with his parents, William John Ratt and Alice Emily Ratt, 1976.

Courtesy of the author.

"namôtha nîtha Indian" Solomon ikwa Kawlaca iyinîhkân Capilano âsokanihk.

"ᓇᒨᖬ ᓃᖬ ᐃᐣᑏᔭᐣ" ᓲᕒᐊᒧᐣ ᐃᑿ ᑲᐤᕒᐋᑿ ᐃᔨᓃᐦᑳᐣ Capilano ᐋᓱᑲᓂᕽ

"I'm not an Indian." Solomon with Kawliga statue on the Capilano Bridge. Vancouver, February 1994.

Courtesy of the author.

Solomon kikiskam osâwi-papakiwayânis osâwi-papakiwayânis kîsikâw ohci.

ᓴᕒᐊᒧᐣ ᑭᑭᐢᑲᒼ ᐅᓵᐏᐸᐸᑭᐘᔮᓂᐢ ᐅᓵᐏᐸᐸᑭᐘᔮᓂᐢ ᑮᓯᑳᐤ ᐅᐦᒋ᙮

Solomon wearing his Every Child Matters shirt on the National Day for Truth and Reconciliation, 2021.

Courtesy of the author.

kâ-pî-isi-kiskisiyân

The Way I Remember

tâpika âcathôhkîwina ta-kî-pî-kîwîmakahki

kâwi mihtotihk pîtohtî wîsahkîcâhk,
wîsahkîcâhk kâwi mihtotihk pîtohtî.
nitayamihcikîwin kakîpiskam
nikiskinwahamâkosiwin;
nipîkiskwîwin, ninîhithawâtisiwin,
nayîhtâwihikow âkathâsîmowin.
kâwi mihtotihk pîtohtîw wîsahkîcâhk,
wîsahkîcâhk kâwi mihtotihk pîtohtî
kâ-matwî-camohkahahk nipiy amisk osoy ohci.

WISHING THE STORIES TO RETURN

Come back to the raft, Wisahkecahk
Wisahkecahk, come back to the raft.
My schooling blocks
My education,
My language, my Cree culture,
Is hampered by the English language.
Come back to the raft, Wisahkecahk
Wisahkecahk, come back to the raft.
In the distance, the beaver splashes the water with his tail.

kiskisiwina / Memories

1
î-âpasâpahtamân

1. î-ati-powâtamân

nikî-kitahamâkwak îkâ ta-pîkiskwîyân nîhithowîwin
nipîkiskwîwin ita
kâ-kiskîthihtamân ikwa kâ-wihtamân nitaskiy.
ninahastâsowin,
nitithinîsiwin,
kâ-isi-nîhithawâtisiyân
kî-nitonamwak – mâka kî-pwâhpinîwak –
ta-mîskotastâcik nititîthimisowin
kâ-isi-nîhithawâtisiyân
masinahikanâpisk ta-pisikwastîk
ita ta-ohpikihtânowik oskiyâtisiwin
ikwa oski-itakisowin
ita ninîhithawâtisiwin
î-mîstahikâtîk ikwa î-kâsîhikâtîk
ikwa anihi itîthimisowina,
"okîskwîpîsk," "okihtimiw," "macâyisiwin," ikwa kahkithaw kîkway
kâ-isi-maci-itîthihcikâsot "ithiniw"
ana okimâwiwin kâ-othastât

1
LOOKING BACK

1. On the Threshold of a Dream

They forbade me the use of my language
My language through which
I know and name the world.
My terms of order,
my metaphysical system,
my expressive cultural practices,
They sought – but failed –
to make my consciousness
of my cultural self
A tabula rasa
– a blank slate –
on which to build a new cultural
and social order
On which my Creeness was obliterated
and erased,
And the concepts of "drunkard," "lazy," "evil"
And every negative connotation of "Indian"
that "Western culture" could create

ikota pisikwastî-masinahikanâpiskohk ta-othastânowik.
kî-pwâhpinîwak!

2. î-maskamiht ocawâsisîwiwin

cikôci:
î-awâsisîwiyan, î-papâmi-mîtawîyan,
î-papâmi-kwâskohtiyan, î-iskwâhtawîyan mistikwak,
poko kîkway î-mâmaskâtaman,
î-kihcinâhoyan î-sâkihikawiyan
... kîtahtawî ayamihikimâwak kâ-pî-kwâsihiskwâw.

3. kâkikî nika-kiskisin

kâkikî nika-kiskisin
kâ-kî-awâsisîwiyân
ispî kâ-kî-kwâsihikawiyân nîkihk ohci
ta-nitawi-ayamihcikîyân ohpimî, wâhthaw nîkihk ohci.
kîspin wanikiskisiyâni
nika-mîtawâkâtâwak
kahkithaw awâsisak kâ-kî-wanihihcik,
kahkithaw awâsisak kâ-kî-nipahihcik,
namwâc nika-kistîthimihâwak
kîspin wanikiskisitotawakwâwi.
kîspin wanikiskisiyâni nika-wanihon.
kîspin wanikiskisiyâni nika-wanihâw nitahcahk.

4. atôspîwinâkwan-papakiwayâni-kîsikâw

anohc ôma atôspîwinâkwan-papakiwayâni-kîsikâw ita kâ-kiskisiyahk awâsisak kâ-kî-kwâsihihcik wîkiwâhk ohci ohpimî ta-nitawi-ayamihcikîcik, ayamihâwi-kiskinwahamâtowikamikohk î-isi-kwâsihihcik mitoni wâhthaw wîkiwâhk ohci. mistahi mâna kî-kâh-kitimahâwak ikota awâsisak, ahpô mîna âtiht ikota kî-nipahâwak.

Would be reinscribed on that blank slate.
They failed!

2. Stolen Childhood

Imagine:
you are a child, playing about,
jumping, climbing trees,
marvelling at everything in the world,
secure in the love you feel from others
... then the priests came to kidnap you.

3. Lest I Forget

Forever I will remember
As a child
When I was kidnapped from my home
To go to school elsewhere, from my home.
If I forget
I will disrespect
All the children who were lost,
All the children who were killed.
I would not show them honour
If I forget about them.
If I forget, I will be lost.
If I forget, I will lose my soul.

4. Orange Shirt Day

Today is "Orange Shirt Day" to remember the children who were taken away to residential schools. Many children were abused, and some were even killed there.

nîsta nikî-kwâsihikawin. ispî nikotwâsik î-itahtopiponîyân nikî-kwâsihikawin kistapinânihk isi. tahto-askiy, ikota nikî-nitawi-ayamihcikân. mitâtaht pîsim ikota nikî-kitinikawin. kâ-nîpihk mâna poko kâ-kî-kîwîyân. namwâc nîtha nikî-ohci-kitimahikawin, namwâc mîna nikî-ohci-wanihtân nipîkiskwîwin. kiyâpic ninîhithowân wîtha kapî mâna î-kî-nîhithowîcik ninîkihikwak ispî kâ-kîwîyân kâ-nîpihk.

mâka ôma kâ-mâmitonîthihtamân; nikitâpahtîn nipimâtisiwin. mistahi kîkway nipî-wâpahtîn kâ-kî-isi-wanâhikoyân nikiskinwahamâkawin ikota ohpimî ayamihâwi-kiskinwahamâtowikamikohk.

namwâc awasimî ikota nikî-ohci-pîhtîn âcathôhkîwina. iyakoni anihi âcathôhkîwina kâ-kî-kiskinwahamawâcik onîkihikwak ocawâsimisiwâwa tânisi ta-isi-ohpikihâwasocik, mîna tânisi ta-isi-pimâtisik ôta askîhk. kahkithaw kîkway ikota âcathôhkîwinihk kî-kiskinwahamâkîwak onîkihikomâwak. namôtha kî-ispathin iyakoni kiskinwahamâkîwina ta-kiskinwahamâkawiyân wîtha kâ-pipohk mâna kâ-kî-âcathôhkânowik, ispî ohpimî kâ-kî-ayâyân.

namôtha mâmaskâc kâ-pî-kitimâkisiyân nipimâtisiwinihk: nikî-kitimahikon minihkwîwin mîna maci-maskihkiya; nikî-wîpinâwak niwâhkômâkan ikwa mîna nitawâsimisak; namôtha nikî-ohci-miciminîn atoskîwin. pîthisk namôtha ahpô nânitaw ita nikî-ohci-wîkin. ôtînâhk mîskanâhk pîthisk nikî-wîkin. pâtimâ kâ-nakatamân minihkwîwin ikwa maci-maskihkiya kâ-ati-kaskihtâyân atoskîwin ta-miciminamân; pâtimâ kâ-nakatamân minihkwîwin ikwa maci-maskihkiya kâ-kî-kaskihtâyân ta-mitho-pimâtisiyân; pâtimâ kâ-nakatamân minihkwîwin ikwa maci-maskihkiya kâ-kî-kaskihtâyân ta-mitho-pamihakwâw nicawâsimisak ikwa nôsisimak. kayâs, mitoni kîkâc nistomitanaw askîwin, kâ-kî-nakatamân iyako nipimâtisiwin.

I too was taken away. When I was six years old I was taken away to go to school in Prince Albert. Every year, I was in school there. I was kept there for ten months of the year. It was only in the summer that I got to go home. I was not abused, and I did not lose my language. I still speak Cree because my parents spoke Cree to me when I would go home in the summer months.

But this is what I am thinking about; I look at my life. I have come to see a lot of things where I have been hindered by my residential school experience.

There (at the school) I was no longer able to hear the traditional sacred stories. These traditional stories were used by the parents to teach their children how to raise children, as well as how to live in this world. Everything parents needed to teach their children were in those traditional stories. It was not possible for those stories to teach me because it was in the winter when those stories were told, when I was away from home.

It is no wonder that I came to suffer during my life: alcohol and drugs made my life pitiful; I abandoned my wife and my children; I was unable to hold down a job. Eventually I had nowhere to live. I lived on city streets. Not until I walked away from alcohol and drugs was I able to hold down a job; not until I walked away from alcohol and drugs was I able to live a good life; not until I walked away from alcohol and drugs was I able to take care of my children and my grandchildren. A long time, almost thirty years now, since I left that life behind.

ninanâskomon anohc kâ-isi-pimâtisiyân: namwâc awasimî niminihkwân mîna namwâc nitâpacihtân maci-maskihkiya, ikwa mîna nistomitanaw askîwin nipî-atoskâtîn ôma nitatoskîwin. nama wîhkâc nika-wanikiskisin ita kâ-pî-ohci-pasikoyân, ita kâ-pî-isi-kitimâkisiyân. tahto-kîsikâw nikakwî-mitho-pimâtisin.

5. kîspin îkâ î-kî-ocawâsimisiyân

otâkosîhk nikî-nitawi-âcimostawâwak okiskinwahamâkanisisak tânisi kâ-kî-ispathihikoyân ispî kâ-kî-sipwîhtahikawiyân ta-nitawi-ayamihcikîyân ayamihâwi-kiskinwahamâtowikamikohk. ispî kâ-pôni-âcimoyân nikî-kâh-kakwîcimikwak awâsisak nanâtohk kakwîcihkîmowina.

piyak awâsis nikî-kakwîcimik: "mosôm, kikî-mithwîthihtîn cî kâ-kî-kîsi-ayamihcikîyân?"

"îhî," nikî-itâw, "nistam oti. mâka nikî-miskâson îkâ nânitaw ita î-kî-ohci-tîpiskamân, îkâ nânitaw ita î-kî-tipîthihtâkosiyân. namôtha awasimî nikî-tipîthihtâkosin nitiskonikanihk, namôtha mîna nikî-tipîthihtâkosin ôtînâhk, âyîtawâyihk ikota nikî-miskâson, î-kî-wanihoyân âyîtawâyihk askiya."

kotak awâsis kâ-kakwîcimit: "mosôm, tânisi mâka kâ-kî-isi-paspîyan?"

"kinwîsk nikî-wâh-wanohtân," nikî-itâw, "mâka pîthisk nikî-miskîn nitatoskîwin, ôma atoskîwin î-mithwîthihtamân. ôma kâ-pî-kiskinwahamâkiyân mîna kâ-nâh-nîhithawasinahikîyân. iyakoni ôho kâ-kî-paspîhikoyân. ninanâskomon wîtha athisk mihcît niwîci-kiskinwahamâkanak ikotî ohci ayamihâwi-kiskinwahamâtowikamikohk kî-osâmi-wanihowak, âyîtawâyihk nîso askiya wîthawâw î-kî-micimwâcîcik."

kîspin êkâ ohci nitawâsimisak nika-kî-micimosinihtay âyîtawâyihk askiya. ninanâskomon: *I am grateful.*

I give thanks for the life I have today: I no longer drink and I no longer use drugs, and it's been thirty years in which I have been working at my job here. I will never forget from where I have risen, where I have had a pitiful life. Every day I try to live a good life.

5. If Not for My Children

Yesterday I went to share my experiences at the residential school with some elementary students. When I finished telling my story the children asked me all sorts of questions.

One child asked: "Grandfather, were you happy when you finished school?"

"Yes," I said. "That is, at first. But then I found that I did not fit in anywhere. I felt that I did not belong on the reserve, nor did I belong in the city. I found myself betwixt and between two worlds, lost."

Another child asked: "Grandfather, how did you survive?"

"I wandered about lost for a long time," I said to her, "but I eventually found my work, this work that I enjoy. All the years I spent teaching and my writing in Cree. These were the things that saved me. I am grateful because many of my fellow students from the residential school were lost, stuck in between two worlds."

If not for my children, I would have been caught in the wastelands between two worlds. *ninanâskomon*: I am grateful.

6. kakîpâtisak

kî-kakwî-nipahtâwak nipîkiskwîwin
ispî kâ-kî-kiskinwahamawicik:
kakîpâtisak!
nikî-kiskinwahamâkwak
tânisi kita-isi-pasikôhtâyân
anima kâ-kî-nâspitihkwâmiskahkwâw.

6. Fools

They tried to kill my language
When they were educating me:
The fools!
They taught me
how to raise
That which has been in a trance.

2
î-mwayî-nitawi-ayamihcikîyân

1. nicâhkosîwikamikos

iskwîyânihk kâ-kî-kiyokawak nikâwîpan nikî-âcimostâk ispî kâ-kî-nihtâwîkiwak:

ikospî îsa î-kî-mikiskâk, kaskatinowipîsim î-kî-akimiht, kâ-kî-pimohtîhocik ninîkihikwak ikwa otôtîmiwâwa, wanihikîskanâhk î-kî-itohtîhocik. tâwic ôma îsa î-kî-otâpahastimwîcik ispî kâ-kî-ati-âhkosit nikâwîpan, athisk îsa ikospî î-kî-kikiskawâwasot; nîtha ôma îsa ikota î-kî-kikiskawit. wihtamawîw nohtâwîpana î-wî-âhkosit, ocâpânâskosihk îsa î-kî-pôsit îskwâ nohtâwîpan. î-pimitisahastimwît.

sîmâk tîpwâtîw owîcîwâkana nohtâwîpan, î-wihtamawât î-wî-âhkosithit nikâwîpana. tâpwî-pokâni nâtakâm isi-otâpahastimwîwak. ikotî nîtî kîwîtinohk, sîpânakiciwanohk kâ-kî-ati-kipihcîcik. wâsakâm ikota î-kî-ati-mânokîcik.

2
LIFE BEFORE SCHOOL

1. My Little Hospital

The last time I visited my late mother she told me the story of the time I was born:

At that time it was freeze-up, during the Freeze-up Moon (November) when my parents and their friends were travelling, they were travelling to the trapline. They were way out in the lake, driving a dog team when my late mother began labour, as she was with child; it was me she was carrying. She told my late father that she was going into labour, she was in the dogsled while my late father was driving the dog team.

Right away my late father calls his companions telling them that my late mother was going into labour. Immediately they drove their dog teams to shore. It was there to the north at the place where the current goes underground where they stopped. It was there they set up camp.

wâhay, kwayask îsa kî-sôhki-atoskîwak aniki nâpîwak, î-kîskatahihtakwîcik, î-wî-wâskahikanîstamawâcik nikâwîpana ita kita-nihtâwikiwak. miscikosa î-kî-apahkwêcik kisik mîna maskîkwa î-tahkohtastâcik apahkwânihk. namôtha kinwîsk ispî kâ-kîsi-wâskahikanihkîcik ispî kâ-pî-nihtâwikiyân.

nikâwîpan nikî-itik: "î-kî-âhkosîwikamikohkâkawiyan ikospî."

2. salamô ikwâni poko *Ratt*

namôtha kîkway kotak niwîhthowin athisk ispî kâ-kî-nihtâwîkiyân piyak awa ayamihikimâsis (onâpîma ana iskwîw kâ-kî-pamihiwîwit "*Solomon*" kî-isithihkâsothiwa, iyako î-kî-okwîmîsiyân) nikî-kiskinawâcihik, tâpiskôc î-kî-sîkahahtawit nîtî wanihikîskanâhk î-kî-itwît "salamô ikwâni poko *Ratt*."

ispî tâpwî takî-sîkahahtâkawiyân, nîtî ayamihikamikohk âmaciwîspimowinihk, ayamihikimâw namwâc kî-ohci-pakitinam kotak wîhthowin kita-mîthikawiwak athisk sâsay î-kî-kiskinawâcihikawiyân "*Solomon*." "ikwâni poko" kâ-âkathâsîmonânowik "*that is all*." nîtha ôma *Solomon* ikwâni poko *Ratt*.

3. acoskîwinisa

kâ-kî-awâsisîwiyân mistahi mâna nikî-atoskîhikawin. ôho acoskîwinisa nikî-itôtîn: nikî-nâcinihtân, nikî-nikohtân, nikî-tâpakwân. nikî-wîcihâw nohtâwîpan ta-pakitahwât ikwa ta-nâtathapît. nikî-pîkwatahôpân ta-kwâpikîyân. nikî-nakwatison.

kahkithaw ôho acoskîwinisa nikî-wîcihikon. ikosi ôma kâ-kî-wâpahtamân ikota î-tipîthihtâkosiyân, î-wîcihowîyân.

Wow, these men worked very hard cutting down trees, as they were set on building a cabin for my late mother where I would be born. They used small trees for the roof and put moss on top for the roof. Not long after they were finished building the cabin I came to be born.

My late mother told me: "They had built a hospital for you at that time."

2. Just Solomon

I have no middle name because the lay preacher (the husband of the midwife who delivered me, his name was Solomon. I was named after him) "baptized" me at the trapline saying, "Solomon *ikwâni poko* Ratt."

When it was time for me to get baptized for real, in the church at Stanley, the minister refused to add another name since I was already "marked" as just Solomon. "*ikwâni poko*" means "that is all." I am Solomon *ikwâni poko* Ratt.

3. Chores

When I was a child I was given lots of chores. These are the chores I did: I fetched firewood, I made firewood, I set snares. I helped my late father setting nets and fetching nets. I chiselled a hole in the ice to haul water. I fetched meat from a kill site.

All these chores helped me. In that way I came to see that I belonged, that I was helping.

4. wîcisâni-kahkwîthihtowin

ispî kâ-kî-awâsisîwiyân mihcîtwâw mâna nikî-kitimahikwak nîtisânak. namôtha mâna nikî-pakitinikwak ta-wîci-mîtawîmakwâw.

piyakwâw ôma î-pipohk î-kî-sâh-sôskwaciwîcik, mâka namôtha nikî-pakitinikwak ta-wîcimîtawîmakwâw. nikî-kîwîtisahikwak. nikî-ati-kîwî-mâton ikota ohci. nikî-kitimâkinawik nohtâwîpan. ikota sîmâk kî-ati-othataham mistik, napakitâpânâskwa î-wî-othatahîstamawit. namôtha kinwîsk sâsay kâ-kîsi-othatahwât ninapakicâpânâskosa. kwayask nikî-cîhkîthihtîn ispî kâwi kâ-nitawi-sôskwaciwîyân ita kâ-sôskwaciwîcik nîtisânak.

nikî-nanôthacimâwak athisk nîtha poko î-ayâwak napakicâpânâskos. ikwâni nitati-sôskwaciwân. wahwâ nipistahwâw mistik! mitoni î-nâhtwâsimak ninapakicâpânâskos. kwayask kî-matwî-pahpiwak nîtisânak.

5. wîsahkîcâhk twîhow wanihikîskanâhk

hâw, wîsahkîcâhk:

apisîs ka-masinahamâtin.

nikiskisin niyânan î-kî-itahtopiponîyân wanihikîskanâhk î-mîtawîyân miskwamîhk, î-makosîkîsikâk ispî kâ-twîhoyan pimithâkanis î-âpacihtâyan. kiwathawîyâhtawân misiwî î-miskosîhoyan misi-maskimot î-nayahtâyan. ikota ninîpawinân, î-mâmaskâtamâhk. ikwa kâ-otinaman kîkwaya kimaskimotihk ohci, kimâh-mîthinân kâ-itahtwasiyâhk nîthanân awâsisak, sîwicîsak ikwa mîtawâkana. ikwa kâ-ohpahoyan, kîwîtinohk isi. kikî-itîthimitin î-kîwîkociniyan, mâka îtokî kotakihk wanihikîskanâhk î-itakociniyan ta-pahpihkwîhacik kotakak awâsisak.

nîtha kitôtîm,

salamô

4. Sibling Rivalry

When I was a child there were many times when my siblings picked on me. Usually they wouldn't let me play with them.

One winter they were out sliding, but they wouldn't let me play with them. They sent me home. I headed home crying. My late father took pity on me and immediately began to hew out a log, hewing out a toboggan for me. It wasn't long before he finished hewing out a little toboggan for me.

I was very happy when I went back to slide where my siblings were sliding. I teased them because I was the only one with my own toboggan. Right away I began to slide downhill. Holy, I accidentally hit a tree! I broke my little toboggan in half. In the distance I heard my siblings laughing it up.

5. Santa Visits the Trapline

Dear Santa:

I will write to you a bit.

I remember when I was five on the trapline. While I was playing on the ice on Christmas day, you landed your bush plane close to us. You climbed out in your red suit, carrying a huge bag. We stood in awe. Then you reached into the bag and gave each of us children bags of candy and toys. Then you took off, north. I thought you were heading home, but you probably went to the next trapline to make other kids smile.

Your friend,

Solomon

6. tâpokîthihtamowin

kayâs kâ-kî-awâsisîwiyân nikî-pâh-pimohtîhonân mâna misiwî itî mâhtâwisîpîhk. piyakwâw î-sîkwahk nikî-wâpamânân môswa î-âsowahahk sâkahikan. kîsiskaw kî-otihtinam pîminâhkwân nôhkomis ikwa kî-ati-tâpakwîwîpinîw iyakoni môswa. mâka ana môswa kwayask nikî-sîkihik athisk mitoni kihciwâk cîmânihk ita kâ-apiwak î-pî-isicimît. pîthisk âtawîtha kî-nipahîw iyakoni môswa nôhkomis î-mwayî-kwatapiskamwak cîmânis ispî kâ-kî-kakwî-tapasîhak ana môswa. awîna îtokî nawac kî-sîkisiw, nîtha awîkâ cî ana môswa? matwân cî î-kî-nitawi-wâpamât nôsî-môswa ministikohk ita kâ-kî-nihtâwikithit oskâyisisa?

7. ohpahowipîsim

tahto-askiy, anohc kâ-ispathik, nikî-pî-nâtahokawinân mâna ta-nitawi-ayamihcikîyâhk wâhthaw nîkinâhk ohci. ikospî namwâc kî-ohci-takwamon mîskanaw âmaciwîspimowinihk. ohcitaw poko mâna ta-pî-nâtahokoyâhk pimithâkana, kita-ohpahoyâhk. piyakwâw nikî-kakwîcimâw nikâwîpan kîspin iyak-ohci "ohpahowipîsim" kî-icikâsot awa pîsim. kî-mitho-pahpiw mâka nikî-wîhtamâk "ohpahowipîsim" awa pîsim itâw athisk ikospî mâna sîsîpisisak ikwa niskisisak î-ati-nihtâ-ohpahocik.

6. Faith

A long time ago, when I was a child, we travelled all over the Churchill River. One time, in the spring, we saw a moose crossing the waters of a lake. Quickly my uncle grabbed a rope and lassoed that moose. But that moose scared me because he would swim close to where I was sitting in the canoe. Eventually my uncle killed that moose before I tipped the canoe from my attempts at getting away from it. I wonder who was more scared: me, or the moose? I wonder if it was going to go see a female moose on the island where the young moose was born?

7. Flying Up Moon

Every year, about this time, they came for us to go to school far away from our homes. At that time there was no road to Stanley Mission. They had to come get us by plane, to fly us out. Once I asked my late mother if that was why this month was called "The Flying Up Moon." She had a good laugh but told me this month was called "The Flying Up Moon" because it was the time when the ducklings and goslings were able to fly.

3
nistam wîsakîthihtamowin

1. mâmitonîthihta ôma!
cîst!

mâmitonîthita ôma:

î-awâsisîwiyan. kîwîtinohk pikwataskîhk î-wîcâyâmacik kinîkihikwak, kîtisânak, mîna kiwâhkômâkanak, kanâtaskîhk î-pimâcihoyîk. mâhtâwisîpîhk î-papâmohtîhoyîk, mâmihk isi ikwa kâwi natamihk, âskaw mâna î-nitawi-kiyôtîyîk mistahi-sâkahikanihk. kikî-mitho-pimâtisinâwâw. kikî-cîhkîthihtîn î-wîcihowîyan ita kâ-pimahkamikisicik kinîkihikwak mîna kiwâhkômâkanak. kikî-cîhkîthihtîn î-mîtawîyan pikwataskîhk, kanâtaskîhk.

namôtha kikî-ohci-âkathâsîmon, kikî-nîhithowân poko. kikî-mâh-mithohtîn âcathôhkîwina ispî kâ-pipohk.

3
PAINFUL FIRSTS

1. Think on This!

Listen!

Think on this:

You are a child. In the north country you are living with your parents, your siblings, your relatives, living off the sacred land. You travel along the Churchill River downriver then back upriver, and sometimes travel to Lac La Ronge to visit. You have a good life. You are happy to help your parents and relatives with their work. You are happy to play in the wilderness, on the sacred land.

You don't speak English, only Cree. You like listening to the sacred stories told in the winter.

kâ-pî-isi-kiskisiyân

kîtahtawî kâ-pî-nâtikawiyân, î-sipwîhtahikawiyan ta-nitawi-ayamihcikîyân ayamihâwi-kiskinwahamâtowikamikohk.

pîtos askîhk kikî-itohtahikawin.

2. kiskinwahamâtowitâpânâsk

kî-mitho-kîkisîpâyâw ispî nistam kâ-kî-sipwîhtahikawiyân nîkihk ohci, ohpimî kita-nitawi-ayamihcikîyân. nikotwâsik ikospî nikî-itahtopiponân. namôtha nikî-pî-wîcîwikonânak ninîkihikonânak misi-tâpânâskohk isi wîtha nikâwîpan âhkosîwikamikohk î-kî-ayât, î-kî-katôhpinịt ikwa nohtâwîpan î-kî-pôsit îkâ î-kî-nohtî-wâpamikoyâhk ta-sipwîhtîyâhk.

ikwâni nitôsisinânak misi-tâpânâskohk nikî-isi-wîcîwikonânak. nîtha ikwa nistîs ikwâni nistam î-kî-sipwîhtîyâhk, î-ati-wîcîwâyâhkwâw nimisinânak, sâsay wîthawâw kî-sâh-sipwîthîwak, kistapinânihk sâsay î-kî-nitawi-ayamihcikîcik.

ikwâni nikî-pôsinân misi-tâpânâskohk. mistahi-sâkahikanihk ohci isko kistapinânihk. *All Saints Indian Student Residential School* kî-icikâtîw ikota kistapinânihk anima *residential school* kâ-kî-itohtahikawiyân. kinwîsk ikospî nikî-pimitâpâsonân, namôtha kî-ohci-mithwâsin mîskanaw tâpiskôc anohc.

ispî kâ-kî-ati-sipwîtâpâsoyâhk pôsotâpânâskohk nikî-ati-mâcosin, î-mawihkâtakwâw niwâhkômâkanak. piyak awa oskinîkîs nikî-kitimâkinawik; kapî nikî-ati-otamihik ikospî, î-âh-âcimostawit poko kîkway. pîthisk nikî-takotâpâsonân kistapinânihk.

pîthisk nitakotâpâsonân kistapinânihk. wahwâ! nikî-mâmaskâtîn ithikohk î-kî-mâh-misâki wâskahikana.

Eventually they came for you, to take you away to go to school in the church run schools.

You were taken to a different world.

2. School Bus

It was a beautiful morning when first I got taken away from my home to go to school far away. I was six years old at the time. Our parents did not accompany us to the bus because my mother was away at the hospital. She had tuberculosis and my father had gone off in his canoe because he did not want to watch us getting taken away.

So it was, my aunts took us to the bus. It was the first time for me and my older brother to be taken away, and we were going without our older sisters, who had gone away before. They had already gone to Prince Albert to go to school.

So we boarded the bus. We went from La Ronge to Prince Albert. All Saints Indian Student Residential School was the name of the residential school in Prince Albert where I was taken. It was a long ride back then because the roads were not as good as they are now.

When we drove away on the bus I started to cry quietly, crying over my relatives. There was this one teenager who took pity on me; he spent time entertaining me, telling me stories about all sorts of things.

We eventually arrived in Prince Albert, and I was amazed at all the big buildings.

kîtahtawî nitakotâpâsonân nikiskinwahamâtowikamikonâhk. nikî-kapânân misi-tâpânâskohk ohci ikwa nikî-nîpawihikawinân î-pîhoyâhk kita-nitomikawiyâhk ita ôma kâ-wî-kitîthimikawiyâhk. nikî-pîhtîn nimisak î-matwî-tîpwâtihcik ikwa ikotî nîsta nikî-kakwî-itohtân mâka nikî-kipihtinikwak nîci-nâpîsisak.

ikota *residential school* nikî-ayân mitâtaht pîsim tahto-askiy, nama wihkâc nikî-ohci-kîwân kâ-makosîkîsikâk pâtimâ nikotwâsikosâp kâ-kî-itahtopiponîyân.

âtawîtha tahto-nîpin mâna kâwi nikî-kîwân.

3. nikî-tâtopitikawin

kikâwînaw askîhk ohci:
kanâtaskîhk î-kî-wîkiyân.
nikî-tâtopitikawin ikota ohci
ta-nitawi-ayamihcikîyân
ayamihâwi-kiskinwahamâtowinihk.

4. nimasinahamawâw nikâwiy

nikiskisin ispî ohpimî nîkinâhk ohci kâ-kî-nitawi-ayamihcikîyâhk:

"tânisi mâmâ,

tânisi ikwa? nîtha wîtha nimithwâyân. môcikan nitayamihcikîwin mâka mistahi nikâh-kaskîthihtîn. mahti pî-itisahamawin pahkwîsikan."

nistam ikosi nikî-isi-kîwî-masinahikân mayaw î-kaskihtâyân ta-masinahamân âkathâsîmowin. tahtwâw kâ-kîwî-masinahikîyân tâpitaw mâna nikî-masinahîn "pî-itisahamawin pahkwîsikan."

All of a sudden, we arrived at our school. We got off the bus and were made to stand by as we waited to be called to our dorms. I heard my older sisters' names being called and I tried to go with them, but the other boys held me back.

I stayed in the residential school for ten months of the year, never going home for Christmas until I was sixteen.

At least I went back home every summer.

3. I Was Torn

I was torn from Our Mother Earth
as I was living on sacred land.
I was torn from there
to go to school
at the Residential School.

4. Letter to Mama

Memory from residential school:

"Dear Mom,

How are you? I am fine. School is fun but I am homesick a lot. Please send bannock."

My first letter home once I knew how to print in English. Each letter ended with "please send bannock."

5. môniyâw pîsimoyâpiya

nikotwâsik poko nikî-itahtopiponân nistam kâ-wâpahtamân ôtînaw. mistahi kîkway nikî-mâmaskâtâpahtîn.

"tâpwî môniyâwak!" nikî-itîthihtîn ispî î-kî-ati-pimitâpâsoyâhk kiskinwahamâtowitâpânâskohk kiskinwahamâtowikamikohk isi. î-kî-kanawâpahtamân wâskahikana ikwa î-kî-koskwâpisiniyân pîsimoyâpiy mohcihk î-ohcipathik owathawîtimiskwâtîmihk piyak môniyâw.

"mâmaskâc ôko! î-kaskihtâcik ta-osîhtamâsocik pîsimoyâpiy!"

mitoni mwîstas kâ-kî-ati-kiskîthihtamân ôma nipiy-sisiwîwîpinihkân îsa î-kî-âpacihtâcik.

6. î-kîwîhtahikawiyân

kika-âcimostâtinâwâw:

ispî kâ-kî-awâsisîwiyâhk ohpimî nikî-kwâsihikawinân kita-nitawi-ayamihcikîyâhk nîtî kistapinânihk. mitâtaht pîsimwak ikotî nikî-ayânân ikwa ispî î-ati-pôni-akimiht opiniyâwipîsim nikî-kîwî-tâpâtikawinân mistahi-sâkahikanihk isi, misi-tâpânâskohk î-pôsiyâhk.

ikwâni nimisak nikî-itohtahikonân nimosômipan wîkihk, ikwa kî-mâci-nitonawîwak ninîkihikonâna. mitoni nîso tipiskâw nitonawîwak, pîthisk âtawîtha kî-miskawîwak, akâmihk îsa î-kî-wî-nîpinisithit, nîtî kayâsi-wâskahikanihk kâ-icikâtîk.

ikwâni kâ-pî-wâpahk nisisipan nikî-itâhothikonân otôtihk, mâka nikî-ati-kitistinâhokonân âsowahonânihk sôskwâc ikota nikî-kapîsinân piyak tipiskâw. ikota nikapîsîwininâhk nikî-sâsakitisinin kâ-tipiskâk, î-kanawâpamakwâw acâhkosak ikwa tipiskâwi-pîsim.

5. Man-made Rainbows

I was six years old when I first saw a town. I looked at many things with wonder.

"These white people are truly gifted!" I thought when we were riding on a school bus to the school. I was watching the houses and I was surprised by a rainbow coming out of the ground just outside of one white person's house.

"Holy, these people! They are able to make rainbows for themselves!"

Much later I came to realize that they were using water sprinklers.

6. Home for the Summer

I'll tell you all a story:

When we were children we got kidnapped to go to school away from home, at Prince Albert. We were there for ten months, and toward the end of June we were sent back home riding on a bus.

My older sisters took us to my late grandfather's home, and they started looking for my parents. In a couple of days they found them across the lake, at Old House (Rapid River Lodge) where they had gone to spend the summer.

The next morning my late uncle took us in his boat to go there, but we couldn't cross the huge body of water known as "the crossing" because the waves were too big. We camped overnight, and there I lay on my back watching the stars and the moon.

kâ-pî-wâpahk nikî-misakânân kayâsi-wâskahikanihk.
ikota nâtakâm kâ-wâpamak nikâwîpan î-nîpawit, kwayask
nikî-cihkîthihtîn ispî kâ-wâpamak.

7. iskwâyâc tipiskâw î-mwayî-ohpahoyâhk

ikospî ôma mâna kâ-kî-ihkihk kâ-kî-pî-nâtikawiyâhk kâwi kita-nitawi-ayamihcikîyâhk kistapinânihk, ayamihâwi-kiskinwahamâtowikamikohk.

kî-mâh-misakâwak mâna ithiniwak ohpimî ohci itî kâ-kî-nîpinisicik. nitôtîminânak mâna nikî-pî-nâtikonânak ta-wîci-mîtawîmâyâhkwâw, aspin kâ-kî-pî-kîwîyâhk kâ-kî-ati-nîpihk iskwâyâc kâ-kî-wâpamâyâhkwâw. kapî-nîpin mâna nîthanân âmaciwîspimowinihk nikî-nîpinisinân, nîthanân nîcisânak ikwa ninîkihikonânak kapî î-otâkosik.

nikî-mâh-mîtawânân. nikî-môcikihtâkosinân îtokî. kâ-pî-kîkisîpâyâk nika-ohpahonân ikota ohci.

kayâs kâ-awâsisîwiyân, namwâc nohci-mâmitonîthimâwak aniki niwâhkômâkaninânak kâ-kî-nakatâyâhkwâw.

mâka anohc ôma nimâmitonîthihtîn:

piyak î-otâkosik kî-môcikihtâkosiwak awâsisak î-mîtawîcik;

kotak î-otâkosik kî-kipihtowîw; kipihtowîwin poko astîw.

When morning came, we arrived at Old House. My mother was standing at the shore waiting. I was so happy to see her.

7. Last Night of Summer

This is the time of the year when we were fetched to go back to school in Prince Albert, to the residential school.

The people would arrive by boat from their summer camps where they had spent their summers. Our friends, whom we had not seen since we came home at the beginning of summer, came to get us to play with them. Me and my siblings and my parents spent the summer in Stanley Mission.

We played all evening. Maybe we sounded joyful. In the morning we would fly away from there.

Long ago when I was a child, I never thought of the relatives we had left behind.

But today I am thinking of this:

one evening the joyful sounds of children playing;

the next evening silence; only the silence remains.

8. kicohcikanis

piyakwâw nikî-kimotin kitohcikan âmaciwîspimowin-*Co-op*-ihk ohci. nikî-itâw nistîs ta-asawâpamât okimâwa ikwa nîtha nikî-sîkowîpinîn kitohcikan nipapakiwayânihk ikwa nikî-wathawân atâwikamikohk ohci.

mitoni î-kî-nanamipathiki niskâta ispî kâ-nâsipîyân ta-pîhoyân ta-ohpahoyân mistahi-sâkahikanihk isi ita ta-pôsiyân âwatawâsiswâkan ayamihâwi-kiskinwahamâtowikamikohk ta-itohtahikoyâhk. niskâta kî-nanamipathinwa ispî kâ-kapâyân pimithâkanihk ohci ikwa kâ-pôsiyân âwatawâsiswâkan.

î-kî-itîthihtamân ta-kahcitinikawiyân nikimotiwin kitohcikan ohci, mâka namwâc nikî-ohci-kahcitinikawin ikospî nikî-kîmôci-nitohtîn kitohcikan ispî kâ-tipiskâk mihtawakay-nitohcikâkanisa î-âpacihtâyân. *Beatles, Cream, Hendrix* nikî-mithohtawâwak ikota nikimoti-kitohcikanihk ohci.

8. Transistor Radio

I stole a transistor radio from the Stanley Mission Co-op store once when we were headed back to the residential school. I told my brother Obie to keep six while I stashed the radio under my shirt and walked out the store.

My legs were shaking all the way to the shore of the lake where we were waiting for the plane to take us to the buses waiting in La Ronge. My legs were shaking as I got off the plane and onto the bus.

I thought I was going to be caught at any point with my stolen radio, but I wasn't caught. That year I listened to the radio's top forty countdown in the dark of night with earphones: Beatles, Cream, Hendrix. Got to love them through my stolen radio.

4
kâ-ati-oskinîkîsiyân

1. î-maskamikawiyân nipâhkîkinaskisina

ohpahowipîsim:

nikâwîpan mîkisihkâcikîw; î-kaskikwâtamâkoyâhk oski-pâhkîkinaskisina kita-kikiskamâhk kâwi itohtîyâhki *residential school* kistapinânihk.

nôcihitowipîsim:

nikikiskîn nitoski-pâhkîkinaskisina kistapinânihk isi. ikota kâ-takosiniyâhk nimîskotayawinisânân. nimaskamikawin nitoski-pâhkîkinaskisina.

4

MIDDLE YEARS AT SCHOOL

1. Stolen Moccasins

August:

My late mother beads: she is sewing new moccasins for us to wear when we go back to residential school in Prince Albert.

September:

I wear my new moccasins to Prince Albert. When we arrive there we change clothes. My new moccasins are taken away from me.

2. *"Dog Biscuits"*

ispî kâ-kî-awâsisîwiyân nikî-nitawi-ayamihcikân ohpimî nitiskonikanihk ohci. kistapinânihk mâna kâ-kî-nitawi-ayamihcikîyân, ikota *residential school* î-kî-itohtahikawiyân. mistahi mâna nikî-kitimahikawinân, mâka namôtha iyako niwî-âtotîn, niwî-âcimâwak nîci-kitimâkisak, nîci-kiskinwahamâkanak.

pâh-piskihc mâna nikî-kitîthimikawinân; piyakwan ka-itahtopiponîyâhk î-isi-kitîthimikawiyahk. ikwa mâna âtiht kâ-misikiticik nâpîsisak kî-kâh-kitimahîwak anihi nâpîsa nawac kâ-apisîsisithit. ikwa mîna kî-nâh-nôtinitowak nâpîsisak mahti awîna nawac kâ-maskawisît.

ikosi ôma kâ-kî-ati-ihkihk. ana nawac kâ-maskawisît "*First Boss*," kî-itâw ikwa mîna kotak "*Second Boss*," ikwa mîna kotak "*Third Boss*." nîtha wîtha "*Last Boss*," athisk î-kî-apisîsisiyân ikwa mîna î-kî-pâwanîsiyân ikospî mîna. nama nânitaw, kiyâm, nikî-itîthihtîn mâna wîtha mâna nistîs î-kî-nâh-nâtamawit.

piyak awa nâpîsis nikî-pakwâtik; kapî mâna î-kî-kakwî-nôtinit. mâka kî-kostîw nistîsa. nikî-paspân. piyak askiy mâka nistîs namwâc kî-pî-nitawi-ayamihcikîw, ayayâ, nikî-kostâcin, nikî-kostâw awa nâpîsis kâ-kî-kakwî-nôtinit. ohcitaw poko ta-kakwî-kaskimak ana *First Boss* ta-nâtamawit.

"*Frank* misti-sikâk" nika-isithihkâtâw ana nâpîsis kapî kâ-kakwî-nôtinit, ikwa "*Joseph* misti-kiyâsk" nika-itâw ana *First Boss*.

nikî-âh-awihâw mâna ana *First Boss* ni*comic book*ima, ikwa mîna nikî-kakwî-asotamawâw ta-atoskâtamowak otatoskîwin. pihtaw mâka kî-âtawîthihtam kahkithaw kîkway, ahpô mîna anihi nisîwi-mîciwina kâ-kî-itisahamawak tahtwâw kâ-kî-mîcisoyâhk. hay, nikî-ati-wawânîthihtîn athisk kîtahtawî nika-kahcitinik ana *Frank* misti-sikâk. tânisi mâka ôma takî-itôtamân?

2. "Dog Biscuits"

When I was a child I went to school away from my reserve. It was at Prince Albert where I went to school, there was a residential school there where I went. There was a lot of ill treatment, but I'm not going to talk about that, I'm going to tell a story about my fellow pitiful ones, my fellow students.

We were kept separate from each other; according to age we were kept that way. Some boys who were bigger than the rest would be mean on the smaller boys and they would fight amongst themselves to see who was the strongest: this was the way of it.

The one who was the strongest we called "First Boss," the next was "Second Boss," and another was "Third Boss." Me, I was "Last Boss" because I was small and skinny even then. It didn't matter. No worries, I thought, because I had an older brother to look out for me.

There was this one boy who disliked me; he always tried to fight me. But he was afraid of my older brother so I was safe. But one year my older brother did not come to school. Uh-oh, I was afraid of that boy who always tried to fight with me. I would have to try to convince the First Boss to look after me.

I will call that boy who tried to fight me "Frank Bigskunk," and "Joseph Biggull" is what I will call the First Boss.

I would lend my comic books to First Boss, and I also promised that I would do his work for him. Unfortunately he rejected everything, even that dessert I would send him every time we ate. Hey, I began to be in a fuddled state of mind because eventually Frank Bigskunk would catch me. What then should I do?

tahto tipiskâw mâna, î-mwayî-kawisimoyâhk nikî-asamikawinân mâna piyak î-misikitit piskit. kwayask mâna nikî-wîhkipwâw iyako. "*Dog biscuits*" mâna nikî-isithihkâtânânak iyakonik piskitisak.

hâw, piyakwâw nikî-itisahamawâw *Joseph* misti-kiyâsk iyakoni, kî-mithwîthihtam! nikî-ati-nipân ikospî î-nohtîhkatîyân mâka nikî-cihkîthihtîn athisk ikwâni î-kaskimak *Joseph* misti-kiyâsk ta-nâh-nâtamawit ispî ana *Frank* misti-sikâk kakwî-nôtinici. ikwâni, ikospî ohci tahto-tipiskâw nitisahamawâw *Joseph* misti-kiyâsk ni*dog biscuit*ima. namôtha awasimî nikî-kostâw *Frank* misti-sikâk.

kinwîsîs ikosi nikî-itôtîn.

tahto mâtinâwikîsikâw mâna nikî-kanawâpahtînân cikâstîpathihcikana. ikwa mâna kâ-kîsi-kanawâpahtamahk iyako nikî-mîtawânân iyakoni cikâstîpathihcikana î-nanâspitâtamâhk ikosi mâna, *Pirates, Cowboys and Indians*: kahkithaw kîkway. nikî-nanâspitâtînân. piyakwâw nikî-kanawâpahtînân *The Great Escape*.

ayâyihkwinî! ikospî kâ-tipiskâk, kinwîsîs aspin ohci kâ-kî-ati-kawisimoyâhk nipîhtawâwak nâpîsisak î-wâh-wathawîyâhtawîcik wâsînamânihk ohci. kîtahtawî *Joseph* misti-kiyâsk kâ-pî-nâsit.

"hâw, âstam! wîcîwinân!" nititik.

"namôtha-katâc, osâm nohtâwiy kâwi nika-pî-itisahok" nititâw. niwâpahtîn kîkway î-miciminahk, maskimocis îsa.

"kîkwây anima?" nititâw, î-itwahamwak omaskimocis.

"ninîmâwin ôma," itwîw, "*Dog biscuits!*" ikwâni, aspin kâ-wathawîyâhtawît wâsînamânihk.

Every night, before we went to bed, we were fed one big biscuit. I really liked the taste of that biscuit. We called those biscuits "dog biscuits."

Okay, once I sent Joseph Biggull that biscuit, he liked that! I began to sleep then, hungry but happy because I was successful convincing Joseph Biggull to look out for me when that Frank Bigskunk tried to fight me. There, from then on, every night I sent my dog biscuit to Joseph Biggull. I was no longer scared of Frank Bigskunk.

I did that for a while.

Every Saturday we watched a movie and when we finished watching, we would role-play those movies, copying the movie that way. Pirates, Cowboys and Indians: everything. We copied them all. Once we saw *The Great Escape*.

Uh oh! That night, a little after we went to bed, I heard boys climbing out the window. All of a sudden Joseph Biggull came to get me.

"Okay, come! Come with us!" he says to me.

"Not even, my father will only send me back," I say to him. I see that he is holding something, a small bag apparently.

"What is that?" I say to him, pointing to his bag.

"This is my lunch," he says, "Dog biscuits!" Then he was off, out the window.

ikwâni iskwâyâc î-kî-wâpamak. kahkithaw aniki nâpîsisak kâ-kî-tapasîcik kâwi kî-pî-itohtahâwak, mâka namwâc *Joseph* misti-kiyâsk.

ikospî kâ-tipiskâk namwâc nikî-ohci-nipân. nikî-kostâw *Frank* misti-sikâk.

3. î-kîmôci-ayamihcikîyân

namôtha nikî-nisitohtîn âkathâsîmowin ispî ohpimî kâ-kî-nitawi-ayamihcikîyân. mâka namôtha kinwîsk nikî-ati-nisitohtîn wîtha tahto-kîsikâw î-kî-pîhtamân, ikwa mîna tahtwâw kâ-mâtinâwi-kîsikâk î-kî-kanawâpahtamâhk cikâstîpathihcikana. nikî-mithwîthihtîn mîna kita-ayamihcikîyân. tahto-tipiskâw nikî-ayamihtân âcimowini-masinahikanisa ikwa mîna kihci-masinahikan, sîpâ nitakohpimihk mâna î-âpacihtâyân wâsaskocîpicikanis ta-kîmôci-ayamihcikîyân.

piyakwâw î-tipiskâk nikî-ayamihtân *comic-book*a sîpâ nitakohpimihk.

kîtahtawî kâ-pîhtawak ana kâ-kanawîthimikoyâhk nâpîw î-pî-itohtît ninipîwinihk isi. kîsiskaw nipakiciwîpinîn anima *comic-book* kâ-kî-ayamihtâyân ikwa nitotihtinîn kihci-masinahikan. ispî kâ-îkatîpitahk nitakohpim, ana nâpîw nimiskâk î-ayamihtâwak kihci-masinahikan.

"hâw, hâw-mâka, tâpwî-kihci, kiyâm ayamihcikiyâni."

ati-sipwîhtîw ikwa kâwi-nitotinîn ni*comic-book*im. ikospî kâ-askîwik mihcît kwâmik-poka nikî-ayamihtân, nama wîhkâc nikî-pisiskîthimik ana nâpîw kâ-kî-kanawîthimikoyâhk.

namôtha kinwîsk kâ-ati-nisitohtamân âkathâsîmowin.

That's the last I ever saw of him. All the boys got brought back, but not Joseph Biggull.

That night I did not sleep. I was afraid of Frank Bigskunk.

3. Undercover Reading

I did not understand English when I went to school far away from home. However, it did not take me long to begin understanding because I would hear it every day and every Saturday we'd watch movies. I also liked to read. Every night I read stories and even the Bible under my blankets using a flashlight to read in secret.

One night I was reading comic books under my blankets.

I heard the supervisor who looked after us approaching my bed. I quickly dropped the comic book and picked up the Bible. When the supervisor pulled my blanket off, he found me reading the Bible.

"Okay, okay then, very good. It's okay if you keep on reading."

He left and I picked up my comic book once again. That year I read lots of comic books. The supervisor never bothered me again.

It wasn't long before I started understanding English.

4. î-kîmôtâpiyân

cikôci! kîspin î-pimithâyan, tâpiskôc pithîsîs, ikotî ispimihk ohci kakî-wâpahtîn anihi wâskahikana ita kâ-kî-kanawîthimikawiyâhk ispî ohpimî kâ-kî-nitawi-ayamihcikîyâhk. kika-wâpahtîn nîso kinokamikwa ikwa anita âpihtawâyihk î-âniskôstîki, piyakwan anima âkathâsîmowin-masinipîhikanis "*H*" kika-isinîn. piyakwâyihk kinokamikohk iskwîsisak kî-kanawîthimâwak, ikwa anima kotak kinokamikohk nâpîsisak, kî-kanawîthimâwak ikwa anita âniskîkâkanihk kanâcihcikîwikamikwa kî-astîwa.

mâka mîna ôma nikî-piyakwahkamikisin ispî kâ-kî-miskamân pohtâhtawîwin ita ohci ispimihtakohk ta-itohtîyân. ikotî ispimihtakohk nikî-pimitâcimon î-nitawi-kanawâpamakwâw iskwîsisak okanâcihcikîwikamikowâhk, wahwâ! kwayask nikî-mithwâpisinin.

ikwâni ikosi nikî-ay-itahkamikisin, mâka piyakwâw î-kîsahkamikisiyân, î-pî-nihtâhtawîyân, kâ-mostinit piyak niwîcîwâkan. nikî-kakwîcimik tânisi ôma kâ-itahkamikisiwak. niwîhtamawâw î-kî-nitawi-kîmôtâpamakwâw iskwîsisak î-mîkwâ-sîpîkinastîcik. nititik kita-wîcîwit kîhtwâm ikosi itôtamâni.

ikosi mâni mâka nikî-pî-wîcîwik kîhtwâm kâ-nitawi-kîmôtâpamakwâw iskwîsisak. kwayask nikî-mithwâpisininân.

ikwa ispî kâ-pôni-kitâpimâyâhkwâw iskwîsisak nikî-ati-nihtâhtawânân ispimihtakohk ohci, wîtha nîkân niwîcîwâkan. kîtahtawî kâ-pîhtawak ana nâpîw kâ-kî-kanawîthimikoyâhk, î-matwî-tîpwît. kîsiskaw nikî-kâsôpathihon awasîwiwâwikanihtakohk.

"tânisi ôma î-itahkamikisiyan?" isi tîpwâtîw awa nâpîw niwîcîwâkana.

4. "Jeepers Creepers"

Listen! If you were flying, like a bird, from above you can see those houses where we were taken care of when I went to school far from my home community. You will see two long buildings and they were connected in the middle. It looks like the English letter "H." At one of the long buildings the girls were kept, and at the other long building the boys were kept, and in the middle connection were the washrooms.

As usual, I was doing things on my own when I discovered a hole through which I could get up to the attic. In the attic I crawled to go look at the girls in their washroom. Whoa! I liked what I saw.

I did that for a while, but once when I was done, as I was climbing down, a friend of mine caught me. He questioned me about what I was doing. I told him I had gone to spy on the girls while they were taking their shower. He told me that he would accompany me the next time I did that.

For sure then, he accompanied me the next time I went spying on the girls. We sure liked what we saw!

When we were done watching the girls we started to climb down from the attic, with my friend going first. All of a sudden I hear the supervisor, yelling in the distance. I quickly hid behind a rafter.

"What were you doing?" yelled the supervisor to my friend.

"namôtha kîkway. î-nitawâpînikiyân ôma mahti kîkway ispimihtakohk astîw," kâ-itwît niwîcîwâkan.

"nama-kîkway ikota astîw," kâ-itwît ana nâpîw. "kotak cî awiyak ispimihtakohk ayâw?" kâ-isi-kakwîcimât niwîcîwâkana.

"namôtha. nipiyakon anima," kâ-matwî-itwît niwîcîwâkan, îkâ î-misimit. ikwa sâkistikwânîw awa nâpîw î-nitawi-kihcinâhot, mâka namwâc nikî-ohci-wâpamik.

ikwâni ati-sipwîhtîwak ikwa acithaw nipîhon, mâka pîthisk nipî-nihtâhtawân nîsta.

kîhtwâm kâ-kocihtâyâhk ta-iskwâhtawîyâhk ispimihtak nimiskînân î-kipo-sakahikâtîk nipohtâhtawîwininân. wîspinac!

5. mistatimotôn

ohpimî kiskinwahamâtowikamikohk kî-astîw mînisihtakâw ikota mâna kî-ohci-mawisowak okiskinwahamâkîwak wîsakipicikwâsa, î-âh-asamikoyâhkwâw ispî kâ-atihtîki. mâka mâna mihcîtwâw nikî-nitawi-kimotinân.

iyak-ohci îtokî piyakwâw ikota mînisihtakâhk kâ-kî-kitîthimiht piyak mistatim, îkâ kita-kimotiyâhk wîsakipicikwâsa, îtokî, mâka nama-nânitaw.

piyakwâw î-otâkosik, nikî-nitawi-kimotinân iyakoni wîsakipicikwâsa. kiyâm ana mistatim. nikî-sîpâhtawânân mînikan ikwa pâh-piyak mistik nikî-iskwâhtawâtânân. namwâc nânitaw ita nikî-ohci-wâpamânân ana mistatim.

ikwâni ôma î-akosiyâhk mistikohk î-mâh-môminiyâhk, kîtahtawî kâ-pîhtawakwâw niwîcîwâkanak.

"Nothing. I was just checking to see what was up there in the attic," said my friend.

"There's nothing there," said the supervisor. "Is there anyone else up in the attic?" he asks my friend.

"No. I am alone," said my friend, not wanting to tell on me. Then the supervisor poked his head up to be sure, but he didn't see me.

They leave from there and I wait a little while, but I too eventually climbed down.

The next time we tried to climb up we found that our crawling-in space had been nailed shut. What a waste!

5. Horse Lips

At the residential school there was an orchard from where the teachers would harvest crabapples, which they fed us when they were ripe. But many times we would go and steal those crabapples.

Maybe that is why they kept a horse there one time, so that we would not go in to steal the crabapples. Maybe, but no matter.

One evening we went to steal some of those crabapples, never mind the horse. We sneaked under the fence and each of us climbed a tree. We didn't see the horse anywhere.

And there we were, up in the trees, when I heard my buddies.

"mâk-âwa! ikwa tapasîtân!" î-matwî-itwîcik. nipîhtawâwak î-sipwîpâhtâcik.

"ahpô îtokî piyak nâpîw kâ-kitîthimikoyâhk," nititîthihtîn. "misawâc ispimihk mistikohk nitakosân, namwâc nika-wâpamik," nititwân. nitâhkami-môminân.

ikwâni ôma watihkwanihk ohci nitisi-kwakwî-ohcipitîn wîsakipicikwâs kâ-sâminamân kîkway î-sâpopîk! kîtahtawî kâ-ôtot mistatim. "nihihihî!" nikoskomik!

mitoni î-nihcipahkisiniyân mistikohk ohci ithikohk î-koskomit! okot îsa î-kî-kakwî-môminiyân!

6. kâ-makosîkîsikâk

ispî kâ-kî-awâsisîwiyân nîsta nikî-kwâsihikawin ohpimî nîkihk ohci ta-nitawi-ayamihcikîyân, kistapinânihk nikî-nitawi-ayamihcikân, mihcîtwâw mâna nikî-kaskîthihtîn nîki. ikwa ôma, î-pî-makosîkîsikâk niwî-âtotîn tânisi mâna kâ-kî-itahkamikahk ispî kâ-makosîkîsikâk ikota kiskinwahamâtowikamikohk.

âtiht mâna awâsisak kî-pî-nâtitisahokowak onîkihikowâwa ta-kîwîcik, ta-nitawi-wîci-makosîkîsikanimâcik owâhkômâkaniwâwa. namwâc mâna nîthanân. nîkân nistîs ikwa nimisak ikwa nisîmisak (mwîstas wîthawâw kâ-kî-pî-ayamihcikîcik) nikî-kisâcânân, osâm î-kî-mihcîtiyâhk, osâm kî-mistakisow pôsotâpânâsk, namwâc kî-ispathihikowak ninîkihikwak ta-tipahahkwâw ta-kîwîyâhk nîstanân. ikwâni ikota kiskinwahamâtowikamikohk nikî-makosî-kîsikanisinân.

kî-nâh-nitomâwak mâna aniki awâsisak kâ-kî-pî-nâtitisahohcik. âta mâna nikî-nitohtîn nânitaw-isi nîstanân nitomikawiyâhki, mâka nama-wîhkâc ikosi kî-ispathin. piyakwâw mâka, î-pôni-âpihtâ-kîsikâk, nipîhtîn nimis î-matwî-nitomiht.

"Here he comes! Come on, let's run!"

"Maybe it's one of the supervisors," I think. "In any case I am up a tree; he won't see me," I say. I continue to pick crabapples to eat.

And as I was reaching into the branches to pick another crabapple I felt something wet. All of a sudden a horse neighed "nihihihihih!" He surprised me!

I was so surprised that I fell out of the tree. Apparently I was trying to pick his nose to eat!

6. Christmas at School

When I was a child I too got taken away to go to school away from my home, to Prince Albert (Prince Albert Indian Students Residential School.) A lot of times I was lonesome for home. Now that Christmas is coming I want to tell a story about what went on during Christmas at that school.

Some children's parents were able to send for their children to go home to spend Christmas with their relatives. Not us. First my older brother, and my older sisters and later my younger siblings (when they too came to school), we stayed behind because there were too many of us, the bus was too expensive, and it was not possible for my parents to be able to afford the bus for all of us to go home too. So there we stayed to spend Christmas.

The children who were sent for would be called (to the office). Although I listened hard, always hoping to hear us too being called, that was never the case. Once, however, I heard my older sister being called.

kwayask nikî-kisowâsin, ikwa pîthisk nikî-mâton. wîtha poko nimis î-pî-nâtitisahoht: mistahi nikî-pakwâtîn.

ispî kâ-nitawi-otâkwani-mîcisoyâhk, awîna mâka kâ-wâpamak? nimis! tâpokâni ninâcipahâw. nikakwîcimâw tânihki îkâ kâ-kî-kîwît. nikî-wîhtamâk tîpithahk î-kî-nitomiht ta-nitawi-wâciyîmât owîcîwâkana onîkihikothiwa.

ikwâni osâm poko kahkithaw awâsisak kî-kîwîwak, âtiht poko nîthanân nikisâcânân. ispî kâ-kihci-tipiskâk, î-mwayî-makosîkîsikâk, nikî-pôsinân pôsotâpânâskohk î-nitawi-kâh-kanawâpahtamâhk makosî-kîsikani-wâsaskocînikanisa ôtînâhk. nikî-môcikinîn. ikwa kâ-takosiniyâhk kiskinwahamâtowikamikohk nikî-akotânânak nitasikaninânak.

ispî kâ-makosîkîsikâk, nitasikanininâhk nikî-miskînân mîthikowinisa, ikwa sîwicîsak. kapî î-kîkisîpâyâk nikî-mîtawâkânân nitoski-mîtawâkaninâna. ikwa kâ-âpihtâ-kîsikâk nikî-misi-mîcisonân. ispî kâ-pôni-âpihtâ-kîsikâk nikî-mâmawihitonân ta-nâh-nikamoyâhk. ikwa kîtahtawî mâna kâ-pî-takosihk wîsahkîcâhk, î-mâh-mîthikoyâhk mîthikowinisa.

7. kinîkânîskawâwak kitithinîmak

ispî kâ-kî-ati-pônipathik nitayamihcikîwinân nikî-mâmawihitonân mâna. kahkithaw okiskinwahamâkanak mîtawîwikamikohk kî-itohtîwak.

okiskinwahamâkîwak ikwa okitîthimâwasowak nâh-nitomîwak okiskinwahamâkana tahto-itakisowinihk ohci î-mâmîthâcik iyakoni kâ-nîkânîthit otayamihcikîwiniwâwa otawihowîwina: kaskihtamâkîwin-masinahikanîkinwa ikwa masinahikan ikwa *cowboy*-astotina kî-otahikîwak iyakonik.

I was so angry, and I eventually cried. Only my older sister gets to go home: I hated that so much.

When it was time to go for supper, who did I see? My older sister. I ran to her right away. I asked her why she hadn't gone home. She told me that she was called only to go shake hands with her friends' parents.

Now then most of the children had gone home, just a few of us left behind. When it was time of the Great Night (Christmas Eve) before Christmas Day, we went on a bus to view the Christmas lights in town. I loved the sights! When we got back to the school we hung our stockings.

When it was Christmas Day in our stockings we found toys and candy. All morning we played with our new toys. At noon we had a big meal. In the afternoon we were gathered together and sang songs, and who should arrive but Santa, giving toys to all of us.

7. "A Credit to Your Race"

Near the end of each school year, the teachers would organize an assembly. Every student in the school was gathered in the gym.

Teachers would stand at the front to announce which students had done best in each grade, and in each subject. All the best students would be called up to shake hands with the teachers and principal. Sometimes we were given certificates, books, and cowboy hats as awards.

âskaw mâna nîsta nikî-nitomikawin athisk î-kî-ati-nakithâskâtamân ayamihcikîwin ikwa mîna âskaw î-kî-mitho-nâpîsisiwiyân.

(*heh, heh,* kîspin poko kî-kiskîthihtahkwâw! matwân cî kî-ohci-kiskîthihtamwak awîna kâ-kî-kimotit tî ikwa sîwihkasikanisak okiskinwahamâkîw-athwîpîwikamikohk ohci? aniki sîwihkasikanisak kî-wîhkicisiwak!)

kâ-wâciyîmâyâhkwâw okiskinwahamâkîwak kî-itwîwak "kimamihcihinân" ikwa mîna "kimamihcihâwak kitathisitinîmak."

î-kî-kakwî-takahkimikoyâhkwâw aniki. namôtha kî-ohci-kiskîthihtamwak î-mâci-itwîcik. nîstanân mîna nikî-mithohtînân iyakoni.

8. pakwanita-itwîwin

ispî kâ-kî-ayamihcikîyân nikî-nihtâ-atoskâtîn nikiskinwahamâkîw-atotamâkawin. ikwa mâna kâwi kâ-mîthikawiyân nitatoskîwin mihcîtwâw mâna nikiskinwahamâkîmak nikî-itikwak. î-âkathâsîmocik: "*Excellent work, Solomon! You are a true credit to your race.*" nikî-mithohtîn mâna iyako. mâka ispî kâ-ati-kîsohpikiyân nikî-nisitawinîn iyako nawac poko î-nihtâtawîhikawiyân. ikwa mîna kâ-ati-kîsi-ohpikiyân, ispî kâ-wâpamak ithiniw î-kaskihtamâsot kîkway kâ-sôhkanithik, mâna nikî-itwân: "*Not bad for an Indian.*"

I was called up several times at those assemblies because I was getting accustomed to school and sometimes I was the best-behaved boy of the dorm.

(Heh, heh, if they only knew! I wonder if they ever found out who stole the tea and cookies from the teachers' lounge? Those cookies tasted so yummy!)

As I shook hands with the teachers, they would tell me I had done well. They would say, "Congratulations." And when they were especially proud, they would always say, "You are a credit to your race."

They meant it in a good way. They didn't know that it was mean. And we, who didn't know better, also thought it was praise.

8. Backhanded Compliment

When I was in school I was good at working on my homework. And when I got my work back my teachers would say, in English: "Excellent work, Solomon. You are a true credit to your race!" I used to like hearing that. It was not until I became an adult that I came to understand that the phrase was in effect putting me down. And when I became an adult, when I saw a First Nations person being successful at something difficult, I would say: "Not bad for an Indian."

5
nîkihk kâ-nîpihk

1. ka-ispitisicik isîhcikîwin

kayâs mâna mihcîtwâw nikî-nitawiminânân natamihk ita ohci kâ-kî-wîkiyâhk. nîtha, nîtisânak, nikâwiy ikwa piyak nôhkom nikî-pôsinân mâna cîmânihk natamihk î-isicimîyâhk ta-nitawiminîyâhk nohcimihk ita î-ispatinâk. nikî-kospinân mâna ikwa nikî-mâh-mawisonân. namôtha mâna kinwîsk sâsay kâ-iskatîthihtamâhk ta-mawisoyâhk, nîtha, nistîs ikwa piyak nisîmis. nikî-mâh-mâci-mîtawânân îskwâ î-mawisocik nikâwiy, nôhkom ikwa nisîmisak, aniki iskwîsisak. mitoni mâna kapî-kîsik î-mâh-mîtawîyâhk. pîthisk kâ-ati-otâkosik nitîpwâtikonân nikâwiy, ikwa kâ-takopahtâyâhk nititikonân ta-nayahtâyâhk mînisa nâsipîtimihk isi. mitoni mâna mistahi miscikowacisa î-kî-sâh-sâkaskinâhtâcik ithinimina ohci. kî-kosikwanwa mâna anihi mînisa ikwa wâhthaw ta-isi-nayahtâyâhk nâsipîtimihk isi, mâka namôtha nânitaw nikî-itîthihtînân athisk ikosi mâna kapî î-kî-isi-atoskîhikawiyâhk nîthanân nâpîsisak.

5
SUMMERS AT HOME

1. Protocol: Age-Appropriate Conduct

A long time ago there were a lot of times we'd go berry picking upriver from where we lived. Me, my siblings, my mother, and one of my grandmothers went on board a canoe and paddled upriver to go berry-picking inland where there are high hills. We went inland into the bush and picked berries. It wasn't long before I, my older brother, and one of my younger siblings got tired of picking berries. We played while my mother, my grandmother and my younger siblings, those girls, picked berries. We played practically all day. Eventually, in the late afternoon our mother called for us, and when we arrived running, she told us to carry the berries on our backs to the shore of the lake. There were a lot of little boxes filled with blueberries. Those berries were heavy and we had to carry them far to the shore, but we thought nothing of it because this was the way we boys were always made to work.

2. nakwâtisowin ikwa mâtinamâkîwin

nikiskisin kâ-kî-awâsisîwiyâhk nikî-nitomikawinân nîtha mîna nistîs ta-nitawi-nakwâtisoyâhk. piyak awa niwâhkômâkaninân î-kî-nipahât môswa ikwa wâhthaw nohcimihk sakâhk î-kî-nakatât î-kî-pî-nâtât owâhkômâkana ta-nakwâtisothit, ikosi mâna kayâs omâcîwak î-kî-itôtahkwâw. tahto-wîtisânîhtowinihk ohci nitomîw kanakî piyak nâpîsisa ta-nitawi-nakwâtisothit. nistîs kî-wîsâmâw niwîtisânîhtowininâhk ohci ikwa nîsta nikî-wîsâmikawin ta-nâtamawak môso-wiyâs piyak nohkom kâ-piyakowîkit. wîpac î-kîkisîpâyâk nikî-sipwîhtânân, nîthanân nâpîsisak mîna nâpîwak. kinwîsk nohcimihk sakâhk nikî-pimohtânân. nikî-môcikihtânân, î-âh-âcimocik nâpîwak mîna î-nâh-nanôthacihikoyâhkwâw. pîthisk nitakohtânân minahowinihk. nâpîwak kî-mâh-manisâwâtîwak anihi môswa ikwa nikî-âh-asiwatânân môso-wiyâs nimaskimotinâhk. kâwi nikî-kîwânân. ispî kâ-takohtîyâhk nikapîsîwininâhk nikî-wîhkohkânân. ana nohkom kâ-kî-pîtamawak wiyâs nikî-kîsisamâk môso-wiyâs, î-kî-nawacîstamawit. wahwâ! kwayask nikî-wîhkistîn iyako môso-wiyâs! kwayask mîna nikî-môcikihtân ikospî kâ-kî-nitawi-nakwâtisoyâhk.

3. kisîwâtisiwin

kayâs kâ-kî-awâsisîwiyâhk nikî-wîcihinân nohtâwîpan ta-nikohtawât atâwîwikimâwa. osâm poko kapî-nîpin nikî-nikohtânân natamihk nîkinâhk ohci. nohtâwîpan kî-kâh-kîskatahâhtikwîw ikwa nîthanân nikî-nâsipiyâwatânân anihi mihta. nikî-sôhki-atoskânân mâna. pîthisk mihcît mihta nikî-âwatânân ikwa mihtot nikî-osîhtânân. nîstâw nikî-pî-wîcihikonân ta-pimitâpîpahtwât otôt ohci, ta-sakahpitahk anima mihtot otôtihk. nikî-itikawinân ta-pôsiyâhk ôsihk mâka nikî-akâwâtînân tahkohc mihtotihk ta-pôsiyâhk. kî-pahpisiw nohtâwîpaninân mâka nikî-pakitinikonân tahkohc mihtotihk ta-pôsiyâhk. wahwâ! kwayask kî-môcikan!

2. Sharing and Generosity

I remember when we were children, me and my older brother, we were invited to go fetch meat from a kill. One of my relatives had killed a moose and it was deep in the forest where he had left it to come get his relatives to go fetch the meat. This is what hunters did a long time ago. From every family he invited at least one boy to go fetch meat. My older brother was invited from my family and I was also invited so I could fetch moosemeat for a grandmother who lived alone. Early in the morning we left, us boys and the men. We walked in the forest for a long time. We had fun, the men would tell stories and they would tease us boys. We eventually arrived at the kill site. The men cut up the moose and we filled our bags with moosemeat. We went back home. When we arrived at out camp we made a feast. That grandmother for whom I brought moosemeat cooked the moosemeat for me, she had roasted it for me on a stick. Holy! I really liked the taste of that moosemeat. I had lots of fun at that time when we went to fetch meat at the killing site.

3. Kindness

A long time ago, when we were children, we helped our father to cut wood for the store keeper. We worked almost all summer at cutting wood upriver from our home. My father would chop down the trees and we would haul them down to the river. We worked hard. Eventually we had a lot of wood, so we made a raft. My brother-in-law came to help us to drag the raft with his motor boat, to tie the raft to his boat. We were told to get into the boat but we wanted to ride on top of the raft. My father laughed but he let us ride on top of the raft. Holy! It was a lot of fun!

4. kistîthihtamowin

ispî kâ-kî-awâsisîwiyâhk nîtha ikwa nimis nikî-kanâcihtânân thikwahaskân akâmihk ita ohci kâ-kî-wîkiyâhk. cîmânihk nikî-pôsinân î-âsowahamâhk sîpiy. kî-mitho-kîsikâw.

nikî-mâci-kanâcihtânân thikwahaskân. kapî-kîsik nikî-kanâcihcikânân. kîtahtawî, î-pôni-âpihtâ-kîsikâk, kâ-ati-sôhkithowîk ikwa î-pîtânaskwâk. kwayask kî-kaskitîwânaskwâw ikwa mîna kwayask kî-sôhkithowîw! pithîsiwak kî-kâh-kitowak ikwa kî-wâh-wâsaskotîpathin!

mâka mîna nîtha nikî-nôhtî-mâthîthihtîn ôma kâ-isi-kîsikâk, nikî-kaskimâw nimis kita-kakwî-âsowahamâhk kiyâm ôma kâ-isi-kîsikâk. ikwâni nikî-pôsinân. wahwâ! kwayask kî-mâh-misi-mamahkâhan mâka kiyâpic nipimiskânân, î-nanimahamâhk! kwayask nimâh-mâkwahikonân thôtin ithikohk î-mâh-misi-mamahkâhahk mâka pîthisk nimisakânân nîkinâhk. nikî-mâh-mamihcihisonân kâ-kî-isi-mâthîthihcikîyâhk. mâka nohtâwînân nikî-kihkâmikonân, î-kî-itikoyâhk ta-kî-kistîthihtamahk anima kâ-kî-isi-kîsikâk, namôtha pakwanita ta-kî-pôsiyâhk ispî kâ-sôhkithowîk mîna kâ-mâh-misi-kîstihk.

5. 1969 askîwin kâ-kî-akihtîk

1969 askîwin kâ-kî-akihtîk: nâpîw kî-pimohtîw tipiskâwi-pîsimohk, kî-mâmawihitonâniwin kita-kitohcikânowik *Woodstock*ihk. ikwa kîwîtinohk, nîtha niyânanosâp nikî-itahtopiponân î-wîcihakwâw nistîs ikwa nisîmisipan ikwa nohtâwîpan kita-wâskahikanihkîyâhk âmaciwîspimowinihk.

tahto-kîkisîpâyâw mâna nikî-pôsinân natamihk î-nitawi-kîskatahâhtikwîyâhk. nikî-nîmânân mâna ikotî ohpimî ta-âpihtâ-kîsikani-mîcisoyâhk. ispî kâ-misakâyâhk nikî-kospinân î-nitonawâyâhkwâw minahikwak î-kwayaskosicik ikwa iyakonik nikî-kîskatahwânânak. nikî-manahkwatatahwânânak minahikwak ikwa nikî-nâsipîtahânânak mistikwak, wâsakâm î-ahthâyâhkwâw.

4. Respect

When I was a child, me and my older sister cleaned the graveyard which was across the water from where we lived. We boarded a canoe and crossed the river. It was a good day.

We started to clean the cemetery. We cleaned all day. All of a sudden it was afternoon when a big wind picked up and clouds rolled in. They were very dark clouds and it was very windy. Thunder started to roll and lightning flashed.

As usual, I wanted to challenge the weather. I convinced my older sister for us to try to go across the water in spite of the weather! We got on board (the canoe). Holy! The waves were huge but still we paddled on, we paddled against the wind! The wind gave us a real tough time because of the big waves but we eventually arrived on shore where we lived. We were so proud of ourselves for meeting the challenge. But our father scolded us, told us to respect the weather when it was storming, to not go on board a canoe for any reason when it was storming.

5. 1969

1969: man walks on the moon, Woodstock happens, and in the north, I was 15 years old helping my older brother, my late younger brother, and my late father build a cabin in Stanley Mission.

Every morning we would set out upriver to go chop down trees. We took our lunch so we would have lunch away from home. When we arrived (by canoe) we would go inland looking for spruce trees that grew straight and it was those we chopped down. We peeled the spruce then carried the logs down to the shore and laid them down there.

mwîstas, kâ-kîsi-kîskatahâhtikwîyâhk nîstâpan nikî-pî-wîcihikonân, î-sakahpitât mistikwa otôtihk ikosi î-isi-otâpît itî kâ-kî-wî-wâskahikanihkîyâhk. niciwâmipan nikî-pî-wîcihikonân kita-kospihtatâyâhk mistikwa. nîstâpan kî-othastâw mistikwa ita kâ-wî-wâskahikanihkîyâhk ikwa ikota ohci nîthanân nâpîsisak kâ-kî-ati-wâskahikanihkîyâhk.

osâm poko kapî-nîpin nikî-otamithonân iyako. ispî kî-ihkin kâwi kita-nitawi-ayamihcikîyâhk kistapinânihk âpihtawithikohk poko î-kî-kîsi-astâyâhk apahkwân. kâ-ati-ohpahoyâhk opimithâw nîswâw wâskâkocin niwâskahikanisinân kita-wâpahtamâhk kâ-kî-isi-atoskîyâhk. î-kî-wâpamikoyâhk îtokî î-kî-wâskahikanihkîyâhk ispî mâna kâ-kî-tâh-twîhot.

ikospî 1969 nistam kâ-kî-kîwîyân aspin ispî kâ-kî-kwâsihikawiyân kita-nitawi-ayamihcikîyân ohpimî, nîtî kistapinânihk. nikî-mamihcihon athisk nohtâwîpan, nikâwîpan, ikwa nisîmisak ikota î-wîkicik, anima wâskahikanis kâ-kî-osîhtâyâhk.

ikospî mâna awiyak kâ-kî-wâskahikanihkît kahkithaw athisitiniwak kî-pî-wîcihowîwak. nohtâwîpan îtokî î-kî-itât namôtha katâc ta-pî-wîcihikoyâhkwâw athisk î-nitawîthimikoyâhk nîthanân nâpîsisak poko kita-wâskahikanihkîyâhk. ikosi kita-ati-kiskîthihtamâhk iyako kîkway. tâpwî mâni mâka: nistîs ikwa nisîmisipan kî-mistikonâpîwiwak ikwa nîtha nitohpikihtân itwîwina masinahikanihk.

Later my late brother-in-law came to help us, tied the logs to his boat, and dragged them to where we were going to build our cabin. My late cousin came to help carry the logs. My late-brother-in-law laid out the logs where we were going to build the cabin and from there us boys began building the cabin.

We were busy at this for most of the summer. When it was time for us to go back to school in Prince Albert we had only half the roof done. When we started to fly away the pilot circled our cabin twice so we could have a look at our work. Maybe he had seen us working at it when he would land during the summer.

1969 was the first time I came home for Christmas since I was kidnapped in 1960 and taken away to residential school in Prince Albert. I was proud when I saw that my mother, my father, and my younger siblings were living in the cabin, the cabin we had built.

At that time, when someone was building a cabin, all the people in the community came over to help. My late father must have told them not to bother since he wanted only us boys to build the cabin. In that way we would learn how to do that. And it was true: my older brother and my late younger brother became carpenters and I build with words in books.

6
î-ayahcitiniîwiyâhk nitaskînâhk

1. *Canada, Oh Canada*, 150 askîwina

Canada, Oh Canada, mitâtahtomitanaw mîna
niyânanomitanaw askîwina

î-kitinihcik ithiniwak

î-othasowâtacik îkâ kita-pimitisahahkwâw ithiniw-isîhcikîwina:

nakwâtisowina, pwâtisimowina, matotisâna;

masinahikanîkinos poko ta-ayât kîspin ta-nakatahk iskonikan –
ta-nitonahk atoskîwin –

âta nîstanân nikî-nitawi-nôtinikânân ispî kâ-nôtinitonânowik.

mâka nîkân poko ta-pakitinamâhk
nitiskonikan-akihtâsowininâna,

6
STRANGERS IN OUR HOMELAND

1. Canada, Oh Canada, 150 years

Canada, Oh Canada, 150 years

Of suppression of First Nations peoples

By outlawing cultural practices:

The potlatches, the powwows, the sweat-lodges;

By the pass system needed to leave the reserve – to seek work –

Although we too went to fight in your wars.

But first we had to give up our Treaty rights,

kâ-pî-isi-kiskisiyân

ikwa ispî kâ-pî-kîwîyâhk namwâc nimîthikawinân
simâkanisihkân-mitho-tôtâkîwina,

namwâc nikakî-kîwânân: namacî nikî-pakitinînân
nitiskonikan-akihtâsowininâna.

Canada, Oh Canada, mitâtahtomitanaw mîna
niyânanomitanaw askîwina

î-mîscihiwîyan: nîkân kimîscihâwak paskwâwi-mostoswak,

ikwa awâsisak kikî-kwâsihâwak ohpimî
ta-nitawi-kiskinwahamâkocik ayamihikimâwa

ita kâ-kî-nôcihiyâhk ispî kâ-pîkiskwîyâhk nipîkiskwîwininâna.

ikosîsi nikî-kipihtinikawinân îkâ kita-kiskîthihtamâhk
nitithiniwi-isîhcikîwina mîna nikâkîsimowininâna

kâ-kî-ânisko-kiskîthihtamâhk âcathôhkîwinihk ohci:

âcathôhkîwina kâ-kî-kiskinwahamâkoyâhk kita-isi-pimâtisiyâhk
ôta askîhk.

ohpimî-kiskinwahamâtowikamikohk ita awâsisak
kâ-kî-nâh-nôcihihcik ikwa kâ-kî-âh-otihtinihcik;

awasimî kihci-mitâtahtomitanaw kî-pôni-pimâtisiwak – mihcît
namwâc kiskîthihtâkwan ita kâ-kî-nahahthihcik.

kâ-kîsi-ayamihcikîyâhk nikî-wâh-wanihonân, kapî athisk
î-kî-kitîthimikawiyâhk namwâc nikî-kiskîthihtînân tânisi
kita-isi-pamihisoyâhk.

mihcît nikî-nisiwanâtahkamikisinân ikosi kipahotowikamikohk
kita-ayâyâhk: kita-kipahokawiyâhk namacî mâka poko
kâ-kiskîthihtamâhk.

And when we returned we were denied veteran benefits,

And we could not return home: after all we gave up our
Treaty Status.

Canada, oh Canada, 150 years

Of genocide: First you killed the buffalo,

Then kidnapped the children to go to church-run
residential schools

Where you beat us for speaking our languages.

Thus we were denied learning our cultural teachings and
spiritual beliefs

Which were passed on through our traditional stories:

Traditional stories which taught us how to live on this earth.

Residential schools where children were physically and
sexually abused;

Thousands died – many buried in unmarked graves.

After leaving the schools we were lost, so institutionalized that we
did not know how to live.

Many of us turned to crime so we'd go to jail: being inside is
something we knew.

mihcît minihkwîwin ikwa maci-maskihkiya kî-nisiwanâcihikowak ikwa kâkikî nâh-nôtinikîskowak.

Canada, Oh Canada, mitâtahtomitanaw mîna niyânanomitanaw askîwina

î-pî-ayahcitinîwiyâhk nitaskînâhk.

2. môtha nîtha *Indian*

kayâs mâna kâ-kî-awâsisîwiyân, ôtî mâna nikî-nitawi-ayamihcikânân kistapinânihk ikotî mâna î-nitawi-kiskinwahamâkosiyâhk. tahto-askiy mâna takwâki-pîsim kâ-kî-mâcihtâyâhk î-kî-nitawi-kâh-kiskinwahamâkosiyâhk ikota ôma *residential schools* kâ-kî-icikâtîki, ikotî kâ-kî-itohtîyân, âh, *Prince Albert Indian Student Residences* kî-isithihkâtîw iyako ânima. ikwa ikota mâna mistahi mâna awâsisak kî-kitimâkisiwak mistahi mâna kî-mâh-mawîhkâtîwak onîkihikowâwa.

aya, mîna mistahi mîna mâna nikî-môcikihtânân mâna tahtwâw kâ-mâtinâwi-kîsikâk, ikospî mâna nikî-kanawâpahtînân, âh, cikâstîpathihcikana, *picture shows* nikî-isithihkâtînân mâna. iyakoni mâna, mitoni mâna nikî-mâh-môcikihtânân kâ-pôni-wâpahtamâhk wîtha athisk mâna î-nitawi-mîtawîyâhk wathawîtimihk tâpiskôc mâna nîthanân, âh, *Pirates* mâna nikî-mîtawânân ikwa mîna *Cowboys and Indians*. ikosi mâna kâ-kî-isi-mîtawîyâhk, ikwa ôma kâ-kî-pî-isi-ohpikiyâhk ôma mitoni mâna, âh ..., nikî-wînîthimisonân, môtha nîthanân nîhithawak ta-kî-isi-pimâtisiyâhk î-itikawiyâhk mâna. ikosi mâna kâ-kî-isi-ohpikihikawiyâhk îkota kiskinwahamâtowikamikohk.

Many were destroyed by alcohol and drugs and are forever fighting.

Canada, oh Canada, 150 years

Of being strangers in our homeland.

2. I'm Not an Indian

Long ago when I was a child, we used to go to school over here, over there in Prince Albert was where we attended school. Every year we'd start in September, we'd go off to attend school there at the "residential schools" as they were called. That's where we went, it was called Prince Albert Indian Student Residences, that's what it was called. And while there the children used to be really desolate and they used to really cry for their parents, missing them a great deal.

Well, we also used to have a great deal of fun every time Saturday came around, for at that time we used to watch, uh, movies, we used to call them "picture shows." Those were the ones, we really used to have fun when we finished watching them for we'd go and play outside just like we were, well, we used to play "Pirates" and also "Cowboys and Indians." That's how we used to play, and at that time as we were growing up we really used to, uh ... we had a very poor opinion of ourselves. We used to be told that we shouldn't live like Cree people, that's the way we were raised there at that school.

mâka piyakwâw ôma î-kî-nitawi-kanawâpahtamâhk *Cowboys and Indians* cikâstîpathihcikan, *John Wayne* ikota mîna kâ-kî-ayât, î-kî-nôkosit, nikî-cîhkinîn, iyakw-ânima nikî-cîhkâpahtîn, nimithwîthihtîn ta-wâpahtamân, *John Wayne* ta-kanawâpamak. ikwa mâna kâ-kî-pôni-wâpahtamâhk iyakoni aya mâna nikî-nitawi-mîtawânân *Cowboys and Indians* mâka mâna î-kî-mâwasakonitoyâhk. âh, piyakwâyihk ita *Indians* ikwa piyakwâyihk kotak *Cowboys*; ikwa mâna nîtha kapî mâna nîtha iskwiyânihk kâ-kî-otinikawiyân. ikwa kîtahtawî ôma ôta piyak kîsikâw nikî-ati-otinikawin, *Indians* îsa nîtha ta-ayâyân. âh, namôtha nikî-cîhkîthihtîn, namôtha nîtha *Indian* nikî-nohtî-itakison ikota.

"môtha nîtha *Indian*," nikî-itwân. "namôtha niwî-*Indian*-iwin!" î-itwîyân.

"êy," itwîw ôta piyak nâpîw kâ-kî-kanawîthimikoyâhk, *supervisor* kâ-kî-itiht; "êy, tâpwî kikitimâkisin ikosi î-itîthihtaman. *Indian* athisk ôma kîtha ta-kî-itîthimisoyan ikosi isi î-itakisoyan," nikî-itikawin.

ikosi

3. âhkîtâp ithiniwak, cikâstîpathihcikan ithiniwak

hê! wîpac wî-nanâskomowikîsikâw!

ikospî ka-wîci-mayawâtamâyahkwâw kiwâhkômâkaninawak sawîthihtowina kâ-pî-wâpahtamahk kipimâtisiwininâhk.

tânihki mâka îkâ ka-tâpwî-itahkamikisiyan?

îhî, tâpiskôc aniki opîtatowîwak nistam kâ-kî-nanâskomowikîsikâk kayâs.

tânisi mâka? kitisi-kakwîcimon.

But this one time we were going to watch this Cowboys and Indians movie, and it had John Wayne in it. I liked it, I really enjoyed watching those ones, I liked to watch those, to watch John Wayne. Then when we had finished watching those ones, we used to go to play Cowboys and Indians and we'd gather ourselves together [choosing sides]. Ah, on one side were the Indians and on the other were the Cowboys. And I used to always be the one chosen last. Well, eventually on this one day I came to be chosen, and apparently I was supposed to be an Indian. Oh, I didn't like that, I really didn't want to be considered an Indian.

"I'm not an Indian," I said. "I'm not going to be an Indian," I was saying.

"Hey," said this one man who looked after us, he was called the "supervisor." "Hey, you're really pitiful thinking that way. You should think of yourself as an Indian because that's what you are," I was told.

That's all.

3. "Reel Injuns"

Hey! Thanksgiving is just a few days away!

A time to celebrate with family, giving thanks for the blessings in our lives!

Why not make it more authentic?

Yes, just like the Pilgrims on that first Thanksgiving back in the day!

How, you ask?

kâ-pî-isi-kiskisiyân

wîhcasin!

atoskîhik *Reel Injuns*!

kiyâpic cî pimahkamikisiwak? kitisi-kakwîcimon.

îhî! pî-sîwîpitamawinân ikwa ka-kî-itisahamâtinân *Reel Injuns*!

mâwaci wîhtakisowak tîpithâhk nanâtohk *Reel Injuns da Rez* ohci, ahpô mîna *da Hood* ohci.

ikwa nawac mistakisowak *Reel Injuns* kâ-wawîsîhocik.

ikwa kîspin namôtha nânitaw ta-mistahi-mîstinikîyan kika-kî-itisahamâtinân *Reel Injuns* kiyâpic î-pîkiskwîcik *Injun*!

îhî! cikôci!

Reel Injuns î-wawîsîhocik î-nîminikîcik kinanâskomowini-mîcisowinihk î-pîkiskwîcik anima kayâs pîkiskwîwin *Injun* kâ-itwânowik!

sîwîpicikî sîmâk *REE-LIN-JUNS*.

ikwa ka-mosci-mîthikosiwin kîkway.

cikôci, wâpamiskwâwi kiwâhkômâkanak, mîna kisiwâk kâ-wîkicik kitôtîmak: î-natomacik *Reel Injuns* kîkiwâhk ta-kihcinâhowak îkâ kîtha î*racist*owiyan!

Simple!

Get yourself Reel Injuns!

Are they still around, you ask?

Yes! Call us for your Reel Injuns for Thanksgiving!

For a standard price we can get you Reel Injuns from da Rez, even from da Hood!

And for a few dollars more we can get you Reel Injuns in Regalia!

And if you don't mind paying extra we can get you Reel Injuns who still speak Injun!

Yes! True! Why just imagine!

Reel Injuns in full dress saying the blessings over your Thanksgiving dinner speaking in that ancient language known as Injun!

Call now! Dial REE-LIN-JUNS.

And there's a bonus!

Just imagine having Reel Injuns over at your house: your family and your neighbors will see that you aren't racist!

4. kâ-papâmi-atâwîyan ispî kâ-wîskwastîwinâkosiyan

piyakwâw î-kî-nitawi-papâmi-atâwîyân ispî kâ-kî-mâtinâwikîsikâk. ayânisa î-kî-nohtî-atâwîyân. atâwikamikohk nikî-isi-pamihcikân. nikî-kapân otâpânâskohk ohci ikwa nikî-pîhtokân atâwikamikohk. otinikîwi-âwacikan nikî-nawasônîn ikwa nikî-ati-papâmi-atâwân ayânisa.

papiyâhtak nikî-thahkowîpinîn otinikîwi-âwacikan. ayânisa nikî-nâtîn. nikî-nawasônâw î-sîpihkosit mitâs. nikî-nawasônâwak î-kaskitîsicik asikanak ikwa mîna âtiht î-sîpihkosicik. nikî-pôsihâwak otinikîwi-âwacikanihk. nikî-nawasônîn î-mithkwâk papakiwayân ikwa miskotâkay î-sîpihkomithkwâk. iyakoni mîna nipôsihtân otinikîwi-âwacikanihk.

mwihci î-wî-nawasônakwâw tâpiskâkanak î-wâpiskisicik kâ-wâpamak atâwikamik-simâkanis î-kâh-kîmôtâpamit. nipakitinâwak tâpiskâkanak, namôtha katâc niwî-otinâwak.

mîciwina nikî-ati-nâtîn. ikotî nikî-isi-pimitisahok ana atâwikamik-simâkanis. kapî nikî-pimitisahok awa atâwikamik-simâkanis.

nikî-nawasônîn wâwa, napatâkwa, kâ-kâspâk mînis, nanâtohk kotaka mînisa, ikwa nîpiya. nikî-nawasônâwak pîswîhkasikanak mîna kohkôsiwîthin. âhci-poko nikî-pimitisahok awa atâwikamik-simâkanis.

nikî-kisowâhik!

sôskwâc poko kîkway nikî-ati-asowatân nitotinikîwi-âwacikanihk. mitoni î-kî-sâkaskinâhtâyân nitotinikîwi-âwacikan. ikosi nikî-nakatîn ikota.

namôtha katâc kîkway nikî-atâwân ikota ohci. nikî-wathawân ikwa nikî-pamihcikân kotakihk atâwikamikohk isi.

misawâc mihcîtinwa atâwikamikwa.

4. Shopping While Brown

Once I went about shopping on a Saturday. I wanted to buy clothes. I drove to the store. I got out of the car and entered the store. I selected a shopping cart and went shopping for clothes.

I carefully pushed my shopping cart. I went to where the clothes were. I chose a pair of blue pants. I chose black socks and some that were blue. I put those into the shopping cart. I chose a red shirt and a purple coat. I put those into the shopping cart too.

Just as I was going to choose white scarves I saw a store detective watching me on the sly. I put down the scarves, not wanting to buy them.

I headed for the food. The store detective followed me over there. This store detective was always following me.

I chose eggs, potatoes, various foods, and lettuce. I chose bread, apples, and bacon. Still the store detective followed me.

He made me angry!

So I started to put in all sorts of stuff into my shopping cart. Eventually I filled up my shopping cart. In that way I left it there.

I didn't bother buying anything from there. I walked out of there and drove to another store.

Anyway, there are a lot of stores.

5. âniskô-kiskinwahạmâkîwin

piyakwâw î-nîpîhk nikî-nitawi-papâmiskânân mâmihk âmaciwîspimowinihk ohci, î-pimitisahamâhk mâhtâwisîpiy. nikî-cîmâwak nitôtîmak. nikî-ati-kapîsinân pâwiscikosihk nistam kâ-tipiskâk ikwa î-ati-wâpahk kîhtwâm nikî-pôsinân, î-âsowahamâhk sâkahikanisîs. pîthisk wapâsihk nikî-takocimânân, kâ-mâthiciwasik isithihkâtîw anima wapâs. kîtahtawî kâ-matwî-tîpwîcik nitôtîmak. "ohcistin kitôtinaw!"

nikî-itâpin mostitakohk, wahwâ! tâpwî mâni mâka, nikî-ohcistinisinân.

"ahâw, cîskwa. kika-sîskipitînaw cîmân miniscikosihk misakâyâhki," nikî-itâwak.

ispî kâ-miskwâyâhk miniscikosihk nikî-sîskipitînân cîmân ikwa nikî-kwatapinînân. nikî-itâwak nitôtîmak ta-kotawîcik ikwa nîtha nikî-kospin î-nitonawak pikiw minahikohk. nikî-miskawâw.

ispî kâ-pî-nâsipîhtîyân kî-takahki-kwahkotîw kotawân. ikota nikî-ati-tihkiswâw ana minahik-pikiw. kâ-kî-kîsi-tihkisot ana pikiw nikî-ati-mîsahîn nicîmâniminân iyako pikiw î-âpacihak. nikitâpamikwak nitôtîmak tâpiskôc nawac poko î-ânwîhtahkwâw ôma kâ-itahkamikisiyân. nipîhonân ta-pâsot ana pikiw, pîthisk pâsow ikwa kîhtwâm nipôsinân. kâ-matwî-tîpwîcik nitôtîmak.

"namôtha awasimî ohcistin! wahwâ! tânisi ôma î-isi-kiskîthihtaman ta-mîsahaman cîmân?"

"kayâs ithiniw mamahtâwisiwin anima. kayâs ithiniw î-kî-kiskinwahamawit: nohtâwîpan."

5. Passing on Teachings

One summer we went canoeing downriver from Stanley Mission, following the Churchill River. I went with my friends. We camped at Little Stanley Rapids the first night and went on our way the next day crossing the little lake eventually arriving at a narrows, known as "place of difficult currents" (Frog Narrows). All of a sudden my friends hollered, "Our boat is leaking!"

I looked at the bottom of the canoe and sure enough, we were leaking!

"Okay, just wait. We'll pull the canoe to shore at a little island when we arrive there." I told them.

When we arrived at the little island we pulled the canoe to shore and tipped it over. I told my friends to build a campfire and I went inland looking for pitch on a pine tree. I found some.

When I went to the shore there was a good fire going, so there I began to melt the pine pitch. When it was done melting I began to patch our canoe using that pine pitch. My friends looked at me as if they doubted that I knew what I was doing. We waited for the pine pitch to melt and once again we boarded the canoe. My friends called out.

"There is no more leak! Holy! How did you know how to do that to patch the canoe?"

"It's an old Indian trick. An old Indian taught me: my late father."

kâ-pî-isi-kiskisiyân

6. âhkami-nîhithowîtân

âhkami-nîhithowîtân:

kipîkiskwîwininâhk astîw kinisitohtamowininaw.

âhkami-nîhithowîtân:

kipîkiskwîwininâhk astîw kinisitawîthimitowininaw.

âhkami-nîhithowîtân:

kipîkiskwîwininâhk astîw kipimâtisiwininaw.

âhkami-nîhithowîtân:

kipîkiskwîwininâhk astîw kinîhithâwiwininaw.

6. Let's Keep on Speaking Cree

Let's keep on speaking Cree:

In our language is our understanding.

Let's keep on speaking Cree:

In our language is our recognition of who we are.

Let's keep on speaking Cree:

In our language is our life.

Let's keep on speaking Cree:

In our language is our Cree essence.

7
tâpwîwin nîkân î-mwayî-mînosihtamâhk mitho-wîcîhtowin

1. tâpwîwin

tâpwîwin: awâsisak kî-sipwîhtahâwak;

tâpwîwin: onîkihikomâwak kî-maskamâwak otawâsimisiwâwa;

tâpwîwin: âtiht awâsisak namwâc kî-ohci-kîwîwak;

tâpwîwin: awâsisak kî-nanôthacihâwak ispî kâ-kî-pîkiskwîcik opîkiskwîwiniwâwa;

tâpwîwin: âtiht awâsisak kî-otihtinâwak;

tâpwîwin: âtiht awâsisak kî-nipahâwak;

tâpwîwin: awâsisak kî-wanihtâwak opîkiskwîwiniwâwa;

tâpwîwin: awâsisak kî-wanihtâwak otisîhcikîwiniwâwa;

7
TRUTH BEFORE RECONCILIATION

1. Truth

Truth: Children were taken away;

Truth: Parents had their children taken away from them;

Truth: Some children never went home;

Truth: Children were punished when they spoke their languages;

Truth: Some children were raped;

Truth: Some children were killed;

Truth: Children lost their languages;

Truth: Children lost their cultures;

tâpwîwin: namwâc wâhkôwîcihiwîwin ta-kî-ispathin pâtimâ naskwîwasihtâtwâwi ayamihikimâwak mîna okimâwak okimânâhk ohci ôho tâpwîwina.

2. kithâskiwin

ay-asastîwa kithâskiwin
ispî awasimî awâsisak
î-miskawihcik wâtihkânihk
oskaniwâwa î-asastîthiki.

3. namôtha âhkîtâp *Indian*

Solomon nitisithihkâson. âmaciwîspimowinihk ohci nîtha. *William John Ratt* (osowathîkis) kî-itâw nohtâwîpan, ohtâwîpana *Patrick* (oskâtâsk) kî-itimâwa, âmaciwîspimowinihk ohci. *Alice Emily Ratt* (pahkahk) kî-itâw nikâwîpan, okâwîpana *Maggie McKenzie* kî-itimâwa, mistahi-sâkahikanihk ohci.

4. kipihtowîwin

kikî-kakwî-kipihtowînikonawak:
kî-nisiwanâcihtâwak kiwâhkôhtowininaw;
kî-nisiwanâcihtâwak kipîkiskwîwininaw;
kî-nisiwanâcihtâwak kitisîhcikîwininaw;
kî-nisiwanâcihtâwak kitahcahkowininaw.
âtiht kikî-nisiwanâcihisonaw;
âtiht kikî-pôni-pîkiskwânaw kipîkiskwîwininaw;
âtiht kikî-wanihonaw
kâ-pîhtâkwahk kipihtowîwinihk.
mâka kîtahtawî
apisci-pîkiskwîwinis kîmwîw
"kimiskâkonawak."
kîtahtawî
kâ-pîhtâkwahk kipihtowîwin
kâ-kisîwîk.

Truth: Reconciliation will not happen until the churches and government are accountable to these truths.

2. Lies

Lies pile up
as more children
are found in graves
their bones in piles on top of each other.

3. Not a Pretendian

My name is Solomon. I am from Stanley Mission. William John Ratt (*osowathîkis*) was my late father's name, his late father's name was Patrick (*oskâtâsk*), from Stanley Mission. My late mother's name was Alice Emily Ratt (*pahkahk*), her late mother was Maggie McKenzie from Lac La Ronge.

4. The Sound of Silence

They tried to silence us:
They ruined our families;
They ruined our talk;
They ruined our culture;
They ruined our spirit.
Some of us destroyed ourselves;
Some of us stopped speaking our language;
Some of us were lost
In the sound of silence.
But suddenly
A small voice whispers
"They found us."
Suddenly
The sound of silence
Is loud.

5. î-nisiwanâcihtâyahk kipîkiskwîwininaw

tânihki ôma kipîkiskwîwininaw kâ-ati-wanihtâyahk?
wîtha kîthânaw î-itôtâsoyahk:
tahtwâw îkâ kâ-nîhithowîmititoyahk;
tahtwâw îkâ kâ-nîhithowîyahk ispî kâ-mâmawihitoyahk;
tahtwâw îkâ kâ-nîhithowîyahk ispî kâ-mâmawapiyahk;
tahtwâw îkâ kâ-nîhithowîyahk ispî kâ-kiskinwahamâkîyahk;
tahtwâw îkâ kâ-nîhithowîyahk ispî kâ-âcathôhkîyahk;
tahtwâw îkâ kâ-nîhithowîyahk ispî kâ-kâkîsimoyahk;
tahtwâw kâ-kitimâkimâyahk oskâya kâ-kakwî-nîhithowît:
"kimôniyâwihtâkosin mâna," î-isi-nanôthacimâyâhk.
ikosi kitisi-nisiwanâcihtânaw kipîkiskwîwininaw:
mitoni tâpiskôc î-ati-nisiwanâcihisômakahk kipîpiskwîwininaw.

6. tâniwî sâkihiwîwin?

cîst! mâmitonîthihta ôho:
ôma:
î-tipiskâk kîkiwâhk:
kipônînâwâw kotawânâpiskos;
kisaskahînâwâw wâsiskocînikanis;
kitanâskânâwâw ikwa kitakwanahonâwâw
opîwayakohp ohci;
mâci-âcathôhkîw kikâwiy.
ôhô matwî-kitow wathawîtimihk;
kotawânâpisk matwîhkahtîw;
wâsiskocînikanis cikâstîpathiw;
kikâwiy papiyâhtak âcathôhkîw.
kitati-nipân.
ahpô ôma:
ê-tipiskâk ayamihâwi-kiskinwahamâtowikamikohk:
kinîpitîkâpawinâwâw kita-otinamâsoyêk piskitis (*dog biscuit*);
kitayamihânâwâw;

5. Linguicide

Why is it that we are losing our language?
because we are doing it to ourselves:
every time that we don't speak Cree to each other:
every time that we don't speak Cree when we are at gatherings;
every time that we don't speak Cree when we are at meetings;
every time that we don't speak Cree when we are teaching;
every time that we don't speak Cree when we are telling
sacred stories;
every time that we don't speak Cree when we are praying;
every time that we bully a young person when he/she tries to
speak Cree:
"You sound so white," we tease them.
These are ways we kill our language:
it's like our language is beginning to commit suicide.

6. Where Is the Love?

Listen! Think on these:
This:
it is night at your home:
you put wood into the stove;
you light the candle;
you lay out the blanket and cover yourselves
with a down quilt;
your mother starts telling stories.
outside an owl hoots;
the fire in the stove crackles;
candle casts shadows;
softly your mother tells stories.
you begin to sleep.
Or this:
it is night at the residential school:
you line up to choose a biscuit, dog biscuit, for yourself;
you say your prayers;

kâ-pî-isi-kiskisiyân

kikawisimonâwâw;
âstawîhikâtîw.
kinwêsk kikanawâpahtên cikâstêsiniwina tahtwâw sêhkêpayîs
kâ-pimakocihk wayawîtimihk.
piyisk kinipân.

you lay down to sleep;
lights are turned off.
for a long time you watch the shadows every time a car drives
by outside.
eventually you sleep.

8
î-kîwîhtotahitoyahk

1. askiy kitohtâpamihikonaw

askiy kitohtâpamihikonaw;
thôtin kitohtâthîhthîhikonaw;
iskotîw kitohtâkîsôwihikonaw;
nipiy kitohtâminihkwînaw;
kipîkiskwîwininawa, kitâcathôhkîwininawa,
kiwâhkômitowininawa, kimâmawihitowininawa
kahkithaw ôho kitohtâpamihikonaw, kahkithaw
kipimâcihikonaw.

2. âniskôhtowin

iyako ôma âniskôhtowin:

pimitisahamani mitho-mîskanaw kika-wîcîwikon kahkithaw kihci-kiskinwahamâkîwina:

8
RECLAIMING OURSELVES

1. Earth Nourishes Us

Earth nourishes us;
Wind gives us air to breathe;
Fire gives us warmth;
Water quenches our thirst;
Our languages, our sacred stories, our kinship systems, our communities
All of these things nourish us, they all give us life.

2. Interconnectedness

This is interconnectedness:

If you follow the good road then all sacred teachings will accompany you:

sîpîthihtamowin, kisîwâtisiwin, sîpithawîsiwin, sâkihitowin, sôhkisiwin, sîpihkosiwin, nanâskomowin, kanâcihowin, mithwîthihtamowin, kistîthihtamowin, tâpowakîthihtamowin, nanahihtamowin, mâtinamâtowin, manâcihitowin, pakosîthihtâkosiwin, tapahtîthimisowin.

3. ninanâskomon

anohc ikwa tahto-kîsikâw:

ninanâskomon î-mithwâyâcik nicawâsimisak ikwa nôsisimak; ninanâskomon îkâ awasimî î-âpacihtâyân minihkwîwin ikwa maci-maskihkiya; ninanâskomon î-kaskihtâyân ta-kanawâpahtamân askiy tâpiskôc awâsis: ita kahkithaw kîkway î-mâmaskâtâpahtamân kahkithaw kîkway î-mithonâkwahk.

mitho-nanâskomowikîsikanisik tahto-kîsikâw

4. kâ-ohtâwîmâwi-kîsikâk

ispî kâ-kî-awâsisîwiyân kapî mâna nikî-wîcîwâw nohtâwîpan kâ-papâmahkamikisit. nikî-wîcîwâw kâ-nitawi-tâpakwît ikwa mîna kâ-kî-nâtakwît; nikî-wîcîwâw kâ-kî-nitawi-pakitahwât ikwa mîna kâ-kî-nâtathapît; nikî-wîcîwâw kâ-kî-nitawi-wanihikît ikwa mîna kâ-kî-nitawi-nâciwanihikanît; nikî-wîcîwâw kâ-kî-nâcinihtîyâhk ikwa kâ-nitawiminît. kahkithaw iyakoni kîkwaya nikî-ati-kiskîthihtîn, î-kî-kiskinwawâpamak nohtâwîpan. ikwa ispî kâ-kî-mâci-ayamihcikîyân tâpiskôc îkâ kîkway î-kiskîthihtamân nikî-isi-pamihikwak okiskinwahamâkîwak, î-kî-kakwî-nîpîwihicik kâ-kî-pî-isi-nîhithawi-pimâtisiyân.

anohc ôma kîthânaw kâ-ati-kiskinwahamâkîyahk kanawâpahtîtân itowihk kiskîthihtamowin awâsis kâ-pîtât okiskinwahamâtowinihk ikwa ikota ohci ati-takwastâtân kotaka kiskîthihtamowina.

tîniki nohtâwîpan.

Patience, kindness, tolerance, love, strength, resilience, gratitude, cleanliness, happiness, respect, faith, obedience, sharing, protection, hope, humility.

3. I Give Thanks

Today and every day:

I give thanks that my children and my grandchildren are healthy; I give thanks that I no longer use alcohol and drugs; I give thanks for the ability to look at the world as would a child: looking at all things in wonder and all things are beautiful.

Happy Thanksgiving every day!

4. For Father's Day

When I was a child I always accompanied my late father as he went about doing the things he needed to do. I went with him when he went setting snares for rabbits and when he went to check on the snares; I went with him when he went to set the net and when he went to fetch the net; I went with him when he went setting traps and when he went to check the traps; I went with him when he went in the canoe for firewood and when he went berry picking. I came to know how to do all those things by watching my late father. So then, when I started school it was like I knew nothing, that is how the teachers treated me, as they tried to make me feel ashamed of my Cree way of life.

Today, those of us who are beginning to teach, let's look at what knowledge the child brings to the classroom and from there we can add to further his knowledge.

Thank you, my late father.

5. nahîwin

okiskinwahamâkanak nikâh-kakîskimâwak, aniki kâ-nohtî-nîhithowîcik:

nohtâwîpan nikî-kiskinwahamâk ta-isi-tâpakwîyân. nikî-mîthik âpacihcikana ta-ohci-tâpakwâkiyân: cîkahikanis ta-kîskatahwakwâw miscikosak, tâpakwâniyâpiy, ikwa môhkomân ta-manisamân miscikosa ta-sihtoskahamân tâpakwân. nikî-kiskinohtahik ita ta-miskamân wâposo-mîskanâsa ikwa mîna ta-isi-nisitawinamân iyakoni. nikî-kiskinwahamâk ta-isi-othastâyân tâpakwâniyâpiy ikwa tânisi ta-isi-akotâyân wâposo-mîskanâsihk.

nistam kâ-akotâyân wâposo-tâpakwân nikî-mamâthân, mâka mihcêtwâw kâ-ati-tâh-tâpakwîyân nikî-ati-nahân. mâka anohc nimamâthân athisk kayâs aspin kâ-kî-tâpakwîyân. kapî mâna poko ta-tâh-tâpakwîyân kîspin ninohtî-nahân.

ikosi anima kahkithaw kîkway: kîspin nohtî-nahîyâni ohcitaw poko kapî ta-pimi-atoskâtamân.

6. kiskîthihtamowin

nika-kî-masinahikân
 âkathâsîmowin mîna nîhithawasinahikîwin
mâka namôtha nika-kî-pakitahwân
 ahpô namôtha nika-kî-wanihikân
 tâpiskôc kîtha.

nika-kî-kiskinwahamâkân
 nanâtohk masinahikîwin
 mîna tânisi ta-isi-kiskinwahamâkânowik
mâka namwâc nika-kî-mâcân
 namwâc nika-kî-mâtâhwâw môswa
 sâpo sakâhk ahpô akâmi-maskîkohk
 tâpiskôc kîtha.

5. Proficiency

My advice to students, those who want to learn Cree:

My late father taught me how to set snares. He gave me the tools with which to set snares: a small axe for cutting down saplings, snare wire, and a knife to cut sticks to brace the snare. He led me to the rabbit trails and showed me how to recognize them. He taught me how to shape and tie the snare wire across the rabbit trail.

The first time I hung a rabbit snare it was awful, but as I set more rabbit snares I became proficient at it. But today I am not good at it anymore as it's been a long time since I set a rabbit snare. I have to continually set rabbit snares if I want to be good at it.

It is this way for all things: if I want to be proficient at anything, I have to continually work at it.

6. Knowledge

I can write
    English and Cree writing
But I can't set gill nets
    Nor can I go trapping
    Just like you.

I can teach
    All sorts of ways to write
    or how to teach
But I can't hunt
    I can't track a moose
    Through the forest and across the muskeg
    Like you.

kâ-pî-isi-kiskisiyân

nitaspîthimon masinahikana ta-wîcihikoyân
 kâ-isi-kaskihtâyân;
kîtha wîtha, kitaspîthimon kikiskisiwin
 kâ-pî-isi-kiskinwahamâskwâw
 kitâniskô-wâhkômâkaninawak.

7. kiskîthihtamowin ohci

kiyâm âta î-mithwâsiki itwîwina mîna pîkiskwîwina apisîs poko ikota kâ-astîki ithiniw-kiskîthihtamowina, ithinîsiwina, ikwa mâmitonîthihcikîwina, nawac mistahi kiskîthihtamowin astîw âcathôhkîwinihk, âcimowinihk, ikwa nikamowinihk ikota kâ-isi-mâmawinamâhk kahkithaw kikiskîthihtamowininawa.

ikota ka-miskînaw kahkithaw kîkway kâ-ohci-kiskîthimisoyahk, ita kâ-ohci-nîhithawâtisiyahk, nanâtohk itîthihcikîwina, nanâtohk itîthihtamowina, nanâtohk môsihtâwina, ikwa nanâtohk âcimisowina kâ-pî-isi-itahkamikisiyâhk ta-ohpinamâhk kiskinwahamâtowina ikwa nîhithaw-isîhcikîwina ikwa nanâtohk isîhcikîwina.

Basil H. Johnston

8. nitohta!

kâwitha nakata ithiniwâtisiwin:
kapî ka-wîcîwikon;
kapî ka-wîcihikon.
tîpithahk acithaw nakata wanîwitowin:
kâkito!
nitohta!
kipihtowîwinihk ka-pîhtawâwak kitâniskô-wâhkômâkaninawak
î-âcathôhkâtikoyâhkwâw.
kâmwâtan.

I rely on books to help me
    With what I can do;
And you, you rely on memory
    The way you were taught
    By our ancestors.

7. About Knowledge: Basil H. Johnston

As rich and full of meaning as may be individual words and expressions, they embody only a small portion of the entire stock and potential of tribal knowledge, wisdom, and intellectual attainment, the greater part is deposited in myth, legends, stories, and in the lyrics of chants that make up the tribe's literature.

Therein will be found the essence and substance of tribal ideas, concepts, insights, attitudes, values, beliefs, theories, notions, sentiments, and accounts of their institutions and rituals and ceremonies.

Basil H. Johnston

8. Listen!

Don't leave First Nations traditions behind:
They will always accompany you;
They will always help you.
Just for a bit leave the noisy confusion behind:
Be quiet!
Listen!
In the silence you will hear our ancestors
Telling us sacred stories.
It is quiet and peaceful.

âcathôhkîwina / Sacred Stories

9
nîhithaw kiskinwahamâkîwin: nistam mâmitonîthihcikîwin

1. tânisi mâna kâ-kî-isi-kiskinwahamâhcik awâsisak kayâs?

kayâs mâna, î-mwayî-kwâsihihcik awâsisak ohpimî kita-nitawi-ayamihcikîcik ikwa î-mwayî-kiskinwahamâhcik kiskinwahamâtowikamikohk, î-mwayî-ihtakohki kiskinwahamâtowikamikwa, kî-kâh-kiskinwahamawâwak awâsisak kâ-mîkwâ-pimahkamikisicik tahto-kîsikâw.

kahkithaw kîkway kî-kiskinwahamawâwak: nâpîsisak kî-papâmi-wîcîwîwak ohtâwîmiwâwa î-wîcihâcik kîkwaya kâ-atoskâtamithit. ikosîsi wîthawâw kî-ati-kiskîthihtamwak tânisi kita-isi-pimâcihisocik. kî-kiskinawâpahcikîwak tânisi kita-isi-nôcihcikîcik, kita-isi-mâcîcik, kita-isi-nâcinihtîcik ikwa kita-nikohtîcik, kita-isi-nôcikinosîwîcik, kita-isi-osîhtâcik cîmâna ikwa wâskahikana; kita-isi-osîhâcik asâma, apoya, âhcâpiya, ikwa akaskwa.

ikwa iskwîsisak kî-papâmi-wîcîwîwak okâwîmiwâwa î-wîcihâcik kîkwaya kâ-atoskâtamithit. ikosîsi wîthawâw kî-ati-kiskîthihtamwak tânisi kita-isi-pimâcihisocik.

9

CREE EDUCATION: FIRST THOUGHTS

1. How Then Were Children Taught Long Ago?

Long ago, before the children were kidnapped to go to school away from home, and before they went to school in schools, before there were any schools, they were taught as they went about with their daily activities every day.

They were taught everything: the boys went about with their fathers helping with whatever they were working on. In this way they came to know how to keep their livelihood. They learned by watching on how to go about hunting, hunting big game, how to fetch firewood and make firewood, how to fish, how to make canoes and houses, how to make snowshoes, paddles, bows and arrows.

And the girls went about with their mothers helping them with whatever they were working on. In this way they came to know how to keep their livelihood. They learned by watching on how to kî-kiskinawâpahcikîwak tânisi kita-isi-piminawasocik, kita-isi-pâhkîkinihkîcik, kita-isi-mîkisihkâcikîcik, kita-isi-maskisinihkîcik, kita-osîhtâcik mîkiwâhpa, ayânisa, tihkinâkana ikwa kita-isi-mawisocik ikwa kita-manâhocik maskihkiya. mîna kiskinawâpahkîwak tânisi kita-isi-wîcihowîcik ispî oskawâsisa kâ-nihtâwîkithit.

kahkithaw kîkway kî-kiskinwahamawâwak kâ-kîsikâthik. ikwa kâ-tipiskâthik kî-kiskinwahamawâwak tânisi kita-isi-wîci-pimâtisîmâcik wîci-athisitinîmiwâwa, âcathôhkîwina ohci kî-kiskinawahamawâwak iyakwîthiw kiskinwahamâkîwin. kâ-piponithik mâna kâ-kî-âcathôhkânowik.

ispî kâ-kî-kwâsihihcik awâsisak ohpimî kita-nitawi-ayamihcikîcik namôtha awasimî ôho kiskinwahamâkîwina kî-ohci-kiskinwahamowâwak. namôtha awasimî kî-pîhtamwak âcathôhkîwina wîtha athisk kâ-pipohk poko kâ-kî-âcathôhkânowik ikwa ikospî wâhthaw ohpimî kî-ayâwak awâsisak.

mâka ôho âcathôhkîwina kî-mitho-âpatanwa kita-kiskinwahamâkîmakahki. anohc ôma mihcît athisitiniwak namwâc kiskîthihtamwak ôho âcathôhkîwina. ikwa âtiht ithiniwak itwîwak îkâ kitakî-âcathôhkîcik wîtha namôtha wîthawâw otâcathôhkîwak, ikosi î-itîthimisocik. mâka kayâs onîkihikomâwak mâna kâ-kî-âcathôhkîcik, namôtha katâc kî-pîhîwak otâcathôhkîwa, kitakî-iskacipîhîwak iyakoni awiya.

ikwa kayâs kâ-pipohk mâna kî-âcathôhkânowin. mâka anohc mistahi wanihtâniwin kipîkiskwîwininaw, ohcitaw poko pokîspî kitakî-âcathôhkîyahk awikâcî kika-wanihtânaw kahkithaw kikiskinwahamâkîwininawa.

cook, how to make leather, how to bead, how to make moccasins, how to make tipis, clothes, cradle boards, and how to harvest berries and medicines. And they learned by watching how to help bring a newborn into the world.

They were taught everything during the day. And at night they were taught how to live with their fellow tribespeople. Through the sacred stories they were taught this education. Winter was the time for the telling of sacred stories.

When the children were kidnapped to go to school far away from home, this education was no longer available. They no longer heard the sacred stories because winter was the time for the sacred stories and that was when the children were far away from home.

But these sacred stories were essential for education. Today many people do not know these sacred stories. Some people say they cannot tell the stories because they are not storytellers, that is what they think of themselves. But long ago it was the parents who told the sacred stories, they didn't have to wait for a storyteller, they would have waited for a long time for such a person.

Long ago winter time was the time for the telling of sacred stories. However, since today we have lost much of our language, we have to tell these sacred stories whenever we can or we will lose all our education.

2. kîkwây kiwîhtamâkonaw âcathôhkana? cihcipiscikwân
tânisi mâka kayâs î-kî-itâpatahki âcathôhkana?

spî mâna kâ-kî-pipohk onîkihikomâwak mâna kî-mâh-mâci-âcathôhkîwak, î-otamihâcik ocawâsimisiwâwa ispî kâ-pihcâ-tipiskâthik. nistam kâ-mispok mâna kâ-kî-mâci-âcathôhkânowik.

nikiskisin kâ-kî-awâsisîwiyân: ikota niwâskahikanisinânihk ninîkihikonânak kî-misi-pônamwak kotawânâpisk, kî-saskahamwak wâsiskocînikanisa, nikî-kîsôsimikonânak, ikwa kî-mâci-âcathôhkîwak. wîsahkîcâhkwa nîkân kâ-kî-âcimâcik.

tâpiskôc mâna tîpithahk î-otamîhâwasocik ispî kâ-âcathôhkîcik, wîtha mâna î-wawiyasîhtâkwahki anihi âcathôhkîwina, ithikohk î-kâh-kakîpâtisit wîsahkîcâhk. namôtha mâka anima iyak-ohci poko: kî-kiskinwahamâkîmakanwa anihi âcathôhkîwina. iyakoni ôho âcathôhkîwina î-ohci-kiskinwahamâkîcik tânisi kita-isi-pimâtisicik ôta askîhk kâkikî kâ-pimipathik.

mâmiskôtîtân nistam anima wîsahkîcâhk âcathôhkîwin, "cihcipiscikwân" kâ-icikâtîk. ikota âcathôhkanihk kikakî-miskînaw kahkithaw kiskinwahamâkîwina wâsakâm-pimâtisiwin ohci:

1. nîwayak isi-tapasîwak wîsahkîcâhk ikwa osîmisa, ispî kâ-tapasîhâcik cihcipiscikwâna:

2. kiwâpamânawak kahkithaw itowihk pisiskiwak: kâ-pimohtîcik, kâ-pakâsimocik, kâ-pimithâcik, kâ-pimitâcimocik;

3. kâ-ati-isi-pimâtisinânowik: oskawâsisiwin, oskâyiwin, kîsohpikihowin, ikwa kisiyayawin;

4. niyo itowihk kâ-ihtânowik: athisitinîwin, pisiskiwin, oskihtîpakiwin, ikwa asinîwin;

2. What Do Our Stories Tell Us? The Rolling Head

How were sacred stories used long ago?

When winter set in it was the time for the parents to tell sacred stories to their children, thus entertaining their children on long winter nights. They started to tell the sacred stories at the first fall of snow.

I remember when I was a child: there in our cabin our parents would put lots of wood in the stove, light the candles, bundle us up in warm blankets, then start telling the sacred stories. First they told stories about wîsahkîcâhk.

It is as if the stories were told to merely entertain the children because the stories were funny and wîsahkîcâhk did many silly things. But that was not their only purpose: the stories were educational. These stories contain lessons on how to survive in our world which is always in flux.

Let's talk about the first story in the wîsahkîcâhk cycle called *cihcipiscikwân* "The Rolling Head." In this story we can find all the teachings of the Circle of Life:

1. there are the four cardinal points in the flight of wîsahkîcâhk and his younger brother as they flee from the evil Rolling Head:

2. in the various characters who are in the story are represented four modes of mobility: walkers, swimmers, flyers, and crawlers;

3. four stages of life: infancy, adolescence, adulthood, and old age;

4. four orders of life: human, animal, plant, and mineral;

5. niyo-ayâkîhiwin: askiy, iskotîw, nipiy, thîhthîwin;

6. niyo kîkwaya ohcitaw poko ta-ihtakohki ta-mitho-pimâtisinânowik: kanawîthimikosiwin, pimâcihiwîwin, ohpikiwin, ikwa misiwîyâwin;

7. niyo isi-ayâwinwa: môsihtâwin, sôhkâtisiwin, mâmitonîthihtamowin, ikwa ahcahkowin.

ikwa otapasîwiniwâw î-âtotahkwâw tânisi kâ-pî-isi-pimôtîhocik nîhithawak: sâkâstînohk ohci, sâwanohk isi, pahkisimotâhk isi, kîwîtinohk isi ikwa kâwi sâkâstînohk takopahtâwak. kapî ôta kikî-ayânaw!

kîspin îkâ awasimî âcathôhkîyahki kika-wanihtânaw ôho kiskinwahamâkîwina.

5. four elements: earth, fire, water, and air;

6. four essential requirements for a healthy life: protection, nourishment, growth, and wholeness;

7. four aspects of human nature: emotional, physical, mental, and spiritual.

The flight of the boys is essentially a Cree migration story: from east to the south to the west to the north and back to the east. We were always here!

When we no longer tell our stories we lose all this education.

10
cihcipiscikwân

kayâs îsa, kî-piyakwâhkamikisiwak awa piyak nâpîw ikwa wîwa ikwa mîna nîso ocawâsimisiwâwa, nîso nâpîsisa, piyak nâpîsis mitoni î-ati-oskinîkîsiwit ikwa ana kotak nâpîsis kaciskaw î-kaskihtât ta-pimohtît. î-kî-piyak-ohpikihâwasocik îsa ôko ôtî pikwataskamikâhk, ôtî kanâtaskîhk. kî-mitho-wîcâyâmitowak îsa: tahto-kîsikâw kî-kospiw awa nâpîw, î-mâh-mâcît ikwa namwâc mwâsi kî-kwîta-mîcisowak wîtha ithikohk î-kî-nihtâ-mâcît.

kî-cîhkîthihtam opimâtisiwin, î-kî-mitho-wîcâyâmât wîwa ikwa ocawâsimisa.

kîtahtawî ati-ispathin î-ati-mîscihâwasot ita kâ-kî-wîkicik. ohcitaw poko nawac wâhthaw ta-nâh-nitawi-mâcît. âskaw mâna piyak-tipiskanisiw. ikosi ay-ihkin kinwîsîs ikwa.

10
THE ROLLING HEAD

Long ago, a man and a woman lived on their own along with their two children, two boys. One boy was almost a teen, the other boy a toddler. They raised their children on their own, in the wilderness, on the sacred land. They lived happily with each other: every day the man went into the bush to hunt and they seldom ran out of food to eat because he was a good hunter.

He was happy in his life, happy living with his wife and children.

Eventually a time came when he had killed nearly all the game where they lived. He had to go further and further to hunt. Sometimes he would stay overnight. That's the way things were for some time.

kâ-pî-kîwît miskawîw wîwa î-wawîsîhothit ikwa î-sîhkwîstikwânîthit tâpiskôc îsa î-kî-papâsipathihothit. mâhmaskâtîthihtam kâ-itahkamikisithit. kiskîthihtam wîtha î-ati-pîtosiyayâthit. ita mâna kâ-kî-nahîthihtamithit nawac ikwa kotak kîkway î-otamîthihtamithit. oskîsikothiwa nawac poko kî-kîskwîyâkwanithiwa. î-otamîthihtamithit. oskîsikothiwa nawac poko kî-kîskwîyâkwanithiwa.

kî-ay-apiw piyakwâw î-kanawâpamât ocawâsimisa î-mîtawîthit, kâ-pisiskâpamât wîwa î-ati-wawîsîhothit î-wî-nâcinihtîthit kihciwâk sakâsihk. ikosi âh-itôtamithiwa âta namôtha katâc ta-nâcinihtânowithik.

namôtha nânitaw itwîw awa nâpîw, mâka itasowîw î-wî-nitawâpînikît tânihk-ôma kâ-itahkamikisithit, ta-wîcihât kîspin ispathihikoci. ikosi piyakwâw sipwîhtîw, âhkîtâp î-nitawi-mâcît. kâsôw sakâsihk cîki mîskanâsihk ita mâna kâ-pimohtîthit.

“mahti kâ-itôtahk,” itîthihtam.

wâpamîw î-pî-âstamohtîthit. mitoni papâsohtîthiwa ispî kâ-ati-pimitisahwât, kâh-kâsôpathihow sakâsihk ispî kâ-nisihkâci-pimohtîthit.

wâpamîw î-nakîthit paskwâcîhk. tasopathihisiw ikwa ocihciya âpacihtâw ta-sîkahosot. otinam miscikos mohcihk ohci ikwa pâh-pawaham paskwâciy.

pôm! pôm! – pôm! pôm!

“ninâpîm, kâ-sâkihak, nitakohtân!”

ikota ohci paskwâcîhk kâ-pî-wathawîyâhtawîthit mihcît kinîpikwa. kî-kostâsinam awa nâpîw. misiwî omiyawithihk pimâhtawîthiwa anihi kinîpikwa.

Time came that whenever he would come home he would find his wife dressed in her finery, but her hair would be messed as if she'd been in a hurry. He wondered about her appearance. He noticed that she had changed somehow. Instead of the happy, contented look he used to see on her face, there was now an air of restless preoccupation. A strange light was in her eye.

Staying home one day, watching his children play, he noticed his wife getting done up in her finery to fetch wood in a nearby bush. This she did repeatedly, even when it seemed altogether unnecessary.

The man said nothing but made up his mind to do some investigating in order to help her if it were possible. So one day he went away, merely pretending to go on a hunt. He hid in the bush along the path she usually followed.

"Let me see what she does," he thought.

He saw her coming. Something in her eager gait so aroused his curiosity that he followed her, hiding in the bushes quickly whenever she slowed down.

He saw her stop by an old, decaying stump. She straightened her dress and ran her fingers through her hair. Then she picked up a stick from the ground and tapped on the stump.

Thump! Thump! Thump! Thump!

"My husband, my handsome one, I have come!"

Out of the stump crawled many snakes. The man was horrified! The snakes crawled all around his wife as she fondled them.

namwâc nânitaw itôtam mâka ikota ohci kisowi-sipwîhtîw. piyak-tipiskanisiw.

kîhtwâm kâ-wâpanithik kinwîsk pimohtîw mihcît pisiskiwa miyâskawîw mâka pîthisk nipahîw môswa. namwâc ahpô kî-ohci-pahkonîw ikosi kâ-ati-kîwît. mahkatâmow, tâpiskôc î-kakwâtaki-nîstosit, pîhtokîw wîkihk.

"nikî-nipahâw môswa," itîw wîwa, "mâka osâm nitâhkosin ta-nakwâtisoyân. kîtha poko ta-nâtaman wiyâs."

wîhtamowîw ita kâ-kî-nakatât anihi môswa, wâhthaw okapîsîwiniwâhk ohci, ikwa ohcitaw poko sîmâk ta-sipwîhtîthit kîspin nohtî-pî-kîwîthici î-mwayî-pahkisimothik. nawac poko namwâc nohtî-sipwîhtîw awa iskwîw.

"mahti nîkân nika-nâcinihtân!"

"nama! sîmâk sipwîhtî!"

sakamotîthanîwîw awa iskwîw ispî kâ-ati-sipwîhtît ikwa î-mwayî-sipwîhtît kakwî-kîmôci-pakitinam maskisiniyâpîs kotawânihk ikosi nawac wîpac ta-takosihk. mâka awa nâpîw wâpamîw ikota î-pakiciwîpinamithit maskisiniyâpîs. otinam animîthow maskisiniyâpîs ikwa sâpopatâw mîna ati-sîpîkipitam ikosi nawac kinwîsk ta-pimohtîthit anihi iskwîwa.

tahkohtastâw maskisiniyâpiy nîpîhk anita mohcîhk. kîsiskaw pîhtokîw mîkiwâhpihk î-nitawi-postiskahk wîwa otayânisa, î-iskwîwisîhot. tahkonam môhkomân. ispahtâw sakâhk itî kâ-kî-wâpamât wîwa î-mîtawâkâtâthit kinîpikwa, ikwa tâpiskôc wîwa, pâh-pâwaham paskwâciy.

pôm! pôm! – pôm! pôm!

"ninâpîm, kâ-sâkihak, nitakohtân!"

Not stopping to make his presence known, he went away in anger. He stayed overnight.

The next day he walked a long time passing many animals before he killed a moose. Without even stopping to take out the insides, he went home. Sighing, as if in great weariness, he entered the lodge.

"I have killed a moose," he told his wife, "But I am too sick to fetch it home. You must go for the meat."

He explained to her where the carcass lay, far from camp, so that she must leave right away if she were to return before dark. She showed a marked reluctance to go.

"Let me get some wood first!"

"No! Go at once!"

Mumbling to herself, she started off. On her way out of the camp she paused by the fire, seeming to tie her moccasins tighter for the long journey ahead. As soon as she was out of sight her husband rushed to the fire and saw a piece of sinew from her moccasin lace contracting in the fire. He knew it was an act of magic to make shorter the distance she had to go. He scooped the sinew from the fire with a stick and, wetting it, stretched it to its utmost length, thereby counteracting the effect of her act.

Setting the sinew aside on a wet leaf on the ground, he quickly went into the lodge and dressed in her finery. Arming himself with a knife, he marched into the bush to where he had seen his wife with the snakes and, like her, tapped on the stump.

Thump! Thump! – Thump! Thump!

"My husband, my handsome one, I have come!"

tâpwî mâni mâka, tâpiskôc nistam pî-wathawîyâhtawîwak aniki kinîpikwak paskwâcîhk ohci. mayaw kâ-pî-itohtîthit kîskikwayawîsâwâtîw. kîkâc kahkithaw mîscihîw. piyak poko paspîhîw, anihi î-apisîsisithit, ikwa ikota othasowîw.

"ispî ati-mihcîtitwâwi ithiniwak ôta askîhk namwâc ka-kaskihtân ta-wanâhowiyan. kapî kika-apisîsisin ikwa ta-wîhcasin ta-nipahikawiyan." kâ-pôni-wîhtahk ôma môsahkinîw anihi kâ-kî-nipahât kinîpikwa ikwa kîwîpahtâw, î-nitawi-kwayâtisit, mwayî-takosinithici wîwa.

nitomîw okosisa ikwa wîhtamowîw î-mâthipathihikocik.

"âhkosiw kikâwîwâw," itîw. "niwî-maskihkiwâpôstamawâw ta-nanâtawihahk mâka kîspin kipîhtînâwâw îkâ î-minihkwît, ôta ohci tapasîk! ôho niyo kîkwaya ka-mîthitinâwâw ta-paspîhikoyîk ispî ati-kostâciyîko: ôma oskâcik âpatan kihci-okâwîminakasiyak ta-ohpikicik; ôma âpiht âpatan asiniy-waciya ta-ohpikiki; awa posâkan ka-kwahkotîhkâkân; ikwa ôma amiskowîpit kakî-ohci-osîhtân sîpiy."

"ikwa poko ta-kâsôyîk wâtihkânihk ta-nitohtamîk. kîspin kikâwîwâw îkâ minihkwîci maskihkîwâpoy sîmâk ôta ohci tapasîk namôtha athisk awasimî iyako kikâwîwâw. mitho-pimôtîhok nikosisak! tâpika ta-mithopathihikoyîk kiyâm ôta mîkwâc î-mâthipathihikoyâhk. ispî ôtî nîkân nohtî-wâpamiyîko ispimihk kîwîtinohk isi itâpik, ikota nika-ayân kihciwâk îkâ kâ-ahcît acâhkos athisk wîtha nika-nâkatîthimik."

nâpîw kâtîw okosisa wâtihkânihk ikwa akwanaham iyakwîthiw akohp ohci. itîw otâpacihcikana îkâ nânitaw ta-wîhtamowâthit anihi iskwîwa. pihtaw piyak asinîs wanihow sîpâ akohpihk namwâc ohci-pîhtawîw. ikota ohci ati-pahkwîsikanâpohkâkîw anihi kinîpikwa kâ-kî-nipahât.

And sure enough, as before, the snakes crawled out of the stump. As quickly as they came, the man severed their heads, killing all but one, and a small one at that. To this lone survivor he pronounced his decree.

"When the earth is peopled by men you will not have the power to interfere with them. You will be small and easily conquered." Having made this pronouncement he scooped up some of the dead snakes and hurried to his camp to make preparations for his wife's return.

Calling his sons to him, he told them that a great misfortune had come upon them.

"Your mother is not well," he told them. "I am going to make a broth for her to drink to make her well but if you hear she doesn't drink it, you must run for your lives! Here are things that will be useful when danger approaches: this awl will provide a hedge of thorns; this flint will form mountains; this piece of tree fungus will provide fire; and this beaver tooth will form a great river."

"Now you must hide underground here and listen. Remember, if your mother doesn't drink the broth, flee for your lives, for she will no longer be your mother. Farewell my sons! May your lot be such that good may come to the Earth through this evil that has befallen us. In days to come, should you want to see me, look up to the Northern skies, for I shall be there next to the North Star, for he will protect me."

The man hid his sons in a hole under a blanket and forbade every object that was in their dwelling to tell the woman anything. Unfortunately, he missed a small stone that had slipped under the blanket. Then he made his broth from the dead snakes.

namôtha osâm kinwîsk kâ-takopahtâthit wîwa, î-pâhkwatâmothit ikwa î-apwîsithit. pakiciwîpinam onayahcikan ikwa sakâhk ati-kakwî-ispahtâw, mâka tîpwâtik onâpîma.

"âstam nîwa, api, mâskôc kinohtîhkatân. na, mîci ôma pahkwîsikanâpoy," itwîw nâpîw. nâh-nisihkâc kotawânihk itohtîw iskwîw ikwa nahapiw. ati-mîciw pahkwîsikanâpoy.

"mmm, kîkwây ôma kâ-wîhkasik?"

"omiskôm ana kinâpîm kinîpik," itwîw awa nâpîw î-kisowâhikot. "î-pahkwîsikanâpohkîstamâtân ôma!"

"namôtha tâpwî!" itwîw awa iskwîw î-ispahtât sakâhk ita kâ-kî-ayâthit kinîpikwa.

ikota kâ-takopahtât pâh-pâwaham paskwâciy.

pôm! pôm! – pôm! pôm!

"ninâpîm, kâ-sâkihak, nitakohtân!" mâka namwâc awiya pî-itohtîthiwa.

pôm! pôm! – pôm! pôm!

"ninâpîm, nitakohtân!" kiyâpic namwâc awiya pî-itohtîthiwa.

pôm! pôm! – pôm! pôm!

"ninâpîm, kâ-mithosit, nitakohtân!" mitoni ati-wawânîthimow, î-mâtot. kîhtwâm kocihtâw.

pôm! pôm! – pôm! pôm!

"ninâpîm, kâ-sâkihak, nitakohtân! âstam!"

Some time passed before his wife arrived, panting and covered with perspiration. She dropped her load and started for the bush, but her husband called her back.

"Come, my wife, sit, you must be hungry. Here, eat this broth I made for you," the man said. Reluctantly the woman came back to the campfire and sat down. She began to eat the broth.

"Mmmmm, what is this that tastes so good!"

"It's the blood of your husband the snake," the man said, angered by her manner. "From it I have made a stew for you!"

The woman got up quickly, angered that this might be so! "It is not true!" she said, running to her lovers in the bush.

When she got there she tapped the tree as she had done before.

Thump! Thump! – Thump! Thump!

"My husband, my handsome one, I have come!" But no one came.

Thump! Thump! – Thump! Thump!

"My husband, my beautiful love, I have come!" Still no one came.

Thump! Thump! – Thump! Thump!

"My husband, I have come!" She was now desperate, crying. She tried again.

Thump! Thump! – Thump! Thump!

"My husband, my dear one, my love, I am here! Come!"

nâh-nisihkâc kâ-pî-wathawîyâhtawîthit piyak kinîpikosisa, î-apisîsisithit.

"tâniwîhkâk mâka kotakak?!"

"awiyak ana kî-pî-itohtîw kahkithaw î-nipahât," itwîw ana kinîpikosis. kwayask kisowâsiw ana iskwîw. ispahtâw mîkiwâhpihk î-kakwâtaki-thawîsit.

ikwa mîkiwâhpihk kî-mamanîw îsa awa nâpîw: athapiya kî-âhthîw iskwâhtîmihk ikwa ikota nîpawiw, î-miciminahk cîkahikan, î-pîhât wîwa. pî-pimohtîthiwa, î-kisowâsithit, mâka athapîhk ostikwân otahwâthiw, kisî-tîpwîw! sîmâk nâpîw kîskikwayawîsâwâtîw cîkahikan ohci. ispî î-ati-pâhkihtihk mistikwân mohcihk isi tîpwâtam omiyaw.

"otihtin! nipah! nîtha nika-nawaswâtimâwak ocawâsimisa.

âta athapîhk î-otahwâmakahk miyaw otihtinîw nâpîwa ikwa kinwîsk mâsihitowak, mitoni misiwî pîhcâyihk mîkiwâhpihk î-tâh-tihtipîcik, sâkâstînohk ohci isko pâhkisimonohk; kîwîtinohk ohci isko sâwanohk. pîthisk ispimihk isi ati-ispathiwak ithikohk sôhki î-mâsihitocik, pîthisk ikotî ispimihk ati-acâhkosiwiwak.

ahpô anohc kiyâpic kakî-wâpamânawak: nâpîw ana ocîkatâhk ikwa miyawa kâ-nawaswâtikot, aniki atim-acâhkwak, namwâc kaskihtâw ta-otihtinikot athisk ana îkâ kâ-âhcît acâhkos î-nâkatawîthimikot.

Then very slowly, the small snake, the survivor, crawled out of the stump.

"Where are the others?!"

"Someone came and killed them all," answered the small snake in a querulous voice. The woman was furious! She ran back to the lodge in a rage!

In the meantime, the man had been making preparations: he had pulled a net over the door, and he stood with axe in hand, ready for his wife's return. She approached furiously, but on entering the lodge her head became stuck in the net. She screamed in rage and frustration. Quickly the man severed her head from the trunk. As the Head tumbled to the ground it yelled at the Trunk.

"Grab him! Kill him! I'll go after his children!"

Though enmeshed in the net the Trunk grabbed the man and they struggled inside the lodge, rolling from one side to the other from East to West, from North to South. Their struggle was so fierce that they eventually worked their way into the heavens in their frenzy and they became stars.

Even today you can see them: the man is the Big Dipper and the body of his former wife chasing him is the Little Dipper; the Little Dipper, however, can't get too close to the Big Dipper for the North Star stays close to protect the man.

11
wîsahkîcâhk tapasîw

aspin kâ-at-âtâhkowicik ohtâwîmâw ikwa omiyaw ana okâwîmâw. ikwa mîkiwâhpihk anima mistikwân, cihcipiscikwân awa, ati-tâh-tihtipîpathiw î-kâh-kakwîcimât âpacihcikanisa tânitî î-kî-itohtîthit otawâsimisa. namwâc kotak awiyak pîkiskwîw, awa poko asinîs îkâ î-kî-ohci-pîhtawât anihi nâpîwa kâ-kî-itwîthit.

asinîs wîhtamawîw cihcipiscikwâna anihi nâpîwa î-kî-kâtâthit nâpîsisa wâtihk sîpâ akohpihk. cihcipiscikwân sîmâk ati-nawaswâtîw!

kwayask sôhkîpathiw cihcipiscikwân î-nawaswâtât nâpîsisa. wâpamîw wâhthaw ikwa tîpwîw.

"tânitî, tânitî kakî-isi-tapasânâwâw? kika-nipahitinâwâw!"

aniki nâpîsisak pîhtawîwak cihcipiscikwâna mâka ana ostîsimâw kiskisiw ohtâwîwâwa kâ-kî-itwîthit îkâ awasimî ôho okâwîwâwa, nawac ati-sôhkânîpahtâw.

11

THE FLIGHT OF WISAHKECAHK

So the father and the body of the mother became stars. Meanwhile, inside the lodge the severed head asked the utensils where her children had gone. None spoke except for a stone who had not heard the man's admonishment not to talk.

The stone told the head that the man had hidden the boys in a hole under the blanket. The Rolling Head immediately gave chase!

With great speed *cihcipiscikwân* – the Rolling Head – pursued the boys. She saw them in the distance and hollered.

"Where, where can you flee! I am going to kill you!"

The boys heard the Rolling Head who had been their mother, but the older boy, Wisahkecahk, remembered his father's warning that this was no longer their mother and ran on.

nawac kisiwâk pîhtâkwanithiw okitowinithiw okâwîwa. kiskisiw anihi mîkiwina kâ-kî-mîthikot ohtâwiya ikwa pakitinîw osîmisa ikwa otâhk isi pimosinîw oskâcik. sîmâk ikota ohci ohpikithiwa kihci-okâwîminakasiyak, sâwanohk ohci isko kîwîtinohk î-ohpikicik. kiposkâkow ôho cihcipiscikwân, namwâc miskam ita ta-tawâthik.

ikosîsi misiwî ikota tâh-tihtipîw mâka anihi kihci-okâwîminakasiya ohpikithiwa kihcikamâhk ohci isko kotak kihcikamâhk. kîtahtawî kâ-pîhtahk kîkway kihci-okâwîminakasîhk, tâpiskôc awiya î-kaspâhcikîthit, natohtam. kîtahtawî kâ-wâpamât kihci-mohtîwa î-pî-tâwisithit kihci-okâwîminakasîhk ohci. tâpwî-pokâni nâcipahtwâw anima ita kâ-tawâtahk mîskanâs ana kihci-mohtîw, mitoni î-ati-napakiskawât, kisik î-wiyahkwâtât, iyakoni, ikwa ati-nawaswâtîw nâpîsisa.

cihcipiscikwân ati-pimipahtâw, wâpamîw nâpîsisa wâhthawîs. ikwa mîna tîpwîw.

"tânitî, tânitî kakî-isi-tapasânâwâw? kika-nipahitinâwâw!"

"namôth-âna kikâwînaw!" itwîw osîmimâw. nâpîsisak ati-sôhkipahtâwak wîsahkîcâhk î-nayahthât osîmisa.

nawac kisiwâk pîhtamwak okâwîwâwa opihtâkosinithiw. wîsahkîcâhk otinam kotak kîkway kâ-kî-mîthikot ohtâwiya ikwa pakitinîw osîmisa otâhk isi-pimosinîw âpiht, sîmâk ikota ohci ohpipathinwa asiniy-waciya î-nakiskâkot cihcipiscikwân.

kîhtwâm nakinâw cihcipiscikwân, namwâc kî-miskam nânitaw-ita ta-tawâthik kiyâm misiwî-ita î-isi-tâh-tihtipît. kîtahtawî kâ-pîhtahk kîkway tâpiskôc awiya î-kaspâhcikîthit asiniy-wacîhk. kipihcîw. wâpamîw kihci-amiskwa î-pî-taskamohtîthit asiniy-wacîhk. tâpwî-pokâni ispahtâw mîskanâsihk, ita kâ-tastawâcikîthit kihci-amiskwa, î-nipahi-napakiskawât, ithikohk î-nanihkisit ta-nawaswâtât nâpîsisa.

Ever nearer came the voice of his mother. He remembered the gifts that his father had given him and, setting his brother down, he threw the first of these, the awl – *oskâcihk* – behind him. Immediately a forest of thorns grew, stretching from the south to the north. The Rolling Head was stopped for she could not find an opening anywhere.

She went up and down but the huge hedge of thorns stretched from sea to sea. Then all of a sudden there came a sound from the hedge and Rolling Head stopped to listen. She saw a huge serpent chewing its way through the thorns. Rolling Head ran straight for the path made by the Serpent, crushing it in her hurry to go after the boys.

Rolling Head ran on and spied the boys in the distance. Again she hollered.

"Where, where can you flee? I am going to kill you!"

"That is not our mother!" said the young boy. And the boys ran on with Wisahkecahk now carrying his younger brother on his back.

Ever nearer came the voice of his mother. Wisahkecahk took the second of the gifts that his father had given him, the flint – *ahpit* – and setting his brother down, he threw this behind him. Mountains sprang up from where the flint hit the ground, blocking the Rolling Head. She was stopped once again for she could not find an opening anywhere.

Rolling Head went up and down the mountain range but could not find an opening. Suddenly she heard a sound of someone chewing through the mountains. She stopped and saw a giant beaver coming through the mountains. She immediately ran straight for the beaver's trail, crushing it in her haste to go after the boys.

cihcipiscikwân ati-pimipâtâw, wâpamîw nâpîsisa wâhthawîs. ikwa mîna tîpwîw.

"tânitî, tânitî kakî-isi-tapasânâwâw? kika-nipahitinâwâw!"

"namôth-âna kikâwînaw!" itwîw osîmimâw. nâpîsisak ati-sôhkipahtâwak wîsahkîcâhk î-nayahthât osîmisa.

nawac kisiwâk pîhtamwak okâwîwâwa opîhtâkosinithiw. wîsahkîcâhk otinam kotak kîkway kâ-kî-mîthikot ohtâwiya ikwa pakitinîw osîmisa. otâhk isi-pimosinîw posâkana. sîmâk ikota ohci kwahkotîw iskotîw î-nakiskâkot cihcipiscikwân. kîhtwâm nakinâw cihcipiscikwân. namwâc kî-miskam nânitaw-ita ta-tawâthik.

kiyâm misiwî-ita î-isi-tâh-tihtipît. ohcitaw poko ta-taskamiskahk animîthow iskotîw ta-nawaswâtât nâpîsisa.

cihcipiscikwân ati-pimipahtâw, wâpamîw nâpîsisa wâhthawîs. ikwa mîna tîpwîw.

"tânitî, tânitî kakî-isi-tapasânâwâw? kika-nipahitinâwâw!"

"namôth-âna kikâwînaw!" itwîw osîmimâw. nâpîsisak ati-sôhkipahtâwak wîsahkîcâhk î-nayahthât osîmisa.

nawac kisiwâk pîhtamwak okâwîwâwa opîhtâkosinithiw. wîsahkîcâhk kakwâtaki-nîstosiw athisk î-pâh-pimipahtât ikwa î-nayahthât osîmisa. otinam iskwiyânihk kîkway kâ-kî-mîthikot ohtâwiya, amiskowîpit, mâka î-mwayî-pakitinât osîmisa, kiciskinam iyakwîthiw nîkânihk isi. sîmâk ikota ohci ohpipathin sîpiy, î-nakiskâkocik, î-micimosihkwâw. ikwa ana cihcipiscikwân namôtha osâm wâhthaw î-pî-nôkosit.

Rolling Head ran on and spied the boys in the distance. Again she hollered.

"Where, where can you flee? I am going to kill you!"

"That is not our mother!" said the young boy. And the boys ran on with Wisahkecahk still carrying his younger brother on his back.

Ever nearer came the voice of his mother. Wisahkecahk took the third of the gifts that his father had given him, the birch fungus – *posâkan* – and setting his brother down he threw this behind him. Fire immediately sprang up from where the fungus had hit the ground blocking the Rolling Head. She was stopped once again for she could not find an opening anywhere.

Rolling Head went up and down the edge of the fire but could not find an opening. There was nothing to do but go through the fire in her haste to go after the boys.

Rolling Head ran on and spied the boys in the distance. Again she hollered.

"Where, where can you flee? I am going to kill you!"

"That is not our mother!" said the young boy. And the boys ran on with Wisahkecahk still carrying his younger brother on his back.

Ever nearer came the voice of his mother. Wisahkecahk was so tired from running and carrying his younger brother on his back. He took the last of the gifts that his father had given him, the *amiskowîpit* – beaver tooth. However, before he could set his brother down, he dropped the beaver tooth in front of him. A great river immediately sprang up from where the beaver tooth had hit the ground trapping the boys with Rolling Head not far from them.

kwayask cihcipiscikwân mithwîthihtam î-wâpamât nâpîsisa î-micimosinithit, wîpac ta-kahcitinât. mitoni ati-wawânîthihtamwak nâpîsisak, mwihci kîkâc î-pakicîcik ispî kâ-pîhtawâcik awiya î-pîkiskwâtikocik sîpîhk ohci.

"kika-âsowakâmîhothitinâwâw nôsisimak," itwîw îsa awa kisîtiniw-môskahosiw. "nispiskwanihk tâhkoskîk ikwa kika-âsowahothitinâwâw. mâka piyâhtak tâhkoskîk athisk î-wîsakîthihtamân nikwayaw." nahihtâwîwak anihi ikwa âsowahothikowak anihi kisîtiniw-môskahosiwa.

cihcipiscikwân nitomîw môskahosiwa î-kakwî-kaskimât ta-âsowathîhikot mâka ana môskahosiw namwâc nohtî-âsowahothîw. mâka mistahi mâh-mamihcimîw pîthisk tîpîthimow awa môskahosiw ta-âsowahothât cihcipiscikwâna. wîhtamawîw mâka îkâ ta-tahkoskâtamithit okwayaw. kîkâc î-misakâcik kâ-ati-kâh-kwâskohtipathihot cihcipiscikwân, î-pistiskawât môskahosiwa okwayâthihk, kâ-pakastawîhikot.

mayaw wîsahkîcâhk î-wâpamât nipîhk cihcipiscikwâna pimosinâtîw asiniya î-âpacihât, ikwa itwîw: "ôta ohci 'namîw' kika-itikawin, ta-mowiskwâw ôko ithiniwak kâ-wî-ayâcik ôtî nîkân."

ikosi ânima îsa. nîstosiwak nâpîsisak. athwîpiwak wâsakâm sîpîhk kapî-kîsik, mitoni isko î-tipiskâthik. ispimihk ay-itâpiwak, î-kanawâpamâcik ohtâwîwâwa, anihi ocîkatâhkwa.

Rolling Head was greatly pleased that the boys were within her grasp. The boys were about to give up when they heard a voice from the river.

"I will take you across the river, grandchildren," said an old bittern. "Step on my back and I will carry you across, but don't step on my sore neck." The boys obeyed and the bittern took them across the river.

Rolling Head called the bittern and tried to convince him to take her across but at first the bittern refused. Rolling Head flattered him and flattered him some more until he agreed to take her across. Rolling Head was excited, so excited that she jumped up and down, accidentally stepping on the bittern's sore neck. Reacting to the pain, the bittern dumped her into the water.

As soon as Wisahkecahk saw Rolling Head in the water he shot her with an arrow and pronounced: "From this day forth you shall be a sturgeon providing food for the people to come."

And it was so. The exhausted boys rested along the shore of the river all day and into the night. They looked up at the night sky and watched their father, the Big Dipper.

12
wîsahkîcâhk ikwa wîmisôsoy

ôta âcathôhkîwinihk kiskinwahamâkîwin astîw tânisi îkâ kita-itahkamikisiyâhk ispî kimanâtisimâkaninawak wîtapimikoyahkwâwi: osisa wîsahkîcâhk ôta kakwî-nipahikow. ôta mîna âcathôhkîwinihk kiskinwahamâkîwin astîw tânisi kita-osîhihcik ahcâpiyak ikwa akaskwak.

ikwa ôko nâpîsisak papâmohtîhowak; mistahi î-kakwâtakihtâcik. ikospî kî-sipwîhtîwak osîmisa î-wîcîwât wîsahkîcâhk. mâka kwîtatî-isi-otamihîw. pîthisk manâhow miskwâpîmakohpakwa ikwa wîwîkinam iyakoni. kwâskwînitowâna î-osîhtamawât osîmisa. ikosi î-isi-otamihât. iyakoni ta-mîtawâkîthit.

ikota wâsakâm sîpîhk mâh-mîtawâkîwak anihi kwâskwînitowâna, î-âh-ohpiwîpinâcik ikwa î-nâh-nawatinâcik. kîtahtawî kâ-pîhtawâcik awiya î-pî-natahamithit sîpiy. natamihk itâpiwak. wâpamîwak awiya î-pî-isicimîthit, pâskac mâna î-pakamahamithit âyîtaw otôtithihk ikosi mâna kâ-sipwîkotîthik otôt. kanawâpamîwak îsa ôko nâpîsisak anihi ayahcitiniwa ikota ôsihk kâ-pôsithit. kisâstaw piyakwan wîthawâw kâ-isinâkosicik î-isi nâkosithit, mâka nawac mistahi mîthawîsithiwa.

12
WISAHKECAHK AND *wîmisôsoy*

This cycle of stories shows the conflict between Wisahkecahk and his father-in-law. In effect these are cautionary tales about relationships with one's in-laws (manâtisimâkanak: those whom we avoid speaking to out of respect). His father-in-law tries to kill him. On another level we see that these stories show how to make bows and arrows.

So these boys went travelling about; they had many hardships. When they left there Wisahkecahk went with his younger brother. But he was at a loss as to how to entertain him. Eventually he gathered some red willow bark and bundled it up, making a ball for his little brother. With that he entertained him, to play with it.

They played along the shore of the river, throwing the ball up in the air and catching it. Suddenly they heard someone coming up the river, they look upriver. They see someone coming up the river, hitting the sides of his canoe to move the canoe forward. The boys looked at the stranger sitting in the canoe. He sort of looked the same as them but he had more hair.

kipihcipathiw anima ôsi akâmihk minîwâtimihk ita kâ-ayâcik ôko nâpîsisak. kîhtwâm mâci-mâh-mîtawâkâtîwak anihi kwâskwînitowâna. ispimihk î-âh-isi-wîpinâcik ikwa î-nâh-nawatinâcik. kîtahtawî kâ-ati-wâh-wâkâkocihk ana kwâskwînitowân, mitoni ôsihk î-nitawi-pahkisihk.

"mahti mîthin nikwâskwînitowâninân," isi-tîpwîw wîsahkîcâhk. "iyako ana poko î-isi-otamihak nisîmis."

ana nâpîw ahthîw anihi kwâskwînitowâna otapômihk ikwa itisinamawîw iyakoni wîsahkîcâhkwa.

"hâw, pî-nâs awa," itwîw awa ayahcitiniw. wîsahkîcâhk pahkopîw î-nâtât anihi kwâskwînitowâna. mwihci î-ati-otinât kwâskwînitowâna kâ-pôsowîpahikot anihi ayahcitiniwa otôtithihk. sîmâk pakamaham otôt awa kisîtiniw ikosi î-ati-sipwîcimît. ikosi î-isi-kwâsihiht wîsahkîcâhk. ikwâni î-nakatahoht awa osîmimâw.

"nistîsî!" isi-tîpwîw awa nâpîsis. "kiyâm! nika-mahihkaniwin! a-wô-ô-ô-ô," î-ati-ôthot.

"nisîmî! kâwitha pahkopîhkan ispî nawaswâtatwâwi môswak! kika-nistâpâwân," isi-tîpwîw wîsahkîcâhk.

wîsahkîcâhk wâpamîw mahihkanisa nohcimihk î-ispahtâthit. mistahi mâtow wîsahkîcâhk î-mawihkâtât osîmisa. kinwîsk mâtow. pîthisk ati-nîstosiw ikwa ati-nipâw.

kîtahtawî misakâwak ita wîmisôsoy – iyako mâni mâka awa maci-kisîtiniw – kâ-wîkit. sîskipitam otôt ikwa ati-kwatapinam. ikota sîpâ ôsihk ahthîw wîsahkîcâhkwa, kiyâpic î-nipâthit. kospiw. ispî kâ-takohtît wîkihk nitomîw otânisa, nîso otânisiw.

"hâw nitânisak! nipîsowâw awiyak kita-onâpîmiyîk," itîw otânisa. "niyâ, nitawi-wâpamihk, sîpâ nitôtihk aspin î-nakatak, î-nipât."

The canoe stopped across from the peninsula where the boys were. Once again the boys started playing ball, throwing it up in the air then catching it. Suddenly the ball curved in the air and landed in the canoe.

"Please give me our ball," yells Wisahkecahk. "That is all I have with which to amuse my younger sibling."

That man put the ball on his paddle and put it toward Wisahkecahk.

"Okay, come get it," said the stranger. Wisahkecahk wades into the water to get the ball. Just as he reached for the ball, the stranger scooped him into his canoe. The old man hit the side of his canoe and headed out. That was how Wisahkecahk was kidnapped. And the younger sibling was left on the shore.

"Older brother!" yells the boy. "It's all right! I will become a wolf! aaa-ooooooo," he howled.

"Younger sibling! Don't go into the water when you chase the moose. You will drown," yells Wisahkecahk.

Wisahkecahk sees a young wolf running into the forest. Wisahkecahk cried a lot, mourning his younger brother. He cried for a long time. Eventually became tired and he slept.

Eventually they arrived where *wîmisôsoy* – for this is who the evil old man is – lived. He pulls his canoe ashore and turns it over. There, under the canoe, he places Wisahkecahk still sleeping. He goes inland. When he arrived at his home he calls his daughters, his two daughters.

"Okay my daughters! I brought a person for you to have as a husband," he says to his daughters. "Go ahead, go see, he is under my canoe where I left him sleeping."

ikwâni omisimâw nâsipîw î-nitawâpînawât ôho awiya. wâpamîw ikota sîpâ ôsihk wîsahkîcâhkwa.

kitimâkinâkosiw awa wîsahkîcâhk î-misi-pâkacâpit. mitoni macinawîw awa omisimâw iyakoni. âtawîthimîw. kâwi-kospiw î-kisowi-ayamihât ohtâwiya.

"namôtha nikakî-onâpîmin ana oskinîkîs! osâm macinâkosiw," itwîw awa omisimâw.

ikwâni osîmimâw ati-nâsipîw, î-nitawâpînawât ôho oskinîkîsa. kitimâkinawîw. ikota ati-kâsîhkwînîw, mitoni î-ati-mithonâkosithit. nitomîw ta-wîcîwikot wîkiwâhk isi. ikota pamihîw, î-ati-wîkimât wîsahkîcâhkwa.

ikwa awa omisimâw akâwâtîw ôho oskinîkîsa athisk î-mithonâkosithit. mâka tahtwâw kâ-nâtât âtawîthimik. kahkwîthimîw osîmisa. ana kisîtiniw pakwâtîw onahahkisîma ikwâni î-othîthihtahk tânisi nânitaw takî-isi-nipahât.

piyak kîsikâw îsa wîsahkîcâhk kî-nohtî-ahcâpîhkîw.

"tâpika waskwayak ôta î-ihtakocik ta-ahcâpîhkâkîyân," itîw wîsahkîcâhk wîwa.

"nikiskîthihtîn ita kâ-mihcîticik waskwayak," itwîw wîmisôsoy. "ikota nici wâpahki ka-itahothitin."

kâ-wâpanithik wîsahkîcâhk ikwa osisa isicimîwak ita kâ-itwîthit osisa î-mihcîtithit waskwaya. ispî kâ-ati-misakâcik wâpahtam wîsahkîcâhk tâpwî mâni mâka îsa î-mihcîtithit waskwaya ikota. mayaw kâ-kapât wîsahkîcâhk ati-sipwîcimîthiwa osisa, î-tîpwîthit.

So then the oldest goes down to the shore to go see this person. She sees Wisahkecahk there under the canoe.

Wisahkecahk looks pitiful with swollen eyes. The oldest sister thought he looked ugly. She rejected him. She goes back up berating her father.

"I can't marry that young man! He is too ugly," says the oldest sister.

And so the younger sister goes to the shore to check on the young man. She takes pity on him. She starts to wash his face and truly he starts to look handsome. She invites him to accompany her to their home. There she took care of him. Eventually she made Wisahkecahk her husband.

The oldest sister desired the young man because he was quite handsome. But every time she made advances, he rejected her. The oldest sister was jealous. The old man did not like his son-in-law and plans on killing him somehow.

One day Wisahkecahk wanted to make a bow.

"I wish there were birch trees here so I could make a bow," he says to his wife.

"I know where there are many birch trees," says *wîmisôsoy*. "I will take you there by canoe tomorrow."

The following day Wisahkecahk and his father-in-law travelled by canoe to where his father-in-law said there were many birch trees. As they reached the shore, Wisahkecahk saw that there certainly were many birch trees there. As soon as Wisahkecahk got onto the shore, his father-in-law paddled away, yelling.

"hâw nipowâkan! kitasamitin awa nâpîw kita-mowat!" isi-tîpwîw wîmisôsoy, î-nitomât opowâkana. kâ-matâwisithit wâpaskwa.

wîsahkîcâhk nipahîw wâpaskwa. kîskikwayawîsâwâtîw ikwa tahkonam ostikwânithiw kisik waskwaya î-wî-ahcâpâhtakohkâkît. âsiskawîw ôho kisîtiniwa ikwa wîkithihk akotâw anima mistikwân. ispî kâ-misakât awa wîmisôsoy wâpahtam opowâkana wâpaskwa ostikwânithiw î-akotîthik wîkihk.

"wâh, nipowâkan!" kâ-isi-mawihkâtât îsa opowâkana awa kisîtiniw.

papiyâhtak ati-othahkotam ahcâpâhtik wîsahkîcâhk waskwayâhtik î-âpacihtât.

"tâpika môswak ôta î-ihtakocik ta-otinamân cîstatîyâpiy ta-kîsi-ahcâpîhkâkîyân," itîw wîsahkîcâhk wîwa.

"nikiskîthihtîn ita kâ-ayâcik môswak," itwîw wîmisôsoy. "ikota nici wâpahki ka-itahothitin."

kâ-wâpanithik wîsahkîcâhk ikwa osisa isicimîwak ita kâ-itwîthit osisa î-ayâthit môswa. ispî kâ-ati-misakâcik, kapâpathihow wîsahkîcâhk. mayaw kâ-kapât ati-sipwîcimîthiwa osisa, î-tîpwîthit.

"hâw nipowâkan! kitasamitin awa nâpîw kita-mowat!" isi-tîpwîw wîmisôsoy, î-nitomât opowâkana. kâ-pî-matâwisithit môswa.

wîsahkîcâhk nipahîw môswa ikwa manâhow cîstatîyâpiya. kîskikwayawîsâwâtîw ikwa tahkonam ostikwânithiw kisik cîstatîyâpiya î-wî-ahcâpâhtakohkâkît. âsiskawîw ôho kisîtiniwa ikwa wîkithihk akotâw anima mistikwân. ispî kâ-misakât awa wîmisôsoy wâpahtam opowâkana môswa ostikwânithiw î-akotîthik wîkihk.

"Okay, my spirit guardian! I brought a young man for you to eat!" yells *wîmisôsoy*, inviting his spirit guardian. A white bear comes out of the forest.

Wisahkecahk kills the white bear. He cuts off its head and takes it with him along with the birch that he is going to use as a bow stick. He overtakes the old man and goes to his home where he hangs the head. When *wîmisôsoy* arrives he sees the head of his spirit guardian, the white bear, hanging at his home.

"Oh my spirit guardian!" *wîmisôsoy* cries for his spirit guardian.

Carefully Wisahkecahk prepares the bow stick using the birch wood.

"I wish there were moose here so I could take some sinew to use as bow string," he says to his wife.

"I know where there are many moose," says *wîmisôsoy*. "I will take you there by canoe tomorrow."

The following day Wisahkecahk and his father-in-law travelled by canoe where his father-in-law said there were many moose. As they reached the shore, Wisahkecahk jumped ashore. As soon as Wisahkecahk got onto the shore, his father-in-law paddled away, yelling.

"Okay, my spirit guardian! I brought a young man for you to eat!" yells *wîmisôsoy*, inviting his spirit guardian. A moose comes out of the forest.

Wisahkecahk kills the moose. He cuts off its head and takes it with him along with the sinew that he is going to use as a bow string. He overtakes the old man and goes to his home, where he hangs the head. When *wîmisôsoy* arrives he sees the head of his spirit guardian, the moose, hanging at his home.

“wâh, nipowâkan!” kâ-isi-mawihkâtât îsa opowâkana awa kisîtiniw.

kîsihîw ahcâpiya wîsahkîcâhk. akaskwa ikwa poko kita-osîhât.

“tâpika nîpisiyak ôta î-ihtakocik ta-akaskohkâkîyân,” itîw wîsahkîcâhk wîwa.

“nikiskîthihtîn ita kâ-mihcîticik nîpisiyak,” itwîw wîmisôsoy. “ikota nici wâpahki ka-itahothitin.”

kâ-wâpanithik wîsahkîcâhk ikwa osisa isicimîwak ita kâ-itwîthit osisa î-mihcîtithit nîpisiya. ispî kâ-ati-misakâcik ikota, tâpwî mâni mâka mihcîtithiwa nîpisiya. mayaw kâ-kapât wîsahkîcâhk ati-sipwîcimîthiwa osisa, î-tîpwîthit.

“hâw nipowâkan! kitasamitin awa nâpîw kita-mowat!” isi-tîpwîw wîmisôsoy, î-nitomât opowâkana. kâ-matâwisithit kinîpikwa.

wîsahkîcâhk nipahîw kinîpikwa. kîskikwayawîsâwâtîw ikwa tahkonam ostikwânithiw kisik nîpisiya kâ-wî-akaskohkâkît. âsiskawîw ôho kisîtiniwa ikwa wîkithihk akotâw animîthow kinîpikostikwân. ispî kâ-misakât awa wîmisôsoy wâpahtam opowâkana kinîpikwa ostikwânithiw î-akotîthik wîkihk.

“wâh, nipowâkan!” kâ-isi-mawihkâtât îsa opowâkana awa kisîtiniw.

ati-kîsi-othisâwâtîw akaskwa wîsahkîcâhk. tahkopitam môhkomânatosâpiskwa piyakwâyihk kisipanohk, ikwa kotakihk câskisâwâcîsiw, tîpithahk apisîs.

“tâpika mîkwanisak kita-astâwîyân ôko akaskwak,” itîw wîsahkîcâhk wîwa.

“nikiskîthihtîn ita kâ-mihcîticik mîkwanisak,” itwîw wîmisôsoy. “ikota nici wâpahki ka-itahothitin.”

"Oh my spirit guardian!" *wîmisôsoy* cries for his spirit guardian.

Wisahkecahk finishes the bow. Now he only has to make arrows.

"I wish there were willows here so I could make some arrows," he says to his wife.

"I know where there are many willows," says *wîmisôsoy*. "I will take you there by canoe tomorrow."

The following day Wisahkecahk and his father-in-law travelled by canoe to where his father-in-law said there were many willows. As they reached the shore, there certainly were many willows. As soon as Wisahkecahk got onto the shore, his father-in-law paddled away, yelling.

"Okay, my spirit guardian! I brought a young man for you to eat!" yells *wîmisôsoy*, inviting his spirit guardian. A snake comes out of the forest.

Wisahkecahk kills the snake. He cuts off its head and takes it with him along with the willows that he is going to use to make arrows. He overtakes the old man and goes to his home where he hangs the head. When *wîmisôsoy* arrives he sees the head of his spirit guardian, the snake, hanging at his home.

"Oh my spirit guardian!" *wîmisôsoy* cries for his spirit guardian.

Wisahkecahk finished the preparation of his arrows. On one end he ties a stone arrowhead and on the other end he makes a notch, a small notch.

"I wish there were feathers so I could decorate these arrows," he says to his wife.

"I know where there are many feathers," says *wîmisôsoy*. "I will take you there by canoe tomorrow."

kâ-wâpanithik wîsahkîcâhk ikwa osisa isicimîwak ita kâ-itwîthit osisa î-mihcîtithit mîkwanisa. ispî kâ-ati-misakâcik ikota, mâni mâka mihcîtithiwa mîkwanisa, misiwîskamik ikota nâtakâm î-pimisinithit. mayaw kâ-kapât wîsahkîcâhk ati-sipwîcimîthiwa osisa, î-tîpwîthit.

"hâw nipowâkan! kitasamitin awa nâpîw kita-mowat!" isi-tîpwîw wîmisôsoy, î-nitomât opowâkana. kâ-twîhothit mikisiwa.

wîsahkîcâhk nipahîw mikisiwa. kîskikwayawîsâwâtîw ikwa tahkonam ostikwânithiw. môsahkinîw mihcît mîkwanisa ta-astâwît. âsiskawîw ôho kisîtiniwa ikwa wîkithihk akotâw anima mikisiw-mistikwân. ispî kâ-misakât awa wîmisôsoy wâpahtam opowâkana mikisiwa ostikwânithiw î-akotîthik wîkihk.

"wâh, nipowâkan!" kâ-isi-mawihkâtât îsa opowâkana awa kisîtiniw.

ikwâni kîsihîw ahcâpiya ikwa akaskwa wîsahkîcâhk.

"tâpwî kihci," itwîw wîmisôsoy. "wâpahki nici kika-nitawi-mâcânaw." mâka mîna îtokî î-miskwîthihtahk ta-nisiwanâcihât wîsahkîcâhkwa.

ikwâni kâ-kîkisîpâyâthik nitawi-mâcîwak. kapî-kîsik nôcihcikîwak. kî-ati-wîpâci-kîsikâthiw. mitoni î-sâpopîthiki ocayânisiwâwa. pîthisk î-ati-otâkosinithik ispî kâ-nipahâcik môswa.

"ohcitaw poko kita-kapîsiyâhk osâm ati-tipiskâw," itwîw wîmisôsoy. "kita-pâsamahk poko kicayânisinawa akwâwânisihk."

ikwâni akotâwak ocayânisiwâwa akwâwânisihk, î-wî-pâsahkwâw. ati-kawisimowak. mayaw î-nipâthit kisîtiniwa nihtinam otayânisa wîsahkîcâhk, î-aspaskwîsimonihkâkît.

The following day Wisahkecahk and his father-in-law travelled by canoe to where his father-in-law said there were many feathers. As they reached the shore, there were feathers everywhere along the shore. As soon as Wisahkecahk got onto the shore, his father-in-law paddled away, yelling.

"Okay my spirit guardian! I brought a young man for you to eat!" yells *wîmisôsoy*, inviting his spirit guardian. An eagle lands there.

Wisahkecahk kills the eagle. He cuts off its head and takes it with him. He gathers up many feathers that he is going to use on the arrows. He overtakes the old man and goes to his home, where he hangs the head. When *wîmisôsoy* arrives he sees the head of his spirit guardian, the eagle, hanging at his home.

"Oh my spirit guardian!" *wîmisôsoy* cries for his spirit guardian.

Wisahkecahk finishes his bow and arrows.

"That is truly great!" says *wîmisôsoy*. "Tomorrow we will go hunting." As usual, he is planning on destroying Wisahkecahk.

In the morning they went hunting. They hunted all day. The weather turned nasty and wet. Their clothes got soaked. It was toward evening when they killed a moose.

"We will have to camp overnight because it is already getting dark," says *wîmisôsoy*. "We will dry our clothes on the drying rack."

So then they hung their clothes on the drying rack, drying them there. They lay down to sleep. As soon as his father-in-law was asleep, Wisahkecahk took down his clothes to use as a pillow.

ikwa kisîtiniw waniskâw, î-kîskwîhkwâmihkâsot î-nâtahk ayânisa. otinam ayânisa ikwa macostîham.

"hî, kîkwây ôma kâ-kîsitîk?" isi-tîpwîw.

"kitayânisa anihi! kîtha anihi kitayânisa! nîtha wîtha nitaspaskwîsimon nitayânisa," itîw wîsahkîcâhk osisa. "ikosi athisk î-kî-wî-itôtawiyan!"

ikwâni mosîskatîkâpawiw awa kisîtiniw. mitoni ati-kawaciw.

"âh, kiyâm nika-môsowin," itwîw. mâka namwâc kaskihtâw kita-môsowit.

nitotam kisinâw wîsahkîcâhk, ta-âhkwacithit osisa. ikwâni ikosi isi-nipahîw maci-kisîtiniwa, wîmisôsoya.

So the old man wakes up. He pretends to walk in his sleep as he gets the clothes. He takes the clothes and throws them in the fire.

“Hey, what is it that’s burning?” he yells.

“Those are your clothes! Those are your clothes! I am using my clothes for a pillow,” says Wisahkecahk to his father-in-law. “You would have done that to me!”

And so the old man was standing there naked. He became very cold.

“Ah no matter! I will be a moose,” he says. But he couldn’t turn into a moose.

Wisahkecahk calls the cold to freeze his father-in-law. And that is how he kills the evil old man, this *wîmisôsoy*.

13
thiskipîw

ôma âcathôhkîwin kikiskinahamâkonaw kita-nâkatîthihtamâhk îkâ ayahcitiniw kita-wîhtamawâyahk kihci-isîhcikîwin kiskîthihtamowin. ikwa mîna kiwîhtamâkonaw î-mithwâsik kita-wâh-wîcihitocik athisitiniwak.

kî-pîhtam îsa wîsahkîcâhk î-kî-nipahimiht osîmisa mahihkana. ikwâni îsa kâ-sipwîhtît wîsahkîcâhk. kinwîsk kî-pimohtîw. kîtahtawî otihtawîw okîskimanasiwa nipîhk î-ay-itâpithit.

“kîkwây ôma kâ-kitâpahtaman nisîmî?” itwîw wîsahkîcâhk.

“âhkikwak ôko î-matwî-mîtawâkîcik mahihkani-osoy,” itwîw awa okîskimanasiw.

kisowâsiw wîsahkîcâhk wîtha î-kiskîthihtahk osîmisa î-kî-nipahikothit âhkikwa. nimitâwaham wîsahkîcâhk î-nâtahk mahihkan-osoy. ati-nâh-nipahîw âhkikwa, î-tâh-tahkamât akaskwa ohci. kîkâc iyawis î-mîscihât. paspîhîw mâka anihi okimâwa, cîmisikwanaya. ikwa otinam mahihkan-osoy. kâwi-pimâcihîw osîmisa mahihkana.

13
THE FLOOD

This traditional story teaches us how to guard against revealing sacred teachings to strangers. It also shows the importance of people helping each other.

Wisahkecahk heard that his younger brother, the wolf, had been killed. It was then he decided to leave. He walked for a long time. Eventually he came upon a kingfisher looking out onto the water.

"What are you watching, younger sibling?" asked Wisahkecahk.

"Seals playing with a wolf tail," said the kingfisher.

Wisahkecahk was angry because he knew it was his younger brother the wolf who had been killed by the seals. Wisahkecahk goes out into the water to get the wolf tail. He kills the seals, stabbing them with arrows. He spares the chief, *cîmisikwanay*. He gathers up the wolf tail. He revives his younger brother the wolf.

ikwâni îsa wîsahkîcâhk kâ-papimohtît. kîtahtawî kâ-wâpamât athîkisa î-kwâskohtithit.

"î-nitawi-nipiskîyân, î-nitawi-nipiskîyân, î-nitawi-nipiskîyân," î-isi-nikamot îsa athîkis.

"îy! nohkô, tânitî ôma î-itohtîyan," itîw îsa wîsahkîcâhk anihi athîkisa.

"ôtî ôma. wîsahkîcâhk îsa î-kî-kakwî-nipahât cîmisikwanaya ikwa nîtha poko ta-kaskihtâyân ana ta-nanâtawihak," itwîw îsa athîkis.

"tânisi mâka mâna kâ-itôtaman ispî kâ-nipiskîyan?" kâ-itwît wîsahkîcâhk.

wîhtamawîw athîkis wîsahkîcâhkwa tânisi mâna kâ-itahkamikisit ispî kâ-nipiskît. ikwa mayaw kâ-kîsi-wîhtamawât kâ-nipahikot wîsahkîcâhkwa. ikwa ikota wîsahkîcâhk pahkonîw anihi athîkisa ikwa î-ati-kikiskahk animîthow athîkisayân ikota ohci ati-kwâskohtiw.

"î-nitawi-nipiskîyân, î-nitawi-nipiskîyân, î-nitawi-nipiskîyân," î-itwît aspin î-kwâhci-kwâskohtit. î-nâtât anihi cîmisikwanaya. ikota wîkithihk kâ-takohtît.

"nipî-nanâtawihowân ôma. awas! kahkithaw poko awiyakak ta-wathawîcik ôta ohci mîkiwâhpihk ikwa ikospî nika-nanâtawihâw awa."

ikwâni ikota ohci kahkithaw wathawîwak.

Later, Wisahkecahk was walking along. He saw a frog jumping.

"I am on my way to heal. I am on my way to heal. I am on my way to heal," sang the frog.

"Hey Grandmother, where are you going?" said Wisahkecahk to the frog.

"I am going over there. Wisahkecahk tried to kill *cîmisikwanay* and I am the only one who can heal him," said the frog.

"What do you do when you do the healing ceremony?" said Wisahkecahk.

The frog tells Wisahkecahk what she does when she does the heal healing ceremony. As soon as she tells Wisahkecahk everything, Wisahkecahk kills her. Wisahkecahk skins the frog and puts the skin on himself and hops from there.

"I am on my way to heal. I am on my way to heal. I am on my way to heal," he says, as he hops on to where *cîmisikwanay* was. He arrives at his home.

"I have come here to heal. Go away! Everybody has to go out of the tipi if I'm going to heal this one."

Everybody leaves.

wâwâkohtîw ikota î-kâh-kanawâpamât ôho cîmisikwanaya ita îsa akaskwâhtikwa î-ayâthit osôthihk. ikota tâpokwâni akaskwa kâ-otinât kîhtwâm î-tâh-tahkamât anihi, î-nipahât. mayaw kâ-nipahât ikota ohci î-pî-thiskipîthik. ikota ohci nipiy î-pîcipathithik, anita ohci osôthihk. mitoni kî-ati-thiskipîw. wîsahkîcâhk kî-ati-sipwîpahtâw ikota ohci, ispatinâhk î-ispahtât.

nitomîw kahkithaw pisiskiwa.

"âstamik! wîcihik! mihtot poko ta-osîhtâyahk," î-itât. kahkithaw ôko pisiskiwak pî-ispahtâwak î-pî-wîcihowîcik mihtot kita-osîhtâcik. ikwâni ikota mitoni misiwîskamik î-kî-thiskipîk ikwa ikota mihtotihk pâh-pôsipahtâwak aniki pisiskiwak.

ikwâni ikota ohci papâmâhokowak. kinwîsk ôma ikota kâ-papâmâhokocik. namwâc nânitaw ita askiy ohci-wâpahtamwak.

kîtahtawî wîsahkîcâhk kâ-itwît, "awiyak poko ohcitaw kita-kôkît ta-nâtahk askiy. nikî-wanikiskisin askiy ta-pî-itohtatâyân."

mwâkwa wîtha nîkân kâ-pîkiskwît: "ahâw nîtha nika-kôkân. ninihtâ-kôkân ôma."

ikwâni, aspin kâ-kôkît.

mitoni kinwîsîs ikota kâ-kôkît. kîtahtawî kâ-pîkopît, î-kî-nistâpâwît îsa. wîsahkîcâhk otinîw osîmisa. pôtâtîw. kâwi î-pimâcihât. kâwi ahthîw anita mihtotihk.

"awîna ikwa?" itwîw wîsahkîcâhk.

ikwa nikik ikwa wîsta kâ-pîkiskwît. "nîtha ikwa nika-kôkân. ninihtâ-kôkân ôma," itwîw.

He walks about, stooping, as he looks at *cîmisikwanay* and he sees the arrow sticking in its tail. Right away he takes the arrow out and he stabs *cîmisikwanay*. He kills him. As soon as he kills him, out of the tail comes water and water, more and more water. It starts to flood the earth.

Wisahkecahk runs from there and he runs to the top of the hill.

"Come, help me! We have to build a raft." All the animals came running, coming to help build a raft. So they hurriedly build a raft and the water was everywhere. All the animals board the raft.

They floated from there. They floated for a long time. There was not one sign of earth.

Then Wisahkecahk says, "Someone will have to dive to get some earth. I forgot to bring along some earth."

The loon spoke up first: "Okay, I will dive. I'm a good diver."

So the loon dives into the water.

He dived for quite a while. Suddenly he emerged. When he emerged from the water, he was dead from drowning. So Wisahkecahk picks him up. He blows on him. He brings him back to life. He sets him back on the raft.

"Now who?" says Wisahkecahk.

So the otter comes in. "I'll go now. I'm a good diver," he says.

ikwâni ikota ana kâ-kôkît. kinwîsîs wîsta ikotî ayâw, atâmipîhk. ikwâni kîtahtawî kâ-pîkopît ikota wîsta î-nistâpâwît. wîsahkîcâhk otinîw anihi anita nikikwa. pôtâtîw ikwa mîna pimâcihîw kîhtwâm ahthîw anita mihtotihk.

"awîna ôma ikwa?" itwîw wîsahkîcâhk

amisk awa kâ-itwît "nîtha ninihtâ-kôkân. nika-kôkân."

ikwâni wîsta amisk awa kâ-kôkît. ay kinwîsîs ikwa nawac awa amisk atâmipîhk ayâw. kîtahtawî poko kâ-pîkopît wîsta î-nistâpâwît. ikwâni otinîw wîsahkîcâhk. pôtâtîw ikwa kîhtwâm pimâcihîw ahthîw kâwi mihtotihk.

ikwa ana wacaskos kâ-itwît "nîsta ôma ninihtâ-kôkân. mahti nîtha ikwa."

aspin kâ-kôkît awa wacaskos. mitoni kinwîsîs ikotî ikwa wîtha atâmipîhk kâ-ayât. kîtahtawî poko kâ-pîkopît.

ocihcîsihk îsa ikota askiy astîthiw ikwa mîna wîpitihk. ikwa wîtha wîsahkîcâhk otinam ikwa nahastâw mihtotihk.

"hâw kîhtwâm kôkî. kiyâpic mistahi askiy kinitawîthihtînaw."

ikwa ana wacaskos kîhtwâm kôkîw. ay, kinwîsîs ayâw ikota atâmipîhk. kîtahtawî poko kâ-pîkopît. ikwa mîna kîhtwâm askiy astîthiw ocihcîsithihk. otinam wîsahkîcâhk ikwa askiy mihtotihk nahastâw.

ikwa mîna kîhtwâm kôkîw awa wacaskos. nîswâw kiyâpic î-kî-kôkît. ikwa mitoni mistahi askiy pâh-pîtâw. mâmawi nîwâw î-kî-kôkît. pîthisk nahîthikohk askiy ayâwak.

So he dives in. He too was underwater for a quite a while. Eventually the otter emerged and he too had drowned. So Wisahkecahk picks him up. He blows on him. He gives him back life. He puts him back on the raft.

"Okay, now who?" says Wisahkecahk.

The beaver comes up and says, "I'm a good diver. I'll dive."

And so the beaver goes ahead and dives into the water. And so the beaver was underwater longer than the others. Suddenly he too emerged dead from drowning. So Wisahkecahk picks him up. He blows on him and gives him back his life. He puts him on the raft.

Then the little muskrat comes up and says, "I too am a pretty good diver. Let me go now."

And off he goes into the water. He was underwater for a long time. Eventually he emerged out of the water.

He has bits of earth on his paws and in his teeth. So Wisahkecahk takes that earth and puts it aside on the raft.

"Okay, dive again! We need more earth."

Again the muskrat dives. He is underwater for a long time. Eventually he emerged. Again he had earth in his paws. Wisahkecahk takes the bits of earth and sets it aside on the raft.

The muskrat dives again. Twice more he dives. He brings quite a bit of earth. Altogether he dives four times. Eventually there is quite enough earth.

ikwa wîsahkîcâhk ati-pâh-pôtâtam animîthow askiy. kinwîsk pâh-pôtâtam askiy, î-misisihtât. ikwa ispî î-itîthihtahk nahîthikohk î-misâthik atotîw osîmisa mahihkana kita-wâskâpahtâthit. piyak tipiskanisiw awa mahihkan.

"osâm apisâsin askiy," kâ-itwît wîsahkîcâhk.

kîhtwâm î-mâci-pôtâtahk askiy. kinwîsîs pôtâtam. ikwa mîna sipwîtisahwîw osîmisa mahihkana. nîso tipiskanisithiwa ikwa, kiyâpic osâm apisâsin askiy.

kîhtwâm mâci-pôtâtam askiy wîsahkîcâhk. kinwîsk pôtâtam. ikwa mîna sipwîtisahwîw mahihkana. kinwîsîs ikwa, mâka pîthisk kîhtwâm takopahtâthiwa. kîhtwâm wîsahkîcâhk pôtâtam askiy, nawac î-wî-misisihtât. ikwa mîna sipwîtisahwîw osîmisa.

mitoni kinwîsk kî-pîhîwak mâka namôtha ohci-takopahtâthiwa.

"ikwâni nahîthikohk misâw askiy," kî-itwîw wîsahkîcâhk, î-ati-sipwîhtît.

ikosi pitamâ ikwa anima.

Wisahkecahk blows on the earth. He blows on the earth for a long time, making it bigger. When he thought the earth was big enough, he told his little brother the wolf to run around it to see how big it was. The wolf was gone for one night.

"The earth is too small," says Wisahkecahk.

Once again he blows on the earth. He blows on it for quite a while. Once again he sends his little brother the wolf to run around it. The wolf was gone for two nights. The earth was still too small.

Once again Wisahkecahk blows on the earth. Once again he sends his little brother out. This time he was gone for quite a while, but he eventually arrived. The earth was still too small. Wisahkecahk blew on the earth, making it bigger. Once again he sends his little brother to run around the earth.

They waited for him for a long time, but he never arrived.

"There, the earth is big enough," said Wisahkecahk, leaving from there.

That's it for that one.

14
opasakwâpisimowak

ôma âcimowin kiwîhtamâkonaw ta-aswîthihtamâhk ispî awiyak itwîci î-wî-mîthikoyahk kîkway.

piyakwâw îsa wîsahkîcâhk kî-papimohtîw wâsakâm sâkahikanihk. kîtahtawî îsa kâ-wâpamât sîsîpa ikwa niska î-akwamothit nâtakâm. kîsiskaw kâsôpathihow.

"tânisi ôma ôko ta-kî-isi-nipahakwâw?" itîthihtam.

mâka mîna îsa î-nohtîhkatît. ati-kîmôci-pasikôw, î-ati-sipwîhtît ikota ohci. pîthisk maskîkohk kâ-takohtît.

"iyakoni nika-âpacihtân," itîthihtam, î-ati-mâh-môsahkinahk askiya, î-asiwatât omaskimotihk. sâkaskinahtâw omaskimot. kâwi sâkahikanihk itohtîw î-wâh-wâsakâmît ikota ita kisiwâk kâ-akwamothit sîsîpa ikwa niska. ikota îsa wâh-wâsakâmîw, î-pimowatât omaskimot. kîtahtawî pisiskâpamik sîsîpa ikwa niska.

"cîst! kistîsinaw!" itwîwak. "kîkwây awa kâ-nayahtahk?"

"mahti nika-kakwîcimâw," itwîw awa piyak sîsîp.

"âhâw," itwîwak.

14

THE SHUT-EYE DANCERS

The teaching of this traditional story: Be wary when someone offers you a wondrous gift.

One day Wisahkecahk was walking along the shore of a lake when he suddenly saw ducks and geese on the water, close to shore. He quickly hid.

"How am I going to kill these ones?" he thought.

As usual, he was hungry. He secretly gets up and leaves from there. Eventually he arrives at a muskeg.

"That's what I'll use," he thought. He begins to gather up the moss and puts it in his bag. He fills up his bag. He walks back to the lake going along the shore close to where the ducks and geese were floating. He went back and forth along the shore, carrying his bag on his back. All of a sudden the ducks and geese notice him.

"Look! Our older brother!" they said. "What is he carrying?"

"Let's see, I will ask him," said one of the ducks.

"Okay," they said.

"nistîsî, kîkwây kâ-nayahtaman?"

âhci-poko papimohtîw wîsahkîcâhk, âhkîtâp îkâ î-pîhtawât.

sâsay mîna sîsîp kâ-pîkiskwît.

"nistîsî, kîkwây kâ-nayahtaman?" kâ-itwît.

âhci-poko papimohtîw wîsahkîcâhk. pîthisk nîwâw kâ-kakwîcimikot naskwîwasihîw anihi sîsîpa.

"ninikamona ôho," itîw wîsahkîcâhk.

"mahti mâka nikamostawinân," itwîw sîsîp.

"nama! oski-nikamona ôho î-kî-mîthikawiyân. namôtha pakwanita pokîtî nikakî-nikamon," itwîw wîsahkîcâhk.

"tânisi mâka takî-itôtamahk ta-nikamostawiyâhk?" itwîw sîsîp.

ikwâni wîhtamawîw kahkithaw sîsîpa ikwa niska tânisi kita-itôtamithit kîspin nohtî-wîhtamawîw anihi oski-nikamona. ati-sîhkimâwasow wîsahkîcâhk.

"otâhk askiy ôma nikî-asotamâkon ta-nîmihiwîyân anohc kâ-askîwik. ikwa îkwîthâc anohcihkî î-mîthikawiyân oski-nikamona, iyakoni ôho kâ-pimowatâyân. nikî-sîhkimikawin ôma tânisi ta-isi-nîmihiwîyân ispî nikamoyâni. ohcitaw poko ta-osîhtânowik nîmiwikamik nahîthikohk î-ispîhcâk ikwa piyak iskwâhcîmis sâwanohk ta-itamok. ikwa ispî sipwîsimonânowiki ohcitaw poko aniki onîmiwak kita-pasakwâpicik, ta-pîhtokî-pasakwâpisimocik nîmiwikamikohk. kîspin namôtha awiyak nohtî-pasakwâpisimow ôta ohci ta-sipwîhtîw sîmâk!"

ikosîsi kakwî-pahkacimîw ôho sîsîpa ikwa niska.

"Older brother! What are you carrying on your back?"

Wisahkecahk walks on, pretending not to hear him.

Once again the duck speaks.

"Older brother! What are you carrying?" he said.

Still Wisahkecahk walks along. After four times of being asked he answers that duck.

"These are my songs," he tells him.

"Then please sing them for us," says the duck.

"No! These are new songs that were given to me. I cannot sing them for no reason just anywhere," says Wisahkecahk.

"Then what can we do for you to sing them to us," says the duck.

So he tells all the ducks and geese what they must do if they want to hear the new songs. Wisahkecahk gives instructions.

"Last year I had vowed that I would give a dance this year. And it was just now that I was given new songs, these ones I am carrying. I was instructed on how I was to give a dance when I sing. There has to be a dance lodge built just the right size with one small door facing south. And when the dance starts the dancers must have their eyes closed, entering dancing the shut-eye dance into the dance lodge. If no one wants to dance the shut-eye dance then they must leave from here right away!"

That is how he tried to trick the ducks and the geese.

kahkithaw ôko sîsîpak ikwa niska nohtî-pasakwâpisimowak, î-nohtî-pîhtahkwâw anihi oski-nikamona. kahkithaw ikota kisâcîwak. ati-osîhtâwak animîthow nîmiwikamik. ispî kâ-kîsihtâcik nîmiwikamik ati-wawîsîhîw osîmisa wîsahkîcâhk. î-sâh-sisopîkahwât anihi sîsîpa ikwa niska. anohc aniki sîsîpak ikwa niskak kâ-isinâkosicik ikospî anima ohci, ispî kâ-kî-isi-sisopîkahokocik wîsahkîcâhkwa. kwayask mâh-mithonâkosîhîw osîmisa wîsahkîcâhk. mitoni cîhkîthihtamwak aniki sîsîpak ikwa niskak î-isi-mâh-mithonâkosicik.

ikwâni kîsi-wawîsîhwîw wîsahkîcâhk kâ-pîhtokît nîmiwikamikohk. ikota tâwâyihk nîmiwikamikohk apiw wîsahkîcâhk. ati-sipwîham kisik î-matwîhwât mistikwaskihkwa.

"hay-ya, hay-ya pasakwâpisimowin ninikamohtân," isi-nikamow wîsahkîcâhk. "hay-ya, hay-ya pasakwâpisimowin ninikamohtân."

ikwâni ati-pâh-pîhtokîsimowak ôko sîsîpak ikwa niskak, pâskac î-nanamistikwânîsimocik, î-pasakwâpisimocik. ikota pîhcâyihk apiw wîsahkîcâhk, tâwâyihk nîmiwikamikohk î-ohci-nikamot.

ikwa wâskâsimowak ôko sîsîpak ikwa niskak. kîtahtawî mâna âh-otihtinîw wîsahkîcâhk sîsîpa anihi nawac kâ-wîthinosithit. kîskikwînîw ikwa asiwaciwîpinîw omaskimotihk. âhkami-nikamow ikwa pîthisk otinamâsow mihcît sîsîpa.

ikwa îsa awa piyak sîsîp, awa sihkihp, ati-mâmitonîthihtam tânihki mâna âskaw îkâ kâ-nikamothit wîsahkîcâhkwa. ikwâni kîmôtâpiw. kâ-wâpamât wîsahkîcâhkwa î-otihtinâthit sîsîpa. sîmâk tîpwîw!

"tapasîk nîtisânak! wîsahkîcâhk awa kinipahikonaw," isi-tîpwîw awa sihkihp.

kahkithaw ati-wâh-wathawîpahtâwak aniki sîsîpak ikwa niskak!

All the ducks and the geese wanted to dance the shut-eye dance, they wanted to hear the new songs. They all stayed. They began to make the dance lodge. When they finished the dance lodge, Wisahkecahk began to decorate his younger siblings. He painted those ducks and the geese. The way those ducks and the geese look today is from that day when Wisahkecahk painted them. He painted them very beautifully. The ducks and the geese were happy because they were so beautiful.

When he finished decorating them, Wisahkecahk entered the dance lodge. There in the centre of the dance lodge sat Wisahkecahk. He begins to sing as well as pounding on the drum.

"Hay-ya, hay-ya the shut-eye dance song I sing," is how Wisahkecahk sang. "Hay-ya, hay-ya the shut-eye dance song I sing."

So the ducks and the geese danced into the dance lodge, bobbing their heads, dancing with their eyes shut. Inside the lodge Wisahkecahk sat, from the centre of the dance lodge he sang.

The ducks and the geese danced in a circle. Every once in a while Wisahkecahk grabbed a duck, one that was nice and fat. He wrung the duck's neck and threw it in his bag. He continued to sing and eventually grabbed many ducks for himself.

And there was this one duck, the mud-hen, who wondered why it was that Wisahkecahk would pause once in a while with his singing. He then took a peek. He saw Wisahkecahk grabbing a duck. He immediately shouted!

"Flee, my siblings! Wisahkecahk is killing us," he shouted.

All the ducks and geese started to run out!

ikwa ana sihkihp iskwiyânihk wîtha kakwî-tapasîw. wîsahkîcâhk tahkiskâtîw anihi sihkihpa mwihci î-ati-wathawîpahtâthit. osôkanihk kâ-tahkiskâtât! iyak-ohci anohc sihkihp kiyâpic kâ-nahihtâwihikot ta-pimohtît askîhk: kiyâpic î-mâskisit.

The mud-hen was the last to try to flee. Wisahkecahk kicked him just as he was heading out! He kicked him in the back. That is why to this day the mud-hen is awkward when he walks on land: he is still crippled.

15
mâskikâtîw mahkîsîs

ôma âcathôhkîwin kikiskinwahamâkonaw: îkâ kita-kakwî-cîsihâyâhkwâw kîci-athisitinîminawak.

ikosi wathawîw wîsahkîcâhk, î-pahpit, î-mithwîthihtahk.

"mistahi nika-mîcison," î-itîthihtahk.

ikosi kawinam onîmiwikamik. môsahkinihtîw ikwa ati-kotawîw. âtiht anihi sîsîpa ikwa niska wî-nawacîw. âtiht wâh-wîwîkinîw nîpîhk nîkân ikwa ikota ohci asaskiy ohci wîwîkinîw. ikwa ati-sîkwahkonîw, atâmihk iskotîhk î-kîsiswât.

osâm îsa mistahi kî-pônam, mitoni î-ati-apwîsit. ati-sipwîhtîw.

"pitamâ nika-pôni-apwîsin. ikwathikohk kita-kîsisowak nisîsîpimak ikwa niniskimak," î-itîthihtahk.

namôtha osâm wâhthaw kî-itohtîw ispî kâ-wâpamât mahkîsîsa î-mâskipathithit. î-wîsakîthihtamithit îsa oskâtithiw. wî-tapasîhikow.

"cîskwa, nisîm!" itîw.

15

THE FOX HAS A CRIPPLED LEG

The teaching of this traditional story: Don't try to play tricks on your fellow people.

Then Wisahkecahk goes out, laughing, happy.

"I will eat lots," he thought.

Then he takes down his dance lodge. He gathers up firewood and starts a fire. Some of those ducks and geese he is going roast. Some he is going to wrap, first in leaves, then in clay. He puts those under the ashes, cooking them under the fire.

Apparently he had put too much wood in the fire. He starts to sweat. He begins to leave from there.

"I will quit sweating first. That should be enough time to cook my ducks and my geese," he thinks.

He doesn't go very far when he sees a fox limping. Apparently he had a sore leg. The fox was going to run away from him.

"Wait, younger sibling!" he says.

"awas, namôtha!" itik. "osâm mâka mîna nânitaw kika-itôtawin," itik.

"namôtha!" itîw. "î-wî-âcimostâtân. îh ôma, kiwâpahtîn cî mistahi nîtî kâ-matwî-kaskâpahtîk?"

"îhî," itik.

"ikotî mihcît nikî-nipahâwak niskak mîna sîsîpak. ikotî î-piminawasoyân iyakonik," î-itât. "mistahi kika-mîcisonaw," itîw. "mâka pitamâ kika-mawinîskâtonaw. ôma sâkahikan kika-wâskâpahtânaw. ana paskithâkîci kita-mowîw anihi sîsîpa ikwa niska."

"hâ, namôtha! namacî kiwâpamin îkâ kwayask î-kî-pimohtîyân. niwîsakîthihtîn ôma niskât. nimâskisitân ôma!" itwîw mahkîsîs.

"hâw cîskwa nisîm. asiniyak niskâtihk nika-tahkopitâwak," itwîw wîsahkîcâhk.

"âhâw," itwîw mahkîsîs.

asiniya otinîw wîsahkîcâhk, î-tahkopitât oskâtihk.

"hâw, nisîm, ikwa!"

ikwa sipwîpahtâwak. nakacipahîw mahkîsîsa wîsahkîcâhk.

"hî, âta mâna mîhkawikîw awa mahkîsîs mâka kiyâpic ninakacipahâw âta î-tahkopitakwâw asiniyak niskâtihk! mwîstas nici âtiht nika-asamâw sîsîpa ikwa niska ispî takopahtâci," itwîw wîsahkîcâhk.

"Go away, no!" it says to him. "As usual, you are going to do something to me," it tells him.

"No!" he says. "I want to tell you something. See over there, do you see a lot of smoke over there?"

"Yes," it says to him.

"I killed a lot of ducks and geese over there. I am cooking them over there," he says to him. "We will eat lots," he says to him. "But first let's have a race. We will run around this lake. Whoever wins will eat the ducks and the geese."

"Ah, no! Can't you see that I can't walk properly? I have a sore leg. I am crippled!" says the fox.

"Oh wait, younger sibling. I'll tie rocks to my legs," says Wisahkecahk.

"Okay," says the fox.

Wisahkecahk picks up rocks, tying them onto his legs.

"Okay, younger sibling. Let's go!"

And they run off. Wisahkecahk leaves the fox behind.

"Hey, even though the fox usually runs fast I still leave him behind even though I have rocks tied to my legs. Later I will feed him some of the ducks and geese when he arrives," says Wisahkecahk.

mayaw î-awasîwîthit wîsahkîcâhkwa kîwîpathiw awa mahkîsîs. namôtha îsa kî-ohci-wîsakîthihtam oskât. ôta ôma kâ-pikihtîthik î-ispahtât. ispî kâ-takohtît niska ikwa sîsîpa kâ-wâpamât î-kîsisothit. otinîw ikwa ati-mowîw. wîsahkîcâhkwa î-kimotamawât. kitamwîw kahkithaw. ositithiwa poko ôho niska ikwa sîsîpa kâwi iskotîhk astâw, tâpiskôc î-sâkinisitîsinât sîsîpa ikwa niska.

"ta-wâpahtahk wîsahkîcâhk," î-itîthihtahk. ikosi tapasîw. "nika-kisowâhâw," î-itîthimât wîsahkîcâhkwa.

ikwa ispî wîsahkîcâhk kâ-takopahtât mistahi kî-apwîsiw athisk mistahi î-kî-pimipâhtât.

"hî, âstîpwîsiyâni nika-mîcison," î-itîthihtahk, "âtiht nici sîsîpa ikwa niska nika-asamâw nisîmis," itîw mahkîsîsa, "ispî takopahtâci," itîthihtam.

namôtha kiskîthihtam sâsay îsa î-kî-kitamwâthit osîsîpima ikwa oniskima. ikosi ikwâni otinam ôma ositithiw niska. nama kîkway niska!

"hî hî hî, nitosâmihkaswâw!" itwîw.

pîthisk kahkithaw sîsîpa ikwa niska kakwî-otinîw. mâka kahkithaw nama-kîkway, ositithiwa poko.

"hî hî hî, mâka mîna îcikâni î-wawiyasihit mahkîsîs. wîtha îtokî kâ-kitamwât nisîsîpima ikwa niniskima! ikosi îcikâni kâ-nohtîhkatîyân!" itwîw.

As soon as Wisahkecahk goes out of sight the fox heads back. Apparently he had no sore leg. He runs over to where there was smoke. When he arrives there he sees ducks and geese cooking. He takes them and begins to eat them. He steals Wisahkecahk's cooking. He eats them all. He puts the ducks' and geese's feet back under the ashes, just like their feet were sticking out of the fire.

"That's for Wisahkecahk to see," he says. He flees. "I will make him angry," he thinks of him.

And when Wisahkecahk arrives he was sweating a lot because he had been running.

"When I am cooled down I will eat," he thought. "Later I will feed my younger sibling some ducks and geese," he says of the fox, "when he arrives," he thought.

He doesn't know that the fox had already eaten all of his ducks and geese. So he takes a goose's foot. There was no goose!

"Oh my! I have cooked it too long!" he says.

Eventually he tried to take all the ducks and geese. But there was nothing in all of them, just their feet.

"Hey! As usual, the fox is playing a trick on me. Perhaps it was him who ate all my ducks and geese. I am still hungry!" he says.

16
wîsahkîcâhk ikwa okoskohowîsak

ôma âcathôhkîwin kikiskinwahamâkonaw: nâkatîthihta kinîhithawi-wîhthowin.

piyakwâw îsa wîsahkîcâhk kî-papimohtîw. kîtahtawî îsa wâpamîw pithîsisa.

"ho! nisîmitik!" itîw îsa. kanawâpamikow ôho pithîsisa.

"nisîmitik, pithîsisak, tânisi kâ-itikawiyîk?"

"sâsay kiwîhthinân, 'pithîsisak,' kâ-itwîyan ikosi kâ-itikawiyâhk."

"nama! kahkithaw awiyak awasimîs wîhthâw. tâpiskôc nîtha: 'wîsahkîcâhk' nitisithihkâson mâka 'ostîsimâw' mîna nititikawin. hâw, tânisi kîthawâw kâ-itikawiyîk."

"namôtha nikakî-wîhtînân. ninîkihikonânak ôko nikî-wîhtamâkonânak îkâ ta-wîhtamâhk kotak niwîhthowininân 'okoskohowîsak' î-itikawiyâhk."

16
WISAHKECAHK AND THE STARTLERS

The teaching of this traditional story: Guard your Cree name.

Once, Wisahkecahk was walking about when all of a sudden, he saw some baby grouse.

"Ho! Honorable younger siblings!" says he to them. The baby grouse looked at him.

"Honorable younger siblings, Baby Grouse, how are you called?"

"You already named us when you said 'Baby Grouse.' That's how we are called."

"No, everyone has more than one name. Like me: 'Wisahkecahk' is my name, but I am also called 'Oldest Brother.' Now, how are you called?"

"We can't tell. Our parents told us not to tell our other name, 'Startlers,' as we are called."

"okoskohowîsak! ha!" kâ-isi-pahpihât îsa!

"îsay, okoskohowîsak!"

"nitakisiy, okoskohowîsak," itwîw îsa î-ati-mîsâtât, ikwa anihi kâ-patahwât, otinîw î-ati-kimisâhwâkît!

"okoskohowîsak! osâm kitapisîsisinâwâw ta-koskohowîyîk," itwîw î-ati-sipwîhtît.

onîkihikomâwak koskwâpisinwak ispî kâ-pî-kîwîcik.

"awîna awa kâ-itôtahk! wahwâ! kwayask kiwîhcîkisinâwâw! îsay!" itwîwak îsa.

"wîsahkîcâhk ana," kâ-isi-mâtot îsa piyak pithîsis. "î-pahkacimikoyâhk ta-wîhtamâhk kotak kiwîhthowininaw. mayaw 'okoskohowîsak' î-itâyâhk kâ-mîsâtikoyâhk!"

"haw cîskwa wîsahkîcâhk!" itwîw awa nôsî-pithîw. nitomîw îsa kahkithaw otôtîma ta-mâmawapicik. kî-nitawi-pîhowak pithîwak wâsakâm sîpîhk ita mâna wîsahkîcâhkwa kâ-âsowakâmîkwâskohtit.

kîtahtawî takohtîw awa nâpîw, kiyâpic î-pahpihât pithîsisa.

"okoskohowîsak! ha! îsay!" wâsakâm sîpîhk takohtîw.

"ha! mahti nika-âsowakâmîkwâskohtin!"

nîkân îsa asihtîw ikwa ikotî ohci pîcipahtâw. mwihci sîpîhk î-takopahtât kâ-nakît.

"kîkâc," itwîw îsa; kâ-wâpamât piyak pithîsisa î-ohpahothit sakâhk ohci. kîhtwâm asihtîw ikwa mîna ati-sipwîpahtâw.

"Startlers! Ha!" He laughed at them!

"Bosh, Startlers!"

"My prick, Startlers," he said as he began to shit on them, and those he missed, he picked up and used them to wipe himself!

"Startlers! You are too small to scare anyone," he said, beginning to leave.

The parents were so surprised when they got home.

"Who did this? Holy! You sure stink! Phew!" they said.

"It was Wisahkecahk!" cried one baby grouse. "He tricked us to tell him our other name. As soon as we said 'Startlers,' he shat on us!"

"Just you wait, Wisahkecahk!" said one female grouse. She called all her tribesmen to have a meeting. They went to wait along the river where Wisahkecahk usually jumped across.

Eventually this man arrived, still laughing at the Startlers.

"Startlers! Ha! Bosh!" He arrives along the river.

"Ha! Let's see, I'll jump across!"

First he backed up, then from there he ran and, just as he reached the river, he stopped.

"Almost!" he says. He saw a baby grouse fly up from the bushes. He backs up and again he begins to run.

"kîkâc!" itwîw, ikwa mîna î-nakît. wâpamîw nîso pithîsisa î-ohpahothit sakâhk ohci. kîhtwâm asihtîw, nawac ikwa wâhthawîs ohci ati-sipwîpahtâw.

"kîkâc!" itwîw, î-nakît ikwa mîna. nisto pithîsisa wâpamîw î-ohpahothit sakâhk ohci. kîhtwâm asihtîw, nawac wâhthawîs ohci ati-sipwîpahtâw. mwihci î-ati-kwâskohtit kâ-sasci-ohpahocik mihcît pithîwak! wahwâ! kwayask, koskowithik! mitoni î-ati-pakastawîsihk sîpîhk.

"okoskohowîsak, okoskohowîsak," kâ-isi-pahpihikot îsa anihi okoskohowîsa!

ikwâni î-iskwâhcimihcik okoskohowîsak.

"Almost!" he says, and once again he stops. He sees two baby grouse flying from the bush. He backs up and again he begins to run, this time from a little ways further.

"Almost!" he says, and once again, he stops. He sees three baby grouse flying from the bush. He backs up again, this time he runs from further away. Just as he begins his jump, lots of grouse flew out from the bushes. Wow! He was so startled that he landed in the water.

"*okoskohowîsak! okoskohowîsak!*" The grouse laughed at him saying their name.

That's the length of that story about the Startlers.

17
wîsahkîcâhk ikwa kâ-masinâsocik waskwayak

ôma âcathôhkîwin kikiskinwahamâkonaw: nâkatîthihta kîkwây kâ-pakosîthimoyan.

sâsay mîna wîsahkîcâhk papimohtîw. kîtahtawî otihtawîw maskwa î-môminîthit wîsakîmina. kâsôpathihow sakâsihk wîsahkîcâhk î-mâmitonîthihtahk tânisi ôma takî-isi-nipahât ôho wîtha mâka mîna î-nohtîhkatît. kiskîthihtam tânisi kita-itôtahk!

otinam âtiht wîsakîmina ikwa ati-pimohtîw itî isi kâ-ayâthit anihi maskwa. pâh-pâskicînam wîsakîmina oskîsikohk. tahtwâw kâ-pâskicînahk wîsakîmina oskîsikohk mâh-misi-tîpwî-pahpiw! pîthisk pisiskâpamik maskwa.

"tânisi ôma î-itahkamikisiyan nistîsî?" isi-kakwîcimik maskwa.

"âh, nisîmî! cîst! kihci-kîkway ôma. kîspin pâskicînamani ôho wîsakîmina kiskîsikohk kika-kakwâtaki-cîhkîthihtîn. mitoni î-takahkiskâkoyân iyak-ohci kâ-misi-pahpiyân tahtwâw kâ-pâskicînamân ôho niskîsikohk. cikôci, kocihtâ!"

17

WISAHKECAHK AND THE MARKING OF BIRCH TREES

This teaching of this traditional story: Watch what you ask for.

Once again Wisahkecahk is walking along. All of a sudden he came upon a bear eating cranberries. Wisahkecahk quickly hid behind a small bush thinking about how to kill the bear, because as usual, he was hungry. He knew what to do.

He takes some cranberries and walks toward where the bear was at. He would break open the cranberries in his eyes. Every time he broke a cranberry in his eyes he would holler in laughter. Eventually the bear notices him.

"What are you doing, older brother?" asks the bear.

"Oh younger sibling! Look! This is a great thing. If you break a cranberry over your eyes you will become very happy. This affects me so well that is why I end up laughing with great delight every time I break them open in my eyes. Here, try it!"

maskwa otinam wîsakîmina, nîso ocihciya î-âpacihtât. pâskicînam oskîsikohk. wahwâ! wîsakiskâkow. misiwîta ispahtâw î-mâh-mawimot! namôtha kî-wâpiw.

"ayayâ! ayayâ!"

"hâ nisîm! osâm mistahi kikî-âpacihtân! îh, nisîmis, ôta mistikohk astâ kistikwân. kika-nanâtawihitin!" itwîw wîsahkîcâhk.

ikwâni mistikohk astâw ostikwân awa maskwa. wîsahkîcâhk otinîw asiniya ikwa pakamistikwânîhîw maskwa, î-nipahât.

ati-kotawîw, î-wî-piminawasot, î-wî-mowât anihi maskwa. mitoni misi-pônam, î-misiwîskaswât maskwa. ispî kâ-kîsitîpot namôtha îsa osâm kî-nohtîhkatîw. nohtî-kitamwîw anihi maskwa mâka nîkân kita-nohtîhkatît mwayî-mowâci iyakoni.

wâpamîw waskwaya î-nîsokâpawithit. tâwâyihk ikota nitawi-pimisin.

"âstamik nisîmitik! nawac kisiwâk pî-isikâpawik. pî-miciminik," itîw anihi waskwaya. "kâwitha pakitinihkîk. pâtimâ kakwâtaki-nohtîhkatîyâni ikospî poko pakitinihkîk."

tâpwî mâni mâka kisiwâk nawac wîci-kâpawîstâtowak ôko waskwayak. micimoskawîwak wîsahkîcâhkwa. kîtahtawî kâ-twîhot wîskacânis, watihkwanihk î-ay-apit. kâ-pisiskâpamât wîsahkîcâhk.

"kakîpâtis pithîsîs!" itwîw wîsahkîcâhk. "kâwitha wîhtamawik pisisikiwak î-kîsitîpoyân ôta."

namôtha ahpô ikosi kî-ohci-itîthihtam ta-itôtahk awa wîskacânis. tâpwî-pokâni ikota ohci ohpahow î-nitawi-wîhtamawat wîci-pisiskiwa kita-pî-mîcisothit. mihcît pisiskiwak pî-mîcisowak. pîthisk kitamwîwak anihi maskwa, oskana poko î-iskwastahkwâw.

The bear takes up some cranberries using two paws. He breaks them open in his eyes. Wah! They cause him pain. He runs all over the place yelping in pain. He was unable to see!

"Ouch! Ouch!"

"Ho, younger sibling! You used too many! Here, younger sibling, put your head on this log and I will heal you," says Wisahkecahk.

So the bear puts his head on the log. Wisahkecahk picks up a stone and hits him on the head, killing him.

He starts a fire as he is going to cook and eat the bear. He built a huge fire, cooking the bear whole. When he had finished cooking he wasn't that hungry just yet. He wants to eat all of the bear, but first he has to be very hungry before he can eat that one.

He sees birch trees standing together. He goes and lays down in between them.

"Come, younger siblings! Stand closer! Come hold me," he says to the birch trees. "Don't let me go until much later. Let me go only when I am very hungry."

For sure the birch stood closer to each other. They hold Wisahkecahk tight. All of a sudden a Whisky Jack lands and sits on a branch. Wisahkecahk notices him.

"Silly bird!" says Wisahkecahk. "Don't tell the other animals that I finished cooking here."

The Whisky Jack hadn't even thought of doing that. He immediately flies off, telling the other animals to come eat. Many animals came to eat. Eventually they ate all of the bear and left only the bones.

ikwa awa wîsahkîcâhk mitoni nîstosiw osâm mistahi î-kî-kakwî-tahcipathihot mâka namwâc kî-ohci-kaskihtâw. kwayask sôhki kî-miciminik anihi waskwaya. pîthisk ati-nipâw ithikohk î-kî-nîstosit. mitoni îtokî kinwîsk kî-nipâw.

ispî kâ-koskopathit kî-tahcipathihow ikota ohci. kî-kisowâhikow anihi waskwaya. nâtam nîpisiya î-wî-pasastîhwât waskwaya.

kinwîsk kî-pasastîhwîw anihi waskwaya. pîthisk î-ati-mâh-masinâsothit. piyakwan ikosi isi-masinâsowak waskwayak anohc.

Wisahkecahk was very tired after unsuccessfully trying hard to get loose. The birch held on to him very tightly. Eventually he went to sleep because he was so tired. He slept for a long time.

When he woke up he broke free from there. The birch trees had made him angry. He goes to get some willows to whip the birch.

He whipped the birch for a long time. Eventually they started to have stripes. Those same stripes are on the birch trees to this day.

18
wîsahkîcâhk ikwa picikîskisîsa

ôma âcathôhkîwin kikiskinwahamâkonaw: kâwitha mîtawâkî kihci-isîhcikîwin.

piyakwâw îsa wîsahkîcâhk kî-papimohtîw. kîtahtawî îsa kâ-wâpamât picikîskisîsa î-matwî-môcikihtâthit. î-otinamithit mâna oskîsikothiwa ikwa mâna î-ohpiwîpinamithit. ikwa mâna kâwi oskîsikothihk î-pî-pahkihtinithiki. mitoni mâna î-tâh-tîpwî-pahpithit tahtwâw ikosi kâ-ispathithik. hâw, mamâhtâwinawîw ôho.

"tâpwî kimamâhtâwisinâwâw," itwîw wîsahkîcâhk. "mahti iyako kîkway kiskinwahamawik."

"awas wîsahkîcâhk! kihci-isîhcikîwin ôma! namôtha kîtha pakwanita kikakî-kiskinwahamâtinân!" itik.

ati-sipwîhtîw wîsahkîcâhk, nawac poko î-kisowâsit. ikwâni nitawi-wawîsîhisow. tâpiskôc kisîtiniw î-isîhisot. kîhtwâm ikota pîci-pimohtîw ita kâ-mîtawîthit picikîskisîsa. pâskac î-wâkohtît ôma, tâpiskôc kisîtiniw. ikwa mawimow.

18
WISAHKECAHK AND THE CHICKADEES

This teaching of this traditional story: Don't disrespect sacred ceremony.

Once Wisahkecahk was walking. All of a sudden he saw some chickadees having fun. They would take out their eyes, throwing them in the air. They would fall back into their eye sockets. They would laugh loudly every time this happened. He thought they were doing a wondrous thing.

"Truly you are gifted," says Wisahkecahk. "Please teach me that thing."

"Go away, Wisahkecahk! This is a sacred ceremony! We cannot teach you for no reason," they told him.

He begins to leave from there somewhat angry. He then goes and disguises himself. He dresses himself like an old man. He again goes to where the chickadees are playing. He even bends over just like an old man. He groans in pain.

"ayayâ! nistikwân!" î-itwît. pisiskâpamik anihi picikîskisîsa, kitimâkinâkow ôho.

"hâw, cîskwa nimosôm!" itik. "kika-kiskinwahamâtinân ôma kita-nanâtawihikoyan. kîspin otinamani kiskîsikwa ikwa ispimihk isi-wîpinamani ikwa kâwi ta-pahkihtihki kiskîsikohk namôtha awasimî kika-tîyistikwânân," itik.

"hâw, mahti kiskinwahamawin nôsisim," itwîw wîsahkîcâhk.

ay, ikosi kâ-isi-kiskinwahamâkot. ispimihk î-ay-isi-wîpinahk oskîsikwa ikwa mâna kâwi î-pîhtokî-pahkihtinithiki ostikwânihk.

ay, cîhkîthihtam wîsahkîcâhk.

"îh, ohcitaw poko ikosi ta-itôtaman ispî tîyistikwânîyâni," itwîw awa pithîsîs. "kâwitha mâka pakwanita mîtawâkî."

"ah, namôtha nânitaw nôsisim," itwîw wîsahkîcâhk. "namôtha nika-mîtawâkân iyakw-ânima."

ikwa ikota ohci ati-sipwîhtîw wîsahkîcâhk, kiyâpic î-wâkohtît tâpiskôc kisîtiniw. ikwa wâhthaw ikota ohci kâ-sipwîhtît kâwi wîsahkîcâhk isinâkosiw.

kwayask kîkway kihci-isîhcikîwin î-kî-kiskinwahamâkot pithîsîsa. ispî kâ-wâpahtahk nîpisiya, tâpwî pok-âni mawimow, tâpiskôc î-tîyistikwânît.

"ayayâ! nistikwân! nitîyistikwânân!" itwîw.

ikwâni ikota oskîsikwa otinam ispimihk î-isi-wîpinahk. kâwi mâna kâ-pahkihtinithiki ostikwânihk.

"ha ha ha, ah tâpwî iyako kihci-isîhcikîwin mamâhtâwan," itwîw. ikosi î-ati-sipwîhtît.

"Ouch, my head!" he says. The chickadees notice him and take pity on him.

"Okay, wait, Grandfather!" they say to him. "We will show you this which will heal you. If you take your eyes and throw them up and let them fall back in your eye sockets you will no longer have a headache," they tell him.

"Okay, please teach me, Grandchild," says Wisahkecahk.

And so they teach him the way to do that. He threw his eyes up and they fell back into his head.

Wisahkecahk was so happy.

"Listen, this is what you have to do when you have a headache," says the bird. "Don't disrespect this!"

"Okay, that's all right, Grandchild," says Wisahkecahk. "I won't disrespect that."

And so he leaves from there, still stooped over as he walks, just like an old man. When he was far from where he had left he reverted back to being Wisahkecahk.

It was truly a great ceremony that the birds had taught him. When he saw some willows he immediately began to groan like he had a headache.

"Ouch! My head! I have a headache!" he says.

So he takes out his eyes and throws them up. They fall back into his eye sockets.

"Hahaha, this sacred ceremony is truly marvelous," he says. He leaves from there.

ikwa mîna kâ-wâpahtahk kotaka nîpisiya.

"ayayâ! nistikwân!" kâ-itwît. ikwa mîna otinam oskîsikwa. ispimihk isi-wîpinam. kâwi ostikwânihk kâ-pahkihtinithiki. ati-papimohtîw. kakwâtaki î-cîhkîthihtahk ôma kihci-isîhcikîwin kâ-kî-kiskinwahamâht.

ikwa mîna kâ-wâpahtahk kotaka nîpisiya.

"ayayâ nitîyistikwânân!" kâ-isi-mawimot.

ikwâni ikota otinam ikwa mîna oskîsikwa. ispimihk isi-wîpinam. kâwi pahkitinithiwa ostikwânihk.

"wahwâ! mamâhtâwan anima kîkway. tâpwî kihci-kîkway!" itwîw.

ikwâni ati-papimohtîw. ikwa mîna kâ-wâpahtahk nîpisiya.

"ayayâ! nistikwân!" kâ-itwît. ikwâni ikota ohci kâ-otinahk oskîsikwa. ispimihk isi-wîpinam.

ah! wâh! osâm wâhthaw isi-wîpinam! ohpimî ita kâ-pahkihtinithiki. ikwâni îkâ î-kî-wâpit.

nitonam anihi anita oskîsikwa, î-papâmitâcimot mohcihk. kîtahtawî mâna kâ-cahkâpahokot awiya.

"ayayâ!" itwîw.

ay, ikwa âhci-poko nitonam ôho oskîsikwa ikota mohcihk. kîhtwâm kâ-cahkâpahokot awiya.

"ayayâ!" isi-mawimow.

nitonam ôho oskîsikwa.

Once again he sees some other willows.

"Ouch! My head!" he says. Once again he takes out his eyes and throws them in the air. They fall back into his head. He walks along. He is very happy that he was taught the sacred ceremony.

Once again he sees some willows.

"Ouch! My headache!" he moaned.

And once again he takes his eyes and throws them in the air. They fall back into his head.

"Wow! This is a marvelous thing. It is truly a great thing!" he says.

Once again he starts walking. Once again he sees willows.

"Ouch! My head!" he says. From there he takes his eyes. He throws them up in the air.

Wow! He throws them too far. They fall elsewhere. Now he cannot see.

He looks for his eyes. He is crawling on the ground. Every now and then someone pokes his eye socket.

"Ouch!" he says.

He continues to look for his eyes there on the ground. Once again someone pokes his eye socket.

"Ouch!" he groans.

He looks for his eyes.

"tâniwîhâ? tâniwîhâ niskîsikwa?" itwîw. ikwa mîna kîhtwâm kâ-cahkâpahokot awiya.

"ayayâ!" itwîw.

ita kâ-cahkâpahoht mitoni î-ati-tîyistikwânît. âh kîtahtawî poko kâ-pîhtawât ôho awiya ita î-pahpithit. "hî hî hî hî hî hî!"

iy! nisitohtawîw iyakoni ôho! mahkîsîsa îsa mâka mîna î-nanôthacihikot.

"ah, cîskwa mahkîsîs, kika-kiskinwahamâtin," itwîw. ikwa ikota ati-pimitâcimow. mistikwa miskawîw ikota.

"awîna ôma kîtha?" itîw.

"waskway ôma nîtha," itwîw awa waskway.

"namôtha kîtha kâ-nitawîthimitân," itwîw wîsahkîcâhk. kîtahtawî kâ-tâwistikwânîsihk.

"awîna kîtha?" itwîw.

"mîtos ôma nîtha," itwîw mîtos.

"namôtha kîtha kâ-nitawîthimitân," itwîw wîsahkîcâhk. sipwîtâcimow. kîtahtawî kîhtwâm kâ-tâwistikwânîsihk.

"awîna ôma kîtha?" itwîw wîsahkîcâhk.

"minahik ôma nîtha," itwîw minahik.

"hâw kîtha kâ-nitawîthimitân," itwîw wîsahkîcâhk. "pikiw nika-otinâw ikota ohci."

"Where are they? Where are my eyes?" he says. Once again someone pokes his eye socket.

"Ouch!" he says.

He starts to get a headache from where his eye socket is being poked. All of a sudden he hears someone laughing. "Heh heh heh heh."

Wah! He recognizes whose voice this is. The Fox is once again teasing him.

"You just wait, Fox! I'll teach you a lesson yet!" he says. He crawls along there. He finds a tree.

"Who are you?" he says.

"I am a birch," says the birch.

"It is not you whom I want," says Wisahkecahk. Suddenly he knocks his head on something.

"Who are you?" he says.

"I am a poplar," says the poplar.

"It is not you whom I want," says Wisahkecahk. He begins to crawl away from there. Suddenly he again knocks his head on something.

"Who are you?" says Wisahkecahk.

"I am a pine," says the pine.

"Ah, it is you whom I want," says Wisahkecahk. "I'll take some pine pitch from there."

ikota pikiwa otinîw minahikohk ohci. ikwa mâh-mâkwamîw ikwa pitikonîw. wâwiyiyâs îsa î-osîhtât. ispî kâ-kîsihtât î-wâskâ-pitikwâthik kîkway ostikwânihk astâw. kotaka îsa oskîsikwa î-osîhtamâsot. kîhtwâm wâpiw.

"ah, tâniwâ ana mahkîsîs," kâ-itwît.

papimohtîw, î-nitonawât osîmisa mahkîsîsa. iy, wâpamîw ikotî î-matwî-nipâthit.

"tânisi mâka ôma kâwi ta-isi-kiskinwahamawak awa? kita-kî-nipahak cî?" itwîw. "hâw namwâc! nawac nânitaw ta-itôtawak. hâw, mahti nika-pônîn ita kâ-nipât kita-wâskâ-kwahkotîk ikota iskotîw. kita-nipahihkasot awa mahkîsîs," itwîw.

ikwâni ikota pônam. ikota î-kotawît wâsakâm ita kâ-nipâthit ôho osîmisa mahkîsîsa. ikwa ati-kwahkotîw anima iskotîw ikota. kîtahtawî poko mahkîsîs kâ-koskopathit. wâpahtam iskotîw misiwî itî î-wâskâ-pasitîthik ita kâ-kî-nipât.

"iy, namôtha nânitaw," itîthihtam. tâpwî pokw-âni kwâskohtiw, omisi isi ikota ispimihk isi. î-awasiwî-kwâskohtit animîthow iskotîw. wacihpîw athisk. ikota ohci ati-pahpiw. ikwa osôsihk poko kâ-ati-pasisot. âhci-poko ikota anohc ka-wâpahtînaw î-wâpiskâthik osôs awa mahkîsîs.

From the pine he takes some pine pitch. He chews it then rolls it into a ball. He is making it round. Once he finishes he puts the round pine pitch into his eye sockets. Apparently he had made himself another set of eyes. Once again he can see.

"Now where is that fox?" he says.

He walks along, looking for the fox. He sees him sleeping in the distance.

"How can I get back at him to teach him a lesson? Should I kill him?" he says. "Okay, no! It would be better if I do something else to him. Let's see, I'll build up a fire where he sleeps, so that the fire goes around there. The fox will die from the heat," he says.

And there he builds up a fire. He builds up the fire around where the fox is sleeping. The fire begins to burn around the fox. Suddenly the fox wakes up. He sees the fire all around where he had been sleeping.

"Well, it doesn't matter," he thinks. He immediately jumps up, up into the air. He jumps over the fire. He can jump high. He laughs. Only his tail got singed. And today you can still see that he is white at the tip of his tail.

19
wîsahkîcâhk omikiy mîciw

ôma âcathôhkîwin kikiskinwahamâkonaw: namôtha kahkithaw kîkway kâ-miskamâhk kimîskanâminâhk î-mîthikoyahkwâw kimosôminawak.

piyakwâw îsa wîsahkîcâhk mihcît sîsîpa kî-nipahîstamâsow. kî-pîhkinîw anihi sîsîpa. ikota kî-ati-kotawîw.

"âh, kwayask niwî-misi-mîcison," itîthihtam.

ikwâni ikota ohci âtiht ati-nâh-nawacîw. miscikosa î-âpacihtât ta-nawacît ikota kotawânihk. ikwa anihi sîsîpa âtiht î-wâh-wîwîkinât nîpiya î-âpacihtât ikwa mîna asiskiy. ikwa sîhkwahkinîw, sîpâ iskotîhk î-ahthât iyakoni sîsîpa. ikwâni ati-kîsisowak sîsîpak. wîsahkîcâhk pâh-pîhow. mitoni ati-iskaci-pîhow.

"âh, sôskwâc pitamâ niwî-nipâsin," itwîw. "mahti, kohcâk!" itwîw, î-wî-atotahk ôma okohcâk.

"kohcâk! koskonihkan ispî sîsîpak kîsisotwâwi!" itwîw îsa. ikwâni ati-nipâw ikota.

kîtahtawî okohcâk kâ-pîhtâkwanithik "pôk! pôk!"

19

WISAHKECAHK EATS HIS SCAB

The teaching of this traditional story: Not all things we find on our road are gifts from the grandfathers.

Once Wisahkecahk had killed many ducks for himself. He cleaned those ducks then he made a fire.

"Ah, I am really going to eat lots," he thinks.

There he began to roast some of those ducks. He used sticks to roast them over the fire. And some of those ducks he wrapped in leaves and also in clay. He put those ducks under the ashes, under the fire. The ducks began to cook. Wisahkecahk waits. He gets tired of waiting.

"Ah, I may as well take a nap for now," he says. "Let's see, hey! Rear end!" he says, asking his rear end to do something for him.

"Rear end! Wake me up when the ducks are done cooking!" he says. He goes to sleep there.

Suddenly his rear end makes a sound. "Poke! Poke!"

âhci-poko awa wîsahkîcâhk kâ-nâh-nipât.

“pôk! pôk!”

âhci-poko awa wîsahkîcâhk kâ-nâh-nipât îkâ î-pîhtahk okohcâk.

kîtahtawî awa kâ-waniskât. kanawâpahtam okotawân. wahwâ! î-mîstâskasothit îsa ôho sîsîpa osâm kinwîsk î-kî-nipât. kwayask kisowâhik okohcâk. ikwâni ikota ohci tâpokâni ikota iskotîhk itisinam okohcâk.

“kika-kiskinwahamâtin kîtha îkâ î-nitohtawiyan,” itîw.

mitoni î-kîsisahk okohcâk. ikota ohci ati-sipwîhtîw. kwayask wîsakîthihtam okohcâk wîtha î-ati-omikît. kinwîsk pimohtîw. kwayask wâh-wîsakîthihtam okohcâk. ati-câh-cihcîkinam okohcâk. pîthisk siyâkîth isiyayâw.

ikwâni mâni mâka kiyâpic pâh-pimohtîw awa. ati-kakwâtaki-nohtî-mîcisow. kîtahtawî kâ-wâpamât asinîwâhkwana. nawakîw î-wî-otinât.

“kâwitha mowinân!” itwîwak ôko asinîwâhkwanak.

“tânisi wîth-ôma kâ-itwîyîk,” itîw. “ninohtîhkatân ôma.”

mitoni mistahi manâhow, î-mowât. mâka kiyâpic nohtîhkatîw. kîtahtawî kâ-wâpamât okiniya. nawakîw î-wî-otinât.

“kâwitha mowinân!” itwîwak ôko okiniyak.

“tânisi wîth-ôma kâ-itwîyîk,” itîw. “ninohtîhkatân ôma.”

mitoni mistahi manâhow, î-mowât. ati-sipwîhtîw.

kîtahtawî kâ-wâpamât pithîwa. otinîw otahcâpiya ikwa mwihci kâ-ati-pimotahkwîw kâ-misi-pwîkitot. osahwîw anihi pithîwa.

Still Wisahkecahk sleeps on.

"Poke! Poke!"

Still Wisahkecahk sleeps on not hearing his rear end.

Suddenly he wakes up. He looks at his fire. Wah! All his ducks have all burned to a crisp because he had slept too long. His rear end really made him angry. Right away he puts his rear end toward the fire.

"I'll teach you for not listening to me," he says.

He very much cooked his rear end. He leaves from there. He had a very sore rear end because it had begun to scab. He walks for a long time. He had severe pain in his rear end. He began to scratch his rear end. Eventually he began to feel better.

So he continues walking. He very much wanted to eat. Suddenly he sees some rock lichen. He stoops intending to pick some.

"Don't eat us!" say the rock lichen.

"What is it that you say," he says. "I am hungry."

He harvests quite a lot, eating them. But he was still hungry. Suddenly he sees rosehips. He stoops to pick some.

"Don't eat us!" say the rosehips.

"What is it that you say," he says. "I am hungry."

He harvests quite a lot, eating them. He leaves from there.

Suddenly he sees some grouse. He takes his bow but just as he was about to let an arrow go his rear end let go a big fart! It scares away the grouse.

ati-pâh-pimohtîw, î-pâh-pwîkitot athisk asiniwâhkwana î-pwîkitiskâkot ikwa î-kithakikohcâkît athisk okiniya î-kithakikohcâkîskâkot. kakwâtaki-nohtîhkatîw.

kîtahtawî kâ-wâpahtahk kîkway mîskanâhk, tâpiskôc kâskîwak ôma î-isinâkwanithik. ikwâni ati-otinam.

"âyî, tâpwî kihci! nimosômak î-asamicik ôma kâskîwak!" î-itwît. otinam ikwa ati-mîciw iyakwîthiw. kîtahtawî poko kâ-pîhtawât pithîsîsa.

"wîsahkîcâhk omikiy mîciw! wîsahkîcâhk omikiy mîciw!"

"ay awas! nimosôm awa î-pî-asamit ômîthow kâskîwak!"

"wîsahkîcâhk omikiy mîciw! wîsahkîcâhk omikiy mîciw!"

ati-nitohtawîw ôho pithîsîsa. pasow animîthow kâskîwak. iyaw! tâpwî mâni mâka îsa omikiy î-kî-mîcit. âh kisîmik ôho pithîsîsa. pimosinâtîw mâka patahwîw. ikota waskwâhk anima kâ-micimopathithik animîthow omikiy.

ikota posâkan anohc kitisi-kiskîthimânaw iyakw-âna waskwâhk mâna kâ-ayât. iyako maskihkiy mithwâsin.

ikwa mâna kâ-wapahtamân iyako ikosi mâna, "wîsahkîcâhk omikiy" nitititthihtîn.

He continues to walk, farting because the rock lichen give him gas, and he has an itchy rear end because the rosehips make him itch in the rear end. He was very hungry.

Suddenly he sees something on the road looking like dried meat. He picks it up.

"Wow, truly great! My grandfathers have fed me some dried meat!" he says. He takes it and begins to eat it. Suddenly he hears a bird.

"Wisahkecahk is eating his scab! Wisahkecahk is eating his scab!"

"Go away! My grandfather fed me this dried meat!"

"Wisahkecahk is eating his scab! Wisahkecahk is eating his scab!"

Eventually he listens to this bird. He smells the dried meat. Oops! It is true that he was eating his scab. The bird makes him angry. He throws the scab at the bird but misses it. The scab gets stuck on the birch tree.

It is from there that we get touchwood (chaga) as we know it today. That is good medicine.

Whenever I see that today I think, "Wisahkecahk's scab."

20 wîsahkîcâhk pimihamow

ôma âcathôhkîwin kikiskinwahamâkonaw: nahîthimisow.

piyakwâw îsa wîsahkîcâhk kî-pâh-pimohtîw wâsakâm sâkahikanihk. kâ-wâpamât îsa niska î-âh-ohpahothit ikwa mâna kâwi î-twîhothit. mâmaskâtîw.

"tânisi ôma î-itahkamikisiyîk, nisîmitik?" isi-kakwîcimîw îsa ôho niska.

"iyaw, î-takwâkik ôma. wîpac ta-pipon ikwa kita-tâh-tâhkâyâw! ohcitaw poko sâwanohk ta-isi-pimohtîhoyâhk îkâ kita-nipahâskaciyâhk," itwîw îsa awa piyak niska.

"mahti nîsta! kika-wîcîwitinâwâw!" itwîw wîsahkîcâhk.

"mâka wîtha îkâ î-otahtahkwaniyan!" itwîw îsa awa niska.

"hâ, tâpwî-wîspinac!"

20

WISAHKECAHK MIGRATES SOUTH

The teaching of this traditional story: Accept yourself.

Once Wisahkecahk was strolling along, around a lake, when he saw some geese flying up and then landing again. He wondered what they were doing.

"Little brothers, what are you doing?" he asked the geese.

"Well, it's autumn now, but soon it will be winter and very cold. We must travel south so that we don't freeze to death," one of the geese replied.

"Me too! I'll come with you!" said Wisahkecahk.

"But you don't have any wings," replied the goose.

"Hmm, truly this is tragic."

"haw cîskwa, kika-mâmawi-wîcihitinân," itwîw awa niska. nitomîw owâhkômâkana ikwa itîw ta-tâh-tahkwamâthit wîsahkîcâhkwa omiyawithihk. ôta tâh-tahkwâmik ôho niska: piyak ostikwânihk, ikwa âtiht ospitonihk, ikwa mîna kotakak oskâtihk. ikosi isi-kaskihtâwak ta-pimohtahâcik ostîsiwâwa, wîsahkîcâhkwa. ispimihk pâskac î-itâpithit ôho, î-sâsakicisinithit.

"kâwitha waskawî nistîsi," itîw îsa awa niska ostîsa. "kika-kiciskinitinân kîspin waskawîyani!"

"hâw, namwâc nika-waskawân," itwîw îsa wîsahkîcâhk. ikosi ati-sipwîpithâwak ôko niskak, î-tahkonâcik ostîsiwâwa. mithwîthihtam wîsahkîcâhk athisk wîsta sâwanohk î-wî-itohtîhot.

kîtahtawî kâ-pîhtawât iskwîwa î-matwî-môcikihtâkosithit. kisâstaw î-pakâsimothit, itîthihtam. sîmâk waskawîw, î-kwîskipathihot, î-kakwî-wâpamât anihi iskwîwa. mayaw kâ-waskawît, kâ-kiciskinikot anihi niska.

mitoni î-pakastawîsihk ita ôko iskwîwak kâ-pakâsimothit. kwayask pahpihik!

ikwâni namwâc sâwanohk ohci itohtîhow wîsahkîcâhk. mâka kiyâpic ôko niskak sâwanohk âh-itohtîhowak tahto-takwâkin ikwa tâpiskôc kiyâpic î-miciminâcik wîsahkîcâhkwa î-isi-pimithâcik.

"Okay, wait. All together we will help you," said the goose. So the goose called his relatives and told them, using their mouths of course, to grab a hold of Wisahkecahk's body. So the geese did just that: one at his head, a few at his arms and others at his legs. In this way, the geese were able to carry their older brother Wisahkecahk: who was facing upwards, he was on his back.

"Don't move, older brother," said the goose. "If you move, we might accidently drop you!"

"Okay, I won't move!" Wisahkecahk replied as the geese began to fly away holding on to him, their older brother. Wisahkecahk was glad as he too was going south.

Suddenly Wisahkecahk heard some women, and it sounded like they were having fun. "Perhaps they are swimming," he thought. Quickly he moved, twisting to try to see those women. As soon as he moved, the geese dropped him.

Wisahkecahk fell right into the water where the women were swimming. Truly they laughed at him.

So Wisahkecahk never made it south. But still, when migrating, geese fly in this same formation: as if still holding Wisahkecahk.

21
wîsahkîcâhk ikwa wîhtikow

ôma âcathôhkîwin kikiskinwahamâkonaw: sâpohtatâ kitasotamâkîwin.

piyakwâw îsa wîsahkîcâhk kî-papimohtîw kîtahtawî îsa kâ-wâpamât wîhtikowa. kîsiskaw kâsôpathihow, athisk î-kostât iyakoni. ikosi ikota sakâsihk ohci-kanawâpamîw, î-kakwî-paspîhot. kîtahtawî poko wîhtikow kâ-matwî-ayamit.

"wîsahakîcahk, kipaswâtitin. âstam! ninohtî-mîcison ôma."

ikosi wîsahkîcâhk ati-nâtîw wîhtikowa, î-mâh-mâcosit pâskac. î-mawihkâtisot, athisk î-wî-mowiht.

"wîsahkîcâhk! nâcinihtî ikwa kotawî ikota ohci kika-mowitin."

ikosi wîsahkîcâhk kospiw, ikota ohci, î-nâcinihtît. kîtahtawî poko kâ-wâpamât sihkosa.

"âstam, nisîmis!" itîw

ikwa ana sihkos,

21
WISAHKECAHK AND *wîhtikow*

The teaching of this traditional story: Carry through on your promises.

Once Wisahkecahk was walking along. All of a sudden he sees *wîhtikow*. Quickly he hid because he was afraid of that one. From the small bush he watches him, trying to be safe. All of a sudden *wîhtikow* speaks from the distance.

"Wisahkecahk, I smell you. Come! I want to eat!"

Wisahkecahk goes to *wîhtikow*, crying a bit. He was crying over his fate because he is going to be eaten.

"Wisahkecahk! Fetch firewood and make a fire and then I will eat you!"

So Wisahkecahk goes into the forest from there fetching firewood. All of a sudden he sees an ermine.

"Come younger sibling!" he says.

And the ermine says:

"kîkwây? kîkwây, wîsahkîcâhk?"

"cîstî, nâha nîtî wîhtikow. î-wî-mowit ana. niyâ! ikotî ispahtâ. nâcipah! sihkâhtawâs okohcâkihk ikota ohci kita-nitawi-paskîhtaman otîhiyâpiy."

ikwa awa sihkos:

"î." ânwihtam, "awas nika-nipin!"

"namô-witha, sihkos. misawâc kâwi kika-pimâcihitin. ikwa kîspin omisi itôtamani kika-osîhtamâtin nawac kita-mâwaci-mithwâsik kitahtay."

mithohtam awa sihkos. ati-nâcipahîw wîhtikowa.

ikosi awa sihkos ispahtâw itî wîhtikowa kâ-ayâthit. nitawi-sîkopahtâw okohcâkithik ikota ohci iskwâhtawîw, î-nitawi-tâh-tahkwamât otîhiyâpîhk. ikwa kîtahtawî poko kâ-tîpwît wîhtikow.

"wîsahkîcâhk kithipa! ninohtîhkatân ôma. wîsahkîcâhk kithipa! ninohtîhkatân ôma!"

ikwâni kîtahtawî poko kâ-pahkisihk awa wîhtikow, î-nipit.

wîsahkîcâhk kwayask mithwîthihtam. nâcipahîw anihi wîhtikowa. ikota ohci pahkonîw, î-otinât anihi sihkosa. ikwa îsa awa sihkos î-nipit, î-kî-nistâpâwît.

ikota ohci wîsahkîcâhk kâ-itohtahât sâkahikanihk, î-nitawi-sîpîkinât anihi sihkosa. î-wâh-wâskânât nipîhk. ikwa mâna î-pâh-pôtâtât, î-kakwî-pimâcihât. hâ! kinwîsk awa ikosi itôtam. osôsithik î-miciminât, î-sîpîkinât anihi sihkosa. î-pâh-pôtâtât mâna, ikwa mâna kîhtwâm î-sîpîkinât.

kîtahtawî kâwi kâ-pimâtisithit anihi sihkosa.

"What? What, Wisahkecahk?"

"Look, over there is *wîhtikow*. He is going to eat me. Go! Run over there. Run to him! Crawl up his anus and from there go and chew off his heart strings.

And the ermine says:

"Ew." He rather doubts that. "Go away, I'll die!"

"No, not so, Ermine. In any case I will give you back your life. And if you do this I will make you a coat of fur that is more beautiful than the one you have."

The ermine likes the sound of that. He runs to *wîhtikow*.

So then the ermine runs to where *wîhtikow* is at. He runs into his anus and climbs up to go chew on his heart strings. All of a sudden *wîhtikow* hollers.

"Hurry up, Wisahkecahk! I am hungry! Hurry up, Wisahkecahk! I am hungry!"

And all of a sudden *wîhtikow* falls down, he is dead.

Wisahkecahk is very happy. He runs to *wîhtikow*. There he cuts him open, taking the ermine. The ermine is dead, he had drowned.

From there Wisahkecahk takes him down to the lake, going to wash the ermine clean. He swishes him around and around in the water. Once in a while he would blow on him, trying to give him life. Ha! He does this for a long time. Holding him by the tail he cleans the ermine. He blows on him and once again he cleans him in the water.

Suddenly the ermine comes back to life.

"cîstî, nisîmis. kanawâpamiso nipîhk!" itîw osîmisa sihkosa.

awa sihkos kanawâpamisow nipîhk. ikota wâpamisow, î-wâpiskisit. kwayask î-mithonâkosit ana sihkos. ikwa ita kâ-kî-miciminikot wîsahkîcâhkwa wanaskoc osôhk, ikota kaskitîsiw.

kiyâpic wanaskoc osôhk kaskitîsiw anohc kâ-kîsikâthik.

"Look, younger sibling. Look at yourself in the water!" says Wisahkecahk to the ermine.

The ermine looks at himself in the water. There he sees himself, he is white. The ermine looks very beautiful. And there, where Wisahkecahk had held him by the tip his tail, he is black.

The tip of Ermine's tail is still black today.

Notes to the Texts

Many of the texts that appear in this book have been previously published electronically, accompanied by corresponding audio recordings. The following notes include URLS to locate those recordings, as well as original publication dates, and brief contextual comments. A Cree genre label is suggested for each individual text, though some pieces, with their layers of teachings and memory, may deserve several.

Following is an index of the genre labels in Cree (SRO and Syllabic) and in English. In the notes below, the label is provided only in Cree (SRO).

âcimisowina	ᐋᒋᒥᓱᐃᐧᓇ	personal, autobiographical stories
âcathôhkîwina	ᐋᒐᖪᐦᑮᐃᐧᓇ	sacred, traditional stories
nikamowini-pîkiskwîwin	ᓂᑲᒧᐃᐧᓂ ᐲᑭᐢᑹᐃᐧᐣ	poetry
kiskinwahamâkîwina	ᑭᐢᑭᓇᐧᐦᐊᒫᑮᐃᐧᓇ	lessons
sîhkimâwasowina	ᓰᐦᑭᒫᐊᐧᓱᐃᐧᓇ	lectures, counselling speeches
kiskisiwinisa	ᑭᐢᑭᓯᐃᐧᓂᓴ	little memories
mâmitonîthihcikana	ᒫᒥᑐᓃᖨᐦᒋᑲᓇ	thoughts

kiskisiwina / ᑭᐢᑭᓯᐃᐧᓇ / Memories

CHAPTER 1: *î-âpasâpahtamân* / ᐄ ᐋᐸᓵᐸᐦᑕᒫᐣ / Looking Back

TEXT 1.1: ***î-ati-powâtamân*** / ᐄ ᐊᑎ ᐳᐋᐧᑕᒫᐣ / On the Threshold of a Dream (2013) ***nikamowini-pîkiskwîwin***. Originally published in y-dialect. https://creeliteracy.org/2014/01/15

TEXT 1.2: ***î-maskamiht ocawâsisiwin*** / ᐄ ᒪᐢᑲᒥᐦᐟ ᐅᒐᐋᐧᓯᓯᐃᐧᐣ / Stolen Childhood (2021) ***mâmitonîthihcikan***. https://creeliteracy.org/2021/06/25

TEXT 1.3: ***kâkikî nika-kiskisin*** / ᑳᑭᑮ ᓂᑲ ᑭᐢᑭᓯᐣ / Lest I Forget (2017)

nikamowini-pîkiskwîwin. https://creeliteracy.org/2017/04/17

TEXT 1.4: *atôspîwinâkwan-papakiwayâni-kîsikâw* / ᐊᑑᐢᐲᐘᐋᐧᓈᑲᐧᐣ ᐸᐸᑭᐘᐋᐧᔮᓂ ᑮᓯᑳᐤ / Orange Shirt Day (2016)
âcimisowinis. https://creeliteracy.org/2016/10/01

TEXT 1.5: *kîspin îkâ î-kî-ocawâsimisiyân* / ᑮᐢᐱᐣ ᐄᑳ ᐄ ᑮ ᐅᒐᐚᓯᒥᓯᔮᐣ / If Not for My Children (2021)
mâmitonîthihcikan. https://creeliteracy.org/2021/09/30

TEXT 1.6: *kakîpâtisak* / ᑲᑮᐹᑎᓴᐠ / Fools! (2019)
nikamowini-pîkiskwîwin. https://creeliteracy.org/2019/03/19

CHAPTER 2: *î-mwayî-nitawi-ayamihcikîyân* / ᐄ ᒣᐧᔩ ᓂᑕᐏ ᐊᔭᒥᐦᒋᑮᔮᐣ / Life before School

TEXT 2.1: *nicâhkosîwikamikos* / ᓂᒑᐦᑯᓰᐏᑲᒥᑯᐢ / My Little Hospital (2014)
âcimisowinis. https://creeliteracy.org/2014/09/09

TEXT 2.2: *salamô ikwâni poko* Ratt / ᓴᕒᐊᒨ ᐃᒁᓂ ᐳᑯ ᐊᕒᐊᐟ / Just Solomon (2020)
âcimisowinis. Because "r" is not a regular part of the Cree sound system, writers like Solomon's late mother would use a vowel before the "r" character. The Syllabic spelling of the name "Ratt" becomes ᐊᕒᐋᐟ. https://creeliteracy.org/2020/01/23

TEXT 2.3: *acoskîwinisa* / ᐊᒍᐢᑮᐏᓂᓴ / Chores (2021)
kiskisiwinis. https://creeliteracy.org/2021/12/07

TEXT 2.4: *wîcisâni-kahkwîthihtowin* / ᐑᒋᓵᓂ ᑲᐦᑹᖨᐦᑐᐏᐣ / Sibling Rivalry (2014)
âcimisowinis. Not previously published.

TEXT 2.5: *wîsahkîcâhk twîhow wanihikîskanâhk* / ᐑᓴᐦᑮᒑᕽ ᑣᐦᐅᐤ ᐘᓂᐦᐃᑮᐢᑲᓈᕽ / Santa Visits the Trapline (2021)
kiskisiwinis. https://creeliteracy.org/2021/11/18

TEXT 2.6: *tâpokîthihtamowin* / ᑖᐳᑮᖨᐦᑕᒧᐏᐣ / Faith (2014)
âcimisowinis. Y-dialect version published in Solomon Ratt, 2022: *âhkami-nêhiyawêtân* / *Let's Keep Speaking Cree*. Regina: University of Regina Press, pp. 241–242. https://creeliteracy.org/2014/06/09

TEXT 2.7: *ohpahowipîsim* / ᐅᐦᐸᐦᐅᐏᐲᓯᒼ / Flying Up Moon (2018)
kiskisiwinis. https://creeliteracy.org/2018/08/02

CHAPTER 3: *nistam wîsakîthihtamowin* / ᓂᐢᑕᒼ ᐑᓴᑮᖨᐦᑕᒧᐏᐣ / Painful Firsts

TEXT 3.1: *mâmitonîthihta ôma!* / ᒫᒥᑐᓃᖨᐦᑕ ᐆᒪ! / Think on This! (2021)
mâmitonîthihcikan.
https://creeliteracy.org/2021/09/30

TEXT 3.2: *kiskinwahamâtowitâpânâsk* / ᑭᐢᑭᓌᐦᐊᒫᑐᐏᑖᐹᓈᐢᐠ / School Bus (2019)
âcimisowinis. Not previously published.

TEXT 3.3: *nikî-tâtopitikawin* / ᓂᑮ ᑖᑐᐱᑎᑲᐏᐣ / I Was Torn (2021)
nikamowini-pîkiskwîwin.
https://creeliteracy.org/2021/04/07

TEXT 3.4: *nimasinahamawâw nikâwiy* / ᓂᒪᓯᓇᐦᐊᒪᐚᐤ ᓂᑳᐏᕀ / Letter to Mama (2015)
kiskisiwinis. Not previously published.

TEXT 3.5: *môniyâw pîsimoyâpiya* / ᒨᓂᔮᐤ ᐲᓯᒧᔮᐱᔭ / Man-made Rainbows (2017)
kiskisiwinis. https://creeliteracy.org/2017/10/18

TEXT 3.6: *î-kîwîhtahikawiyân* / ᐄ ᑮᐑᐦᑕᐦᐃᑲᐏᔮᐣ / Home for the Summer (2015)
âcimisowinis. https://creeliteracy.org/2015/05/29

TEXT 3.7: *iskwâyâc tipiskâw î-mwayî-ohpahoyâhk* / ᐃᐢᑹᔮᐨ ᑎᐱᐢᑳᐤ ᐄ ᒷᔩ ᐅᐦᐸᐦᐅᔮᕽ / Last Night of Summer (2021) *mâmitonîthihcikan*. https://creeliteracy.org/2021/08/26

TEXT 3.8: *kicohcikanis* / ᑭᒍᐦᒋᑲᓂᐢ / Transistor Radio (2020) *âcimisowinis*. https://creeliteracy.org/2020/11/02

CHAPTER 4: *kâ-ati-oskinîkîsiyân* / ᑳ ᐊᑎ ᐅᐢᑭᓃᑮᓯᔮᐣ / Middle Years at School

TEXT 4.1: *î-maskamikawiyân nipâhkîkinaskisina* / ᐄ ᒪᐢᑲᒥᑲᐎᔮᐣ ᓂᐹᐦᑮᑭᓇᐢᑭᓯᓇ / Stolen Moccasins (2017) *mâmitonîthihcikan*. https://creeliteracy.org/2017/09/30

TEXT 4.2: "Dog Biscuits" (2014) *âcimisowinis*. This story provided the earliest testing material for the Cree language tools developed by Alberta Language Technology Laboratory at the University of Alberta (AltLab). Both y- and th-dialect versions of this story have been published. https://creeliteracy.org/2014/01/14

TEXT 4.3: *î-kîmôci-ayamihcikîyân* / ᐄ ᑮᒨᒋ ᐊᔭᒥᐦᒋᑮᔮᐣ / Undercover Reading (2015) *âcimisowinis*. https://creeliteracy.org/2015/04/28

TEXT 4.4: *î-kîmôtâpiyân* / ᐄ ᑮᒨᑖᐱᔮᐣ / "Jeepers Creepers" (2015) *âcimisowinis*. This story was titled first, jokingly, in English. The Cree title might be translated literally as "peeking." https://creeliteracy.org/2015/05/02

TEXT 4.5: *mistatimotôn* / ᒥᐢᑕᑎᒧᑑᐣ / Horse Lips (2018) *âcimisowinis*. Although the story clearly refers to the horse's nose, "Horse Lips" was chosen for the English title simply because it sounds funnier, and was eventually translated directly into Cree. https://creeliteracy.org/2018/06/07

TEXT 4.6: *kâ-makosîkîsikâk* / ᑳ ᒪᑯᓰᑮᓯᑳᐠ / Christmas at School (2015) *âcimisowinis*. https://creeliteracy.org/2015/12/16

TEXT 4.7: *kinîkânîskawâwak kitithinîmak* / ᑭᓃᑳᓃᐢᑲᐚᐘᐠ ᑭᑎᖩᓃᒪᐠ / "A Credit to Your Race" (2019)
âcimisowinis. Not previously published. The residential school teachers who made this comment sincerely meant it in a good way when they congratulated Solomon and others on their school successes. But racism as so deeply ingrained that it was invisible to the teachers and supervisors who worked there. At the time, students who received comments like this as praise understood they were meant well. They were also conditioned to accept this kind of racism as normal.

TEXT 4.8: *pakwanita-itwîwin* / ᐸᑿᓂᑕ ᐃᑏᐧᐃᐧᐣ / Backhanded Compliment (2021)
kiskisiwinis. https://creeliteracy.org/2021/10/07

CHAPTER 5: *nîkihk kâ-nîpihk* / ᓃᑭᕽ ᑳ ᓃᐱᕽ / Summers at Home

TEXT 5.1: *ka-ispitisicik isîhcikîwin* / ᑲ ᐃᐢᐱᑎᓯᒋᐠ ᐃᓰᐦᒋᑮᐃᐧᐣ / Protocol: Age-Appropriate Conduct (2014)
âcimisowinis. Y-dialect version published in Solomon Ratt, 2022: *âhkami-nêhiyawêtân* / *Let's Keep Speaking Cree*. Regina: University of Regina Press, p. 235. https://creeliteracy.org/2014/06/03

TEXT 5.2: *nakwâtisowin ikwa mâtinamâkîwin* / ᓇᑳᐧᑎᓱᐃᐧᐣ ᐃᑲᐧ ᒫᑎᓇᒫᑮᐃᐧᐣ / Sharing and Generosity (2014)
âcimisowinis. Y-dialect version published in Solomon Ratt, 2022: *âhkami-nêhiyawêtân* / *Let's Keep Speaking Cree*. Regina: University of Regina Press, pp. 241-242. https://creeliteracy.org/2014/06/06

TEXT 5.3: *kisîwâtisiwin* / ᑭᓰᐋᐧᑎᓯᐃᐧᐣ / Kindness (2014)
âcimisowinis. Y-dialect version published in Solomon Ratt, 2022: *âhkami-nêhiyawêtân* / *Let's Keep Speaking Cree*. Regina: University of Regina Press, pp. 246. https://creeliteracy.org/2014/06/10

TEXT 5.4: *kistîthihtamowin* / ᑭᐢᑏᖧᐦᑕᒧᐃᐧᐣ / Respect (2014)
âcimisowinis. Y-dialect version published in Solomon Ratt, 2022: *âhkami-nêhiyawêtân / Let's Keep Speaking Cree*. Regina: University of Regina Press, p. 232.
https://creeliteracy.org/2014/06/02

TEXT 5.5: *1969 askîwin kâ-kî-akihtîk* / 1969 ᐊᐢᑮᐃᐧᐣ ᑳ ᑮ ᐊᑭᐦᑏᐠ / 1969 (2019)
âcimisowinis. https://creeliteracy.org/2019/04/12

CHAPTER 6: *î-ayahcitiniwiyâhk nitaskînâhk* / ᐄ ᐊᔭᐦᒋᑎᓂᐃᐧᔮᕽ ᓂᑕᐢᑮᓈᕽ / Strangers in Our Homeland

TEXT 6.1: *Canada, Oh Canada*, *150 askîwina* / *Canada, Oh Canada*, 150 ᐊᐢᑮᐃᐧᓇ / Canada, Oh Canada, 150 years (2017)
An Indigenous response to sesquicentennial celebrations.
https://creeliteracy.org/2017/05/16

TEXT 6.2: *môtha nîtha* Indian / ᒨᖫ ᓃᖫ Indian / I'm Not an Indian (2012)
âcimisowinis. Also published in Arok Wolvengrey, 2007: *wawiyatâcimowinisa / Funny Little Stories* Narrated by Cree-speaking students, instructors and Elders. Regina: University of Regina Press, pp. 41–45. Deanna Reder and Sophie McCall, eds., 2017: *Read, Listen, Tell: Indigenous Stories from Turtle Island*. Waterloo: Wilfrid Laurier University Press, pp. 170–172. https://creeliteracy.org/2012/01/20

TEXT 6.3: *âhkîtâp ithiniwak, cikâstîpathihcikan ithiniwak* / ᐋᐦᑮᑖᑊ ᐃᖧᓂᐊᐧᐠ, ᒋᑳᐢᑏᐸᖧᐦᒋᑲᐣ ᐃᖧᓂᐊᐧᐠ / "Reel Injuns" (2016)
mâmitonîthihcikan. Solomon responds with satire (sort of) in response to traditional North American Thanksgiving celebrations. Originally published in y-dialect. https://creeliteracy.org/2016/10/06

TEXT 6.4: *kâ-papâmi-atâwîyan ispî kâ-wîskwastîwinâkosiyan* / ᑳ ᐸᐹᒥ ᐊᑖᐑᔭᐣ ᐃᐢᐲ ᑳ ᐑᐢᑲᐢᑏᐃᐧᓈᑯᓯᔭᐣ / Shopping While Brown (2019)
âcimisowinis. An unpleasant, all-too-frequent experience is reported in the style of a classroom lesson. https://creeliteracy.org/2019/03/03

TEXT 6.5: *âniskô-kiskinwahamâkîwin* / ᐋᓂᐢᑰ ᑭᐢᑭᓇᐧᐦᐊᒫᑮᐃᐧᐣ / Passing on Teachings (2014)
âcimisowinis. https://creeliteracy.org/2014/06/11

TEXT 6.6: *âhkami-nîhithowîtân* / ᐋᐦᑲᒥ ᓃᐦᐃᖬᐑᑖᐣ / Let's Keep on Speaking Cree (2015)
nikamowini-pîkiskwîwin. This poem is included in—and also provides the title for—Solomon Ratt, 2022: *âhkami-nêyiyawêtân* / *Let's Keep Speaking Cree*. Regina: University of Regina Press. https://creeliteracy.org/2015/03/31

CHAPTER 7: *tâpwîwin nîkân î-mwayî-mînosihtamâhk mitho-wîcîhtowin* / ᑖᐲᐃᐧᐣ ᓃᑳᐣ ᐄ ᒪᐧᔩ ᒦᓄᓯᐦᑕᒫᕽ ᒥᖪ ᐑᒌᐦᑐᐃᐧᐣ / Truth before Reconciliation

TEXT 7.1: *tâpwîwin* / ᑖᐲᐃᐧᐣ / Truth (2021)
nikamowini-pîkiskwîwin.
https://creeliteracy.org/2021/09/22

TEXT 7.2: *kithâskiwin* / ᑭᖭᐢᑭᐃᐧᐣ / Lies (2021)
nikamowini-pîkiskwîwin.
https://creeliteracy.org/2021/06/16

TEXT 7.3: *namôtha âhkîtâp* Indian / ᓇᒨᖬ ᐋᐦᑮᑖᑊ Indian / Not a Pretendian (2021)
mâmitonîthihcikan. Reacting to yet another "pretendian" controversy, Solomon demonstrates an authentic style of self-identification.
https://creeliteracy.org/2021/04/06

TEXT 7.4: *kipihtowîwin* / ᑭᐱᐦᑐᐑᐃᐧᐣ / The Sound of Silence (2021)
nikamowini-pîkiskwîwin. Originally published in

y-dialect. Written in reaction to the May 2021 discovery of the first 215 unmarked residential school graves near Kamloops. https://creeliteracy.org/2021/06/06

TEXT 7.5: *î-nisiwanâcihtâyahk kipîkiskwîwininaw* / ᐄ ᓂᓯᐘᓈᒋᐦᑖᔭᕽ ᑭᐲᑭᐢᑸᐏᓂᓇᐤ / Linguicide (2020) *nikamowini-pîkiskwîwin*. Linguicide, or language death, was clearly part of the residential school agenda; today, we can and must choose differently for the Cree language to thrive. https://creeliteracy.org/2020/03/12

TEXT 7.6: *tâniwî sâkihiwîwin?* / ᑖᓂᐑ ᓵᑭᐦᐃᐑᐏᐣ? / Where Is the Love? (2021) *nikamowini-pîkiskwîwin*. https://creeliteracy.org/2021/10/18

CHAPTER 8: *î-kîwîhtotahitoyahk* / ᐄ ᑮᐑᐦᑐᑕᐦᐃᑐᔭᕽ / Reclaiming Ourselves

TEXT 8.1: *askiy kitohtâpamihikonaw* / ᐊᐢᑭᐩ ᑭᑐᐦᑖᐸᒥᐦᐃᑯᓇᐤ / Earth Nourishes Us (2021) *nikamowini-pîkiskwîwin*. Originally published in y-dialect. https://creeliteracy.org/2021/03/31

TEXT 8.2: *âniskôhtowin* / ᐋᓂᐢᑰᐦᑐᐏᐣ / Interconnectedness (2019) *mâmitonîthihcikan*. https://creeliteracy.org/2019/05/29

TEXT 8.3: *ninanâskomon* / ᓂᓇᓈᐢᑯᒧᐣ / I Give Thanks (2019) *mâmitonîthihcikan*. https://creeliteracy.org/2019/10/12

TEXT 8.4: *kâ-ohtâwîmâwi-kîsikâk* / ᑳ ᐅᐦᑖᐑᒫᐏ ᑮᓯᑳᐠ / For Father's Day (2018) *mâmitonîthihcikan*. https://creeliteracy.org/2018/06/14

TEXT 8.5: *nahîwin* / ᓇᐦᐄᐏᐣ / Proficiency (2021)
sîhkimâwasowina.
https://creeliteracy.org/2021/02/24

TEXT 8.6: *kiskîthihtamowin* / ᑭᐢᑮᖨᐦᑕᒧᐏᐣ / Knowledge (2021)
sîhkimâwasowina. Originally published in y-dialect.
https://creeliteracy.org/2021/10/12

TEXT 8.7: *kiskîthihtamowin ohci* / ᑭᐢᑫᖨᐦᑕᒧᐏᐣ ᐅᐦᒋ / About Knowledge: Basil H. Johnston (2020)
mâmitonîthihcikan. This thought is translated from Basil H. Johnson, 1990: "One Generation from Extinction" in *Native Writers and Canadian Writing: Canadian Literature Special Issue*. Vancouver: University of British Columbia Press. https://creeliteracy.org/2020/01/12

TEXT 8.8: *nitohta!* / ᓂᑐᐦᑕ! / Listen! (2020)
nikamowini-pîkiskwîwin.
https://creeliteracy.org/2020/06/17

âcathôhkîwina / ᐋᒐᖫᐦᑮᐏᓇ / Sacred Stories

PREFACE: *tâpika âcathôhkîwina ta-kî-pî-kîwîmakahki* / ᑖᐱᑲ ᐋᒐᖫᐦᑮᐏᓇ ᑕ ᑮ ᐲ ᑮᐑᒪᑲᐦᑭ / Wishing the Stories to Return (2022)

nikamowini-pîkiskwîwin.
https://creeliteracy.org/2022/03/13

CHAPTER 9: *nîhithaw kiskinwahamâkîwin: nistam mâmitonîthihcikîwin* / ᓃᐦᐃᖬᐤ ᑭᐢᑭᓌᐦᐋᒫᑮᐏᐣ: ᓂᐢᑕᒼ ᒫᒥᑐᓃᖨᐦᒋᑮᐏᐣ / Cree Education: First Thoughts

TEXT 9.1: *tânisi mâna kâ-kî-isi-kiskinwahamâhcik awâsisak kayâs?* / ᑖᓂᓯ ᒫᓇ ᑳ ᑮ ᐃᓯ ᑭᐢᑭᓌᐦᐋᒫᐦᒋᐠ ᐊᐚᓯᓴᐠ

ᑲᔮᐢ? / How Then Were Children Taught Long Ago? (2019)
kiskinwahamâkîwina. Not previously published.

TEXT 9.2: *kîkwây kiwîhtamâkonaw âcathôhkana? cihcipiscikwân* / ᑮᒁᐩ ᑭᐑᐦᑕᒫᑯᓇᐤ ᐋᒐᖫᐦᑲᓇ? ᒋᐦᒋᐱᐢᒋᒁᐣ / What Do Our Stories Tell Us? The Rolling Head (2019)
kiskinwahamâkîwina.
https://creeliteracy.org/2019/02/21

CHAPTER 10: *cihcipiscikwân* / ᒋᐦᒋᐱᐢᒋᒁᐣ / The Rolling Head (2016)

âcathôhkîwin. First presented orally in a 2016 storytelling performance, then transcribed and translated from video. Solomon blends childhood memories of his mother's telling with details of the English-only edition of the same story published in Edward Ahenakew, 1929: "Cree Trickster Tales," in the *Journal of American Folklore*, Vol. 42, No. 166 (Oct.–Dec., 1929), pp. 309–353. Some of Ahenakew's phrases are so memorable, they are incorporated verbatim.
https://creeliteracy.org/2016/03/09

CHAPTER 11: *wîsahkîcâhk tapasîw* / ᐑᓴᐦᑮᒑᕽ ᑕᐸᓰᐤ / The Flight of Wisahkecahk (2016)

âcathôhkîwin. Usually told as a second segment of The Rolling Head. First presented orally in a 2016 storytelling performance, then transcribed and translated from video. Solomon blends childhood memories of his mother's telling with details of the English-only edition published in Edward Ahenakew, 1929: "Cree Trickster Tales," in the *Journal of American Folklore,* Vol. 42, No. 166 (Oct.–Dec., 1929), pp. 309–353. Some of Ahenakew's phrases are so memorable, they are incorporated verbatim. (Told as a continuation of The Rolling Head on video). https://creeliteracy.org/2016/03/09

CHAPTER 12: *wîsahkîcâhk ikwa wîmisôsoy* / ᐑᓴᐦᑮᒑᕽ ᐃᑿ ᐑᒥᓲᓱᐩ / Wisahkecahk and *wîmisôsoy* (2019)

âcathôhkîwin. Not previously published.

CHAPTER 13: *thiskipîw* / ᖨᐢᑭᐲᐤ / The Flood (2016)

âcathôhkîwin. First presented orally in a 2016 storytelling performance, then transcribed and translated from video. Solomon blends childhood memories of his mother's telling with details of the English-only edition recorded in Edward Ahenakew, 1929: "Cree Trickster Tales," in the *Journal of American Folklore*, Vol. 42, No. 166 (Oct.–Dec., 1929), pp. 309–353. Some of Ahenakew's phrases are so memorable, they are incorporated verbatim. https://creeliteracy.org/2021/01/28

CHAPTER 14: *opasakwâpisimowak* / ᐅᐸᓴᒀᐱᓯᒧᐘᐠ / The Shut-Eye Dancers (2016)

âcathôhkîwin. First presented orally in a 2016 storytelling performance, then transcribed and translated from video. https://creeliteracy.org/2021/02/17

CHAPTER 15: *mâskikâtîw mahkîsîs* / ᒫᐢᑭᑳᑏᐤ ᒪᐦᑮᓰᐢ / The Fox Has a Crippled Leg (2019)

âcathôhkîwin. Not previously published.

CHAPTER 16: *wîsahkîcâhk ikwa okoskohowîsak* / ᐑᓴᐦᑮᒑᕽ ᐃᑿ ᐅᑯᐢᑯᐦᐅᐑᓴᐠ / Wisahkecahk and the Startlers (2016)

âcathôhkîwin. Also published as "Wîsahkîcahk and the Startlers" in Solomon Ratt, *nîhithaw âcimowina / Woods Cree Stories*, Regina: University of Regina Press, pp. 39–46. https://creeliteracy.org/2016/02/15

CHAPTER 17: *wîsahkîcâhk ikwa kâ-masinâsocik waskwayak* / ᐑᓴᐦᑮᒑᕽ ᐃᑿ ᑳ ᒪᓯᓈᓱᒋᐠ ᐘᐢᑿᔭᐠ / Wisahkecahk and the Marking of Birch Trees (2016)

âcathôhkîwin. First presented orally and recorded in a 2016 storytelling performance, later transcribed and translated. https://creeliteracy.org/2021/02/03

CHAPTER 18: *wîsahkîcâhk ikwa picikîskisîsa* / ᐑᓴᐦᑮᒑᕽ ᐃᑿ ᐱᒋᑮᐢᑭᓰᓴ / Wisahkecahk and the Chickadees (2017)

âcathôhkîwin. First presented orally in 2017 at a winter storytelling camp. The video recording was then transcribed and translated by Solomon's student, Ben Godden. https://creeliteracy.org/2017/04/19

CHAPTER 19: *wîsahkîcâhk omikiy mîciw* / ᐑᓴᐦᑮᒑᕽ ᐅᒥᑭᐩ ᒦᒋᐤ / Wisahkecahk Eats His Scab (2016)

âcathôhkîwin. First presented orally in 2016, then transcribed and translated from video. https://creeliteracy.org/2021/02/17

CHAPTER 20: *wîsahkîcâhk pimihamow* / ᐑᓴᐦᑮᒑᕽ ᐱᒥᐦᐊᒧᐤ / Wisahkecahk Migrates South (2016)

âcathôhkîwin. First presented orally in February 2016. The video recording was then transcribed and translated by Solomon's student, Ben Godden. https://creeliteracy.org/2021/01/14

CHAPTER 21: *wîsahkîcâhk ikwa wîhtikow* / ᐑᓴᐦᑮᒑᕽ ᐃᑿ ᐑᐦᑎᑯᐤ / Wisahkecahk and *wîhtikow* (2016)

âcathôhkîwin. Originally presented orally in February 2016. The video recording was then transcribed and translated by Solomon's student, Ben Godden. https://creeliteracy.org/2017/01/11

ABOUT THE SERIES

Our Own Words

University of Regina Press's book series, *Our Own Words*, publishes the personal stories of members from the Indigenous Nations of the Great Plains in their Indigenous language.

The books in the series provide longer, more extensive Indigenous texts for both the intermediate and advanced learners of the Indigenous language, and are presented, where appropriate, in Syllabics, Standard Roman Orthography, and English translation.

Series Editor

AROK WOLVENGREY

A linguist noted for his work with Indigenous Languages of the Americas, Arok Wolvengrey is a professor of Algonquian Languages and Linguistics in the Indigenous Languages Program at the First Nations University of Canada in Regina, Saskatchewan, located on Treaty 4 territory.

For more information about publishing in the series, please contact:

Karen May Clark, Senior Acquisitions Editor
University of Regina Press
3737 Wascana Parkway
Regina, Saskatchewan S4S 0A2 Canada
karen.clark@uregina.ca
www.uofrpress.ca

SOLOMON RATT kî-nihtâwikiw nâtakâm mâhtâwisîpîhk namôtha wâhthaw kîwêtinohk âmaciwîspimowinihk ohci. onîkihikwa kî-wanihikîthiwa ikwa kî-pakitahwâthiwa î-nôcihcikîthit pikwâc-askîhk, wanihikîskanâhk î-wîkicik ispî kâ-piponithik ikwa kâ-nîpinithik î-pakitahwâcik misti-sâkahikanihk. nistam nikotwâsik askiy kâ-pimâtisit kî-wîcâyâmîw onîkihikwa, iyakoni namôtha kî-ohci-âkathâsîmothiwa. kî-kiskîthihtamwak ta-pimâcihocik askîhk ikwa mîna kî-kiskîthihtamwak âcathôhkîwina kâ-pî-âniski-wîhtamawihcik otâniski-wâhkômâkaniwâwa. iyakoni kî-âh-âcathohkawîwak Solomona ikwa wîtisâna.

ᓱᕒᐅᒧᐣ ᕒᐋᐟ ᑮ ᓂᐦᑖᐏᑭᐤ ᓈᑕᑳᒼ ᒫᐦᑖᐏᓰᐲᕽ ᓇᒨᖬ ᐚᐦᖬᐤ ᑮᐍᑎᓄᕽ ᐋᒪᒋᐑᐢᐱᒧᐏᓂᕽ ᐅᐦᒋ᙮ ᐅᓃᑭᐦᐃᑿ ᑮ ᐘᓂᐦᐃᑮᖨᐘ ᐃᑿ ᑮ ᐸᑭᑕᐦᐚᖨᐘ ᐄ ᓅᒋᐦᒋᑮᖨᐟ ᐱᒁᒐᐢᑮᕽ, ᐘᓂᐦᐃᑮᐢᑲᓈᕽ ᐄ ᐑᑭᒋᐠ ᐃᐢᐲ ᑳ ᐱᐳᓂᖨᐠ ᐃᑿ ᑳ ᓃᐱᓂᖨᐠ ᐄ ᐸᑭᑕᐦᐚᒋᐠ ᒥᐢᑎ ᓵᑲᐦᐃᑲᓂᕽ᙮ ᓂᐢᑕᒼ ᓂᑯᒙᓯᐠ ᐊᐢᑭᐩ ᑳ ᐱᒫᑎᓯᐟ ᑮ ᐑᒑᔮᒦᐤ ᐅᓃᑭᐦᐃᑿ, ᐃᔭᑯᓂ ᓇᒨᖬ ᑮ ᐅᐦᒋ ᐋᑲᖭᓰᒧᖨᐘ᙮ ᑮ ᑭᐢᑮᖨᐦᑕᒷᐠ ᑕ ᐱᒫᒋᐦᐅᒋᐠ ᐊᐢᑮᕽ ᐃᑿ ᒦᓇ ᑮ ᑭᐢᑮᖨᐦᑕᒷᐠ ᐋᒐᖫᐦᑮᐏᓇ ᑳ ᐲ ᐋᓂᐢᑭ ᐑᐦᑕᒪᐏᐦᒋᐠ ᐅᑖᓂᐢᑭ ᐚᐦᑰᒫᑲᓂᐚᐘ᙮ ᐃᔭᑯᓂ ᑮ ᐋᐦᐋᒐᖪᐦᑲᐑᐘᐠ ᓱᕒᐅᒧᓇ ᐃᑿ ᐑᑎᓵᓇ᙮

SOLOMON RATT was born on the banks of the Churchill River just north of the community of Stanley Mission. His parents were hunters and fishers who lived off the land, spending their winters on the trapline and summers fishing in La Ronge. Solomon spent the first six winters of his life with his parents, who didn't speak English. They knew the ways of the land, including the traditional stories passed down through generations, which they told to Solomon and his siblings.